FOOTBALLISTICS

FOOTBALLISTICS

JAMES COVENTRY
(AND A TEAM OF FOOTY'S SHARPEST THINKERS)

ABC
Books

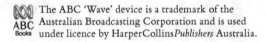 The ABC 'Wave' device is a trademark of the
Australian Broadcasting Corporation and is used
under licence by HarperCollins*Publishers* Australia.

First published in Australia in 2018
by HarperCollins*Publishers* Australia Pty Limited
ABN 36 009 913 517
harpercollins.com.au

HarperCollins*Publishers*
Level 19, 201 Elizabeth Street, Sydney, NSW 2000, Australia
Unit D1, 63 Apollo Drive, Rosedale, Auckland 0632, New Zealand
A 53, Sector 57, Noida, UP, India
1 London Bridge Street, London, SE1 9GF, United Kingdom
Bay Adelaide Centre, East Tower, 22 Adelaide Street West, 41st floor,
Toronto, Ontario, M5H 4E3, Canada
195 Broadway, New York, NY 10007

A catalogue record for this book is available
from the National Library of Australia

ISBN: 978 0 7333 3844 1 (paperback)
ISBN: 978 1 4607 0871 2 (ebook)

Cover design and illustration: Design by Committee
Cover images by shutterstock.com
Typeset in Sabon by Kirby Jones
Printed and bound in Australia by McPherson's Printing Group
The papers used by HarperCollins in the manufacture of this book are a natural, recyclable
product made from wood grown in sustainable plantation forests. The fibre source and
manufacturing processes meet recognised international environmental standards, and carry
certification.

Contents

Introduction

2015 AFL Grand Final
Hawthorn 9.3 (57) leads West Coast 3.8 (26)

As Hawthorn forward Jarryd Roughead swooped on a bouncing ball in front of the MCG's Great Southern Stand, the mercury touched 31 degrees Celsius. The 2015 AFL Grand Final was officially the hottest on record. Even though it was only 30 seconds into the third quarter, and Roughead was feeling refreshed after the half-time break, he was careful to follow his coach's instructions. 'If you were to play full throttle for the full four quarters in those type of conditions, which were very oppressive, no team in the competition would be able to withstand that for long,' said Hawks coach Alastair Clarkson. 'At different stages you need to conserve your energy and just try to control the ball, so that was the plan.' Roughead, with no obvious option ahead of him, turned and kicked the ball 20 metres backwards to his teammate Ben Stratton. It gave the Eagles time to set up their famed 'web': a zonal defence that weaved around the ball carrier. West Coast coach Adam Simpson had served his coaching apprenticeship as an assistant to Clarkson, and the web was an evolutionary version of the rolling zone the Hawks had used during his time there.

Stratton hesitated behind the mark. The web was strangling his usable space, denying him the option of a short kick. Umpire Jeff Dalgleish raised his arms to call play on, and Stratton kicked long to a one-on-one contest between Cyril Rioli and Brad Sheppard. The Eagles defender managed to get his fist to the ball first, knocking it forward to midfielder Matthew Priddis. Within seconds it had passed through the hands of three West Coast players, and Mark LeCras was lining up for goal. 'It's in good hands, you would think,' said Channel Seven commentator Bruce McAvaney. 'Sixty-seven per cent of the time this year he has goaled from a set shot.' McAvaney was never short of a convincing statistic, but this one let him down. From about 45 metres out, on a slight angle, LeCras's shot faded left and hit the post. 'It's a behind, so it's 3.9 to 9.3 – they've had the same number of scoring shots,' said McAvaney. The Hawks led by five goals, but the Eagles had posted five of the last six scores. It felt like the game was still alive.

A few boxes down from McAvaney, another commentator was hard at work. Daniel Hoyne's call wasn't being broadcast, but his potential audience was just as big.

'Burgoyne. Kick-in, long, right, rebound.'

'Shiels, contested mark. Kick, short.'

'Lewis, mark. Kick, clanger, out on the full.'

Hoyne was calling the game for Champion Data, the AFL's official statistics provider. 'When we started in 1999, we only had three people working on each match,' said the company's senior analyst, Glenn Luff. 'Now we have 10 people involved in capturing the data for each game – five at the ground and five at the bunker.' The bunker was the company's headquarters in Southbank, where Amanda Parker was sitting in front of a patchwork screen of coloured boxes. Like a hyperactive stenographer, Parker was translating Hoyne's staccato call into raw numbers with a flurry of mouse clicks and keystrokes. The data she entered was instantaneously transmitted to fans' smartphones, the press tribunes, the TV and radio broadcasters, fantasy football sites, and the two competing teams. 'Our mission statement is to tell the story of the game,' said senior statistician Karl Jackson. 'We try to do that through data. In any 30-second passage of play, there's just so much information that we can collect. Even if you haven't seen a single second, you can always go back and look at a stats sheet or a running sheet and know what happened.'

'Butler, mark. Play on, handball,' continued Hoyne, binoculars pressed firmly to his eyes.

'Hurn, receive. Kick, long, inside.'

'Darling, contested mark.'

'Kick, short. Goal. 57 to 33.'

Down the corridor, McAvaney's call was somewhat more animated. 'They've kicked the last three goals of the match!' he cried. 'Forty-four points was the big margin, now it's back to 24!'

By now, the warning signs were beginning to crystallise in Hawthorn's coaches' box. The Hawks' Head of Strategy and Innovation, David Rath, had in front of him a screen that showed what were called 'drive chains'. It was a visual representation of how the game was being played, and was powered by the information delivered by Champion Data. The Hawks had taken the idea from similar systems used in American football's NFL. A vertical line ran down the middle of Rath's monitor, halfway between two lines marking the goals. Colour-coded horizontal bars – orange for the Hawks and blue for the Eagles – indicated how far a team had moved the ball each time it had taken possession. In the background, there was a peach-coloured graph that was charting the game's ebbs and flows. 'Basically, it was a formula we came up with to measure periods of dominance,' said Hawks analyst Darren O'Shaughnessy. 'By looking at the display, the coaches are able to see whether a team has been able to take advantage of when it's had possession and territory.'

It was Rath's job to monitor and interpret this information. 'I use the bespoke dashboards that Darren has created for us to define the structure of the game, and to see where we're going well and where we're not going so well,' he said. 'I then try to distil that information for Clarko.' In this instance, the picture that was being painted by the drive chain data was unambiguous. 'We were actually giving West Coast a genuine chance to get back into the contest because we weren't taking ground with the ball,' explained Clarkson. 'We had control of the ball a couple of times across halfback and kicked backwards to guys who couldn't play on. Even though we had the ball in our hands, we were giving them territory rather than taking it ourselves. It can be a fine line between controlling the ball and carrying it forward. If you look like you're going to be too conservative, opposition teams are able to press the man on the mark and cut down his exits.'

The message went out to Hawthorn's players to be braver when they had the ball, and to take the game on. Hot weather be damned, they had another cup to win. 'Once we were taking some ground with the ball, from about the 10-minute mark from the third quarter onwards, we became a bit more potent and found some avenues towards goal,' said Clarkson. In fact, from that point they kicked 5.2 to the Eagles' 1.0 for the rest of the term. 'We ended up winning the scoreboard in the third quarter, which was obviously critical,' said Clarkson. 'If the Eagles were going to get back into the game, it needed to be in the third that they did it.'

Hawthorn great Leigh Matthews knew what it was like to hold an unassailable three-quarter-time lead in a Grand Final. He had described walking over to the huddle during the final change of the 1983 decider as 'the most surreal moment of my entire football life'. 'A quarter to go in a Grand Final and we couldn't lose,' he said. 'What a fantastic, euphoric feeling that was.' Now it was Clarkson and Rath's turn to experience that rare form of ecstasy. Their team's 50-point lead over West Coast wasn't quite the 87-point buffer Matthews's side had enjoyed over Essendon, but it was still more than enough. The celebrations were already well underway as Hoyne dictated the closing stages to Parker.

'Priddis, hard. Handball.'

'Gaff, receive. Handball.'

'Priddis, receive. Kick, long, inside.'

'Gibson, spoil.'

'End quarter. End game. Score is 107 to 61.'

In the coaches' box, Clarkson and Rath embraced. It was the fourth premiership they had won together, and their third in the past three years. It was the culmination of a plan they had hatched more than a decade earlier to establish a new way of thinking about Australian football. They had joined Hawthorn as the *Moneyball* revolution was sweeping professional sports in the United States. Both had been enthralled and inspired by the Michael Lewis bestseller, which detailed how baseball manager Billy Beane had transformed the Oakland A's by using statistical analysis to challenge the sport's conventional wisdom. 'There was definitely an awareness of the *Moneyball* idea at that time, and I think there was hope that we could "*Moneyball*" the AFL,' said Rath. 'I suppose there was a feeling of optimism, like "Oh wow, this is a great idea. Let's see if we can apply it to our game".'

The wise men of the Wimmera

If it wasn't love at first sight between Clarkson and Rath, it was probably the next best thing. Rath was lecturing at an advanced coaching course at the Australian Institute of Sport in 2003. Clarkson was an uninvited participant. 'He'd found out about the course and that he wasn't on it, but he just turned up in Canberra anyway,' said Rath. Some of the coaches were slow to arrive on the first day after going out for drinks the night before, so there were plenty of spare seats for Clarkson to choose from. When the instructor began handing out the coursework, he mistook Clarkson for his former North Melbourne teammate Anthony Rock. 'He gave him all of Rocky's stuff,' said Rath. 'Clarko didn't say a word.' When Rock arrived later and asked for his paperwork, the instructor told him, 'I've just given it to you!' It didn't take long for them to realise there was an interloper.

Clarkson, as was his way, managed to talk himself onto the course. He was captivated by Rath's presentation, which was all about the science of kicking a football. Rath had worked at the AIS for nine years as a biomechanist and performance analysis expert. He had developed an interest in biomechanics as a sports-crazed kid growing up in Nhill, in Victoria's Wimmera grain belt. 'I was one of those kids who always wanted to work out how to kick a footy further, or how to bowl faster, or how to hit a golf ball further,' he said. 'I was always technically minded with sport, and was driven to distraction working out how to do things better.' Clarkson approached Rath at the end of the day and they immediately found common ground. He, too, had studied sports science at university. Clarkson was from Kaniva, which was only a half-hour drive from Nhill down the Western Highway. They were also the same age, and they figured out that Rath had gone to primary school with Clarkson's wife, Caryn. 'I struck up a strong rapport with him straight away,' said Rath. 'There are usually a couple of stand-outs at those courses who are perhaps a little bit more inquisitive, and he was definitely one of those.' When Clarkson returned home, he mentioned to Caryn that he had met one of her former classmates. 'If I ever get a senior job, I'm going to employ that bloke,' he told her.

About a year later, sports agent Liam Pickering was sitting in his Melbourne office, when his boss, Martin Jolly, walked in. As well as being the managing director of talent agency IMG, Jolly was also the vice-president of Hawthorn. The Hawks had just sacked their coach, Peter Schwab, and Jolly was on the committee tasked with finding a replacement. Former Hawthorn players Terry Wallace, Rodney Eade and Gary Ayres were reported to be the three men vying for the position, but Jolly had other plans. 'I've got an idea,' he told Pickering. 'Rather than getting someone who has already had a go, why don't we try to find the next Kevin Sheedy?' He rattled off a list of names that included John Longmire, Daryn Cresswell, and Shaun Rehn. 'I know someone else who'd be good,' said Pickering. 'You should look at Alastair Clarkson.' Jolly's expression went blank. 'Who is he?'

Clarkson's relatively low profile belied the fact he had played 134 games in 11 seasons of senior football. He had spent nine years with North, playing mostly as a midfield tagger. He had a reputation for constant on-field chatter. 'Like a lot of chaps under six foot, he always had a fair bit to say,' said his former teammate Wayne Schwass. 'There was a fair bit of Tony Shaw and Tony Liberatore about him.' As a 19-year-old in 1987, Clarkson had infamously broken the jaw of Carlton player Ian Aitken with a king hit during an exhibition match in London. Although he later admitted it had been a 'cowardly act', he also counted having to face the fierce retribution of Aitken's teammates as a formative experience. When he eventually fell out of favour at the Kangaroos, he all but talked his way onto Melbourne's list. 'He wasn't a priority but we thought if he wanted it that badly we couldn't lose,' said former Demons coach Neil Balme. 'He turned out to be a terrific contributor.' After two seasons he was delisted at the end of 1997, worked as Melbourne's runner for a year, and then spent a season as an assistant to Tim Watson at St Kilda. His first experience coaching his own team was with Werribee in the VFL in 2000, and the following year he coached Central District to an SANFL premiership. When Central lost the 2002 SANFL Grand Final to Sturt, he returned to the AFL as an assistant coach under Port Adelaide's Mark Williams.

Shortly after Clarkson arrived at Alberton, *Moneyball* was released. It quickly became a must-read among AFL coaching personnel. One the biggest beneficiaries of the buzz surrounding its publication was Champion Data. '*Moneyball* was huge for us,' said Glenn Luff. 'We went from being purely data collectors to also becoming analysts.' Fortunately for Clarkson, the club he had just joined was already at the forefront of the changing landscape. Clarkson's fellow Power assistant coach, Phil Walsh, was regarded as one of the league's sharpest analytical minds. 'We felt at that stage we were constantly a step behind Port because of the innovation they were bringing to the game,' said Luff. 'Phil was amazing with that. He was my favourite person in the footy industry to talk to during the 2000s, because he just spoke a different language to everyone else.' Two years learning at the knee of Williams and Walsh put the polish on Clarkson's football education.

In August 2004, just weeks before the Power would defeat Brisbane in the Grand Final, Clarkson met Pickering over coffee in Adelaide. 'I remember he was disappointed that he hadn't been interviewed for the Western Bulldogs job, which had just gone to Rodney Eade,' said Pickering. 'I asked him, "Well, have you got a résumé?" and he said, "No, but I'm definitely ready to go".' Despite Jolly's ignorance of Clarkson's career up to that point, Pickering convinced the Hawks to give him a hearing. At the time, the club was being criticised for dawdling in its search. 'Rodney Eade: gone; Terry Wallace: gone; Gary O'Donnell: not interested; Mark Harvey: feeling rejected and refusing to respond to calls,' wrote Mike Sheahan in the *Herald Sun*. 'The facts are Hawthorn is on the bottom of the ladder, doesn't have a permanent chief executive, and can't find a coach. That's crisis territory.'

Hawks great Jason Dunstall, who was acting as chief executive, conceded the club was at a low point. 'We were rock bottom,' he said. 'You talk about risk-taking, but we were in a position where we had no option.' That is not to say, however, that Clarkson's appointment was a fait accompli. Gary Ayres was still considered the frontrunner for the job, even though his friend and former teammate Dermott Brereton had stood down from the selection subcommittee to remove any perceived conflict of interest. Longmire, Cresswell, Rehn, and Matt Rendell were all interviewed, while Donald McDonald, who had taken over as caretaker coach after Schwab's departure, also applied. It was Clarkson, though, who stood out from the pack. 'I remember

Jolly coming back to the office and saying, "He was impressive, really impressive",' recalled Pickering. 'I said, "I told you! He's smart!"' Hawks president Ian Dicker described Clarkson's presentation as 'invigorating', while Dunstall said he had been attracted by the 36-year-old's long-term vision. 'He was a fresh-faced young fella with some pretty exciting ideas,' he said. 'He knew how he wanted to run a footy club, and how the game needed to be played.'

The Hawks had finished the 2004 season second-bottom, avoiding the wooden spoon by less than one percentage point. Clarkson made it his priority to restructure the club's underperforming football department. McDonald and assistants Gavin Crosisca and George Stone were not offered new contracts, with Clarkson opting to bring in his own staff. He upset his most recent employer, Port Adelaide, by poaching its fitness coach, Andrew Russell. He also appointed the recently retired Power defender Damien Hardwick as an assistant coach, along with Todd Viney and Ross Smith. He put a broom through the playing ranks, delisting several veterans, including defender Mark Graham. Key forward Nathan Thompson was traded to North Melbourne, and the Hawks went to the national draft armed with three top-10 picks. There, they selected Jarryd Roughead (2), Lance Franklin (5), and Jordan Lewis (7).

Still, the new coach wasn't satisfied. He remembered what he had told his wife after returning from the course at the AIS, and he was determined to keep his word. 'He was really keen to get David Rath,' said Pickering, who had become Clarkson's manager. 'Unfortunately, Hawthorn were a bit broke back then. They didn't have much money.' Clarkson, though, would not be so easily deterred. 'I just remember when his first contract came through, it was at least $20,000 short of what we had negotiated,' said Pickering. 'I rang the club and said, "Hey, what's going on here? We didn't agree on this number." And they said, "Didn't Alastair tell you? He's given up that money to employ another bloke".' Mark Evans, who had just been appointed the club's new football manager, had signed off on the deal. 'It was an unusual approach,' he admitted. 'But Alastair was less driven by money, and more driven around the type of people he wanted to bring into the organisation.' Pickering was flabbergasted. 'Basically, Clarko gave up at least $20,000 of his own money, maybe even more, to make sure that he got David Rath,' he said. 'He did it to get him up to the salary he'd promised he could get him. I told him, "Mate, my role is to get you as much money as you can. That's why you have a manager. It's not for you to give it away!" Clarko just laughed and said, "Yeah, but this guy is going to help me win".'

For Clarkson, the decision had been easy. 'We were pretty down as a footy club at that point in time,' he said. 'When you're appointed to a role you need a fair amount of support, and if the club couldn't pay for it, then I didn't want to go without that resource.' Drawing on the lessons from *Moneyball*, he knew that he needed to surround himself with people who had a broad range of experiences, and who were capable of independent thought. 'Alastair was keen to bring in some diversity in the coaching mix,' said Evans. 'David has a wide-reaching analytical brain, and that was something Alastair was keen on. He had some people who had come through direct coaching pathways within football, but he was looking to see what else he could add.' Rath's lack of AFL experience was considered a positive. 'I knew with Hardwick, Viney and Smith, we had the same mould of guys who had come through the normal route,' said Clarkson. 'What we didn't have to complement those guys was someone with a different slant.'

Rath was made an assistant coach, and put in charge of the Hawks' 'game style'. He scoured other sports for tactics that could be applied to Australian football, and developed a variety of internal metrics by which the club could analyse its performances. 'Previously there had been basic tally stats like kicks, marks, handballs, and inside 50s, but there wasn't a lot more than that,' said Rath. 'We started going to Champion Data and saying, "We want to do this …" and they would help us develop something for it.' Glenn Luff believes it was the behind-the-scenes men, such as Rath and Phil Walsh, who pushed Champion Data to expand its horizons. 'It was around that period when we started to get a lot of feedback from clubs giving us specific instructions about what they wanted,' said Luff. 'Things started to change with analytics and the way clubs were embracing it. We had to get smarter in terms of what we captured, and how we looked at the data.'

Rath's biomechanics background also came to the fore, as he became the key figure in developing the precision kicking that would become Hawthorn's trademark. 'I have very strong views that some old coaching mantras are totally wrong,' Rath told the *Age*, a few weeks after his appointment. 'I think we know now that kicking isn't just a straight-line skill where you must hold the ball rigidly over your kicking leg, guiding the ball as closely to your foot as possible. It's a much more complex skill than that.' Midfielder Brad Sewell, who was in his third season at the club when Rath arrived, was one of several players to benefit from his expertise. 'Because my kicking was sub-par I spent a lot of time with him, just mucking around with different strategies and techniques to try and bring my kicking up to scratch,' he said. 'He was particularly important in developing different kicking drills, recognising what types of kicks are important in each part of the ground, and understanding the players' strengths and weaknesses.'

In addition to improving the skills base of their existing list, the Hawks made a deliberate decision to recruit players who could already kick the ball well. 'For quite a few years, there had been an emphasis upon recruiting athletes, often at the expense of skilled footballers,' said Rath. 'We definitely recruited with an eye to getting good kickers in, and I think our game style then evolved with an appreciation of possession and time on the ball. The principle was that the ball was king, and being able to control the play was a good thing.' The Hawks ranked last in the league for kicking efficiency in Rath and Clarkson's first season in 2005. By 2008, when they shocked the football world by beating Geelong in the Grand Final, they ranked number one.

Of the AFL's 16 senior coaches and 52 assistant coaches in 2005, just seven, or 10%, hadn't played in the AFL/VFL. The only senior coach was Neil Craig, who had recently replaced Gary Ayres as coach of the Adelaide Crows. Although a lot was made of Craig's sports science background, he had also played 319 games in the SANFL, and had represented South Australia 11 times. Similarly, half of the assistant coaches without any AFL playing experience had enjoyed productive careers in the WAFL. It was only Rath, Geelong's Brendan McCartney, and the Western Bulldogs' Matthew Drain who had managed to break into the coaching ranks without having played anything more than country or amateur football. Rath admits there were times he felt self-conscious about his outsider status. 'I'd be lying to say I always felt like I belonged, because I didn't feel like that at first,' he said. 'In the early days I felt way out of my depth at times. I remember Shane Crawford coming up to me in the huddle during a practice match in my first year and saying, "Isolate me, isolate me". I was so green that I wasn't exactly sure what he meant.'

Clarkson, however, understood that Rath was on a steep learning curve, and he was prepared to give him time to carve out his niche. 'Historically, every footy club had pretty much said that a prerequisite for being an assistant coach at AFL level was that you needed to have played 100 games of AFL footy,' said Clarkson. 'I didn't think that was true, particularly when there were guys out there like David Rath.' Of course, success breeds imitation, and as Hawthorn started its steady ascent under the new regime, other clubs began to search for their own David Raths. By 2018, when Rath left Hawthorn to become the AFL's Head of Coaching, a quarter of all coaches employed at the top level had no AFL playing experience. 'Maybe our success with my role has contributed to that,' said Rath. 'I think there's now an understanding that there's value in getting a different look at things. There's no doubt data is being used to ask more specific questions than it once was.'

The new football

The aim of this book is to provide you, the reader, with an insight into the new way of thinking about Australian football that has been pioneered by coaches such as Rath and Clarkson. We have put together a crack team of football analysts, data scientists, and sports economists to ask our own questions of the data. Which clubs are the masters of drafting and trading? Is momentum real? How much does home-ground advantage matter? We will also examine some of the AFL's most famous shibboleths and truisms. Are blond-haired players more likely to poll Brownlow Medal votes? Can you accurately judge a team's chances of making a comeback by using the 'Leigh Matthews Theory'? Is goal kicking really the only aspect of the game that hasn't improved? Along the way we will meet some of the other outsiders who have infiltrated the inner sanctums of the AFL's 18 clubs, and who are now busily uncovering the sport's hidden truths.

Chapter One
Goal Kicking

Heartbreak

There was a funereal air in Adelaide Oval's media room, as a procession of grim-faced reporters awkwardly deposited their digital recorders between the Channel Seven microphones and Gatorade bottles that were set before Ken Hinkley. When all was in place, the Port Adelaide coach waited impassively as an awkward stillness descended. It seemed nobody wanted to ask the first question. What could you say to a man who had just watched his side's season ended by an after-the-siren goal in extra time of an elimination final? Eventually, and inevitably, it was the *Advertiser* scribe and lifelong Port supporter Michelangelo Rucci who broke the silence. 'Ken, if there was one moment or one thing you could do again, what would that be?' Rucci asked. A sardonic half smile briefly flickered across Hinkley's face. 'Kick straight, probably,' he deadpanned. 'That's been our problem for large parts of the year.'

Hinkley's pain was amplified by the fact the Power had looked all but home when it surged to a 13-point lead over West Coast early in the first extra period. But the Eagles had refused to go quietly, and stole an improbable victory when the unflappable Luke Shuey drilled a 40-metre set shot from a controversial high-contact free kick in the dying seconds. 'The Eagles found a way to win and I give them great credit for being able to do that,' said Hinkley. 'There were opportunities for both sides, but they kicked straight and we didn't.' His summary was simplistic but indisputable. Port had kicked 10 goals 16 to West Coast's 12 goals 6. It was, in a way, a microcosm of the season. On a basic measure of goals as a proportion of scores, the Eagles had ended the home-and-away season as the league's fourth most accurate side, while the Power had ranked 13th. Port's woes were embodied by its leading goal kicker, Charlie Dixon. His performance against the Eagles had been outstanding in every regard bar accuracy. He had booted three goals six, with two of those behinds recorded during the tense final minutes.

As the veteran football writer Ashley Porter cleared his throat, Hinkley braced for the question he knew was coming. 'What did you think of Charlie Dixon's game, his performance?' Hinkley turned his head, raised his eyebrows, and scratched his neck. 'He's not overpaid, is he?' said the coach. But before Porter could reply, Hinkley had swivelled back to address him directly. 'He's not overpaid, is he?' he repeated, a defiant note in his voice. Hinkley rested his chin on his left fist as if pondering his own rhetorical question. Clearly, he had not forgotten the scathing criticism recently levelled at Dixon by Porter's Fairfax colleague Caroline Wilson, in which she had raised his reported salary of $650,000 to $700,000 per season. 'No,' said Porter, slightly taken aback to suddenly find himself answering questions rather than asking them. Hinkley sat up in his chair. He maintained eye contact with Porter, but was now plainly addressing the room. 'This wonderful place here, they tend to whack people for unknown reasons,' he said. 'I couldn't be prouder of Charlie Dixon, and I, like a lot of people, get sick to death of the stuff that gets thrown around in this game.'

If Hinkley sounded like a protective father, it was because in many ways he was. In his previous role as the Gold Coast Suns' forward-line coach, he had nurtured Dixon since he was a precocious, if sometimes unruly, teenager. After taking on the Port job, it had been he who had convinced the Queenslander to join him at Alberton, and then defended him throughout an underwhelming first season. And now, at the end of a year in which Dixon had proven his worth, he would not allow him to be blamed for the team's heartbreaking exit. He had just come from the team's dressing room, where he had seen the two-metre-tall forward openly sobbing. 'People sometimes think they don't care or that it doesn't mean enough to them, but I wish they could go and watch our players now and understand the hurt they're going through,' said Hinkley. 'We've worked really hard at it [goal kicking] all year and we just haven't been able to quite convert the way we should.' As the press conference lurched to a close, Rucci made one last attempt to coax a more expansive explanation. 'Do you become as puzzled as everyone has been for more than a century about goal kicking?' Hinkley looked down at his clasped hands and let out a world-weary chuckle. 'We all do,' he conceded. 'The amount of work that gets done on it is unbelievable. You've just got to factor in that thing called pressure.'

The one thing ...

Two months earlier, the Western Bulldogs had trudged off the same ground after an even more wretched performance in front of goal. The reigning premiers had conspired to kick a pitiable five goals 15 in a 59-point thrashing at the hands of the Adelaide Crows. ABC Grandstand pundit and four-time premiership coach David Parkin was merciless in his assessment. 'I've been part of this game for 50 or 60 years now, and the one thing that hasn't got better during that time is the players' ability to kick the ball between two white posts that don't move,' he raged. 'Every other element of Australian football in my lifetime has gone up by hundreds of per cent, but that's the one thing we can't control.' It was a familiar refrain. In fact, just that week, Cats forward Daniel Menzel had penned an article for his club's newspaper of record, the *Geelong Advertiser*, in which he wrote: 'As our game changes, adapts, improves, and evolves over the years, there is one thing that remains constant and hasn't progressed – goal kicking.'

When considering these statements from Parkin and Menzel, not to mention the countless others who have argued the same line, it seems reasonable to assume they are referring to the league-wide conversion rate. In analytics, as in arguments, it is important to define your terms, so let us begin by initially describing a team's or player's goal-kicking accuracy as the percentage of scoring shots that are registered as goals. Under this definition, the accuracy of the Bulldogs when they kicked 5.15 was $5 / (5 + 15) \times 100$, or 25%. The team to which they lost, the Crows, kicked 16.8, which made their accuracy 16 / (16 + 8) x 100, or 66%. Accuracy, defined in this way, will always lie between 0% and 100%. It is easy to contemplate ways in which this definition might be improved upon. For example, we could include attempted scoring shots that went out on the full, or exclude rushed behinds. However, these statistics are not available for the entire history of the sport, making any evaluation of long-term trends problematic. Later we will use more advanced data to discover how factors such as shot location can impact accuracy, but for now we will stick with the simplest, most intuitive definition.

Each of the dots in the chart below represents the season-long accuracy of a single team, while the squiggly line traces the average accuracy of all teams from 1897 to 2017. It is obvious to see that modern teams are, on average, considerably more accurate than those prior to about 1980. There has been a broadly upward trend in accuracy since 1950, with a slight dip during the 21st century. The spread of dots in any given year reveals how variable accuracy was in

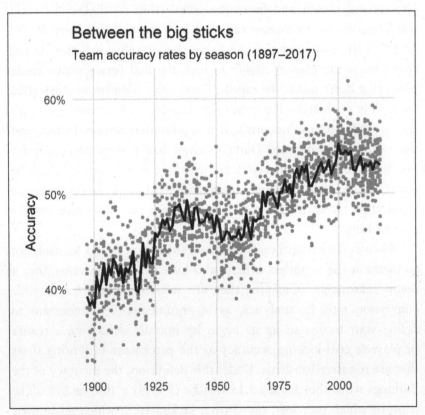

Between the big sticks

Team accuracy rates by season (1897–2017)

that season. The 1916 regular season and finals produced the smallest range, spanning just 2.6 percentage points from 42.9% to 45.5%, while 1950 produced the largest range of 15.2 percentage points from 39.8% to 55.0%. It should be noted, however, that there were only four teams in the 1916 competition compared to 12 in 1950. In the VFL's earliest years, even the best teams converted less than half of their scoring shots into goals. It took until 1920 for a team to end a season with a 50% accuracy level, with Fitzroy achieving the feat after kicking 3.5 in a losing semifinal to finish with a ledger of 185.185. Geelong's premiership team of 1925 was the first to go above 50%, its 10.19 performance in the Grand Final leaving it with a 248.241 (51%) record for the season.

Since 2000, the difference between the most and least accurate teams in a season has ranged from six percentage points to about double that. The low came in 2009 and the high in 2004, when St Kilda became the only side in the competition's history to record a season-long conversion rate of more than 60%. Grant Thomas's side finished the year with 409.253 (62%), including 39.30 during the finals, where it lost to the eventual premier, Port Adelaide. Thomas believed accurate goal kicking to be a football fundamental. He ignored his sports scientists' warnings against overwork, conducting lengthy goal-kicking sessions both before and after training. One of his favourite drills was called 'the gauntlet', which involved players walking through a tunnel of jeering teammates before taking their shots. Thomas was what might be termed a confidence coach, in that he placed the highest value on spirit and morale. To that end, he never monitored or recorded whether his players were missing or scoring at practice. 'Goal kicking is an outcome, but we wouldn't talk about the outcome or effects, we'd only talk about the inputs and causes,' he said. 'It's only when you bring the outcome into a skill that you have problems, whether that be with a golf putt, a smash in tennis or a shot at goal, because you're then thinking about the consequence rather than the cause.'

The Saints were also blessed with a supremely talented trio of forwards. The powerful Fraser Gehrig notched a century of goals, finishing with 103.39 (72.5%). The club's future captain Nick Riewoldt kicked 67.32 (67.7%) and the opportunistic Stephen Milne booted 46.22 (67.6%). Between them, they had contributed well over half the Saints' majors. In no other season have three players kicked more than half of their side's goals at a higher conversion rate (69.9%) than Gehrig, Riewoldt, and Milne did in that season. To put their extraordinary accuracy into some context, consider the following table. We have compiled a list of the 30 best career conversion rates since 1965, which is the year from which reliable

Highest conversion rates from at least 100 scoring shots, 1965–2017					
Rank	Player	Seasons	Goals	Behinds	Conversion
1	Tory Dickson	2012–2017	149	52	74.13%
2	Shane Loveless	1979–1981	72	28	72.00%
3	Peter Jones	1966–1979	284	113	71.54%
4	Tim Membrey	2014–2017	91	39	70.00%
5	Mike Green	1966–1975	83	36	69.75%
6	Tony Lockett	1983–2002	1,360	590	69.74%
7	Bob Heard	1970–1979	155	68	69.51%
8	Aaron Edwards	2005–2014	139	61	69.50%
9	Mark Seaby	2004–2012	69	31	69.00%
10	Peter Hudson	1967–1977	727	330	68.78%
11	John Anthony	2008–2012	83	38	68.60%
12	Matthew Lloyd	1995–2009	926	424	68.59%
13	Mark Johnson	1999–2008	100	46	68.49%
14	Ross Ditchburn	1982–1983	91	42	68.42%
15	Darryl White	1992–2005	165	77	68.18%
16	Mark Jackson	1981–1986	308	144	68.14%
17	Greg Stafford	1993–2006	141	66	68.12%
18	Mark Scott	1978–1989	175	82	68.09%
19	Frank Goode	1965–1967	95	45	67.86%
20	Jason Heatley	1995–2000	171	81	67.86%
21	Paul Puopolo	2011–2017	151	72	67.71%
22	Luke Breust	2011–2017	304	145	67.71%
23	John Barnes	1987–2001	90	43	67.67%
24	Matthew Wright	2011–2017	115	55	67.65%
25	Jay Schulz	2003–2016	333	160	67.55%
26	Ben Brown	2014–2017	154	74	67.54%
27	Matt Campbell	2007–2012	79	38	67.52%
28	Brodie Holland	1998–2008	141	68	67.46%
29	Daniel Chick	1996–2007	210	102	67.31%
30	Daniel Bradshaw	1996–2010	524	255	67.27%

information about individual behinds scorers is available. To avoid the results being skewed by players with a small sample size, we have omitted those who recorded fewer than 100 scoring shots. Although Gehrig, Riewoldt and Milne failed to make the cut over the course of their whole careers, their 2004 accuracy levels all comfortably fell within the elite bracket. Viewed on its own, Gehrig's 72.5% would have placed him behind only Western Bulldogs sharpshooter Tory Dickson, who sits well clear on top with a freakish 74.13%.

It is perhaps unsurprising to learn that Dickson had missed the Dogs' inaccurate performance in Adelaide that had so incensed Parkin. A combination of injury setbacks and patchy form meant Dickson only managed nine games during the 2017 season, during which his team slid from 13th (52%) to last (47%) on our basic measure of accuracy. Still, when he was on the park, he contributed a typically precise 11.3 (79%). 'It's something that I take a lot of pride in,' said Dickson. 'I always want to finish off my work because as a forward you have limited opportunities, and you want to make the most of the ones you get.' Dickson's philosophy has been to keep his goal-kicking process as simple as possible. He follows a three-item checklist: forward momentum, a short ball drop, and a pointed toe on impact. 'My strength is that even if I miss one of those things, as long as I get the other two right, it will usually still go through.'

Charlie Dixon's routine, like his surname, is similar but distinct from Dickson's. Dixon's key thought when lining up for a set shot is 'right shoulder, right foot, right post', a mantra that had been taught to him by Malcolm Blight during his time at the Suns. 'It doesn't matter about the wind, I'll still always aim around there,' he said. 'Then it's basically my right foot in front of my left, a couple of breaths to make sure I'm settled, and then my left foot steps first, a small step into four big steps, into a stride until I feel comfortable, and then I kick the ball.' At face value, it may seem odd to compare the mechanics of Dickson (the AFL/VFL's most accurate goal kicker of the past half century) to those of Dixon (the sometimes maligned forward who kicked 3.6 in an elimination final), but the Port player's occasional bouts of waywardness have masked an otherwise strong conversion rate. Indeed, at the end of 2016 he would have ranked 12th on our accuracy table at 68.51%, and second behind only

Dickson among active players. His 2017 haul of 49.30 (62%) saw his career percentage drop to 66.5%, which was still good enough for 41st overall across our 53-season sample period.

Dixon blamed the small downturn on straying from his normal process. He said he had allowed his mind to become cluttered by the advice and opinions of others. 'Everyone loves to tell you how to kick goals, and I was hearing stuff like, "You should only try and kick it mid- goal-post height", "You're kicking it too hard", all this sort of stuff,' he said. 'In the end I was like, "Oh, stuff that, I'm not going to listen to you guys, I know what I'm doing".' Dixon remedied himself by watching YouTube clips of goals he had kicked for the Suns. 'When I was playing for Gold Coast it was just natural, it was fluent,' he said. 'I didn't just try to poke at it, I *kicked* the footy, and that's enough for me now.'

Fatigue

By his own admission, Dixon was exhausted when he marked strongly in front of Cats defender Lachie Henderson, 35 metres from goal, late in the last quarter of the Power's round-10 match in Geelong in 2017. Port led by three points with less than four minutes to play, and Dixon knew that another goal would likely be enough to lift his side into the top four. 'I reckon this is the biggest kick he's had in a Port Adelaide guernsey,' enthused Channel Seven commentator Bruce McAvaney. Dixon slowly got to his feet and walked back to take his shot. 'I looked up and saw I had about 15 seconds left on the shot clock,' he said. 'But I went back and just sort of stood there – I was gassed.' As he attempted to settle into his usual routine, he was also oblivious to the field umpire cautioning that his allotted time was running out. 'I had a deep breath, another deep breath, took a step, and suddenly there was a Geelong player running at me.'

Cats midfielder Mitch Duncan had heard the umpire's warnings and was first to react when he raised his hands to signal play on. Under pressure, Dixon fired a handball to his teammate Justin Westhoff, whose hurried kick was rushed through for a behind. Two minutes later Patrick Dangerfield kicked a goal at the other end to snatch a two-point victory for the Cats. 'Everyone knows I stuffed that up,' said Dixon. 'But it was late in the quarter and I was gassed.' Dixon had covered 12.63 kilometres during the match, marginally below his season average of 12.94, although the GPS data showed he had run particularly hard immediately prior to his botched set shot. On average, a Port Adelaide player covered 13.27 kilometres per game during 2017, up from an average of 12.48 kilometres per match in 2013. The Power says the increase was linked to the introduction of the interchange cap, with players spending a greater proportion of each game on the ground.

We can try to quantify the effect that fatigue has on goal-kicking accuracy. Across the 1,993 home-and-away and finals matches played between 2008 and 2017, there was a total of 98,847 scores recorded – each with an individual time stamp to indicate exactly when they occurred during a match. It is unfortunate for our purposes that these are based on a 'count-up' instead of a 'count-down' clock, meaning they show the amount of time that has elapsed in a quarter rather than the time that remains. The 20-minute count-down clock that is used by the timekeepers and shown on the television broadcasts is stopped during breaks in play. The count-up clock continues ticking regardless of stoppages, measuring the total duration of a quarter from the opening bounce to the siren. The length of a quarter can be highly variable when timed in this way. For example, there was just one goal and 11 stoppages during the opening quarter of a 2015 match between Essendon and Western Bulldogs, which as a result ran for just 23 minutes and 23 seconds. At the other extreme, the second quarter of a match between Brisbane Lions and Adelaide Crows the previous year had clocked 39 minutes 43 seconds, after two players had been taken from the field on stretchers.

To conduct our analysis, we therefore need to standardise the time stamps by scaling the duration of each quarter to 25% of its corresponding match. This enables us to consider each scoring event as having occurred at a certain percentage on the timeline of a match. By using this method, we find that accuracy does tend to fade during each quarter. On average, the conversion rate falls by about one percentage point for every five minutes of play. Tiredness could be one reason for this. The general negative trend is observed across all quarters and for both the winning and losing teams, with the exception being

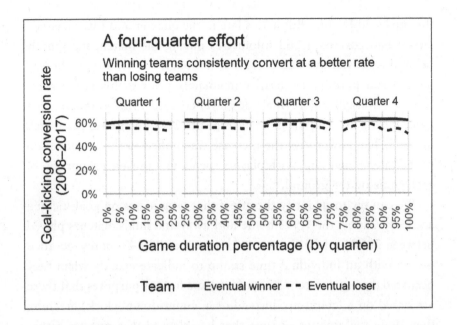

A four-quarter effort

Winning teams consistently convert at a better rate than losing teams

Goal-kicking conversion rate (2008–2017)

| Quarter 1 | Quarter 2 | Quarter 3 | Quarter 4 |

Game duration percentage (by quarter)

Team — Eventual winner - - Eventual loser

that winning sides tend to improve their accuracy during the last quarter. Intriguingly, average accuracy was at its lowest during the first quarter, although this does not necessarily refute the influence of fatigue. In this case, it could be argued that teams are harder to score against when they are fresh at the start of a game.

The impact of the opposition's defensive incentive or ability also appears evident when looking at the influence of in-game margins on conversion rates. In general, we find that players are more accurate when their team is ahead on the scoreboard. However, when a deficit is greater than 50 points, the trend reverses and the accuracy of the trailing side tends to improve. This might be an indication that teams that are winning comfortably lose motivation to maintain the same level of defensive effort, allowing their opponents to secure better quality chances on goal.

Crunch time

If there is anyone who doesn't need to be convinced about the effect of incentive on performance, it is Port Adelaide's Chad Wingard. 'I don't like playing games where we're smashing teams. I don't get into them,' Wingard admitted. 'I prefer the closer games. That's what I live

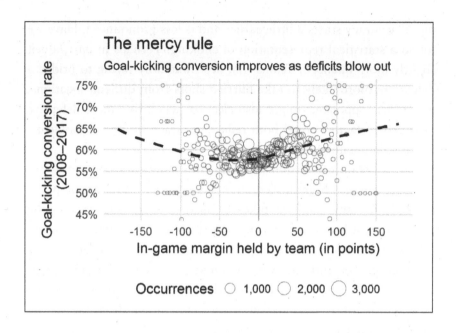

The mercy rule

Goal-kicking conversion improves as deficits blow out

Goal-kicking conversion rate (2008–2017) vs In-game margin held by team (in points)

Occurrences ○ 1,000 ○ 2,000 ○ 3,000

for.' Such is his affinity for the big stage that he asked his teammates to call him 'LeBron' in honour of his hero, the NBA superstar LeBron James. He was only half joking. 'Everyone wants to be that guy,' he said. 'The guy who has done extraordinary things and dominates.' David Steventon, a trained psychologist, has the somewhat New Age job title of mindset performance coach at the Power. He believes Wingard's fearlessness is inspirational. 'He certainly does embrace the big moment and rarely misfires,' said Steventon. 'Moving toward big moments willingly, almost hungrily, is a great mindset frame as he's essentially saying, "Get the ball to me. I will get the job done". If we are believers in the "you move towards what you think about" theory, then Chad's process is a great example of a player setting himself up for success.'

We can create a picture of the crunch moments to which Wingard aspires by overlaying our analysis of accuracy by time with the patterns of conversion rates by margin. By focusing on just the final quarter, when games are truly on the line, we see a few key trends emerge. Teams trailing by a margin of two goals or fewer in the last 10% of a match, which is roughly eight minutes of playing time, tend to become more inaccurate as the clock ticks by. A similar trend is observed in teams down by between 13 and 24 points, although the dip in accuracy starts a little earlier and is less pronounced. Have we found a statistical representation of choking? Perhaps in part, albeit slightly more nuanced. Teams that are frantically trying to bridge a deficit are more likely to take hurried shots from difficult locations, while their opponents might also elect to switch to a more defensive style. These factors could both reduce accuracy in critical moments, as could late-game fatigue.

The all-team conversion rate also drops steeply when scores are level late in a match. In this situation, it seems that teams are prepared to settle for any score to take the lead. During our decade-long sample size, it is notable that in comparison to 18 draws, there were 29 one-point results, 40 two-point margins and 49 games decided by three points. Indeed, every winning margin between one point and 38 points was more common than a draw between 2008 and 2017. This pattern is strengthened when examining the league's entire history, with every margin between one and 42 points occurring more frequently than a draw. Denis Pagan once famously described the feeling of a draw as like dancing with one's sister, and he and his fellow coaches must believe that is a fate worth avoiding at all costs.

The best footballers are often remembered for delivering when the result is in the balance and the stakes large. In contrast, some

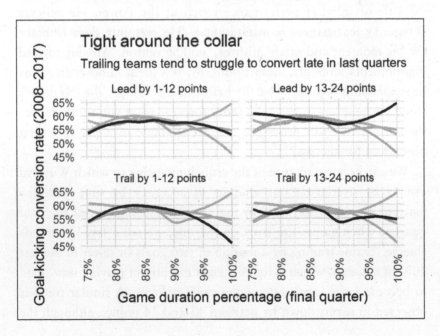

players gain infamy by underperforming in big moments. We have compiled a list of players who have taken at least 20 'crunch' shots since 2008. For this exercise, we have defined crunch time as being any time during the final quarter when the lead to either side is two goals or fewer. The league-wide conversion rate in this situation is 1.8 percentage points worse than the average. Of the 41 players we identified as meeting our 20-shot minimum, only about a third recorded a better conversion rate during crunch time than they did overall. Wingard lives up to his own hype, placing third on the list of players who have performed above themselves, behind only Western Bulldogs midfielder Marcus Bontempelli and Gold Coast captain Tom Lynch.

Players who convert better in 'crunch time' than at all other times, 2008–2017				
Player	Overall conversion	Crunch conversion	Other conversion	Difference
Marcus Bontempelli	54.2%	80.0%	50.0%	+30.0%
Tom J Lynch	62.6%	76.2%	61.8%	+14.4%
Chad Wingard	60.5%	72.4%	59.4%	+13.0%
Jarrad Waite	62.8%	73.3%	61.9%	+11.4%
Jarryd Roughead	61.9%	69.8%	61.4%	+8.3%
James Podsiadly	63.7%	70.0%	63.3%	+6.7%
Nick Riewoldt	61.5%	67.7%	61.2%	+6.5%
Angus Monfries	65.5%	71.4%	65.0%	+6.4%
Stephen Milne	62.6%	67.6%	62.2%	+5.4%
Drew Petrie	61.9%	65.9%	61.6%	+4.3%
Overall	58.5%	56.9%	58.6%	−1.8%

On the other side of the equation, there is a longer list of those who underperformed in crunch moments. Fourteen players recorded a conversion rate that was more than 10 percentage points worse than their average. At first glance, some of the names may seem surprising. The likes of Jack Gunston, Luke Breust, Eddie Betts, and Jay Schulz have enjoyed a healthy reputation for being straight shooters. In fact, all on our list except Michael Hurley and Dustin Martin have recorded an above-average overall accuracy level since 2008, with Gunston, Breust, Betts, Chapman, Fevola, and Motlop each featuring in the top 31 among those who had at least 200 shots.

Players who convert worse in 'crunch time' than at all other times, 2008–2017				
Player	Overall conversion	Crunch conversion	Other conversion	Difference
Jack Gunston	65.0%	41.7%	66.4%	−24.7%
Luke Breust	67.7%	45.5%	69.5%	−24.0%
Michael Hurley	58.4%	40.0%	61.3%	−21.3%
Hayden Ballantyne	59.9%	41.7%	61.2%	−19.5%
Steven Motlop	63.6%	50.0%	65.1%	−15.1%
Eddie Betts	66.5%	52.9%	67.2%	−14.2%
Brendan Fevola	64.0%	51.9%	64.9%	−13.1%
Paul Chapman	65.7%	53.8%	66.8%	−12.9%
Dustin Martin	57.0%	45.5%	58.3%	−12.9%
Jay Schulz	68.1%	57.1%	68.9%	−11.7%
Overall	58.5%	56.9%	58.6%	−1.8%

While both lists include a mix of small, medium, and tall forwards, there is a greater proportion of key targets among the overperformers, and more opportunists among the underperformers. Might it be that the smaller forwards are attempting more difficult shots?

Goal-kicking spread over time

In the 19 AFL seasons between 1999 and 2017, there were exactly 84,441 scores from set shots and 83,640 scores from general play. When rounded, this equates to a 50–50 split. While the world's other football codes mostly afford teams the freedom to choose which players take their set shots at goal, the same cannot be said for Australian football. The penalty takers in soccer, rugby league and rugby union are usually experts at the skill, which they refine through rigorous and repetitive training. American and Canadian football have a specialised position of kicker, which assumes sole responsibility for kicking field goals and extra points. But in Australian Rules, only in the case of injury can a set shot be handed over to a teammate. This results in a much greater spread of goal kickers, which has only expanded over time.

Sports biomechanics lecturer Dr Kevin Ball is one of those well-named people who were born to do their job. In a classic case of nominative determinism, he runs a private kicking consultancy for

AFL players who want to learn how to make a ball sing. He was previously a full-time AFL assistant coach and biomechanist under Chris Connolly at Fremantle, and has also worked for the Melbourne Storm and South Sydney Rabbitohs rugby league teams, as well as rugby union's Melbourne Rebels. 'If you look at the percentages of rugby league and union goal-kicking accuracy compared to the AFL, they're 20 to 30 per cent higher,' said Dr Ball. 'The main difference is that they don't have the ball drop and they're kicking with a place kick, so they've got clarity around where the ball is when they impact it.' Still, Dr Ball is a firm believer that improved accuracy is attainable in Australian football, and he scoffs at the notion that it has been an aspect of the game that has failed to match the advances seen in other areas. 'One thing people don't consider when they say that is there are now more players having shots at goal,' he said. 'There is more of a spread of goal kickers so it's not an accurate comparison, because the strategies and gameplay have changed.' To test Dr Ball's assertion, we will try to quantify how significant that change has been.

Some players, such as Charlie Dixon, Lance Franklin or Jack Riewoldt, are easily identifiable as their team's predominant forward. However, to single out their equivalent in every team since 1897 is a little more ambiguous and difficult. We could rank a team's forwards across a season based on their average number of scoring shots per game, but this might be skewed by players who record extreme results in a small sample. Alternatively, we might assume that the player who recorded the most scoring shots for a team during a season was its main forward, although that would fail to acknowledge that a side's structure can markedly change from one week to the next. For example, Carlton's Stephen Silvagni was selected as fullback in the league's Team of the Century, but still managed to finish his career with 202 goals. Likewise, nobody would question that Tony Lockett was top dog in St Kilda's forward line during the late '80s and early '90s, yet he failed to record the most scoring shots for the Saints in three of the seven seasons between 1988 and 1994 because of a combination of injury and suspension.

Maybe the simplest way is to identify a team's primary forwards on a game-by-game basis, and then aggregate the results to try to assess any trends. For each match, the player with the most goals for his team is ranked first, the player with the next most is ranked second, and so on. It doesn't matter in which order we rank players who kicked the same number of goals, because at the aggregate level it will have no effect on our overall measurement of goal-kicking spread. The following table shows Port Adelaide's rankings from the 2017 elimination final loss to West Coast:

Goals kicked and goal-kicker 'rank' of Port Adelaide players in the 2017 AFL elimination final		
Player	Goals	Goal rank
Charlie Dixon	3	1
Ollie Wines	2	2
Sam Gray	2	3
Chad Wingard	1	4
Brad Ebert	1	5
Sam Powell-Pepper	1	6
All other players	0	7–22

By ranking teams' performances in this way and aggregating the results by season, we find that the average proportion of goals per game kicked by a side's top four scoring forwards has diminished at a relatively constant rate since 1897. St Kilda's Charlie Baker kicked a whopping 47% of his club's goals during the 1902 season, but just over a century later Angus Monfries won Essendon's club

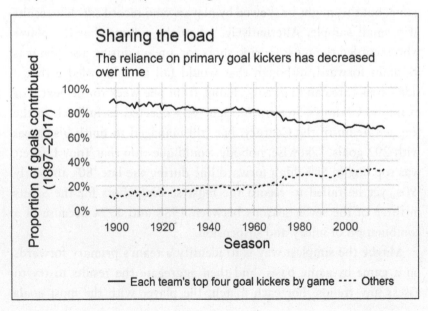

Sharing the load

The reliance on primary goal kickers has decreased over time

Proportion of goals contributed (1897–2017)

Season

—— Each team's top four goal kickers by game · · · · Others

goal-kicking award in a year that he contributed less than 9% of the Bombers' season total. When the VFL's eight teams averaged just under 38 points per game in 1899, each club's top-ranked forward was contributing about 41% of his side's goal tally and about 92% were being kicked by just four players. By 2017, the average team's leading forward was kicking only a quarter of its goals, while its top four were combining for less than two-thirds. This means that, on average, the remainder of the side is now contributing three times the proportion of goals it did 120 years ago.

Goal-kicking spread and accuracy

The dramatic expansion in the spread of goal kickers is one thing, but has this change in team dynamic affected overall accuracy? Do primary goal kickers tend to have better conversion rates? To answer these two questions, we need to change our ranking system to include scoring shots instead of just goals.

Scoring shots and scoring shot 'rank' of Port Adelaide players in the 2017 AFL elimination final					
Player	Goals	Behinds	Scoring shots	Scoring shot rank	Conversion
Charlie Dixon	3	6	9	1	33%
Travis Boak	0	3	3	2	0%
Chad Wingard	1	2	3	3	33%
Sam Powell-Pepper	1	1	2	4	50%
Ollie Wines	2	0	2	5	100%
Sam Gray	2	0	2	6	100%
Jarman Impey	0	1	1	7	0%
Karl Amon	0	1	1	8	0%
Paddy Ryder	0	1	1	9	0%
Robbie Gray	0	1	1	10	0%
Brad Ebert	1	0	1	11	100%
All other players	0	0	0	12–22	–

We can only assess matches since 1965 in this way, because of the availability of data on individual behinds scorers. When two or more players have recorded the same number of scoring shots, this time we randomise their rank to ensure our results are not skewed by the alphabetical arrangement of player names. Through this approach,

Practice makes perfect

Players taking more shots at goal tend to be more accurate

Goal-kicking conversion (1965–2017)

Percentage of scores by each player 'score rank'

Total scores ○ 25,000 ○ 50,000 ○ 75,000 ○ 100,000

we discover a neat correlation between a player's conversion rate and the share of shots that they take. It turns out that a player's accuracy tends to increase by about 1% for every additional 2.5% share of their team's shots.

Dr Ball's explanation for this trend is straightforward. Primary forwards are usually among their team's most highly skilled kickers and are typically stationed near goal. Not only do they take more shots, but they also take them from closer range. He said this is still the case in the modern AFL, although somewhat less pronounced than in years gone by. 'In the days when there was just a dedicated full-forward who would lead out of the goal square, their average kick for goal would probably be about 30 metres and within the 45-degree arc,' he said. 'Those guys wouldn't get up the ground too far and they were the best kicks, so they would take most of the shots.'

As we saw earlier, the league-wide conversion rate climbed steadily throughout the 20th century until hitting a peak of 60.3% in 2000. It has cooled off a little since then, but has still bounced around at historic highs of between 57% and 60%. In fact, the 22 seasons prior to 2018 ranked as the top 22 for conversion on record. It is enlightening, though, to juxtapose the league's average accuracy level with the figures derived from our scoring shot rankings. If we

30

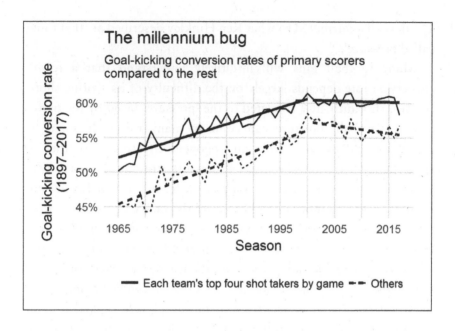

The millennium bug

Goal-kicking conversion rates of primary scorers compared to the rest

Legend: Each team's top four shot takers by game —— Others

split players between those who were among their team's top four shot takers and the rest, we find that while both groups reflect the annual direction of the league-wide trend, the top four always outdo the average while the rest fall below it. Of course, the fact that players who take fewer shots have a lower conversion rate is not particularly revelatory. The noteworthy part is that the period since 2000 marks the longest interval over which the league's average conversion rate has not improved, and that this is mostly attributable to the performance of the fifth- to 22nd-ranked shot takers in each team.

Pressure, scoring spread and accuracy

The way Australian football is played at its highest level has changed dramatically since 2000. The game has transformed from a man-on-man style in which players largely kept to defined positions, to a high-possession running game in which team defence is emphasised. The use of the interchange bench to rest and rotate players has revolutionised the strategies that coaches can employ, with zones and presses becoming staples of most game plans. The number of effective tackles being laid has also skyrocketed, jumping from a team average of 32 per game in 2000 to 69 per game in 2017, an increase of 116%.

This has all contributed to what Ken Hinkley described as 'that thing called pressure'.

Many football fans will intuitively understand that a team's conversion rate depends largely on the difficulty of its scoring shots. In turn, shot difficulty is related to the 'pressure' faced by the player kicking the ball. Pressure can come in many forms. It might be direct physical pressure from an opponent effecting a smother or spoil. Equally, it might be inferred pressure from an opponent who is blocking space, forcing a player to kick from wider or further out from goal. For simplicity, we have used the tackle count as a proxy for the physical pressure in a match. In doing this, we find a clear connection between pressure and accuracy. For every 14% increase in the average tackle rate per season, the league's average conversion rate tends to fall in that season by about one percentage point.

This relationship is accentuated for the players ranked fifth to 22nd in their team for scoring shots per game, who appear to be by far the most sensitive to this pressure factor. Their conversion rate is about four times more adversely affected by pressure than that of their team's top four scorers, falling by about one percentage point for every 8% increase in tackles. This insight falls in line with

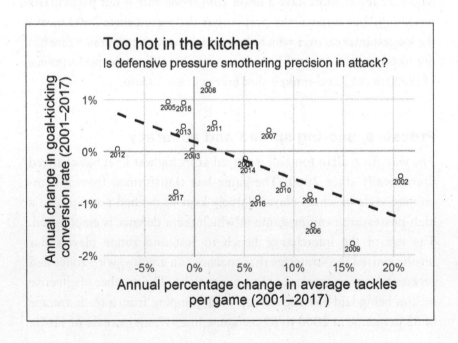

32

Dr Ball's theory that secondary scorers not only are less likely to be permanent forwards, but also usually take harder shots at goal. 'Because the defensive zones are better these days, the profile of where players are kicking from has changed,' he said. 'They're now being forced further from the goal and further towards the sides as well.' Midfielders are also generally required to run harder throughout a match, meaning there is a greater likelihood they will be fatigued when taking their shots.

All of this is not to say that the role of the permanent forward has remained static. Gone are the days of six forwards waiting for the ball to be delivered to them in the 50-metre arc. In the modern era of team defence, every player remains constantly engaged, pushing up or back depending on the game's situation. Charlie Dixon said while he admired the great goal kickers of the past, it was unfair to hold them as a standard for the modern key forward. 'If you watch some of those old guys, sure, they kicked straight, but they also got to stay at home and not really leave the forward 50,' he laughed. 'Kicking 100 goals a season would be nice, but they weren't expected to run up the ground and chase someone as well.'

Does accuracy persist across seasons?

Rightly or wrongly, a team's goal-kicking accuracy is often remembered as its defining characteristic. This was certainly the case for the Power's class of 2017, but not for the reason it would have hoped. 'Port Adelaide did improve on defence and in creating more scoring opportunities, although repetitive lapses in conversion accuracy ultimately proved costly, very costly,' wrote Michelangelo Rucci in his post-season report card. We might wonder, then, how difficult is it for a team to turn around its accuracy from one season to the next? In the chart overleaf we show each team's year-by-year record of 'relative accuracy'. The darker tiles reflect those years in which a team's accuracy level was higher than the all-team average, while the lighter tiles indicate years in which a team's accuracy fell below the average. If accuracy or inaccuracy were defining and persistent characteristics, we would expect to see long runs of both light and dark tiles.

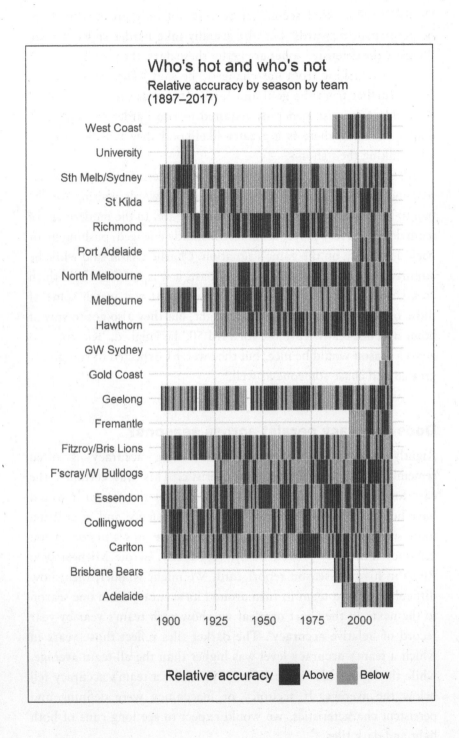

Who's hot and who's not

Relative accuracy by season by team
(1897–2017)

Relative accuracy ■ Above ▨ Below

West Coast
University
Sth Melb/Sydney
St Kilda
Richmond
Port Adelaide
North Melbourne
Melbourne
Hawthorn
GW Sydney
Gold Coast
Geelong
Fremantle
Fitzroy/Bris Lions
F'scray/W Bulldogs
Essendon
Collingwood
Carlton
Brisbane Bears
Adelaide

1900   1925   1950   1975   2000

Clearly, some clubs have enjoyed an above-average conversion rate for more than just one or two consecutive seasons. For example, the Western Bulldogs finished at least one percentage point above average in every season between 2005 and 2011. Other clubs have been below average for extended periods too, and there does seem to be a tendency for runs of lower accuracy to last longer than the above-average streaks. However, the overall pattern appears to be that teams are about as likely to switch from being above average to below average as they are to repeat an above-average year. The largest single-season improvement in accuracy was registered by the St Kilda team of 1908, which raised its conversion rate by more than 13 percentage points from the previous year to 48.6%. Richmond's 1964 side, in contrast, recorded the largest single-season decline. The Tigers' accuracy dropped by almost 12 percentage points that year to 39.7% as they adapted to new coach Len Smith's play-on-at-all-costs game plan.

We can look at the season-by-season picture in another way, by plotting all teams' relative accuracy levels across successive years in a single chart (next page). Here, each dot represents the accuracy displayed by a single team across two consecutive seasons, relative to the all-team accuracy rate in each season. Consider, for example, the Western Bulldogs teams of 2016 and 2017, labelled in the chart and shown with a black dot. In 2016, the Bulldogs recorded an accuracy of 52.2% compared to the all-team average of 53.2%, giving them a -1% relative accuracy for that year. That determines their x-value in the chart. In 2017, they slipped to 46.7% against an all-team average of 53.0%, giving them a -6.3% relative accuracy for that year. That determines their y-value in the chart.

If accuracy and inaccuracy persisted, we would expect to see dots clustering along a line running from the lower left of the chart and rising to the upper right. This would imply that teams carried their relative conversion rates from one season to the next. The black line on the chart is an average of all the points for different relative accuracy levels. It reveals that there is a positive correlation between teams' relative accuracy levels across successive seasons, but only a weak one. Mathematically it is just +0.18, whereas a perfect correlation would be +1. The slope of the line is less than 1, which provides evidence of the phenomenon known as 'regression to the mean', in that relatively inaccurate teams in one season tend to be relatively less inaccurate the following season, and that relatively accurate teams tend to be relatively less so in the next.

We can gain some further insight by answering two simple questions:

1. If a team was more accurate than the average team in one season, how likely is it to be above average in the next?
   Answer: 54%
2. If a team was less accurate than the average team in one season, how likely is it to be below average in the next?
   Answer: 59%

In short, teams that are above average in terms of accuracy in one season are only slightly more likely to be above average in the next. Teams that are below average are somewhat more likely to remain

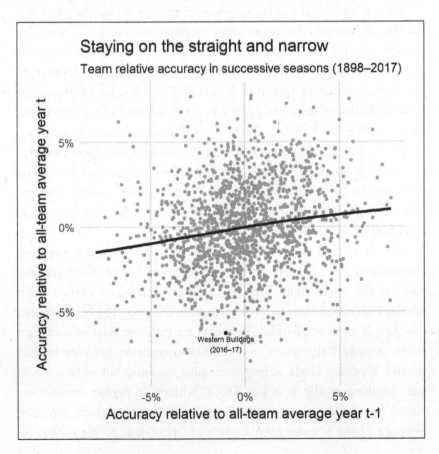

36

so the following year, but still have about a two-in-five chance of becoming above average. The fact that these percentages are both above 50% is why we do see some runs of below- and above-average accuracy for some teams in the earlier chart.

Interestingly, the results for average scoring shot production and concession are quite different:

1. A team that generated scoring shots at a higher than average rate in one season was 70% likely to do the same in the next.
2. A team that generated scoring shots at a lower than average rate in one season was 71% likely to do the same in the next.
3. A team that conceded scoring shots at a higher than average rate in one season was 70% likely to do the same in the next.
4. A team that conceded scoring shots at a lower than average rate in one season was 75% likely to do the same in the next.

All of this strongly hints that there might be a large random component to goal-kicking accuracy. This is certainly the case if we are talking in terms of entire seasons. Instead, it appears that the creation and concession of scoring shots might be a more useful, stable metric.

You always take the weather with you

We have seen that season-to-season accuracy can be fickle, but is it any easier to predict a team's conversion rate from one game to the next? Well, in a word, no. The all-time correlation between a team's accuracy in one game and its accuracy in its previous match is just +0.13, which is barely better than chance. If we only consider matches played since 1980, the correlation is even lower at a mere +0.02. So, what other factors might we look to before a game to forecast the accuracy levels of the participating teams?

An obvious one is the prevailing conditions. The Power's psychologist, David Steventon, has noticed that players often seek his counsel once winter arrives. 'Those down times tend to happen between June, July, and August when it's getting cold, it's getting wet and they're beginning to think it's getting harder to kick goals,' said Steventon. 'Some players start to believe, "I can't really be expected to slot these ones because it's so wet and the ball is so heavy", but is that necessarily the truth? It's probably not.' While it would be too daunting a task to compile detailed weather data for every match, we can use the month and time of day that a game was played as a rough proxy. In analysing these factors, we will consider only games from 2000 to 2017, because the average conversion rate was relatively stable during this period.

What we find is that average accuracy levels vary only a little based on the time of day at which a game starts, and almost not at all by month. Steventon's intuition was right. Games starting before 4.30 pm local time see accuracy levels of about one percentage point higher than in games that start later. One plausible explanation for this is that dew affects at least some games that are played into the evening. This is supported by the fact that twilight and night games also feature fewer scoring shots. A game starting before 4.30 pm will produce, on average, one more scoring shot than a game starting later. The league's fixturing decisions may also be a factor, as the quality of a round's matches is rarely spread evenly throughout the day. Friday and Saturday nights games are more likely, at least in theory, to feature better sides in important games, which may lead to greater defensive pressure and more difficult shots.

To put all of this in some sort of context, we can use the information from these tables to consider the likely total scores in a game given certain conditions. A game starting before 4.30 pm would, on average, produce 51 scoring shots, 53.9% of which would be registered as goals. That would make the average total score (51 x 53.9% x 6) + (51 x 46.1% x 1), or about 188 points. In comparison, a game starting at 7.30 pm or later would, on average, produce 50.4 scoring shots, 53% of which would be registered as goals. That would make the average total score (50.4 x 53% x 6) + (50.4 x 47% x 1), or about 184 points. So, we can say that the difference between a day game and one under lights is slightly more than four points per game. One last thing worth highlighting before we move on is the results for games played during the months of September and October, which would mostly be finals. We see fewer scoring shots (48.8 per game) during these months than in other months, reflecting the

38

Average accuracy by month and start time (2000–2017)

	Before 4.30 pm	4.30 pm to 7.30 pm	7.30 pm or later	All times
March	54.1%	54.0%	53.5%	53.9%
April	52.9%	52.7%	52.9%	52.8%
May	54.2%	53.0%	52.9%	53.7%
June	53.9%	52.9%	54.3%	53.7%
July	54.2%	52.2%	53.4%	53.5%
August	54.3%	53.4%	52.0%	53.7%
September/ October	53.0%	51.8%	52.0%	52.4%
All months	53.9%	52.9%	53.0%	53.4%

Average scoring shots by month and start time (2000–2017)

	Before 4.30 pm	4.30 pm to 7.30 pm	7.30 pm or later	All times
March	54.7	49.8	54.6	53.0
April	52.1	50.4	50.2	51.3
May	50.9	50.9	50.1	50.8
June	49.7	49.6	50.3	49.8
July	50.7	48.6	50.2	50.0
August	50.9	50.1	51.0	50.7
September/ October	49.0	48.9	48.4	48.8
All months	51.0	49.9	50.4	50.6

Average accuracy and scoring shots by venue (2000–2017)

Venue (minimum 30 games)	Games	Average accuracy	Average number of scoring shots	Likely score
Docklands	843	55.2%	52.0	195.4
Princes Park	44	54.5%	51.3	191.0
Sydney Showground	46	53.8%	50.4	185.9
Kardinia Park	137	53.7%	48.0	176.9
York Park	64	53.6%	46.5	171.2
Subiaco	407	53.3%	49.3	180.7
Adelaide Oval	93	53.1%	48.7	178.0
Manuka Oval	43	53.1%	49.3	180.0
MCG	888	52.9%	50.7	184.6
Football Park	325	52.6%	49.6	180.0
Gabba	216	52.4%	53.5	193.5
SCG	171	52.3%	49.3	178.2
Sydney Olympic Stadium	56	51.8%	48.5	174.0
Carrara	84	51.7%	50.0	179.3

more defensive nature of finals contests. We also see lower accuracy (52.4%), which, again, might indicate the effect of pressure.

One of the unusual aspects of Australian football is the variability allowed in the dimensions of the playing field. For example, the dimensions of the playing surface of the MCG at the time of writing were listed as 161 m x 140 m, while Kardinia Park's were 170 m x 115 m. That represents about a 15% difference in area. It seems reasonable to assume that these differences might have some effect on accuracy and scoring.

Looking again at the period since 2000, the data reveals a difference of about 3.5 percentage points in the average accuracy across all venues. Teams were most inaccurate at Carrara, where 51.7% of scoring shots were registered as goals. They kicked straightest at Docklands, with an all-team conversion rate of 55.2%. To the end of 2017, the Bulldogs' renowned marksman Tory Dickson had played more than half of his career games at the roofed venue, kicking 94.28 (77%). 'If you hit the ball well, it doesn't favour a certain direction, which I think happens because you're under a roof and the conditions are great,' said Dickson. 'Brian Taylor once claimed there was a wind or a fade to the right at Docklands, but there's not.'

In terms of scoring shot production, York Park was the most barren venue at 46.5 per game, while the Gabba was the most fertile at 53.5 per game. Combining scoring shot production and accuracy sees York Park emerge as the lowest-scoring ground at 171.2 points per game, and Docklands as the highest-scoring ground at an average of 195.4 points per game. We should note, however, that the variability in these numbers, especially those relating to scoring shot production, can't be attributed to the venue alone. They would also be affected by the average quality of the teams that played at those grounds during our sample period. One way of accounting for this is to develop attacking and defensive ratings for teams – as we will discuss later in this book – and measure the association between those ratings and goal-kicking accuracy. It should come as no surprise that, after doing this, we find that a team's accuracy is positively related to its own attacking ability, and negatively related to its opponent's defensive ability. Again, though, the correlations are modest.

Chapter Two
Expected Goals

Shot selection

David Steventon has a framed quote sitting on the windowsill of his office. It reads, 'When you change the belief, you change the results.' 'That's really the crux of what my work is all about,' said Port Adelaide's mindset performance coach. 'We tend to focus a lot on self-belief, which in turn links in to resilience. We try to instil a resilience within the players, so that whatever they're going through, they feel like they're going to come out the other side.' Steventon works closely with Trent Hentschel and Aaron Greaves, who oversee Port's goal-kicking program. Hentschel joined the Power as a development coach in 2015 after crossing the great divide from the Adelaide Crows, where his own promising career as a forward had been curtailed by injury. 'Basically, we look at two things with goal kicking,' he said. 'Obviously there's the player's routine and biomechanics, which we try to get down pat, and then the second major component to the program is putting the players in every scenario possible that might come up in a game.' To enable the latter, the ground is divided into 12 different zones. In contrast to the successful laissez-faire approach taken by Grant Thomas at St Kilda more than a decade earlier, the Power fastidiously monitors every shot a player takes. 'It's tracked within an inch of its life,' said Hentschel. 'There are folders at each station that the coaches have, and those results then go into a database, which allows us to pull up information on where they've been kicking well, or where they need to improve.'

Greaves, a former schoolteacher, is the Power's head of football development. He believes that players need to be empowered to use different types of kick depending on the situation they face. To explain this point, he uses the analogy of a golfer selecting which club to use from a certain distance or lie. 'Rather than just having your normal sort of set shots all the time, we do snap routine set shots, on the run, left foot, right foot,' he said. 'We'll ask players to consider what they'll do if they, say, mark the ball next to the point post. Will they banana it? Will they kick a left-foot snap? We try to expose the players to all the scenarios they might face in a game, so they'll be ready for them.' There is also an emphasis on teaching them to understand the difference between when they should be taking a shot, and when they should be looking to pass to a better placed teammate. 'It's about minimising the wider and longer kicks and trying to get into good areas,' said Greaves. 'Because of the low percentages of taking long shots on goal, a lot of teams will now just put it back into a contest with a shorter kick to 20 metres out.'

After its disappointing end to 2017, Port Adelaide's football department appointed a new full-time analyst named Robert Younger. It was a bold hire, with the 24-year-old yet to complete his mathematical sciences degree at the University of Melbourne. Younger had attracted the club's attention through his widely read statistical blog, Figuring Footy. Among his most popular posts were those that detailed a concept called 'Expected Score', or 'xSco', which he had adapted from other sports, such as soccer and ice hockey. Younger had developed a model to rate the difficulty of scoring shots in the AFL, enabling him to judge a team's performance by the quality of the chances it created, rather than purely its scoreboard output. The concept aligned well with the message that the Power was already preaching to its players. What can Younger's model teach us about the art of goal kicking?

A model for shot difficulty

In rating the difficulty of a shot for goal, there are two obvious factors to consider. The first is field position, which can be measured by the distance and angle to the centre of the goal. A close, straight kick makes for a much easier shot than one from 40 metres out, on the boundary. The second consideration is the type of shot taken. A set shot, a quick snap, or a soccer-style ground kick will all have varying difficulties at different points on the field. Beyond these two core criteria, a shot difficulty model could also account for some of the influences we have already discussed, such as weather, venue, start time, margin, conditions, and time left in the match. Champion Data uses a model based on its own internal pressure ratings. For the sake of simplicity, the model we will outline here will be contained to the basic 'where' (field position) and 'how' (kick type).

To assign a number to the difficulty of a shot, we can look at how often similar shots have been converted in the recent past. In the five seasons to the end of 2017 there were about 54,000 shots at goal. About 27,000, or roughly half, were goals and about 19,000 were behinds. A further 8,000 missed entirely, either falling short or sailing wide. For each of these shots we note the distance and angle to goal, and classify it as one of six types of kick: ground kick, set shot, set-shot snap, play on from a mark, snap from general play, or shot from general play (or on the run). Once we have this data, we can run a regression analysis to discover the historical accuracy of each different type of shot at varying points on the ground. The competition-wide accuracy for a certain shot is how we determine its difficulty.

For example, consider a set shot that is 30 metres from goal and at an angle of about five degrees from the centre. Our model shows us that similar shots to this in the AFL have resulted in goals about

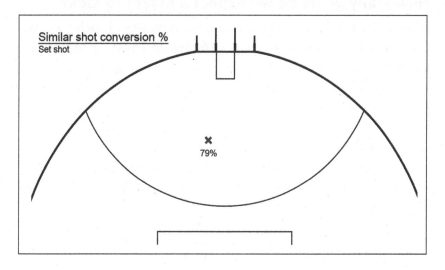

Similar shot conversion %
Set shot

✖
79%

79% of the time, and in behinds 20% of the time. Only one out of 100 shots from this position would fail to register any score. This is a relatively easy kick. If we see a player take a lot of shots from this position and miss them at a rate much greater than one in five, we may start to question their kicking ability.

Next, consider a quick snap from a pack near the junction of the boundary and 50-metre lines. This is a much tougher proposition. On average, only 18% of shots from this position would go through for a major score and 34% would register a behind. Almost half, 48%, wouldn't even trouble the goal umpire.

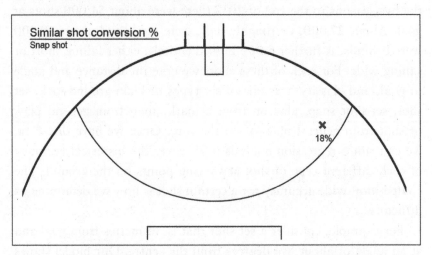

How many goals do we expect a player to kick?

Now that we have a means of rating the difficulty of each shot, we can appraise a player's kicking performance based on what they would have scored if they had met the competition average. The idea is that the numbers we assign to shot difficulty can be added together to give an 'expected' number of goals. In the tradition of similar shot difficulty models in sports such as soccer, we will refer to this value as 'Expected Goals' or, for brevity, 'xG'.

Let's start with a simple example. If an AFL-standard player takes six shots, each with a historical difficulty of 50%, on average we would expect:

$$0.5 + 0.5 + 0.5 + 0.5 + 0.5 + 0.5 = 3 \text{ goals}$$

Their xG for those six shots is three goals. If they score more than that, they have performed above average. If they score fewer, they have performed below average.

A player is unlikely to take several shots of the same difficulty in one match, so let's now contemplate a more realistic scenario. If a player takes four shots with difficulties of 45%, 60%, 70%, and 55%, we would expect:

$$0.45 + 0.6 + 0.7 + 0.55 = 2.3 \text{ goals}$$

Of course, a fraction of a goal makes little sense during a single game. What an xG of 2.3 really tells us is that a player who kicks two or three goals from these four chances has performed at about the competition standard. If they kick four goals, their finishing has been very good. If they kick one or none, it has been poor. With this final piece in place, we now have the framework to judge which players convert at a higher or lower rate than the rest of the league over long periods of time based on the quality of the shots they create. We can also identify the players who take the toughest or easiest shots.

Most teams have a player who revels in the improbable, backing themselves to score from seemingly anywhere in the forward half. For the five years prior to 2018, here are the five players who took the most difficult combination of at least 20 shots in a single season:

Player seasons by hardest average shot difficulty, minimum 20 shots, 2013–2017					
Player	Season	Shots	Average shot difficulty	xG	Goals
Hamish Hartlett	2013	43	33%	14.4	16
Daniel Rich	2017	24	34%	8.2	8
Brodie Smith	2016	24	35%	8.4	7
Matt Suckling	2017	28	35%	9.8	9
Paul Seedsman	2013	23	36%	8.4	9

The list is dominated by halfback flankers and outside midfielders who have big kicks and the confidence to shoot from long distances. While these players may not get forward often, they are happy to blaze away when they do. Of Brodie Smith's 24 shots on goal in

2016, all but one were launched from 40 metres or beyond. Hamish Hartlett took 20 of his 43 shots in 2013 from outside 50, and those that were taken from inside the arc were often from tight angles.

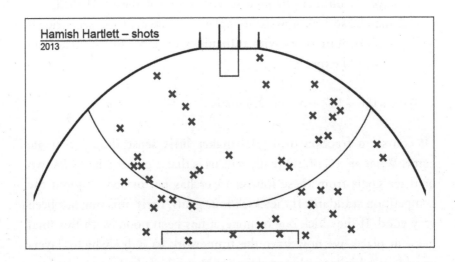

Hamish Hartlett's season-long xG was 14.4, meaning we would have expected the average AFL player to kick 14 or 15 goals from those same chances. Hartlett kicked 16. In the same year, Paul Seedsman finished with a higher conversion rate (39% compared to Hartlett's 37%), but he took fewer shots with a slightly easier average difficulty. This explains why Hartlett's 'goals above expectation' was higher.

Conversely, we have the players who only ever seem to take easy shots. This might be a result of their role, hard work, or conservativeness. Here are the top five player seasons, of those who had at least 20 shots, ranked by easiest average shot difficulty:

Player seasons by easiest average shot difficulty, minimum 20 shots, 2013–2017					
Player	Season	Shots	Average shot difficulty	xG	Goals
Jesse Hogan	2017	28	69%	19.3	20
Tom Boyd	2015	27	67%	18.0	16
Mason Cox	2016	26	66%	17.2	17
Mike Pyke	2013	38	66%	25.0	28
Josh Jenkins	2016	95	65%	61.6	62

This is where we find the ruckmen and the big forwards. Before 2018, Hogan had only kicked two career goals from outside the 50-metre arc. In fact, he did not kick a single point from beyond 50 in his 10 matches in 2017. His only attempt was a kick after the quarter-time siren, which fell about 20 metres short of goal. Instead, he relied on his strong marking in and around the goal square to create chances. Twenty of his 28 attempts were from set shots.

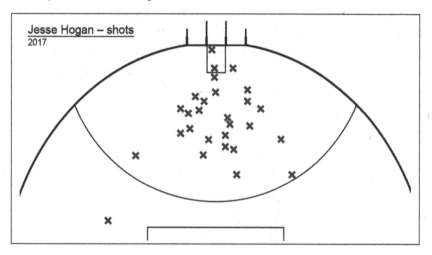

Jesse Hogan – shots
2017

Apart from Hogan, the other four players on the list all spent time in the ruck. Ruckmen who are resting forward often take marks close to goal, and many will prefer passing the ball to a teammate unless they have an easy shot. Interestingly, two North American imports in Mason Cox and Mike Pyke feature on the list, which could indicate that those who are new to the sport are among the most mindful of their limitations. To their credit, both converted their chances at about the AFL average, with Pyke even managing to finish a few goals above his xG. In 2016, Adelaide's Josh Jenkins was the beneficiary of the Crows' strong ball movement and ability to 'slingshot' into an empty forward line. He kicked 30 goals from within 15 metres, which was second only to his teammate Eddie Betts with 31. For reference, the third most goals from inside 15 metres that season was 15, kicked by Greater Western Sydney's Jeremy Cameron.

The deadeyes

We learned earlier that Tory Dickson towers over the rest of the competition on our basic measure of accuracy, defined as goals as a proportion of scores. How, then, does he fare when we factor in our new data relating to shot difficulty? Well, as we will soon see, still extremely well, even if he concedes to being quite conservative in his shot selection. 'I'm probably not one who has shots from ridiculous angles,' he said. 'I'd rather be a team player and put it to a better spot or let someone have a shot who is closer in, because I kind of know my range and know where I want to kick the ball from and have shots from.' This innate cautiousness might in part explain his absence from our top-five list of players whose sharpshooting added the most value to their team in a season:

Player seasons by goals above expectation, 2013–2017						
Player	Season	Shots	Average shot difficulty	xG	Goals	Goals above xG
Luke Breust	2014	78	54%	42.4	57	+14.6
Cyril Rioli	2016	63	54%	34.2	47	+12.8
Josh Kennedy	2013	99	48%	47.7	60	+12.3
Lance Franklin	2014	147	45%	66.9	79	+12.1
Josh Kennedy	2014	103	48%	49.0	61	+12.0

In this table, players have been ranked by their 'goals above expectation' in a single season. In other words, it shows how many more goals they recorded than the average player would have kicked from the same shots. Unsurprisingly, Luke Breust's 2014 season, which saw him tie the AFL record of 29 goals straight without a behind, ranks as the best display of straight kicking in recent history, even though the streak did feature three shots falling short and one going out on the full. The next best was his Hawthorn teammate Cyril Rioli in 2016, narrowly ahead of West Coast forward Josh Kennedy's performance in 2013. Kennedy's return of 60 goals 23 that year looks even more impressive when we consider his xG, which shows that the overall difficulty of his shots was such that the average AFL player would have missed more of them than they kicked.

Breust's goal kicking deserves further analysis. He was easily the AFL's most accurate player in 2014, but how has he fared in other years? Here is his record for the five seasons of our data sample:

Hawthorn forward Luke Breust, 2013–2017						
Season	Games	Shots	Average shot difficulty	xG	Goals	Goals above xG
2013	25	77	55%	42.2	40	−2.2
2014	25	78	54%	42.4	57	+14.6
2015	25	74	59%	43.4	52	+8.6
2016	24	85	54%	48.2	47	−1.2
2017	21	55	51%	28.3	33	+4.7

As we can see, there is little consistency between seasons. Remarkably, his accuracy was below the AFL average the year before his record-equalling streak. He also had a wayward season in 2016. What is the reason for this? Was he not practising as hard in these years? Was he focusing on other aspects of his game? Was his head just not in it? These are all possibilities, although the most likely cause is what statisticians call variance.

What is so hard about kicking goals?

As much as fans, the media, and former coaches and players might deride the current standard of goal kicking in the AFL, in truth it is a vexing skill to master. We have already discussed how the ball drop component distinguishes it from the types of set kicks used in most other codes. The initial release from the hand is a fine motor skill. The ball is dropped to a point at which it can be intercepted by the foot at an average force of 1,000 newtons, or about 100 kilograms. The shape of the ball is also a complicating factor. Unlike Gaelic footballers and soccer players, who also use punt kicks, Australian footballers need to think about the orientation of the ball. The biomechanist and kicking consultant Dr Ball believes it is the combination of the ball drop and orientation that makes kicking such a challenging manoeuvre. Just a minor fault or error in either of these two factors can alter the ball's angle by a few degrees, which could be enough for it to miss its target. 'Certainly, nobody will be able to produce the perfect kick every time,' said Dr Ball. 'I don't think randomness is the word for this. I'd say variability would be the one I use.'

It is this type of variance that could explain the fluctuations in Luke Breust's accuracy. His kicking ability has probably remained relatively constant during his career, but in 2014 he may have significantly benefited from positive variance. His dip in accuracy in 2016 could have been the result of negative variance, missing a few shots that might have previously snuck in. It is important to clarify that this in no way detracts from Breust's status as an above-average finisher. Not all players are equal, and there are some who are genuinely better at converting their chances than others. This is where another valuable tool can be applied: the notion of 'statistical significance'. Statistical significance alerts us to when something happens so often that we can reasonably discount the likelihood of coincidence. The key to determining whether someone is a statistically significant good or bad kick is repetition, meaning that over the course of many shots they have consistently delivered above- or below-average results. Accuracy across a small number of shots may well be evidence of skill, but there is no easy way for us to differentiate a skilled player from a lucky one until we see them take a few more attempts.

Let's consider a non-football analogy. If we are gambling on the toss of a coin with a friend and the first five throws result in four heads and one tail, would this be enough evidence for us to accuse our friend of using a weighted coin? Probably not. The small sample size means the results can be attributed to natural variance. But if we toss it 500 times and see 400 heads and only 100 tails, it is time to take a closer look at that coin. Goal-kicking skill can be viewed in a similar way. We must assume a player is average in ability until they have taken enough shots for their true skill to be revealed. If we witness a player kicking above expectation over many shots, we can begin to suspect that they are playing with their own biased coin. In this case, it will be their natural kicking ability.

Using the concept of statistical significance, we can rank players by how sure we are that they are of above-average ability. In doing this, we will obtain a list of the competition's 'best kicks' over the five seasons prior to 2018. In statistical hypothesis testing, a 'p-value' helps us determine the significance of our results. In this case, low p-values indicate players we can be sure are good kicks. The only way a player can make it onto this list is by kicking straighter than expected over a long period of time. If a player has a p-value of 0.001, it means there is only a 0.1% chance that their results can be ascribed to pure luck.

Player	Games	Shots	Average shot difficulty	xG	Goals	Goals above xG	p-value
Josh Kennedy	108	596	50%	300.7	352	+51.3	0.000002
Lance Franklin	110	652	46%	299.4	340	+40.6	0.0003
Jay Schulz	76	276	52%	144.3	169	+24.7	0.0005
Jack Gunston	116	388	52%	202.4	231	+28.6	0.0007
Tory Dickson	71	190	56%	106.8	126	+19.2	0.001
Jamie Elliott	74	209	54%	113.1	132	+18.9	0.003
Luke Breust	120	369	55%	204.5	229	+24.5	0.003
Cyril Rioli	79	213	54%	114.1	133	+18.9	0.003
Gary Ablett Jr	70	151	43%	64.2	80	+15.8	0.004
Jeremy Cameron	96	422	54%	227.9	252	+24.1	0.005

'Best kicks' by statistical significance, 2013–2017

The list includes a few familiar names, including Mr Accurate himself, Tory Dickson, and a couple of all-time greats in Lance Franklin and Gary Ablett. The rest are all high-quality players. What makes them so good is their ability to match high shot creation with accurate kicking over long periods of time. West Coast's Josh Kennedy marries these qualities perfectly, with only Franklin taking more shots during the five-year period. Surprisingly, Kennedy once had his detractors, who were perhaps preoccupied with his unusual stutter step approach. Our model shows how asinine those critics were. Kennedy not only creates chances at a level few forwards can match, but he is also the AFL's best kick at goal. He has kicked more than 10 goals a season above what an average player would have scored from the same areas. He is undoubtedly one of the best forwards of the modern era.

Under the traditional method of judging goal-kicking accuracy solely from goals and behinds, Franklin would rate as only the 90th most accurate player of those to have taken at least 100 shots during this period. What this fails to consider, however, is the difficulty of his attempts. No other player in the competition has taken nearly as many shots from outside 50 as Franklin. When accounting for difficulty, his record of 340 goals, 231 behinds, and 81 misses is about 40 goals better than we would expect an average player to have kicked if given his chances. His large sample of 652 shots makes us confident that this is much more than just luck.

Ablett is the only non-forward to make the cut. Long noted for his precise field kicking, his performance in front of goal has also been of the highest quality. Unlike the others, who take most of their shots from behind a man on the mark, Ablett usually hits the scoreboard from snaps and shots on the run, which considerably raises his average shot difficulty. Despite this, his finishing ability alone is worth about a goal above average every four games.

At the other end of the spectrum, only six of the players to have taken at least 150 shots had a record so bad that there was a less than 5% chance that an average player would have performed as poorly if given the same chances. Here the p-value signifies the probability of seeing a record as poor, or worse, if the player was an average quality kick. Low p-values indicate the player is more likely to have a below-average kicking ability.

'Worst kicks' by statistical significance, minimum 150 shots, 2013–2017							
Player	Games	Shots	Average shot difficulty	xG	Goals	Goals above xG	p-value
Levi Casboult	88	197	57%	111.4	98	−13.4	0.02
Travis Cloke	82	354	52%	185.1	169	−16.1	0.03
Shane Edwards	98	162	51%	81.9	72	−9.9	0.03
Charlie Cameron	73	199	49%	98.1	87	−11.1	0.04
Josh Caddy	93	185	49%	89.9	80	−9.9	0.04
Luke Dahlhaus	109	191	49%	94.5	84	−10.5	0.05

We uncovered many other notably poor kicks in our five-year sample, including Will Langford, Matthew Kreuzer, Patrick Cripps, Jack Billings, Maverick Weller, Sam Gray, Ollie Wines, Jack Viney, Tomas Bugg, and Elliot Yeo. However, the six players in our table were the only ones who took enough shots to make us statistically confident that they were inherently inaccurate. No-one could be shocked that the maligned Levi Casboult and Travis Cloke rated as the two worst, as small forests have been sacrificed over the years to dissect and debate their goal-kicking woes. In his prime, Cloke was a powerful and influential forward, who was the Magpies' leading goal kicker in four straight seasons after winning a premiership with them in 2010. However, he was plagued by inaccuracy, which steadily worsened as his career progressed. Cloke tried everything to correct the fault. He consulted sports psychologists, listened to music while he practised, and even had finger surgery to improve his ball drop. In the end, nothing was enough. He retired at the end of 2017, after struggling to cope with what he described as a torrent of personal abuse on social media. 'It's death by 1,000 cuts,' said Cloke. 'You read it after a game, week in, week out. You start doubting yourself and having insecurities, and I broke down. Mentally and physically, I was a wreck.'

Besides Cloke and Casboult, the other four players on our 'worst kicks' list all played in a Grand Final in either 2016 or 2017. This surprising fact is a good segue to shift our focus from the individual to the team.

'Expected Goals' into 'Expected Score'

The concept behind Expected Goals should hopefully be making sense by now. To recap, it is simply the average number of goals that will be kicked from a sequence of shots, given some basic information about where and how the shots are taken. But to link xG to a team's score, we will need to introduce a logical complementary model. Expected Behinds (xB) works in the same way as xG, except that it focuses on behinds instead of goals. With both xG and xB in our arsenal, we are now able to work out a player or team's 'Expected Score' (xSco). Expected Score is a measure of what an AFL-average player or team would kick in a match given the chances they created. It is calculated like this:

Expected Score = (6 x Expected Goals) + Expected Behinds

This enables us to break down a team's performance into two elements: how well they created chances (their xSco), and how well they took those chances (their actual score minus their xSco).

The circles on the following chart show the location of every shot taken by Port Adelaide in its extra-time elimination final loss to West Coast in 2017. The dark circles are goals, and the white circles are behinds. The circles with a cross inside show the location of shots at goal that failed to register a score. The size of the circle corresponds to the xG of the shot in question. Charlie Dixon's set shot from 25 m out, dead in front, was the Power's highest xG chance of the game. We would have expected it to be converted into a goal about 86% of the time, a behind about 13.5% of the time, and to miss everything less than one in every 200 attempts. Sam Gray's shot from deep in the right-side pocket was the toughest kick of the game, with the model seeing similar shots converted into goals roughly 22% of the time and behinds 47% of the time. Gray instead fell into the remaining 31%, slicing the shot to the near side and out on the full.

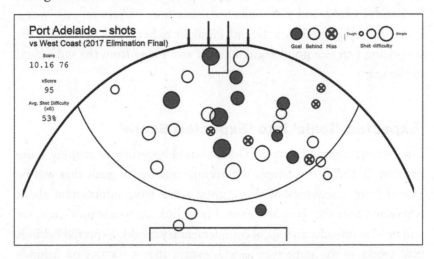

If we sum the xG and xB of every shot the Power took, we get their Expected Score for the match. From Port's 31 shots, its xSco was 95, meaning we would have expected the average team to score 95 points from the same chances. As we heard from Ken Hinkley earlier, his side failed to kick straight. The Power kicked 10.16 (76) through four quarters and two periods of extra time.

West Coast, on the other hand, was clinical. It scored 12 goals from its 19 shots, with only one shot failing to register a score. Josh Kennedy and Jack Darling both kicked three goals straight, while Drew Petrie and Luke Shuey each kicked two straight. The Eagles' 78-point return came from shots worth, on average, about 63 points. The Expected Score for the two sides at the end of the regulation four quarters was 74 to 53 in favour of the Power. While Hinkley

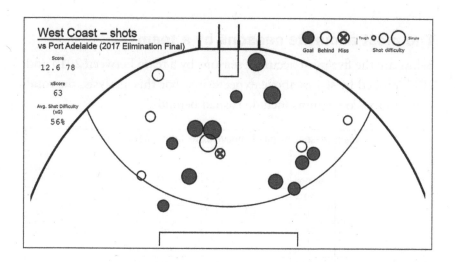

West Coast – shots
vs Port Adelaide (2017 Elimination Final)

Score
12.6 78

xScore
63

Avg. Shot Difficulty
(xG)
56%

Goal   Behind   Miss   Tough   Simple
Shot difficulty

was right to lament his side's goal kicking, its opponent had also converted abnormally well. It is extremely rare for a match with such one-sided shot creation to be lost by the busier team. Only two other games since 2013 have been won by a team with an xSco deficit of more than 30 points.

All teams will experience variations in their conversion from one week to the next, but over the course of a season most will tend to average out to an actual score that is close to their Expected Score. Of the 90 unique team seasons during the period from 2013 to 2017, more than half of the teams finished the year with a 'points for' tally that was within six goals of their xSco. From the hundreds of shots taken by each team throughout a season, xSco can predict how many goals most teams will kick to within six, based on nothing else but the type and location of its attempts. That is a powerful tool. Seventy per cent of all teams will finish a season within 10 goals of their xSco.

It begs the question: if we have so many observably good and bad kicks in the competition, why do most teams still convert their chances at the average rate? The answer to that lies in the AFL's equalisation policy. A salary cap, priority picks, and a draft order determined by ladder position all conspire to ensure that most teams have an equitable mix of above-average and below-average players, which will include a blend of good and bad kicks. Sometimes, though, a team will manage to break the mould.

The most accurate seasons by a team

Below are the five most accurate seasons by a team between 2013 and 2017, ranked by scores above expectation. For this analysis, the total score and xSco columns include rushed behinds.

Team seasons by points above expectation, 2013–2017							
Team	Season	Goals	Behinds	Misses	xSco	Score	Points above xSco
Hawthorn	2014	418	224	90	2,579	2,796	+217
Sydney	2016	376	250	95	2,417	2,558	+141
West Coast	2014	300	193	75	1,905	2,045	+140
Hawthorn	2015	426	234	102	2,718	2,852	+134
Sydney	2014	351	248	102	2,299	2,429	+130

Hawthorn's successful 2014 campaign was unquestionably the season par excellence in our sample. That year's premiers scored more than 200 points above what the average team would have been expected to kick from the same opportunities on goal. They took a mountain of shots too, led by Luke Breust with 57.12 and Jack Gunston with 58.27. The following year they recorded the fourth-biggest margin above expectation, while their 2013 team ranked eighth by this measure, finishing 93 points above its xSco. The triple-premiership-winning Hawks had an unrivalled ability to create high-quality shots through elite ball movement, combined with the skill to convert those chances at a better rate than any other side. The importance of this straight shooting was underlined in the 2014 preliminary final against Port Adelaide, in which they recorded 23 shots on goal to the Power's 30. If both teams had converted their chances at the competition average for their difficulty, Port would have won the match by 20 points instead of losing by three.

In many ways, the Hawks' accuracy was unsurprising considering they had the second (Franklin), fourth (Gunston), seventh (Breust) and eighth (Rioli) best kicks ranked by statistical significance at times during this period. Franklin's move to Sydney also saw him contribute to the second and fifth biggest team margins above expectation, owing primarily to his amazing conversion from outside 50. Perhaps it is to be expected that premiers and runners-up will have had accurate seasons? After all, straight kicking wins matches, and winning matches can win flags. However, a look at the least accurate team seasons shows that isn't always the logical progression.

Team seasons by points below expectation, 2013–2017							
Team	Season	Goals	Behinds	Misses	xSco	Score	Points below xSco
Western Bulldogs	2017	260	240	103	2,045	1,857	−188
Carlton	2016	224	186	96	1,742	1,568	−174
Essendon	2016	200	199	80	1,596	1,424	−172
St Kilda	2017	271	251	75	2,090	1,925	−165
Richmond	2017	331	252	125	2,454	2,294	−160
Western Bulldogs	2016	324	234	124	2,345	2,241	−104

Of the 90 separate team seasons played in the five years prior to 2018, the teams that left the fifth and sixth most points on the table as a result of inaccurate kicking were the 2017 and 2016 premiers, Richmond and the Western Bulldogs. The contrast between those two teams and the Hawks' premiership sides couldn't have been starker. For the Tigers, the major culprits were Josh Caddy (21.22 with nine complete misses), Jason Castagna (26.20 with sixteen misses), and Shane Edwards (11.16 with five misses). All three of these players finished at least five goals below expectation. For the Dogs, Josh Dunkley (9.12 and eight misses), Jordan Roughead (8.10 and four misses), and Lachie Hunter (10.14 and five misses) were the worst offenders. How, then, did these teams achieve ultimate success? Well, there is more to the game than just straight kicking. The Bulldogs consistently created better chances than their opponents, and a well-timed spurt of form in September turned a good season into a great one. Richmond's major strength, along with its solid shot creation, was an ability to pressure opponents and affect their kicks on goal. A look at the conversion rates for the different types of shots conceded by the Tigers highlights just how important their pressure was:

Opposition accuracy by shot type vs Richmond, 2017							
Shot Type	Goals	Behinds	Misses	Average shot difficulty	xSco	Score	Points above xSco
Set shot	141	90	42	52%	942	936	−6
Set snap	5	11	6	50%	73	41	−32
Mark, play on	15	6	1	67%	96	96	0
Off ground	10	4	1	63%	63	64	1
Run/general play	49	49	30	44%	387	343	−44
Snap	44	50	30	43%	361	314	−47

Players are limited in the amount of pressure they can apply to an opponent who is taking a set shot or who has chosen to play on from a mark. Richmond conceded almost exactly as many points as expected from these types of shots. Shots off the ground are usually opportunist in nature, and similarly, opposition sides scored from these about as much as the xSco model predicted they would. But when we look at the types of kicks that defenders can stifle by tackling their opponent or corralling them to a tight angle, the Tigers conceded significantly fewer goals than we would have normally expected. Without even considering the shots that this type of manic defence prevented from being launched in the first place, the pressure the Tigers put on opposition goal kickers may have saved them something in the order of 20 goals during the season. Such frugality can make all the difference.

Alternative ladders

Over the course of 400 or 500 shots in a season, a lot of the luck and natural variance in goal kicking begins to even out. The class of the best finishers will outweigh any poor patches they have endured, while some of the poorer kickers who tumbled a few through early will eventually be found out. The ladder, however, isn't determined on averages. Teams must grind their way through 22 home-and-away games, and then a few more in September if they hope to lift the big cup. An uncharacteristic miss or a fortuitous bounce in any one of those matches could prove the difference between winning and losing.

The fine margins between success and failure make it a worthwhile exercise to examine which team generated the higher Expected Score in each game. Here is what the 2017 ladder would have looked like at the end of the regular season had each team converted its shots at the competition average for difficulty. In this hypothetical scenario, every match was won by the team that created the best chances. For consistency, we have called a game in which a team had a higher xSco than its opponent an 'xWin' for that side. The naming convention has also been applied to draws, losses, competition points and percentage.

	Ladder ranked by competition points if team with best chances won each game, 2017							
	Team	xWins	xDraws	xLosses	xPts	xPerc	Real ladder position	Difference in points from real ladder
1	Adelaide	17	0	5	68	135.8	1	+6
2	Richmond	16	0	6	64	121.1	3	+4
3	Port Adelaide	15	0	7	60	129.6	5	+4
4	Geelong	15	0	7	60	119.5	2	-2
5	Sydney	13	0	9	52	118.5	6	-4
6	GWS	13	0	9	52	109.5	4	-8
7	Melbourne	13	0	9	52	102.4	9	+4
8	St Kilda	12	0	10	48	106.0	11	+4
9	Essendon	12	0	10	48	104.0	7	0
10	Western Bulldogs	11	1	10	46	108.1	10	+2
11	West Coast	10	1	11	42	101.4	8	-6
12	Collingwood	10	0	12	40	100.8	13	+2
13	North Melbourne	9	0	13	36	91.4	15	+12
14	Hawthorn	9	0	13	36	87.4	12	-6
15	Carlton	7	0	15	28	81.2	16	+4
16	Fremantle	6	0	16	24	75.9	14	-8
17	Gold Coast	6	0	16	24	71.3	17	0
18	Brisbane	3	0	19	12	69.3	18	-8

The results of 28 games in 2017 would have been reversed had every team met their xSco in each match. Adelaide would still have claimed the minor premiership, but would have picked up an extra six points through having the better chances in both its draw with Collingwood and loss to Sydney. The only change to the top four would have seen Port Adelaide earn the double chance at the expense of Greater Western Sydney. Before their elimination final horror show, the Power had already lost to the Eagles in a match in which they had created the higher-quality chances. In round seven at Adelaide Oval, Port had created shots with an xSco of 77 points. It finished with a respectable 12.12 (84), with another two shots failing to score. The Eagles, meanwhile, kicked 15.6 (96) from 21 shots, outperforming their xSco of 70 by 26 points. It must be said, though, that aside from a few costly games, poor goal kicking did not particularly plague Port's season. Its own score ended within a goal of its own Expected Score in 13 of its 22 home-and-away games. It significantly outperformed its xSco in five games, and only four times fell more than a goal below its xSco.

At the most basic level, a team will win a football match by kicking more points than its opponent. It can achieve this outcome in three ways. It can: 1) create more chances than its opponent; 2) create higher-quality chances than its opponent; or 3) convert its chances into goals at a higher rate than its opponent. Every match will be decided by at least one of these three factors: quantity, quality, and conversion. Younger hopes his xSco model will help the Power's coaches differentiate between the three, to identify which areas of their game are strong, and which ones need improvement. 'Perhaps we might find there's a problem with the quantity of shots we're creating, and the next step would be to work out why that's the case,' said Younger. 'Are our kicks inside 50 too ambitious, looking for a screamer at the top of the goal square, rather than hitting a short lead in the pocket? Or maybe the problem might stem from further up the ground. Being able to better understand scoring patterns is not an end to itself, but it can lead us in the right direction when trying to understand other things about the game.'

When reporters or fans review why a side won or lost, it is often the team's goal-kicking accuracy that receives the most attention. This is understandable. Watching a player miss an easy chance at an important stage tends to stick in the memory. Statistics show that roughly one match per round will be decided by significantly accurate or inaccurate goal kicking from either side. While this might sound like a lot, it means the other eight games are more often decided by which team created the better chances. 'If you can create many high-quality shots, and restrict the opposition from doing the same, the result will usually fall your way,' said Younger. 'Goal kicking is an important skill to train and perfect, and it can certainly win you games, but if you get to the point as a team where you're relying on accuracy, rather than underlying shot production, that should be setting off all sorts of alarm bells.'

Chapter Three
Score Involvements

The shape of the game

Several new statistical terms have crept into the football lexicon in recent years. In the past, few fans would have given much thought to how many 'rebound 50s' a defender had, or which player had the most 'metres gained'. The usefulness of these modern metrics varies widely, but there is one that has the potential to change the way the game is analysed: 'score involvements'. The appeal of the statistic lies in its simplicity. A player is credited with a score involvement any time they are directly involved in a possession chain that ends in their side scoring points. The player's involvement could range from a handball in the defensive 50, to a mark and kick in the centre square, to snapping a goal from the forward pocket. The number of each player's score involvements reveals much not only about them as individuals, but also about their team. If used correctly, they can tell us a lot about the different styles of play and strategies deployed in the AFL.

Players in high-scoring teams naturally accumulate more score involvements than players in struggling sides, so looking at just the raw counts can be unhelpful. Four of the seven players with the most score involvements in 2017 were from the Adelaide Crows, which averaged a league-high 108 points per game. In such a potent side, a player might only need to complete a few basic passes each game to finish with a healthy involvement total. A more insightful way of using the statistic is to look at the percentage of a team's scores that each player was involved in. For example, in the 23 games that Adelaide captain Taylor Walker played in 2017, he was, on average, involved

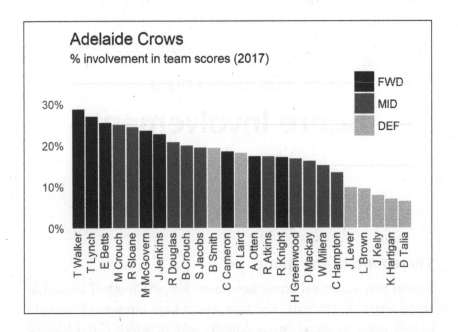

Adelaide Crows
% involvement in team scores (2017)

FWD
MID
DEF

30%

20%

10%

0%

T Walker
T Lynch
E Betts
M Crouch
R Sloane
M McGovern
J Jenkins
R Douglas
B Crouch
S Jacobs
B Smith
C Cameron
R Laird
A Otten
R Atkins
R Knight
H Greenwood
D Mackay
W Milera
C Hampton
J Lever
L Brown
J Kelly
K Hartigan
D Talia

in 28.7% of his side's scores. The next most involved Crow was Tom Lynch, who had a hand – or foot – in an average of 26.9%. The graph above shows the results for every Adelaide player who played at least eight senior games during the season. Players are colour-coded into forwards, midfielders, and defenders, as classified by Champion Data. Bear in mind that some players drift between multiple positions throughout a season.

By analysing every team in this way, we can uncover the distinctive 'shape' of the game plans that exist in the AFL. Our analysis shows that clubs rely on certain types of players in different ways. Some have a key player involved in many of their scores, while others rely on a more balanced contribution.

The centrepiece forward

Clubs most typical of this style in 2017: Sydney, West Coast, Gold Coast.

Sydney's Lance Franklin is the brightest of beacons in the Swans' forward line. The ball is drawn to him like a moth to a flame. He was involved in 219 scoring chains during his 24 games in 2017, at a league-high average of more than nine per game. His involvement in

36% of Sydney's scores was also the highest percentage of any player to play at least eight matches. Franklin is a unique beast when it comes to forward-half engagement. He was 10th on the list of players most targeted inside 50, with an average of eight entries per game directed his way. But he was not just a stay-at-home forward. Instead, he regularly worked up the ground, taking possession outside 50. He ranked eighth on the list of players to average the most forward-50 entries, kicking his side into attack at an average of 4.5 times per match. Almost half of those were direct shots at goal. No other player in the AFL finished in the top 50 for both i50 targets and i50 kicks. The closest were Taylor Walker, who was the 22nd most targeted player inside 50 and the 61st for kicking the ball into attack, and Geelong's Patrick Dangerfield, who was 78th and fifth respectively. Only seven other players were in the top 100 for both.

Sydney's Franklin-centric approach was vastly different to Adelaide's forward set-up. Of the 12 Swans players with the most score involvements, only two were recognised forwards. In contrast, five of the Crows' regular six starting forwards were in their top seven for score involvements. Again, this ignores the fact that midfielders like Heeney and Jack do spend time up forward for Sydney. Nonetheless, it seems clear that negating Franklin would force the Swans to alter their preferred style more than shutting down Walker would for the Crows.

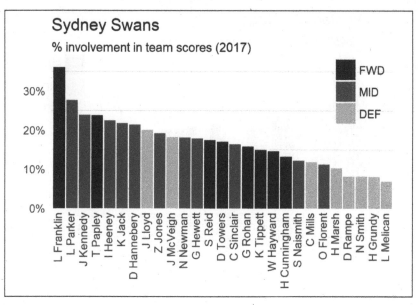

Sydney Swans
% involvement in team scores (2017)

FWD
MID
DEF

The false forward line

Clubs most typical of this style in 2017: Western Bulldogs, Fremantle, Collingwood.

The 'false' forward line represents a style of play where only a small proportion of the scoring is channelled through conventional forwards. Either by design or by circumstance, hybrid midfielders or marauding defenders will instead carry the bulk of their team's attacking responsibility. In 2017, Jake Stringer and Liam Picken were the Western Bulldogs' joint top goal scorers with 24 goals apiece. Only three times in the 21 seasons since Fitzroy departed the competition had an AFL team's leading goal kicker recorded a lower total. Brisbane and Carlton had players with 23 and 22 goals respectively win their goal-kicking awards in 2016, while Danny Stanley kicked a club-high 20 goals for the Gold Coast Suns in their inaugural season in 2011.

Part of the Bulldogs' issue was that they lacked specialist forwards. Travis Cloke had been brought in at the end of 2016, but was unable to reignite his career. The club seemed to make a conscious decision to recruit and field versatile players who could cover several positions. Almost all the darker grey bars on the left-hand side of the Bulldogs'

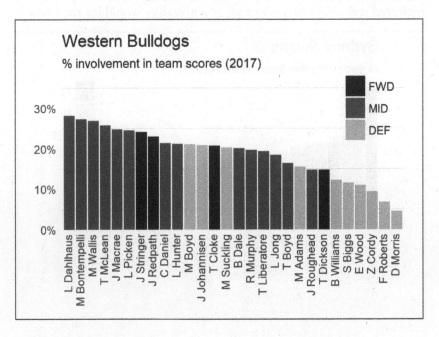

score involvement graph are midfielders capable of spending time forward. The Dogs had won a flag by using a similar style the year before, but their midfield machine broke down in 2017. Only 17.7% of their inside 50s led to goals, which was the lowest conversion rate in the competition. Fremantle and Collingwood were similarly poor in this regard, despite both having classy on-ballers. Although the 2016 premiership had shown that success is attainable without an established forward line, such teams can become vulnerable if other areas are performing at below capacity.

The midfield monster

Clubs most typical of this style in 2017: Richmond, Geelong, Brisbane, Fremantle, Gold Coast.

Closely related to score involvements is another relatively new metric known as score 'links'. Whereas the former is a measure of how many scoring chains a player is involved in, score links are a count of how many times the player touches the ball in those chains. Richmond's Dustin Martin won just about every medal and award on offer in 2017, so it is perhaps no surprise that he recorded more score links than anyone else in the league. Martin handled the ball multiple

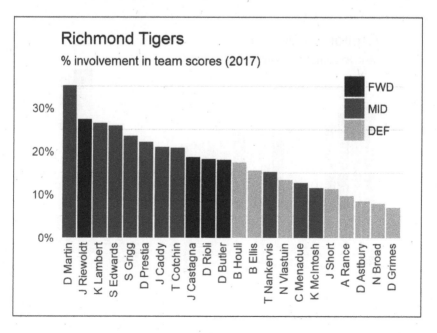

times in a chain more often than Franklin, who was the player with the most score involvements. Many of Franklin's involvements came via a single link, often being the final kick at goal.

Martin's importance to the Tigers cannot be overstated. He averaged almost 10 score links per match during their premiership year, which was three more than any of his teammates. To put that in perspective, the difference between Port Adelaide's most and seventh most involved midfielders, Ollie Wines and Jared Polec, was fewer than one-and-a-half score involvements per game. Martin contributed equally well inside and outside the contest. Other teams needed multiple players to match the same breadth of output. Despite the predictability of so much of Richmond's attacking play flowing through Martin, no team managed to find a reliable way of stopping him.

The launching backmen

Clubs most typical of this style in 2017: Carlton, Brisbane, Adelaide, West Coast.

In 2017, only four teams had two of their regular defenders each involved in at least 18% of their scores. The list included Adelaide

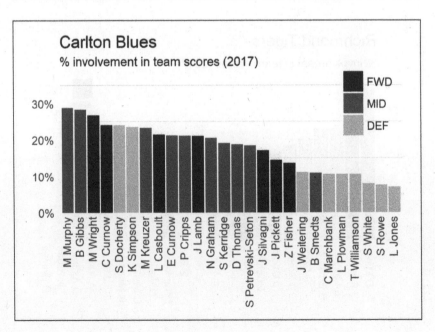

Carlton Blues
% involvement in team scores (2017)

(Brodie Smith and Rory Laird) and West Coast (Elliot Yeo and Jeremy McGovern) from the top eight, and Carlton (Sam Docherty and Kade Simpson) and Brisbane (Daniel Rich and Alex Witherden) from the foot of the ladder.

The key difference between the clubs that used this style was the speed at which they moved the ball from defence to attack. Of the Crows' 209 possession chains that started in their defensive 50 and ended in their attacking arc, 52% of them were shuttled through midfield in 15 seconds or less. Only 13% took more than 30 seconds to travel between the arcs. In contrast, only 44% of Carlton's 158 successful rebounds took 15 seconds or less to reach the forward 50, and 22% took more than half a minute. The Lions were similarly slow, while the Eagles were somewhere in between.

Catching teams off guard by quickly rebounding from the defensive 50 can be a powerful tactic. The defenders who launch these attacks are integral components of the sides that adopt this style. However, having defenders so prominently placed on the score involvement list could also be a sign that the ball is spending too much time in the wrong half of the ground.

Score link footprints

Score involvements and score links can also be used to compare the individual output of players nominally filling the same position. It can be particularly enlightening to break down the two counts by zone. Champion Data uses four zone classifications: forward 50, attacking midfield, defensive midfield, and defensive 50. Visualising the number of score links a player had in each of these zones gives us a picture of their unique 'footprint'. It shows us not only the player's role, but how it fits in their team's game style. Let's look at the players who recorded the most score links per game in each zone during 2017, and compare their contribution to that of other players in the league.

Forward 50

Rank	Player (minimum 8 games)	Club	Forward-50 score links per game
1	Josh Kennedy	West Coast	6.5
2	Eddie Betts	Adelaide	5.9
3	Lance Franklin	Sydney	5.5

Josh Kennedy finished four goals behind Franklin in the race for the 2017 Coleman Medal, which was a remarkable effort considering he missed five games to injury. He arguably has a greater scoreboard impact than just about any other player in the competition. However, that shouldn't be the only gauge of a forward's effectiveness. Kennedy averaged 8.2 score links per game, which was roughly the same as Adelaide forward Tom Lynch. Analysing where the two players recorded their score links gives us an idea of the differences in their roles.

Kennedy is a classic stay-at-home forward and has the score link footprint to prove it. The tall black bar on the left of the graph below represents the nearly six-and-a-half score links per game that he recorded in his side's forward 50. Kennedy had fewer than two score links per game in the other zones combined, of which almost half

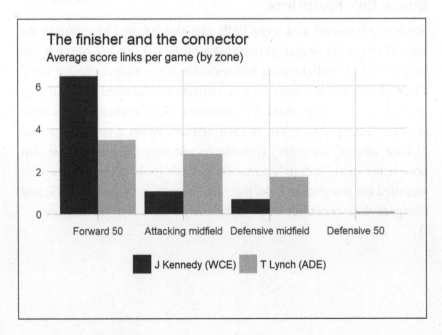

The finisher and the connector
Average score links per game (by zone)

J Kennedy (WCE)   T Lynch (ADE)

were shots on goal. He didn't once register a meaningful attacking contribution in his side's defensive 50. On the other hand, Lynch's footprint shows a forward who ventured a lot further up the ground. Coaches and commentators often refer to Lynch as the 'connector', because he plays a key role in linking Adelaide's defence and attack.

Attacking midfield

Rank	Player (minimum 8 games)	Club	Forward-50 score links per game
1	Dustin Martin	Richmond	4.1
2	Adam Treloar	Collingwood	4.0
3	Mitch Duncan	Geelong	4.0

Martin recorded the most score links in the attacking midfield section of the ground, with his 4.1 per game narrowly ahead of both Collingwood's Adam Treloar and Geelong's Mitch Duncan. However, it was another Cats player, Patrick Dangerfield, to whom his influence was most often compared.

Studying the two stars' score link footprints is an efficient way to establish the subtle differences in their playing style and role throughout 2017.

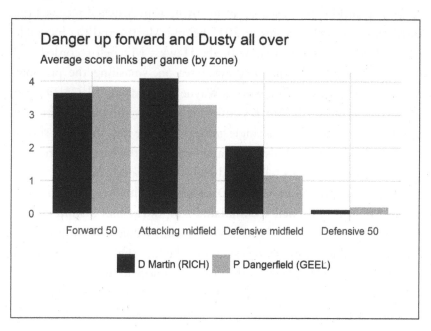

Dangerfield recorded slightly more forward-50 score links per game, and finished with a more forward-heavy score link footprint than Martin overall. This represented a change from previous seasons, reflecting the fact that Dangerfield spent more time as a one-out forward than he had previously. There was no doubt he struck fear in the hearts of many defenders, but it did reduce his overall midfield contribution. During his Brownlow year in 2016, Dangerfield had averaged 3.8 score links per game in the attacking midfield and 2.5 in the defensive midfield. In 2017, those numbers fell to 3.3 and 1.2 respectively, while his forward-50 score links rose from 2.7 to 3.8 per game. Martin also spent significant time as a resting forward, but it had less of an effect on his midfield output. His zonal breakdown illustrates how he won the ball and influenced the game in every part of the field.

Defensive midfield

Rank	Player (minimum 8 games)	Club	Forward-50 score links per game
1	Tom Mitchell	Hawthorn	3.4
2	Seb Ross	St Kilda	3.1
3	Zach Merrett	Essendon	3.0

After a record-breaking season of his own, Tom Mitchell received the third most Brownlow votes in 2017 behind Martin and the ineligible Dangerfield. In his first year with the Hawks, Mitchell recorded 787 disposals during the home-and-away season, smashing the previous record of 748 set by Collingwood's Wayne Richardson in 1971. He also joined the 50 disposals club, becoming only the seventh player in history to notch a half century in a single game. His score link footprint shows us where he did most of his work, and highlights the vast differences in his role compared to his fellow midfield workhorse Martin.

In contrast to Martin and Dangerfield, who are both attack-minded players, Mitchell accumulated a lot of the ball behind centre. It is important to note, though, that an individual's score links are largely a product of his team's success. The fact that Mitchell won so many more of his disposals in the defensive midfield relative to Martin was at least partly because the ball was more often in that part of the ground for Hawthorn than it was for Richmond. That aside, clearly

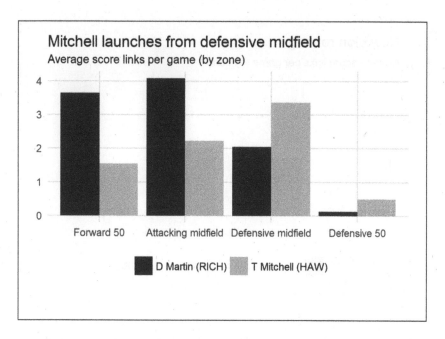

Mitchell launches from defensive midfield

Average score links per game (by zone)

Legend: D Martin (RICH), T Mitchell (HAW)

Zones: Forward 50, Attacking midfield, Defensive midfield, Defensive 50

Mitchell is a different type of midfielder. His kick-to-handball ratio compared to Martin's tells its own story. Martin had a K:H of 1.81, meaning he registered almost two kicks for every handball. Mitchell's was 0.64, showing that he greatly preferred the handball option. He used this style to great effect, recording the most defensive-half score launches – the first possession in a scoring chain – of any midfielder in the competition.

Defensive 50

Rank	Player (minimum 8 games)	Club	Forward-50 score links per game
1	Alex Witherden	Brisbane	2.8
2	Michael Hurley	Essendon	2.6
3	Shannon Hurn	West Coast	2.0

Brisbane's Alex Witherden burst onto the scene after debuting in round 14 against Greater Western Sydney, winning a rising star nomination a few weeks later against Richmond in round 17. He became just the fifth player in the AFL era to amass at least 20 disposals in each of his first six games, joining Essendon ball-magnet Joe Misiti, mature-age St Kilda debutant Dean Greig, and more recently Toby Greene and

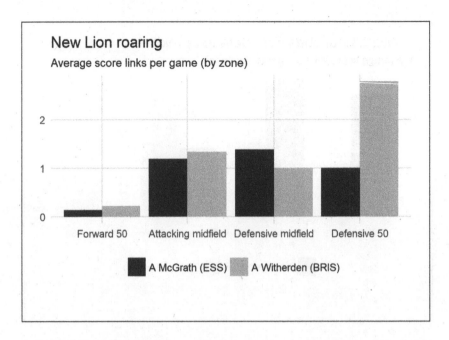

New Lion roaring

Average score links per game (by zone)

Forward 50 · Attacking midfield · Defensive midfield · Defensive 50

■ A McGrath (ESS) ■ A Witherden (BRIS)

Ed Curnow. Greg Williams had also achieved the feat in his debut VFL season with Geelong in 1984.

Defenders should not be rated purely on their contribution to scoring, but if they were, Witherden would be one of the best. In the nine games he played during his debut season, he managed to record more defensive 50 score links than all but 21 other players in the league. Again, this was no doubt helped by the amount of ball in the Lions' defensive 50, but his impact was still exceptional. The above graph compares Witherden's footprint to that of Essendon's number one draft pick and rising star winner Andrew McGrath. Considering the success rate the Lions achieved by using Witherden to launch their defensive rebounds, it would be unsurprising if he became a key cog in their future game plans.

Chapter Four
Win Probabilities

Counting cards

West Coast's Lewis Jetta nestled the yellow Sherrin under his elbow as he stepped slowly backwards. He had just trapped Melbourne captain Jack Viney holding the ball about 30 metres out from goal, and now had the opportunity to put his team 21 points up with less than nine minutes remaining in the final term. Charlie Dixon's shot clock blunder against Geelong was fresh in Jetta's memory as he lingered at the top of his mark, staring at the countdown on the Subiaco Oval scoreboard. Essendon great Matthew Lloyd didn't like it. He thought it was much too early to be concerned with milking the clock. 'Just worry about what you need to do,' he pleaded. 'Who cares about the 30 seconds?' Jetta twirled the ball between his palms, waiting until a tick before zero before starting his slow approach. One step, two steps, three, four, five, six. 'This to make it really difficult for the Demons,' intoned commentator Basil Zempilas. 'Virtually directly in front, and ... what a let-off.' Jetta's kick sprayed off the outside of his boot and whistled wide of the right-hand goalpost. 'That keeps Melbourne well and truly in it,' said Matthew Richardson to Zempilas in commentary. 'It would have been tough if Jetta had scored that, but we all know how quickly goals can be scored.' As the goal umpire waved one flag, the scoreboard flickered and changed. The Eagles led 96 points to 80.

In Melbourne's coaches' box, the Demons' game analyst, Craig Jennings, was sitting in his usual place at the left shoulder of senior coach Simon Goodwin. Jennings had a more thorough understanding of how quickly goals could be scored than perhaps anyone at the ground. He glanced at the timer and ran the sums. Eight minutes and 20 seconds remaining. 16 points. Three scoring shots. He estimated the Demons had a 3% chance of winning from their current position. Not the rosiest of outlooks, admittedly, but he remained resolute. There were still moves to be made. 'If you're a 3% chance of winning, you need to implement higher risk strategies,' Jennings explained later. 'That will increase both your likelihood of scoring and the opposition's, although really it's your team that has nothing to lose.'

About a minute after Jetta's miss, Melbourne ruckman Max Gawn took possession on the right half-forward flank. He kicked long to a large pack in front of the goal square, where his teammate Cam Pedersen flew from three deep to take a strong mark over Eagles captain Shannon Hurn. Pedersen hurriedly popped it through, cutting the margin to 10 points and prompting Jennings to again run the numbers. With one straight kick, according to Jennings, a 3% chance of victory had become a 9% chance. 'I felt okay because I knew that teams go inside 50 about once every minute-and-a-half or two minutes,' Jennings said. 'There were about seven minutes to play, so that meant we were probably going to go inside 50 another three or four times and we were going to get some opportunities.'

The Demons knew, too, that the time had come to seize every one of those opportunities. If there were only a few inside 50 chances left, they needed to have enough players up forward to make the most of them. Instead of playing their usual two men off the back of the square at the bounce, the call went out for them to go man-on-man all over the field. When play resumed, a rushed centre clearance from the Eagles was cut off by the Demons' halfback line, and in a few seconds the ball had been whisked to the other end of the field for Tom McDonald's fourth goal. 'That was great play,' observed Richardson on the broadcast. 'They had even numbers in the forward line, so there were no Eagles players free to come over and intercept.' West Coast now led 96 points to 92.

The television camera flashed to the Demons' coaches' box. Goodwin was busily working the phone, while Jennings sat pensively beside him in the pose of Rodin's *The Thinker*. 'I was calm, and the reason for that was it was just numbers to me at that stage,' said Jennings. 'I was just sitting there doing the math.' Jennings constantly assesses his team's chances in this way, right from the opening bounce. His probabilities are based on the feed of statistical information from Champion Data, but he figures them all out himself without the need of a calculator. He just knows, for example, if his team is a goal down at quarter time that it has a 45% chance of winning. If it is a goal up, it has a 55% chance. While the margin and time left in the game have the most influence on his calculations, Jennings also factors in other variables, such as the venue and the style of the opposing coach. 'My job is to increase our chance of winning, so I always need to know those odds,' he said. It is a similar approach to that used by coaches in American football's NFL, whose play calling is based on field position, margin, and time.

After McDonald's goal, Jennings had estimated the Demons' winning probability had jumped from 9% to 23%, although the new odds were made to feel a little skinny when, in hardly any time, Pedersen was lining up for the chance to put them ahead. He pushed his kick across the face of goal, cutting the Eagles' lead to just three points with four minutes left. The game became tight and congested. West Coast failed to capitalise when it twice went into attack itself, but as time continued to evaporate, the Demons' chances of winning again began to plummet. 'I think every coach would agree that the clock goes quickly when you're behind, and slowly when you're in front,' said Jennings, before letting logic get the better of him. 'Clearly, that's not true, but it's certainly how it feels.'

With 41 seconds left on the clock, the Demons forced a boundary throw-in about 40 metres from goal on the outer side. 'There's heaps of time for Melbourne,' insisted pundit Peter Bell. 'They've got the ball in a dangerous position. There's heaps of time.' Another quick glimpse into the Melbourne box hinted that Goodwin, brow furrowed, wasn't so sure. Eagles ruckman Nathan Vardy outjumped Gawn to win the tap, but it was sharked by Demons midfielder Clayton Oliver. 39 seconds. Oliver freed his arms to handball to the running Michael Hibberd. 36 seconds. Hibberd evaded Luke Shuey to heave a high left-footed kick to the goal square. 33 seconds. Pedersen knocked the ball to McDonald, who trapped it with his back to goal and was immediately tackled by Jeremy McGovern. 30 seconds. With McGovern pulling him to ground, McDonald threw the ball out in front of him and somehow twisted his body to swing through his fifth goal. 24 seconds. Melbourne were in front. 'He's done it!' went up the cry in commentary. 'Tom McDonald, you genius!'

As might be expected, the swings in win probability can be wild and steep after lead-changing goals late in a game. Jennings now put the Demons' chance of victory at 99%, but he was conscious that they still needed to finish the job. 'You certainly don't want to be the one out of 100,' he said. At the next bounce, all but one of Melbourne's players were moved behind the ball. 'Once you're a 99% chance of winning, you don't need to take any risk,' said Jennings. 'You play a much more defensive-focused style of game.' Putting extra numbers around the contest enabled the Demons to soak up the last few seconds by forcing a secondary bounce. Soon, the siren blew for their first win over the Eagles in Perth for 15 years.

The Demons' coaches' box was euphoric. Goodwin pumped both fists in triumph before being embraced by his offensive coordinator, Troy Chaplin. Assistant coaches Jade Rawlings and Ben Mathews both jumped to their feet, roaring in exultation. One man, however, remained as undemonstrative as he had been throughout the febrile closing stages. 'That man is Craig Jennings. He keeps his emotions in check,' explained Lloyd, who knew him from his time at Essendon. 'Keeps them in check?' said Garry Lyon, incredulously. 'Has he got a pulse, that bloke?' Without so much as a grin, Jennings leant back in his chair and brought his hands together for a single clap. He closed his laptop, job done. 'Sometimes people can confuse my demeanour with a lack of competitiveness, but I am highly competitive,' he said. 'I'm just counting the cards and working out the best way to get the odds back in our favour. Emotion doesn't really come in to it.'

The numbers game

Jennings's grounding in probability theory and its applications started during his childhood. When he was just 10 years old, he devised his own fantasy football game in which he would roll dice to simulate entire seasons. Working through the real-life fixture match by match, he would roll once for a team's goals and again for its behinds. The same would be done for the opposing side. He would log the scores and maintain a ladder, complete with percentages. He would even calculate a goal-kicking tally, allocating a quarter of each team's score to its recognised spearhead, so that at the end of the season he could award an imaginary Coleman Medal to Bernie Quinlan or Simon Beasley or Brian Taylor. All this information would be studiously logged in exercise books. Jennings estimates that he filled hundreds of them. 'I think it just taught me about probability and numbers and that kind of thing,' he said.

Jennings had barely outgrown the games of his childhood when he joined North Melbourne as a 16-year-old. The Kangaroos selected him with pick 45 in the 1990 national draft, but he failed to develop as they hoped and was delisted two years later without playing a senior game. After a few seasons plying his trade in the VFL, he came to the realisation that he enjoyed analysing football more than he did playing it. He retired at 23 and focused all his attention on becoming a coach, studying teaching, and working his way through the coaching ranks at the lower levels. His break back into the big time came in 2005, with Essendon's Kevin Sheedy offering him the chance to prove his mettle in the AFL. Initially unsure how best to use his talents, the Bombers had Jennings psychologically evaluated by an external human resources consultancy. He returned the highest abstract reasoning score the company had ever recorded. 'They'd put patterns up on the screen and I could work out what the next pattern should be,' he said. 'How did I do that? I don't know. I guess it sort of just made sense to me.'

In 10 seasons with the Bombers, Jennings rose from the role of Sheedy's opposition scout to become an assistant to Matthew Knights and then James Hird. He spent 2015 under Luke Beveridge at the Western Bulldogs, before joining Melbourne the following year at the invitation of his former Essendon colleague Goodwin. His job of 'game analyst and education coordinator' is unique in the AFL, and involves conveying complex concepts in intuitive ways. 'I'm a coach, but because I'm good with numbers I understand which ones are important,' he said. 'I pick out the crucial bits of information that might tip the odds in our favour and then convey them in a way that the players and other coaches believe and understand.' This comes to the fore on game day, when he uses his strong understanding of data and numbers to inform the tactical advice that he provides to Goodwin. Jennings describes his match-day approach as 'coaching to probability'. He closely monitors the ebbs and flows in a game's patterns to recommend when the coaches need to make changes. At an advanced level, this involves the calculation of his winning probability estimates, but he also employs mental shortcuts known as 'heuristics'. There has been a long tradition of this type of commonsense thinking in Australian football, dating back to well before the onset of detailed statistical analysis.

First to 100 points wins

Probably the simplest example of these unwritten rules is the old commentator's saw that the first team to score 100 points will win the match. Dermott Brereton has arguably been most responsible for propagating this slogan, although he has been far from a lone voice. 'Bicks says first to 100 wins!' declared radio broadcaster Stephen Rowe, as North Melbourne moved towards triple figures against the Crows in 2017. 'Yep, 98.4 per cent of the time,' affirmed Mark Bickley. It was a bold declaration, but the Crows' two-time premiership captain had clearly done his homework. From matches in which at least one side scored 100 points, the team to get there first had a 97.8 winning percentage in the decade prior to 2018.

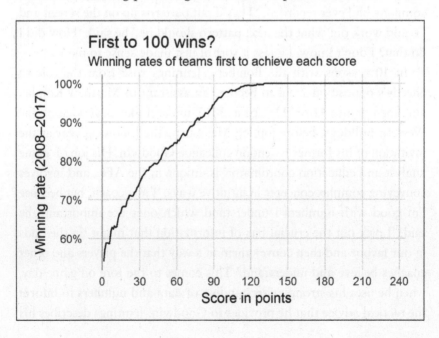

Such a high strike rate would seem to suggest the 100-point rule is well worth monitoring. The average team score in our 10-year sample was about 90 points per game, so any side that reached 100 points had performed almost two goals better than the all-team average. Additionally, when a side hit triple figures, it usually wasn't until about 10 minutes into the final quarter, leaving its opponent little time in which to stage a comeback.

Digging a little deeper, however, reveals the rule's limitations. It couldn't be used in more than a third of matches (35.5%) because neither team reached 100 points. In more than half (57.6%) of games, only one of the two teams notched a century, although if we wanted to be facetious we could argue 'highest score wins' was just as insightful an explanation for those results. In only 6.8% of matches did both teams reach 100 points, which is really the only instance the rule should be used. In restricting our analysis to just those games, the winning percentage of the team that gets to triple figures first falls to 79.4%. Suddenly the rule doesn't look so helpful. We can use it in about 14 games per season, but it will only get about 11 of those right.

The first-to-100-points rule is more of an indicator than a predictor, but not a particularly useful one. Sure, teams will tend to win if they are the first to reach a century, but mostly because it is a high score that is achieved late in a match. On average, teams that won after reaching 100 points first already held a 39-point lead at the time they hit triple figures. In contrast, sides that lost despite scoring 100 points first only led by 11 points on average when they reached the mark. Unsurprisingly, a team's chance of victory depends more heavily on the margin than on just its own score.

The 30-point rule

Craig Jennings was in his third year at Essendon, in 2007, when he experienced a moment of clarity. He turned to his fellow assistant coach Gary O'Donnell at the club's Windy Hill training base. 'Jeez, Gary,' he said, 'it's bloody hard to win when you're five goals down, isn't it?' One imagines O'Donnell might have been a little perplexed by this sudden epiphanic declaration, but he said he agreed with the presumption. 'From there it kind of just cemented for me,' said

Jennings. 'I think there's definitely something psychological to it. If you're five goals down it starts feeling tough, so for me that's when you have to start making some moves.'

Jennings was not alone in noticing the significance of the margin. Not long afterwards, Champion Data began popularising what it termed 'the 30-point rule'. 'The stats guys have all season long been talking about the 30-point rule,' wrote Mark Stevens in 2010. 'If you get 30 or more down, you have got no hope – or so the theory goes.' To test the relative usefulness of the rule, we can calculate the competition-wide winning percentage at every margin. For the purposes of our analysis, we will remove all 'duplicate' margins that a team held within a game. For example, St Kilda led Sydney by five points on a dozen separate occasions on its way to a one-point win at the SCG in 2009, but we will only count it as having held that margin once. Our results for the win rate of teams holding five-point leads would become skewed if we counted all 12 instances for just the one eventual outcome.

Under these criteria, the winning rate for all teams that held an exact 30-point margin at some stage during a match between 2008 and 2017 was 93.1%. That looks solid at first blush, although of course it also means that 6.9% of teams that led by 30 points ended up losing. To put that in perspective, it is about the same probability as landing four heads from four tosses of a coin. Unlikely, sure, but certainly liable to happen from time to time. Across the 10 seasons, 46 teams lost after leading by exactly five goals, and 77 lost after leading by five goals or more. When it happened four times in the opening month of the 2013 season, Jon Ralph was moved to question in the *Herald Sun*, 'What is happening to Champion Data's 30-point rule, where if a side gets 30 points up it's as good as home?'

The greatest comeback in our 10-season sample was St Kilda rallying from 55 points down against the Western Bulldogs in 2015, which, by extension, means that every team that led by at least 56 points went on to win. However, the Saints' recovery was only the equal-fifth greatest comeback in the competition's history. In 2001, Essendon famously overcame a 69-point second-quarter deficit to beat North Melbourne by two goals. Admittedly, the '70-point rule' doesn't sound quite so handy as a heuristic device. But if 70 points is impractical, and 30 points fallible enough to leave room for doubt, is there any single number that is markedly more suitable? Well, at 36 points up, a team's winning percentage is 96.4%. At 42 points, the win rate is 99.6%. At the risk of stating the obvious, a team's chance of victory generally rises in accordance with the size of its lead.

If we graph the relationship between in-game margin and winning percentage, we get what approximates a symmetric S-shaped curve. This curve mathematically fits what is known as a logistic function. The curve starts with a long, flattened tail denoting a 0% winning rate for the largest deficits. The winning percentage then climbs sharply across the middle section for margins of about 40 points either way, before flattening out again at 100% for the biggest leads. We can see that a lead of 30 points sits near enough to where the curve flattens at the top. Here, the win rate is well above 90% and starting to become invariant to any further increase in a team's lead.

So, in this instance, it appears Jennings didn't need to do the maths. He intuitively understood what was going on. 'Remember, when you include the preseason, I see about 100 live games a year,' he said. 'The more footy I watched, the more I began to think if a team was 29 points down, well, that's okay. But as soon as they got 30 points down I was like, oh, they're stuffed now.' Ironically, though,

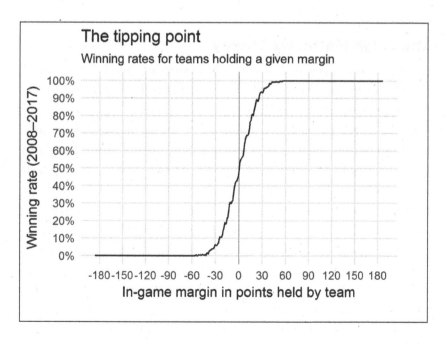

The tipping point

Winning rates for teams holding a given margin

Winning rate (2008–2017)

In-game margin in points held by team

the winning percentage for teams holding 28- or 29-point leads is actually slightly higher than for teams holding a round five-goal lead. It is difficult to distinguish on our graph, but the same pattern occurs for every exact multiple of six up to 36 points. For example, a team leading by 16 or 17 points has a marginally higher winning rate than one leading by precisely three goals. The reason for this is that the number of scoring shots that a team takes is often a better indication of its superiority over an opponent than the margin. Consider a team that has kicked 5.0 (30) to an opponent's 4.5 (29). Although it leads by one point, it has had four fewer scoring shots. Our data shows that this sort of team is prone to being overrun, because its perfect five goals from its first five scoring shots likely reflects an element of luck that might not hold throughout the rest of the contest.

As a mental shortcut, the 30-point rule does a reasonable job. It uses a round number that is easy to remember, and enjoys a success rate of about 93%. But, like the 100-point rule, the number is also relatively arbitrary, and doesn't factor in other important variables such as the scoring rate and time remaining. It should be used with care, and with the expectation that it will let us down about once a month during a season.

The Leigh Matthews Theory

Easily the most discussed of the scoring rules of thumb is the famed 'Leigh Matthews Theory'. Matthews explained the premise in his autobiography, *Accept the Challenge*. 'I developed a simple scoreboard formula I'd run through my mind late in games to assess my team's winning chances,' he wrote. 'If we were more goals in front than there were minutes to go, we'd probably win. In fact, it was not so much about probably winning; it was more about when the possibility of losing no longer existed.' Jennings believes that when someone so well-regarded in the football industry puts forward such an idea, it pays to take heed. 'Leigh Matthews has been involved in thousands of games of footy in terms of playing, coaching, or watching, so that would just make sense to him,' he said. 'It's something that you still see coaches applying, because they look at the clock in the coaches' box all the time. You're definitely thinking in those terms.'

In recent years the Matthews Theory has also become much beloved of television commentators who are calling a tight finish, although they usually apply it in reverse. If a team is trailing by four goals with just over four minutes to play, the commentator might invoke the theory to insist they still have time to snatch victory. Stay tuned, sports lovers, this one is still alive! For example, Bruce McAvaney cited it when Jay Schulz was lining up to cut Port Adelaide's deficit to 17 points with four minutes remaining in its 2013 semifinal against Geelong. 'We keep saying they're going to run out of time,' said McAvaney, 'but if Schulz can dob a third goal here, maybe it will be the "Leigh Matthews Theory", minutes and goals.' It prompted a brusque reply from the theoriser himself. 'We're getting on the edge of that one here tonight, Bruce,' said Matthews, indulging the corruption. We found half-a-dozen similar mentions in Channel Seven broadcasts since 2012, although we suspect that number might be just scratching the surface.

As Matthews points out in his book, his eponymous theory usually only applies late in a game. 'This "no-longer-can-lose" situation is rarely in play at three-quarter time,' he said. 'With 30 minutes left you need a 10-goal lead to be completely safe. Even with a 60-point margin at the final break, my mindset of never expecting and never assuming wouldn't have been totally comfortable that far out from the final siren.' With this caveat in mind, we can test the theory's veracity with the same time-stamped scoring data from 2008 to 2017 that we used in the first chapter. Let's start by looking at the 'broadcast version' of the Matthews Theory: how often does the trailing team win when there are more minutes left than its goal deficit in the final quarter?

Just over 40% of sides that trailed by a goal with at least a minute remaining in the last term went on to taste victory, with the winning rate dropping steadily for every extra goal that was required. Teams that needed four goals in four or more minutes won 8% of the time, while those that needed six goals in at least six minutes had a win rate of 2.5%. While those percentages are small, they do not, in Matthews's words, equate to a 'no-longer-can-lose' situation for the team in front.

We should note, though, that there is no upper bound on the amount of time remaining when the theory is cast in this way. Most teams that won after overcoming a fourth-quarter deficit launched

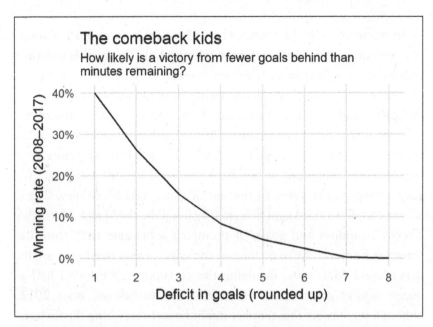

The comeback kids

How likely is a victory from fewer goals behind than minutes remaining?

Winning rate (2008–2017) vs *Deficit in goals (rounded up)*

their comebacks from a point at which they had more than twice as many minutes left as the number of goals they trailed by. When any kind of time limit on the comeback is enforced, the winning percentage of the trailing sides falls dramatically. For example, only 10 teams in the decade prior to 2018 won from three goals down with six minutes or fewer remaining, and only five overcame a four-goal deficit with eight minutes or fewer left.

Implicit in the original version of the Matthews Theory is the assumption that if all goes right, a team will need at least a minute to win possession, move the ball to within scoring range, and kick a goal. Following that logic, a team trailing by four goals could bridge that deficit in as many minutes. That would be pretty good going, by any measure, but how often do these goal-a-minute runs occur at any point during a match? The following graph shows all instances of such streaks during our sample period.

We have timed these streaks from the moment the first goal was scored. A streak of three goals in three minutes or less indicates that two additional goals were kicked within three minutes of the first being scored. We have also included all overlapping streaks, meaning the 717 instances of four goals in four minutes are included in the tally of 2,993 runs of three-in-three. The graph reveals a steady percentage decrease in the number of streaks for every additional

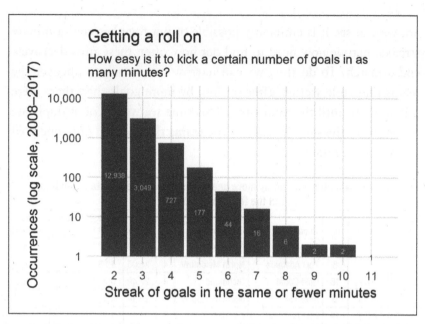

Getting a roll on

How easy is it to kick a certain number of goals in as many minutes?

Occurrences (log scale, 2008–2017)

Streak of goals in the same or fewer minutes

goal. Of the 12,640 teams that scored two goals in two minutes or less, 24% went on to score three-in-three, and 24% of the three-in-three teams continued their streak to four-in-four.

The streaks of nine goals and above all come from one extraordinary match: Essendon's 139-point demolition of Gold Coast in the Suns' inaugural season in 2011. In one of the most staggeringly one-sided quarters in history, the Bombers kicked 15.4 (94) to a solitary behind in the opening term. It included a run of 11 goals in exactly 10 minutes of playing time. West Coast takes credit for the other stand-out streak in our sample, having kicked eight goals in six minutes and 14 seconds in its 98-point victory over the Brisbane Lions in 2012.

Goals	Season	Rd	Team	Opponent	Q	Clock	Actual playing time
3	2009	GF	St Kilda	Geelong	2	1:41	0:40
4	2010	9	Essendon	Richmond	1	3:28	1:16
5	2012	18	West Coast	Brisbane Lions	4	6:25	3:02
6	2012	22	Fremantle	North Melbourne	4	7:44	3:47
7	2012	18	West Coast	Brisbane Lions	4	10:38	4:36
8	2012	18	West Coast	Brisbane Lions	4	13:26	6:14
9	2011	6	Essendon	Gold Coast	1	15:33	7:58
10	2011	6	Essendon	Gold Coast	1	17:27	9:05
11	2011	6	Essendon	Gold Coast	1	19:24	10:00

Exceptional occurrences of a tally of goals kicked in fewer than the same number of minutes, 2008–2017

So, we can see it is eminently possible to put together goal-a-minute streaks, but we now need to find out how often these runs decisively end a match. To do this, we can narrow our search to uncover the teams that stole victory after trailing by more goals than there were minutes left until the final siren. This time we won't count duplicate entries from the same streak, or the teams that needed only one goal in less than a minute.

								Time	In-game	Final
Teams to win after trailing by more goals than there were minutes remaining until the final siren, 2008–2017										
Goals Down	Season	Rd	Team	Opponent	Q	Clock	Time left	In-game margin	Final margin
3	2009	5	Essendon	Collingwood	4	25:33	2:55*	−14	+5
2	2012	8	Port Adelaide	North Melbourne	4	28:05	1:28	−10	+2
2	2012	16	Gold Coast	Richmond	4	27:49	0:26	−10	+2
2	2013	9	Adelaide	North Melbourne	4	26:14	1:49	−12	+1
2	2013	19	Port Adelaide	Adelaide	4	28:18	1:28	−8	+4
2	2014	12	Geelong	Carlton	4	27:28	1:53	−7	+5
2	2015	2	Essendon	Hawthorn	4	25:33	1:21	−10	+2
2	2016	2	Collingwood	Richmond	4	28:27	1:47	−11	+1
3	2017	4	Sydney	Essendon	4	29:01	2:38	−13	+1
2	2017	9	Port Adelaide	St Kilda	4	29:49	0:55	−10	+2

*Time remaining in 2009 Anzac Day game is an estimate. TV broadcast displayed a count-up clock.

Fans of all stripes will be able to instantly recall several of the winning goals from these classic finishes, which serves to emphasise the merit of the accomplishment. Among them are David Zaharakis's buzzer beater in the 2009 Anzac Day game; rugby league convert Karmichael Hunt's goal after the siren for Gold Coast against Richmond; Angus Monfries's incredible 'off-break' in the 2013 Showdown; and Jared Petrenko's hack out of mid-air that capped a five-goal last-quarter turnaround for Adelaide over North Melbourne. 'Well, I guess there's still a little hope, is there?' said McAvaney, when the Crows had narrowed the Kangaroos' lead shortly before Petrenko's sealer. 'What's Leigh's theory?' asked Tim Watson. 'Less goals than minutes?'

Well, sort of. All up, 10 teams defied the bona fide Matthews Theory between 2008 and 2017. Eight fought back from two goals down with less than two minutes left, while only two managed to come back from three goals down with less than three minutes remaining. In short, it does happen, but only about once per season. That is an excellent strike rate for a rule of thumb.

It is also conspicuous that no side overcame a deficit of four or more goals if that number exceeded the minutes left on the clock. Is that the point at which Matthews's 'no-longer-can-lose' utopia is reached? Jennings believes the effects of the 30-point rule are enhanced when time is running out. 'If you're four or five goals up, it gives you plenty of breathing space to be able to gather evidence in what you're seeing, and to be able to change the direction of the game if your opponent starts to fight back,' he said. 'That's why five goals is such a good margin, because it gives you time to be able to halt momentum.'

Chapter Five

Momentum

The irresistible force?

Of all the concepts, theories, and principles in sport, perhaps the hardest to pin down is momentum. No-one can seem to settle on a definition, let alone agree on its importance. This was comically, if unintentionally, illustrated by the *Guardian* in April 2016. 'It's taken 158 long winters, but the AFL world has almost finished figuring out that football is not a ball sport but a game of momentum, involving a ball,' wrote Mick Ellis in a Monday morning article for its online Australian edition. 'Psychological momentum is real. It runs every game.' Unfortunately for Ellis, his polemic against statistics was undermined on the very same day by the site's London-based sports writer Sean Ingle. 'While it [momentum] remains one of football's great shibboleths, there is a problem – a lack of conclusive proof that teams and players get 'hot' due to anything other than talent or luck.'

The confusion about how best to describe the nature, scope, or meaning of momentum has done nothing to slow its use as a catch-all explanation for why a team won or lost. Whether it is a coach sitting in a post-match media conference, a pundit sitting in front of a television camera, or a fan sitting in a bar, momentum has seemingly become the answer to all questions. It is spoken of as an intangible force that lifts a team or player above another, manifesting itself as an implacable streak of dominance. 'Momentum and scoring progression are pretty aligned,' said Jennings. 'If I had to describe momentum, I think it's probably most connected to whether a team is scoring with ease or with difficulty. If a team is scoring with ease then it's probably got a fair bit of momentum.' Fremantle coach Ross Lyon believes it is often a weight-of-numbers effect. 'Momentum is having more players on the field playing well compared to their opponents,' he said. 'Everyone is always giving their best, but sometimes when it all comes together it's a real force.'

How, though, can we measure when this effect begins and ends? If Lyon's Dockers 'seize the momentum' to win an opening quarter six goals to one, at what point did momentum take hold? There are many unpredictable events that can influence the outcome of a football match, from the bounce of the ball, to an untimely injury, or an umpire's mistake. Skill does not always trump luck. Although the better athlete will usually prevail in an individual sport, such as running or swimming, in team sports that have a strong random component we tend to see periods of domination by one side or the other. Are these swings caused by momentum, or can they be better explained by randomness? It is the ambiguity surrounding the concept that makes it so difficult to objectively test. For other topics we can confidently apply statistical models to tease out trends, but studies of momentum often raise more questions than they answer. Nevertheless, it is still worth delving into the numbers to find out what they say.

Peaking at the business end

A good run of form at the right time of year is a crucial ingredient of premiership success. Every premier must, by necessity, play well enough in September to make and win a Grand Final. For some, their finals performances will merely be a continuation of the high standard they have shown throughout the year. But others seem to time their runs to perfection, emerging from a mediocre patch to sweep all before them. The media places a lot of importance on 'peaking at the right time of year'. The inference is that slow starts can be managed, but that a team must be playing its best football by the time the finals arrive.

To gauge whether this is true, we can examine the record of every AFL premier from 1990 to 2017, and compare their win–loss counts from the first and second halves of the home-and-away season. The 2017 premier, Richmond, for example, had a slightly better run of eight wins and three losses before the finals than its seven wins and four losses to open the season. If momentum heading into September is as vital as is often stated, we might expect to see a better overall win–loss record in the second half of the season, as the premiers-in-waiting gear up for their finals tilt.

Season	Premiers	Record in 1st half of season	Record in 2nd half of season
A comparison of premiers' home-and-away records during the 1st and 2nd halves of the season, 1990–2017			
2017	Richmond	7–4	8–3
2016	Western Bulldogs	8–3	7–4
2015	Hawthorn	7–4	9–2
2014	Hawthorn	8–3	9–2
2013	Hawthorn	10–1	9–2
2012	Sydney	8–3	8–3
2011	Geelong	11–0	8–3
2010	Collingwood	8–3	9–1–1
2009	Geelong	11–0	7–4
2008	Hawthorn	10–1	7–4
2007	Geelong	8–3	10–1
2006	West Coast	10–1	7–4
2005	Sydney	6–5	9–2
2004	Port Adelaide	7–4	10–1
2003	Brisbane	8–1–2	6–5
2002	Brisbane	8–3	9–2
2001	Brisbane	6–5	11–0
2000	Essendon	11–0	10–1
1999	North Melbourne	8–3	9–2
1998	Adelaide	5–6	8–3
1997	Adelaide	7–4	6–5
1996	North Melbourne	8–3	8–3
1995	Carlton	9–2	11–0
1994	West Coast	9–2	7–4
1993	Essendon	7–1–3	8–3
1992	Geelong	8–3	8–3
1991	Hawthorn	7–4	9–2
1990	Collingwood	8–3	8–3
Total		228–2–78	235–1–72

It is a close-run thing. In aggregate, the eventual premiers lost a total of six fewer games during the back end of the home-and-away season than in their first 11 games. But a difference of six games in a

616-match sample is not a lot, and there are several exceptions to the overall result. Of the 10 premiers prior to 2018, half started the regular season in better form than they finished it. This doesn't provide much support to the notion that a team needs to be in top form before the finals. Granted, the drawback of this type of analysis is that it treats each group of 11 games as identical. It fails to account for a whole range of factors relating to the relative difficulty of the fixture, or the impact of injuries, suspensions, and players being rested. But then again, it is unlikely that most pundits who declare a team has come into the finals with 'all the momentum' have considered these aspects either.

Jennings believes that in-season tactical innovation can be one of the biggest drivers of a sustained change in form. 'You train new things all the time because from about round seven, if you're not in the top eight, often you've got to change the way that you play,' he said. 'In fact, every six or seven weeks there will be changes in the look of the game and how teams play. It probably won't look much different to most people, but within clubs there are subtle alterations that are being made all the time.' The inherent difficulty in recognising and adjusting to these changes in tactics is part of what makes them effective. If the tweaks go unnoticed by the media or fans, as they often do, it can be easy for any improvement in results to be attributed to an indefinable sense of 'momentum'. It is an explanation that can sell short a team's hard work.

Catching fire

Watching your team catch fire, piling on goal after unanswered goal, is one of the most exciting experiences of being a fan. Depending on which club you support, you may be more acquainted with being on the receiving end of one of these barrages. Either way, you will doubtless be familiar with what coaches and commentators alike refer to as 'in-game momentum'. 'One extraordinary aspect of momentum is the way that it infects the minds of everyone in its presence: not just participants but observers too,' wrote Ellis, in his aforementioned piece for the *Guardian*. 'If you read a little Eastern philosophy, you might think of momentum as the *qi* of the contest.' But what if we told you that these periods of relentless domination were not due to some inscrutable force? Often, they can simply be put down to variance. To better understand this natural 'randomness', let's again take out our lucky coin.

The following experiment is used regularly by 'Probability 101' professors in universities around the world. The class is divided into two groups and, without the knowledge of the professor, the students decide which group will be the 'flippers' and which will be the 'fakers'. The flippers toss a coin 50 times, recording the outcome as heads (H) or tails (T) after each one. Meanwhile, the fakers write down a sequence of H's and T's that they believe is a reasonable simulation of what a series of 50 tosses would look like. It is then the professor's job to identify which of the sequences came from a real coin. Imagine the two groups returned the following sequences. Can you guess which is which?

Sequence A:

TT H T H T HH T H TT HH T H TT HH T H TT H TTT
H TTT H TT HH T H TT H T H T H T H TT

Sequence B:

HHH TTTT H TT HHHH TTTT H T H T H TTTTTTT
HH T H TTT HHH T HHHH T H T HH

If you thought that sequence A was the coin toss, you are not alone, but you are wrong. The answer is sequence B. What makes sequence A unrealistic is its absence of streaks. It might instinctively feel as though a series of coin tosses should result in a reasonably even spread of heads and tails, but it is usually a lot clumpier than that. Even if the average of any sequence will be about 50% heads and 50% tails, there is no correlation between one toss and the next. There will always be a 50% chance of heads, no matter what has come before it. If this were a real probability class, we would now go through the maths of just how clumpy we can expect our sequence to be, but let's spare the finer details and skip ahead to the final numbers. The evenness seen in sequence A, which has many short runs rather than a few long ones, would only happen from a real coin flip about once every 500 tries. In contrast, we would expect to see a run of at least seven consecutive heads or tails about 30% of the time if we tossed a coin 50 times. Even a run of 10 or more heads or tails would not be unheard of, occurring about 4% of the time.

The human brain is wired to spot patterns. If we see even a few people eat wild berries and later get sick, we know to extrapolate the pattern and stay away. Understanding the pattern of other people's emotional reactions allows us to cooperate in groups and society. However, sometimes the desire to find a pattern can lead us astray. It is the reason people lose money on poker machines they think are 'due' to pay out, and why some sportspeople become bogged down by superstitions to which they ascribe their success. If we see long runs of only heads or tails, it is easy to fall into the trap of searching for meaning in the patterns rather than accepting them as natural chance. Real-life randomness is often a lot less random than we might think.

Leaving the classroom and returning to the football field, we can now contemplate whether a run of goals to one team is likely to have just been a case of coin-tossing-type randomness, or whether the team really did have momentum. However, in doing so, we must acknowledge that a football match is not a completely random event. When Hawthorn met Greater Western Sydney for the first time in 2012, the two teams didn't toss coins to decide who kicked the next goal. The Hawks were clearly superior to the young and inexperienced Giants and won by 162 points. This is where we can employ a statistical tool known as a 'runs test'. In the context of analysing momentum swings in football, runs testing looks at the sequence in which goals were kicked during a match. Periods of dominance can typically be seen in streaks of consecutive goals. A runs test can indicate whether there have been more of these streaks than we would expect to see if the goals had been randomly distributed throughout the game.

In round eight, 2008, the Swans thrashed Essendon by 91 points at Sydney's Olympic Stadium. The Swans kicked 21 goals to the Bombers' seven. If an S represents a Sydney goal and an E represents an Essendon goal, the scoring progression from the opening bounce to the final siren looked like this:

SSSS EEEE SSSS EEE SSSSSSSSSSSS

There were only five 'runs' of scoring in the game, making it all but irresistible to describe the match as one of momentum. Sydney kicked four consecutive goals to start, and Essendon responded in kind. Another four-goal spurt from the Swans was then followed by three more from the Bombers, before the home side kicked away with 13 unanswered majors from the 18th minute of the third quarter. If we randomly distributed 21 S's and seven E's, there would be less than a one in 1,000 chance of having as few runs without any sort of underlying momentum causing the pattern. Our probability professor would describe such a sequence as being highly clumpy.

In contrast, when Adelaide beat Fremantle by 28 points at Football Park in round 20, 2012, the scoring progression looked like this:

A F AA FF A F A F A FF AAA F A F A F A F A F A F AA F A

Adelaide kicked 17 goals to Fremantle's 14, and the match had 25 'runs' of scoring. It is hard to see how momentum would have factored in the result. The odds of having more than 25 runs if the 31 goals were distributed randomly are, again, about one in 1,000.

So, which of these two sorts of games do we see more often in the AFL? To find out, we can conduct runs testing on the scoring progression of all games from 2008 to 2017. If we consistently detect games with longer goal-scoring streaks than we would expect from randomness, it will provide strong evidence in favour of the existence of momentum. On the other hand, if there aren't many examples of goal-scoring streaks in the sample, then that suggests that momentum might be overrated as a force in the AFL.

In total, there are 1,993 games for us to analyse. If momentum wasn't really a factor, and any runs of goals were purely driven by random variation, statistical theory tells us we should expect about 5% of those games, or about 100, to feature clumpy scoring like the Swans–Bombers match in 2008. Instead, our runs testing uncovers 127 such games. This is more than 100, so this provides some tentative evidence that momentum is real. Still, the 27-game difference is small enough that the unexpected clumpy streaks could be caused by other things, such as in-game injuries or tactical changes, which are not accounted for in our data. It would be hard to consider this strong evidence that momentum-driven runs of scoring are commonplace in the AFL.

If we include all scores in our runs tests, instead of just goals, the number of games flagged as having statistically significant clumpy streaks rises to 206. However, this might just be an indication that a team is more likely to score next after kicking a behind because the ball is already in its forward 50. As tactics have improved over time, the likelihood of a team scoring from an opposition kick-in has increased. This can be seen in the following graph showing how often a team scores next in the same quarter after it has scored a goal, behind, or rushed behind.

The graph reveals a few interesting trends. Before the practice was banned in 2009, teams were deliberately conceding rushed behinds to relieve pressure on themselves. When they did this, they were often able to quickly clear the ball from their defensive zone before the

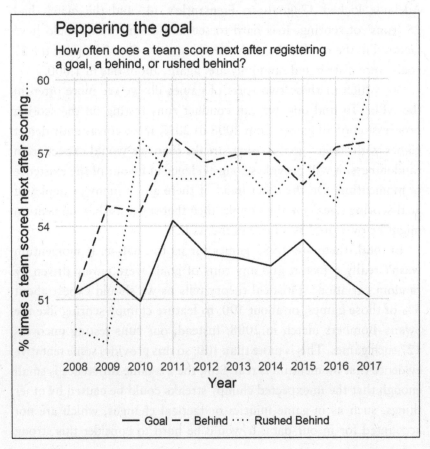

Peppering the goal

How often does a team score next after registering a goal, a behind, or rushed behind?

% times a team scored next after scoring...

Year

—— Goal – – Behind ···· Rushed Behind

opposition had time to react. It meant that in conceding a rushed behind, they increased the chance that they would be the next team to score. In recent years, however, the trend has gone the other way. A team is now more likely to give up the next score if it has just conceded a rushed behind. This is a result of a combination of both the rule change and recent improvements in defensive tactics. Scoring from a kick-in has become harder as teams have become more adept at applying forward presses and locking the ball in their attacking 50. In 2008, a side was just as likely to score next from a centre bounce as it was from an opponent's kick-in.

One of the most significant catalysts for this league-wide tactical improvement was Hawthorn's implementation of 'Clarko's Cluster' in 2008. After making some preseason trips to the English soccer club Bolton, David Rath developed a framework for coding games that showed where the Hawks were winning possession on the field and how far they were moving the ball from those positions. 'It was a visual chart and it showed that we were getting a lot of the ball in our defensive 50,' said Rath. 'If you looked at footy training at an AFL club back then, a lot of it would be practising winning the ball back in the defensive 50 and marching it the whole length of the ground. It was a reasonable thing to do because in those days you got through 50 per cent of the time.' To make it harder for teams to transition the ball from their backline, Alastair Clarkson and Rath developed the Hawks' famous rolling zone. It combined the soccer tactics they had seen at Bolton with a high-pressing strategy that had been implemented by Neil Craig at the Adelaide Crows. 'When we started pressing we found we could stop teams from rebounding so easily. These days if you get through 25 per cent of the time it's a pretty good result, so the ability to get from end to end has been halved.'

The percentage at which a team scores next following a goal is a good proxy for the evenness of the competition. Our graph shows that the AFL was at its most uneven in the years immediately following the introduction of its expansion teams, Gold Coast and Greater Western Sydney. Good sides were thrashing the Suns and Giants, and in doing so they were often kicking consecutive scores. As the two new teams gained experience and improved, the competition began to even out. In 2017, a team that kicked a goal was the next to score

51% of the time, down three percentage points from six years before. Again, this might suggest that momentum plays less of a role in runs of goals than is widely thought.

Another place we can look for signs of in-game momentum is in the length of time between goals. We might expect to see surges in momentum manifested as quick bursts of scoring throughout a game. To study these bursts, we can again use a runs test. For each game in our sample, we can list the amount of time between goals for each team. We can then compare those numbers to the team's median time between goals in the same match. If we find longer than expected runs above or below the median, such as several goals kicked in quick succession followed by long scoreless periods, this might suggest the presence of momentum. For example, when Collingwood played the Western Bulldogs at the MCG in round six, 2011, it had only kicked seven goals by the seventh minute of the last quarter. The average interval between its goals had been 12-and-a-half minutes, and it hadn't kicked two consecutive goals in less than six minutes of game time. From that moment, the Magpies kicked eight unanswered goals to finish the match, with an average interval of about two-and-a-half minutes. Leigh Brown kicked three in just over four minutes. There could be several explanations for this type of scoring pattern, but if we see it repeated consistently over many games it would be foolish to discount momentum as one of them.

Using the data from our 10-year sample, we can analyse 3,986 separate team performances in this way. Of those, only 201 show up as having goal-scoring patterns that are highly unlikely (a less than 5% chance) to have happened randomly. Out of 3,986, 201 is almost exactly 5%, the conventional threshold for statistical significance. We can say the patterns in our sample are close to what we would expect if they were only the result of randomness. This is far from conclusive proof against the existence of momentum, but it is yet another place we have failed to detect it where we might have expected to.

The hot boot

It might be hard to find compelling evidence of team momentum, but what about at a personal level? Do individual players experience sudden boosts in performance above what we would normally expect to see? The barrier to answering these questions, once again, is the difficulty in defining and measuring the concept. Say we wanted to discern momentum-related changes in a midfielder's output. We could begin our investigation by looking at when they recorded contested possessions in a game. If we come across a period during which the player gathered a lot of contested ball relative to their usual output, we might want to infer they were wearing the halo of momentum. But what if they hadn't won as much ball at other times because their teammates had already done so and moved it on? What if the player had been left a step behind play after an awkward bounce of the oval-shaped ball? What if the coaching staff had asked the player to start off in a tagging role, and then switched them to be on the ball? What initially appeared to be momentum might simply have been the player taking advantage of good opportunities.

In basketball there has been a long-running debate about the so-called 'hot hand'. The basic premise of a hot-handed player is that they are more likely to make a successful shot because they have scored from their previous shot. Amos Tversky, an Israeli psychologist who was the protagonist of Michael Lewis's bestselling book *The Undoing Project*, co-authored a 1985 paper entitled 'The Hot Hand in Basketball: On the Misperception of Random Sequences'. After conducting a series of studies, including an analysis of the Boston Celtics' free throw attempts, Tversky and his collaborators found the hot hand was a cognitive illusion. They concluded that the perception of shooting streaks was stronger than any statistical evidence for them. However, more recent research, including a 2002 paper from Australia's Monash University, has questioned the findings. The debate remains unresolved.

Perhaps the most unalloyed display of individual ability in football occurs during a set shot for goal. The player on the mark might be yelling, waving their arms, and jumping up and down, but they cannot physically interfere with the player taking the shot. A set shot, like a free throw in basketball, is essentially a closed skill involving the player, the ball, and the goals. When a player is 'in the zone', we would expect their set-shot kicking to be accurate. 'We sometimes hear footballers and basketballers talk about entering a state of flow,' said Port Adelaide's mindset performance coach, David Steventon.

'When they're in that flow state, everything else tunes out. We've all seen players have a quarter that you just can't believe. Is that momentum? It's certainly belief, and it is certainly energy directed towards an outcome, so maybe it is.'

Channelling Tversky, let's see if we can find evidence of the 'hot boot' in the AFL. We will do this by testing whether players are more likely to convert a set-shot attempt if they kicked a goal from their last shot. Unlike the case of basketball free throws, footballers don't take set shots from the same point on the ground every time, so we will also need to factor in the difficulty of their shots. To begin our analysis, we will list every player from 2013 to 2017 who took at least two shots in a match, with the second being a set shot. This happened 6,123 times during our five-season sample. Of those, 3,099 players scored a goal from their first shot and 3,024 either registered a behind or missed completely. On their second attempt, would we expect the players who kicked their first goal to have a higher conversion rate for their second shot?

	Goal from 2nd (set) shot	Average difficulty of 2nd shot (xG)
Goal from 1st shot (3,099 players)	1,656 (53.4%)	53.4%
Miss from 1st Shot (3,024 players)	1,598 (52.8%)	53.7%

The 'Average Difficulty of Shot' listed in the right-hand column represents the average 'Expected Goals' from all shots. If you skipped chapter two, a shot's xG is essentially the AFL-average conversion rate for shots of that type (here, set shots) from the same angle and distance. So, a 53.4% average difficulty means that of those 3,099 shots, we'd expect 53.4% of them to be kicked if they were converted at the AFL average. In this case, the players who had already kicked a goal with their first shot converted their shots exactly as expected, and at a slightly higher rate than those players who had missed their first shot. This is arguably unsurprising. A lot of players will manage to take two shots in a match, and not all of them will be good goal kickers. We can't say too much about momentum at this stage.

If we look at all instances in which a player created at least three chances, with their third being a set shot, our list is whittled down to 3,473. Of those, 955 players had kicked both of their first two chances, 1,732 had kicked one, and 786 had missed both.

	Goal from 3rd (set) shot	Average difficulty of 3rd shot (xG)
2 goals from first 2 shots (955 players)	528 (55.2%)	54.7%
1 goal from first 2 shots (1,732 players)	940 (54.3%)	53.5%
0 goals from first 2 shots (786 players)	424 (53.9%)	54.5%

The players who kicked goals from their opening two shots had a negligibly higher conversion rate than those who had missed both. Based on these figures, a player who is on fire early will only kick about one more goal every hundred games than players who start slowly. This could be a result of the wide range in ability of players on this list, or even random variation. Regardless, the relationship between past kicking and future kicking on the same day doesn't seem strong.

Finally, let's refine our search to the players who took at least four shots in a game, the fourth of which was a set shot. This reduces the list to 1,988 occurrences, most of them attributable to forwards and attacking midfielders, who are historically slightly better-than-average kicks.

	Goal from 4th (set) shot	Average difficulty of 4th shot (xG)
3 goals from first 3 shots (316 players)	174 (55.1%)	55.2%
2 goals from first 3 shots (792 players)	448 (56.6%)	54.7%
1 goal from first 3 shots (684 players)	393 (57.5%)	55.1%
0 goals from first 3 shots (196 players)	104 (53.1%)	53.3%

After accounting for the quality of shots taken, there is little difference between the set-shot conversion rate of a player who has already nailed three-from-three, and a player who has so far blown every chance. In fact, the most accurate players on this list were those who had missed two of their first three chances. The pattern continues for longer streaks as well, although the sample sizes drop quickly. There is no statistically significant improvement in accuracy from players who convert their shots compared to those who miss. In fact, this is the case for all shot types, not just set shots. Our simple study seems to suggest that a player's ability to kick a goal is not related to how well they have been kicking that day, or any 'momentum' they may or may not have generated.

The fact that none of our studies, imperfect as they are, returned any meaningful suggestion of momentum does not rule out its presence. It is telling, however, that our search came up blank in the places we might have expected to see its effects most prominently. It could be argued that our objective approach fails to properly recognise the subjective nature of the concept, for it is true that it does not account for the players' own experiences and perceptions. We don't know if the players felt like they were experiencing momentum at the time. We could ask them, but we would then run the risk of creating patterns and narratives from random data. Perhaps Ellis's interpretation of momentum as *qi* – a mystical life force that underpins much of traditional Chinese medicine, philosophy, and martial arts – is apt after all. Just because something is not provable and scientifically measurable will not stop some people from believing in it. Whether one wishes to worship at the altar of momentum is ultimately a matter of faith.

Chapter Six

Statistics

The art of saying nothing

An AFL coach's pre-match media conference can be a strange old dance. The participants are rarely in sync, even though there is plenty of time for rehearsal. Factoring in the preseason, they will run through the steps at least 24 times each year. In Melbourne, the size of the media contingent will rest on the team's ladder position, the significance of the match, and how busy the news day is. In other cities, the same core of reporters will be in attendance each week. There will typically be a couple of football writers from the legacy newspapers, a smattering of broadcast journos, a scribe from the AFL's website, and two or three silent staffers from the club's in-house media unit. The dance traditionally begins with one of the young, brash commercial TV reporters trying to seize the lead. The coach's personality, experience, and mood will dictate whether he allows himself to be led, or instead steps on the reporter's feet to wrest the discourse his way.

Much of it is elementary fact finding. How is Easton Wood's hamstring injury? Has Tom Liberatore done enough in the reserves to earn a recall? Depending on when and where the game is being played, even such perfunctory questioning can be enough to raise a coach's hackles.

Journalist: 'Well, Luke, who's on the flight who didn't play last week, and who's not on the flight who did play last week?'

Luke Beveridge: 'I'm not going to answer that, sorry. It's early in the day and I'd rather not send that message to Perth before the teams come out this afternoon.'

Journalist: 'So, you'd rather not reveal even the 25 you're taking?'

Luke Beveridge: 'No, I mean, what – you want me to name the 25 players?'

Journalist: 'Well, no, just a couple of them.'

Luke Beveridge: 'No. I mean, just respect the fact that it's early in the morning on a Thursday. West Coast aren't going to declare their team this early in the day, and I'm not going to either.'

Journalist: 'Does it make much difference, though, really?'

Luke Beveridge: 'Oh, yeah. Yeah.'

One might reasonably assume that if Beveridge believes revealing his emergencies a few hours early will put him at a competitive disadvantage, there is little chance of him ever offering any real insight into his team's tactics and game plan. Anything that might be of practical use to an opposing ear will be met with the straightest of bats. While some coaches, such as Chris Scott, Nathan Buckley, and Damien Hardwick, will at least attempt to address a question and avoid stating the obvious, others seem to revel in being opaque and giving as little as possible. In the lead-up to Alastair Clarkson's 300th game as coach, Hawthorn's media unit put together a video entitled 'Clarko's Clichés'. It was a two-minute 'greatest hits' compilation of his recent banalities.

'We don't discuss anything around selection until the sides come out later this afternoon.'

'We'll reveal our selections at the appropriate time.'

'We'll declare our side tonight.'

'It's a tough competition.'

'Every game you play is tough.'

'It's a tough environment. It's a really close competition.'

'They're a tough opponent.'

'They're such a ferocious side.'

'They're a very, very good side.'

'They're a formidable side.'

'They've got a formidable midfield.'

Clarkson has a way of heaping praise on the Hawks' upcoming opponents that makes it sound as though his side should go into every match as a raging underdog. The benefit of wheeling out such tired and hoary platitudes is that they say nothing, they kill time, and they bore reporters into changing the subject. In Clarkson's case, as the league's longest-serving active coach, it might instead invite questions about the week's burning topics. Should the bounce be scrapped? Has the game become too congested? Has the standard of goal kicking diminished? On these subjects, away from the practical details of the match at hand, he often becomes more expansive. Sometimes he might sense the opportunity to filibuster, and by the time he finishes an impressively thoughtful and detailed response, the microphones will be getting heavy in the reporters' hands. 'That's it?' Clarkson will ask them, as their arms drop. 'Thanks guys, good on you.' Many successful coaches employ this approach. The NRL's Wayne Bennett, the NFL's Bill Belichick, and the NBA's Gregg Popovich are well-known practitioners from other sports.

One of the by-products of cultivating a taciturn media persona is that when you stray from the well-worn lines, the impact can be significant. Before flying out for a Thursday night match against Port Adelaide in 2016, Clarkson raised eyebrows by questioning the Power's consistency. 'We like to think that we've proved ourselves over a long period of time, from week to week, playing tough, hard footy,' he said. 'Port Adelaide are yet to prove that they can do that on a week-to-week basis.' The comment was widely interpreted as being not so much a dig at the opposition, as a thinly veiled message to his own players. The Hawks had lost three of their past four games against Port. 'The real message was: it's time, boys,' wrote the *Herald Sun*'s chief football writer, Mark Robinson. 'It's time to be really unsociable.' Sure enough, the Hawks returned home with the four points.

The following week, Clarkson had another uncharacteristically candid exchange with reporters at Melbourne Airport. Ahead of the Hawks' match against the league's dominant contested possession team, the Sydney Swans, he was asked whether he was concerned that his side ranked last for the statistic. 'Contested ball is just a fancy term for everyone in the media. We don't give a toss about that,' he said. 'We've won five contested ball counts in about two years, but we've still won lots of games of footy.' In this case, the underlying message to his players seemed to be for them to trust their own strengths, such as their ball movement and forward pressure, rather than worry about what the Swans were good at. As if to prove his point, the Hawks won the match by five points despite losing the contested possession count 160 to 123. 'In hindsight, Clarkson's pre-match engagement with the media before both these games was the best tactical move he made,' observed Alex Fair in the *Advocate*.

Whether it's worth wading through the interminable dross for the rare gems is questionable. In England, the quality of Premier League news conferences has plumbed such depths that there has been serious debate about their continuing value. 'The bulk of sports news is quotation, and the bulk of quotation is chronically dull. Dull and omnipresent,' wrote *Guardian* sportswriter Andy Bull. 'Have we lost all judgement of what is actually worth reporting? Or listening to?' To be fair, there is little doubt that most AFL coaches would gladly forego their pre-game responsibilities if they were given the option. It is the AFL media that insist they keep showing up to the dance, with the oft-repeated claim is that it serves an important purpose in connecting fans with their clubs. But what, if anything, can a fan really glean from what a coach says before a match?

What really matters?

In researching this chapter, we watched nearly every pre-match media conference held by a senior coach during the 2017 AFL season. This was made possible because most are uploaded in full each week to the 18 clubs' respective websites. St Kilda seemed to lose interest in this task late in the season, so we missed a few of Alan Richardson's appearances, but in all we sat through more than 65 hours of triteness and triviality, punctuated by flashes of genuine insight and reflection. The aim of this somewhat Augean task was to identify the main potential sources of victory that coaches highlight before games, and to test whether they are accurate predictors of success.

Without putting an exact figure on it, we found that roughly half of the average pre-game presser was devoted to selection matters such as injuries, suspensions, and form. About a quarter of the questions related to general topics, such as rule changes, the state of the game, or the league's latest scandal, and there were usually one or two queries about the club's ongoing list management issues. The rest, or about a fifth of the typical pre-match media conference, addressed how the game would be played. It is this last slice of the pie that we will concern ourselves with here.

'Where's the game going to be won?' Rodney Eade was asked before the Gold Coast Suns' round-one match against Brisbane. This, or a variant of it, is perhaps the most frequent question that a coach will field during a season. Eade's reply was equally standard: 'You win games in the midfield by being able to give your forwards some access and denying the opposition, so that's what we'd like to do.' The following week, ahead of his side's match against Greater Western Sydney, he gave a similar response to the same question: 'I think our midfield is where it's going to be won or lost and that's what we need to get right.' The Suns lost both games.

Closely associated with 'winning the midfield' was the other constant refrain of 'winning the contest'. 'If we don't win the ball in the contest and put pressure on them it's going to be a hard day for our defenders,' Eade told reporters leading into the Suns' round-five clash with Adelaide. 'We need to get our hands on the ball first. We've won contested ball the last couple of weeks and we certainly need to do that again.' Gold Coast lost the contested possession count to the Crows by 10, and the match by 67 points. Eade maintained the message the following week. 'I think the most important thing is the contest,' said Eade. 'I mean, if we can win the footy, we're able to control it.' This time a contested ball deficit of seven translated into a 13-point loss to North Melbourne.

Heading into round 10, with his side struggling at 15th on the ladder, Eade had seemingly downgraded his expectations. 'We just need consistency of effort, and that's what happens with young teams,' he said, before taking on Melbourne in Alice Springs. 'We've got to bridge that consistency gap between our best and worst.' After leading the Demons by 30 points during the third term, the Suns ended up losing by 35. By now edging ever closer to his eventual sacking, Eade used his next pre-match presser to again plead his players for a 'consistent effort for four quarters'. This time he got it, with Peter Wright kicking a late goal to give the club its first win over West Coast. Nine games later, Eade was out of a job.

Eade's various answers to the question 'Where will the game be won?' closely reflected the most common themes we heard during our year of coach watching:

- contested possession
- winning the midfield battle
- consistency.

To help us translate the jargon and cliché of clubland, we have enlisted the services of one of the AFL's most highly rated young analysts and development coaches, Fremantle's Adam Read. Thirty-six-year-old Read has one of the most unusual résumés of any coach currently working in the league. He grew up around the corner from Matthew Pavlich in Adelaide, and used to drive the Dockers great to school. Unlike his friend, he never made Sacred Heart College's First XVIII, and never attracted the attention of AFL talent scouts. He played amateur football while completing a university arts degree, majoring in screen studies. 'As a bright-eyed, early 20s film student, you're thinking you're going to become the next Steven Spielberg,' said Read. 'But then reality sets in that you're in Adelaide and there are no jobs available, so you've kind of just got to get to work.' He spent time as a sales representative, before setting up his own paving business.

Read's break into the football industry came in 2007 when he was offered work as a recruiter for Fremantle. He scouted players in his home town for two years before moving to Perth, where he put his screen studies degree to unexpected use as the Dockers' video analyst. 'I was fortunate that Chris Scott, when he was at Fremantle, was fantastic to work with in that role, which is really where my football education started,' he said. 'He would get me to break down different bits of footage, not only of our team but also the opposition, and was always really keen to have a conversation and teach me new things.' After Ross Lyon's arrival as senior coach at the end of 2011, Read was promoted to the coaches' box in the role of coaches' assistant. It had been a rapid rise, but he never felt his lack of AFL playing experience was a hindrance. 'The Italian soccer club AC Milan used to have this coach called Arrigo Sacchi, who was never a professional player, and when people used to try to pin that on him in the media he'd say, "I never realised that to become a jockey you needed to have first been a horse",' said Read. 'It's a great quote. Anything in this world can be learned.'

Contested possession

Let's begin our tour of Read's world of coach speak and football statistics by learning about the much-discussed contested possession counts. Clarkson's public scorning of the metric made so many headlines because it was counterintuitive to what we usually hear from coaches. 'It's all about the contest, whether that be at a centre bounce or a stoppage,' said Crows coach Don Pyke in 2017. 'Yeah, more than anything, it's the side that wins the contest, to give you the ball where you want it the most,' agreed Power coach Ken Hinkley. 'I think most teams in the competition understand that now.'

As we know, Champion Data collects a huge amount of information from every AFL game, including tallies of when a player gathers a disputed ball at ground level or out of a ruck contest. If a player does this under direct physical pressure from an opponent it is counted as a 'hard-ball get'. If a player gathers a ground ball under no pressure it is called a 'loose-ball get'. A 'contested mark' is recorded when a player takes a pack mark or a one-on-one mark under direct pressure. These three metrics, as well as contested knock-ons and free kicks, all contribute to a team's 'contested possession' total. It is more a statistical grouping than an individual statistic.

Hard-ball gets + Loose-ball gets + Gathers from a hit-out + Contested marks + Contested knock-ons + Frees for = Contested possessions.

According to Read, it is true that contested possession is one of the most closely monitored metrics in the coaches' box. 'It is, because it's a good, broad indicator,' he said. 'With the amount that goes on match day, you can't always drill down into the more advanced stats or proprietary stats that you can look at during the week in review, so you need that broad indicator. It's also important for the players, just to give them an indication of how they're doing or how the team is tracking. You don't want to overload them with too much statistical information, so having that nice, broad number is good for them to look at and say "Hey, we're doing really well here," or "We're not doing so great". The players have a lot going on. They're running 14 kilometres a game, they're making hundreds or maybe thousands of decisions, so the last thing they need is to look at a huge table full of numbers. They just need a simple overview, and contested possession is a really good one for that.'

We might wonder, though, how often does the team that wins the contested possession count also finish ahead on the scoreboard? The following table answers that question, based on the statistics collected from every AFL match from 2007 to the end of the 2017. That's 2,177 games in total, including finals. We should note that drawn games have been excluded, and that ties in the metric counts have been treated as half a win.

Percentage of games in which the winning team won or tied a specified metric count		
Metric	Won or tied the metric	Included ties
Kick	77.9%	1.4%
Inside 50	74.2%	2.7%
Uncontested possession	69.5%	0.7%
Contested possession	69.4%	1.8%
Mark	69.2%	1.1%
Gather	65.2%	5.8%
Loose-ball get	63.3%	3.8%
Contested mark from team	62.4%	10.0%
Clearance	61.0%	4.6%
Handball receive	60.9%	1.1%
Running bounce	59.6%	5.9%
Handball	58.9%	1.0%
First possession	57.3%	4.4%
Hard-ball get	56.2%	3.6%
Tackle	55.6%	2.5%
Contested mark from opposition	55.5%	13.0%
Hit-out to advantage	54.2%	7.5%
Smother	52.5%	10.9%
Free for	52.4%	7.6%
50-metre penalty for	51.6%	30.7%
Hit-out	51.4%	2.4%
Spoil	45.2%	4.4%
Rebound 50	39.4%	3.6%
Turnover	26.8%	4.1%

The metric most closely associated with victory is, in fact, the kick count. The team that had the highest (or equal highest) number of kicks in a match won almost 78% of the time. You can't kick without the ball and, as the saying goes in many sports, you can't win without the ball either. The inside-50 count is second on the list, with the team that recorded the most forward entries enjoying a winning rate of just under 75%. Uncontested possession is third at 69.5%, marginally ahead of contested possession in fourth at 69.4%.

It makes sense that coaches talk so much about the contested possession count when you realise how highly connected it is with winning. Unlike many of the other statistics, it also relates to a possession-instigating act. While kicks are obviously directly related to point-scoring, contested possessions are what lead to a player having the opportunity to kick the ball in the first place. As such, contested possessions are arguably more fundamentally causal of victory. 'Footy is a game of contest and transition,' explained Read. 'It starts with a contest at the centre bounce and continues from there, so contested ball is always an important one to be winning.'

Since 2007, the minor premier has, on average, recorded the third best contested ball differential during the home-and-away season. The average premier has recorded the sixth-best differential during that time, although Hawthorn's four flag-winning seasons are a big factor in that relatively low ranking. The Hawks were ranked 12th for contested ball differential in 2008 (-2.8 per game), seventh in 2013 (+3.5), fifth in 2014 (+4.1), and eighth in 2015 (+1.5). After Clarkson launched his famous tirade about the statistic in 2016, they ranked dead last (-16.7). 'People can make what they want of stats,' Clarkson said at the time. 'We don't like that in a significant, competitive game that we're viewed as being number 18 in one facet, but really it's not talked about internally at our club at all.'

By mid-2017, however, the Hawks were beginning to reconsider their approach. After again ranking last for contested possession differential through the first 12 rounds (-17.1 per game), they significantly lifted their output during the second half of the season to rank ninth from rounds 13 to 23 (+2.4). 'The contested ball style has changed footy considerably in the last couple of years, and what worked for us during 2011 through to 2015 was obviously a different style of footy,' said Hawthorn's former head of strategy and innovation, David Rath. 'We had previously been lower in contested possession for a number of reasons. It's connected to what you choose to do with the ball when you have it, and whether you want to play like the Western Bulldogs and Sydney by keeping it moving to another contested possession situation. That can be okay, but it's also risky because you can cough the ball up. There's a sweet spot, I suppose. Your philosophies around how you want to play can have a big influence on your contested possession numbers.'

Winning the midfield battle

Not all contested possessions are equal, of course, because their influence can vary depending on where they happen, and what they entail. 'A contested possession can be a contested mark in the forward line, or it can be putting your head over the ball and picking it up in the midfield,' said Rath. 'Those two things are tactically and strategically totally different things. Depending on where the ball is, there will be different players involved, different motives, and you will be trying to do different things.' If we are to believe what the senior coaches tell us at their pre-match media conferences, it is the actions that take place in the midfield that are the most critical. 'The midfield is always important, there's no doubt about that,' said Saints coach Alan Richardson. Swans coach John Longmire described the midfield as 'where a lot of games are decided', while Crows coach Don Pyke believed that was especially true during September. 'The reality is that finals come down to winning the contest where it counts, and that's through the midfield,' he said. 'That battle becomes pivotal in most games.'

To analyse this widespread assertion, we have obtained breakdowns of the raw metric counts based on where they occurred. As we discussed in chapter three, Champion Data divides the field into four portions or zones: defensive 50, defensive midfield, attacking midfield, and forward 50. The zone in which an event is designated as having taken place is determined by the perspective of the player performing that action. For instance, a Fremantle player could take a mark in his team's forward 50, seek to play on, and have his kick smothered by a Hawthorn player. That passage of play would result in a mark for Fremantle in the forward 50 and a smother for Hawthorn in the defensive 50, even though both actions took place in the same physical part of the field. 'The zone-by-zone data is really important for coaches,' said Read. 'The ground position has a huge bearing on how much weight you put on a statistic, because there are different circumstances in each zone and they've all got contrasting outcomes that can affect the games in various ways.'

The following table shows the zone-based breakdown for various possession-related statistics in 2007, 2012, and 2017. The two rightmost columns show the percentage change in the relevant metric over the past five and 10 seasons. In 2017, uncontested possessions were up by about 12% on 2007, but the number of contested possessions had risen by less than 1% during the same period. The mix of possession type has therefore swung significantly towards the uncontested, though mostly in the defensive 50 and attacking midfield. We can also see that although the average number of kicks per game has risen overall, the increase has been solely due to teams kicking more in their defensive 50 and attacking midfield. There are generally fewer marks than there were 10 years ago, but more than there were five years ago. The number of handballs has risen in every zone.

Team statistic averages by zone					
				Change % from 2017	
Metric	2007	2012	2017	vs 2007	vs 2012
Points	95.4	91.9	89.1	(6.6%)	(3.0%)
Kick: all	201.9	206.0	211.1	+4.5%	+2.5%
– Defensive 50	34.2	36.6	45.7	+33.5%	+24.6%
– Defensive midfield	78.4	78.7	69.3	(11.6%)	(12.0%)
– Attacking midfield	54.8	56.4	63.2	+15.2%	+12.0%
– Forward 50	34.5	34.2	32.9	(4.6%)	(3.7%)
Handball: all	143.1	151.0	171.1	+19.6%	+13.3%
– Defensive 50	29.3	27.5	32.7	+11.4%	+18.9%
– Defensive midfield	63.2	63.5	69.3	+9.7%	+9.2%
– Attacking midfield	37.4	43.5	51.3	+37.0%	+17.9%
– Forward 50	13.1	16.5	17.8	+36.4%	+8.0%
Mark: all	103.4	88.1	93.3	(9.8%)	+5.9%
– Defensive 50	22.7	18.6	24.2	+6.6%	+30.4%
– Defensive midfield	39.6	35.8	32.4	(18.0%)	(9.3%)
– Attacking midfield	26.9	22.4	24.5	(9.1%)	+9.4%
– Forward 50	14.1	11.3	12.1	(14.6%)	+6.9%

Team statistic averages by zone

Metric	2007	2012	2017	Change % from 2017	
				vs 2007	vs 2012
Uncontested possession: all	226.2	213.5	239.1	+5.7%	+12.0%
– Defensive 50	44.4	39.1	51.6	+16.2%	+32.0%
– Defensive midfield	97.3	91.2	91.6	(5.9%)	+0.4%
– Attacking midfield	61.8	60.0	71.7	+15.9%	+19.4%
– Forward 50	22.7	23.2	24.3	+7.0%	+4.7%
Contested possession: all	117.1	141.7	142.6	+21.8%	+0.7%
– Defensive 50	23.4	25.3	26.6	+13.8%	+5.2%
– Defensive midfield	38.8	48.7	47.8	+23.1%	(1.9%)
– Attacking midfield	33.8	43.2	44.2	+30.8%	+2.4%
– Forward 50	21.1	24.5	24.0	+13.8%	(2.0%)
Hard-ball get: all	41.0	53.7	47.5	+15.8%	(11.6%)
– Defensive 50	7.4	9.3	8.4	+13.9%	(9.8%)
– Defensive midfield	13.8	18.0	15.6	+12.4%	(13.6%)
– Attacking midfield	12.4	16.8	14.9	+20.1%	(11.0%)
– Forward 50	7.4	9.6	8.6	+17.0%	(10.6%)
Loose-ball get: all	39.6	44.8	51.9	+31.0%	+15.8%
– Defensive 50	9.5	9.2	11.0	+15.6%	+19.3%
– Defensive midfield	13.5	15.7	17.4	+29.2%	+11.0%
– Attacking midfield	10.6	12.9	15.5	+46.7%	+20.7%
– Forward 50	6.1	7.1	8.0	+31.9%	+13.1%
Gather: all	21.8	25.7	29.2	+33.7%	+13.5%
– Defensive 50	2.9	3.3	4.6	+60.1%	+41.5%
– Defensive midfield	8.4	9.8	10.7	+26.7%	+9.1%
– Attacking midfield	7.8	9.0	10.1	+30.2%	+12.1%
– Forward 50	2.7	3.6	3.7	+37.8%	+3.8%
Free for: all	19.2	18.9	18.8	(1.8%)	(0.6%)
– Defensive 50	3.5	3.2	3.2	(6.8%)	+1.6%
– Defensive midfield	6.6	6.7	6.6	(0.6%)	(2.7%)
– Attacking midfield	6.0	6.1	6.2	+2.9%	+1.2%
– Forward 50	3.1	2.9	2.8	(8.3%)	(2.2%)
50-m penalty for: all	1.2	1.1	1.0	(22.0%)	(13.5%)
– Defensive 50	0.4	0.3	0.3	(32.8%)	(11.7%)
– Defensive midfield	0.4	0.4	0.3	(15.1%)	(9.0%)
– Attacking midfield	0.2	0.3	0.3	+4.9%	(13.6%)
– Forward 50	0.2	0.2	0.1	(45.5%)	(26.5%)
Contested mark from opposition: all	3.7	4.8	4.6	+24%	(5.0%)
– Defensive 50	2.1	1.9	1.9	(10.5%)	(2.3%)
– Defensive midfield	0.9	1.4	1.2	+25.0%	(18.8%)
– Attacking midfield	0.6	1.4	1.4	+145.9%	+4.3%
– Forward 50	0.1	0.1	0.1	+47.7%	+22.6%

Team statistic averages by zone					
				Change % from 2017	
Metric	2007	2012	2017	vs 2007	vs 2012
Contested mark from team: all	6.4	6.8	6.6	+2.8%	(3.1%)
– Defensive 50	0.0	0.1	0.1	+58.9%	(17.9%)
– Defensive midfield	1.1	1.8	2.0	+81.0%	+6.6%
– Attacking midfield	1.6	1.6	1.5	(3.9%)	(9.4%)
– Forward 50	3.7	3.2	3.1	(17.8%)	(5.0%)

The rest of the metrics are listed below. The rate at which some of these statistics have been recorded has changed dramatically during our sample period. Clearances are up significantly in the defensive midfield, but down in the attacking midfield. Teams have recorded more hit-outs in their defensive half, but fewer in attack. Smothers and tackles are up across the board, and there are more spoils and turnovers everywhere except the attacking midfield. The running bounce has been reduced to a roughly twice-per-quarter phenomenon, which is usually seen in the defensive midfield.

Team statistic averages by zone					
				Change % from 2017	
Metric	2007	2012	2017	vs 2007	vs 2012
Clearance: all	32.0	37.7	36.8	+15.1%	(2.4%)
– Defensive 50	3.8	4.9	4.9	+28.3%	(0.4%)
– Defensive midfield	13.5	15.5	20.3	+50.4%	+31.2%
– Attacking midfield	11.4	13.0	7.7	(32.5%)	(40.8%)
– Forward 50	3.3	4.3	3.9	+20.4%	(9.7%)
Hit-out: all	31.3	39.7	39.9	+27.5%	+0.4%
– Defensive 50	3.6	4.9	5.6	+53.7%	+13.7%
– Defensive midfield	17.9	20.6	21.3	+19.0%	+3.4%
– Attacking midfield	6.3	8.7	8.5	+35.4%	(3.2%)
– Forward 50	3.5	5.4	4.5	+29.2%	(17.0%)
Hit-out to advantage: all	7.4	10.1	11.5	+55.5%	+14.5%
– Defensive 50	0.9	1.1	1.5	+67.6%	+41.8%
– Defensive midfield	2.9	4.0	6.4	+117.0%	+58.9%
– Attacking midfield	2.8	3.8	2.5	(9.7%)	(34.1%)
– Forward 50	0.8	1.1	1.1	+41.5%	(5.1%)
First possession: all	34.4	41.0	40.2	+16.9%	(1.8%)
– Defensive 50	4.3	5.4	5.4	+25.3%	(0.2%)
– Defensive midfield	14.5	16.5	21.9	+51.3%	+32.5%
– Attacking midfield	12.1	14.1	8.4	(30.8%)	(40.3%)
– Forward 50	3.6	5.0	4.6	+29.2%	(8.2%)

Team statistic averages by zone					
				Change % from 2017	
Metric	2007	2012	2017	vs 2007	vs 2012
Smother: all	4.7	7.3	8.4	+80.1%	+16.1%
– Defensive 50	0.9	1.4	1.5	+56.5%	+8.1%
– Defensive midfield	1.5	2.3	2.7	+80.7%	+16.3%
– Attacking midfield	1.6	2.4	2.7	+68.1%	+10.9%
– Forward 50	0.6	1.1	1.6	+143.0%	+35.9%
Spoil: all	25.8	32.5	34.0	+32.1%	+4.6%
– Defensive 50	13.0	13.5	13.9	+7.4%	+3.1%
– Defensive midfield	2.5	5.2	8.8	+246.7%	+68.5%
– Attacking midfield	8.6	11.9	9.1	+6.0%	(23.7%)
– Forward 50	1.6	1.8	2.2	+32.3%	+18.1%
Tackle: all	52.9	63.7	68.5	+29.5%	+7.6%
– Defensive 50	10.2	12.3	13.0	+27.4%	+5.8%
– Defensive midfield	16.6	19.8	21.5	+29.1%	+8.3%
– Attacking midfield	17.9	20.9	22.0	+23.2%	+5.4%
– Forward 50	8.1	10.6	12.0	+47.1%	+12.7%
Turnover: all	58.3	64.6	69.5	+19.2%	+7.6%
– Defensive 50	3.3	3.9	4.4	+33.8%	+13.9%
– Defensive midfield	13.4	17.7	20.2	+51.1%	+13.8%
– Attacking midfield	18.8	20.2	20.2	+7.3%	(0.4%)
– Forward 50	22.9	22.8	24.8	+8.3%	+8.9%
Handball receive: all	118.3	119.9	138.1	+16.7%	+15.2%
– Defensive 50	21.8	20.1	26.1	+19.6%	+29.9%
– Defensive midfield	54.2	52.5	55.9	+3.2%	+6.6%
– Attacking midfield	31.9	34.7	43.5	+36.6%	+25.4%
– Forward 50	10.4	12.6	12.5	+20.2%	(0.2%)
Running bounce: all	19.2	10.0	7.0	(63.7%)	(30.4%)
– Defensive 50	4.2	2.1	1.5	(64.4%)	(27.5%)
– Defensive midfield	12.1	5.9	3.7	(69.4%)	(37.0%)
– Attacking midfield	2.7	1.8	1.5	(45.0%)	(17.2%)
– Forward 50	0.2	0.3	0.3	+29.9%	(3.1%)

With this additional data at our disposal, we can now test how closely a team's chance of winning relates to it recording more of a statistic in a certain zone. We can do this in two ways. Firstly, we can compare how teams fared within their same-named zones. For instance, to find the winning percentage for teams that recorded more kicks in their defensive 50, we can compare the number of kicks that a victorious team recorded in its defensive arc to how many its opponent had in the corresponding zone at the opposite end of the field. We have done this for every match from 2007 to 2017. Like we did before, we have excluded drawn games, and treated ties in the metric counts as half a win.

Overlaying the zonal data in this way adds some interesting nuance to our earlier analysis. It reveals that winning teams only tend to top the kick count in the midfield and attacking zones. Teams that recorded more kicks than their opponents in their respective defensive 50s are marginally more likely to have lost than won, since this suggests they spent more time than their opponents in defence. We also see a similar pattern for several other metrics, including contested possessions.

Percentage of games in which the winning team won the specified metric in a certain zone					
	Defensive		Attacking		
Metric	50	Midfield	Midfield	50	All
Kick	46%	64%	71%	81%	78%
Inside 50	–	–	–	–	74%
Uncontested possession	48%	59%	68%	74%	69%
Contested possession	41%	49%	65%	73%	69%
Mark	50%	62%	66%	76%	69%
Gather	49%	53%	62%	65%	65%
Loose-ball get	45%	53%	62%	65%	63%
Contested mark from team	50%	49%	54%	65%	62%
Clearance	45%	54%	58%	61%	61%
Handball receive	46%	53%	65%	67%	61%
Running bounce	50%	58%	57%	56%	60%
Handball	43%	51%	64%	65%	59%
First possession	45%	52%	56%	60%	57%
Hard-ball get	41%	47%	58%	62%	56%
Tackle	43%	45%	62%	60%	56%
Contested mark from opposition	49%	54%	56%	51%	56%
Hit-out to advantage	48%	46%	58%	56%	54%
Smother	47%	48%	54%	53%	53%
Free for	43%	47%	56%	61%	52%
50 m penalty for	48%	51%	50%	53%	52%
Hit-out	46%	50%	54%	57%	51%
Spoil	38%	44%	58%	53%	45%
Rebound 50	–	–	–	–	39%
Turnover	35%	34%	42%	56%	27%

The other way we can gauge the importance of where statistics are recorded is to compare how teams performed in the same physical portion of the field. The difference from our previous comparison is that now when we look at how often a winning team kicks in its defensive 50, we are contrasting that number with how many kicks a losing team has in its forward 50. In other words, the comparison is being made from the perspective of one team.

We know from our earlier analysis that some statistics are more likely to occur in certain zones. Spoils, for example, are six times more likely to be recorded in a team's defensive 50 than its attacking 50. Therefore, we would not expect even the most dominant teams to win the spoil count in their forward 50. The table opposite shows the relative differences between the rates at which winning and losing teams led the counts for certain statistics in each zone.

By looking at the data in this way, we find that 79% of winning teams have more kicks than their opponent in their own defensive 50. In contrast, only 49% of losing teams record more kicks in their back 50. That is a significant difference of 30 percentage points. About the same disparity is seen in the rates that winning and losing teams finish ahead on the kick count in their attacking 50s. In the two midfield zones the differentials are less prominent, at about 20 percentage points. Unlike for kicks, however, the midfield differentials are larger than in the two other zones for statistics including marks, spoils, tackles, smothers, handballs, running bounces, contested marks, and uncontested possessions. For turnovers, too, almost 60% of which occur in the midfield, we see that losing teams head the count in both their own and their opponent's midfields significantly more often.

So, what does this say about the importance of the midfield battle? Well, the table does indicate that a team's winning rate is generally more strongly associated with recording more of a statistic in the two midfield zones than with recording more in the two 50-metre arcs. However, it also shows that victorious teams lead the statistical tallies more often in almost every metric across all four zones. In short, winning teams tend to win all over the park. Despite the numerous public declarations about how crucial the midfield is, Read believes that few clubs would place more emphasis on one part of the field than any other. 'I would say there's not really any extra focus on the

Percentage of games in which the winning team won the specified metric in a certain zone

Statistics here are for the same portion of the field (e.g. Team A's Defensive 50 is compared with Team B's Attacking 50)

	Defensive 50			Defensive Midfield			Attacking Midfield			Attacking 50			All		
	Winner	Loser	Diff	Winner	Loser	Diff	Winner	Loser	Diff	Winner	Loser	Diff	Winner	Loser	Diff
Kick	79%	49%	+30%	90%	69%	+21%	30%	9%	+20%	48%	19%	+29%	78%	21%	+57%
Inside 50	–	–	–	–	–	–	–	–	–	73%	24%	+48%	73%	24%	+48%
Uncontested possession	97%	91%	+6%	94%	81%	+13%	19%	6%	+13%	46%	26%	+20%	70%	29%	+40%
Contested possession	70%	48%	+21%	78%	59%	+19%	37%	18%	+19%	19%	5%	+13%	69%	29%	+40%
Mark	92%	78%	+15%	89%	66%	+22%	31%	10%	+21%	50%	32%	+18%	69%	30%	+40%
Gather	52%	37%	+15%	61%	44%	+17%	47%	30%	+17%	96%	90%	+6%	63%	31%	+32%
Loose-ball get	1%	0%	+0%	41%	39%	+2%	41%	35%	+6%	24%	15%	+9%	58%	32%	+26%
Contested mark from team	78%	67%	+10%	72%	58%	+14%	35%	23%	+13%	36%	28%	+8%	62%	34%	+28%
Clearance	58%	52%	+6%	77%	66%	+11%	29%	18%	+11%	13%	7%	+6%	59%	36%	+23%
Handball receive	91%	84%	+7%	90%	80%	+9%	18%	9%	+9%	8%	5%	+3%	61%	38%	+23%
Running bounce	75%	69%	+5%	86%	76%	+10%	15%	7%	+8%	10%	5%	+4%	57%	37%	+20%
Handball	93%	88%	+5%	91%	84%	+8%	15%	8%	+8%	39%	31%	+7%	59%	40%	+19%
First possession	57%	49%	+8%	76%	70%	+6%	25%	19%	+6%	51%	41%	+10%	56%	40%	+16%
Hard-ball get	48%	40%	+8%	59%	50%	+9%	42%	34%	+8%	35%	29%	+6%	55%	41%	+13%
Tackle	63%	57%	+6%	47%	37%	+10%	58%	48%	+9%	1%	1%	+1%	55%	43%	+12%
Contested mark from opposition	81%	79%	+1%	43%	34%	+10%	39%	27%	+12%	36%	29%	+8%	50%	38%	+12%
Hit-out to advantage	39%	36%	+3%	59%	53%	+6%	35%	29%	+6%	32%	30%	+1%	51%	42%	+9%
Smother	39%	39%	+1%	40%	36%	+3%	44%	40%	+3%	39%	32%	+6%	48%	41%	+6%
Free for	49%	45%	+4%	52%	48%	+4%	41%	36%	+5%	13%	9%	+3%	49%	43%	+6%
50 m penalty for	21%	21%	(1%)	24%	20%	+4%	17%	17%	(0%)	47%	42%	+5%	37%	33%	+4%
Hit-out	44%	42%	+2%	94%	93%	+1%	5%	4%	+1%	0%	0%	(0%)	51%	47%	+4%
Spoil	99%	100%	(0%)	25%	23%	+3%	72%	69%	+3%	–	–	–	43%	52%	(9%)
Rebound 50	–	–	–	–	–	–	–	–	–	–	–	–	38%	59%	–
Turnover	0%	0%	+0%	21%	43%	(22%)	51%	75%	(24%)	100%	100%	+0%	25%	71%	(46%)

midfield,' he said. 'There's an even spread between defence, stoppage, and ball movement. Stoppages and the midfield are important, but you're never going to win 100 per cent of them. It's just a fact of the game that there's some randomness. The ball can hit the ground and bounce awkwardly and suddenly it will be going the other way, so you need to be ready defensively. When you do win the stoppage, you need to be set up well in attack. It ends up being quite an even split.'

It is also worth noting that no single metric is associated with a winning percentage higher than about 80%. Clearly, no statistic alone, even with zonal overlay, is indicative of certain success. 'Look, to be honest, I don't necessarily think there are key variables,' said Rath. 'It's such an open game and there are so many ways of playing it, there's no one perfect strategy. Teams have distinct styles and signatures, and the game ebbs and flows on the back of teams doing different things.' Fremantle coach Ross Lyon agrees. 'There's never a silver bullet,' he said. 'Everyone looks for one key indicator, but it doesn't work like that.'

With that in mind, it is conceivable that winning certain metrics will be more important to some teams than others. To test this, we can recut the data we already have on a team-by-team basis, to estimate how often each side wins when it records more of a certain statistic. By comparing this rate with the team's average winning percentage, we can get a sense of which metrics are particularly good indicators of heightened or lowered success for each team. Recognising that styles – not to mention coaches – can change regularly, we have reviewed only the period 2015 to 2017.

The following table shows:

- Almost every team wins at a significantly higher rate than usual when it records more kicks, inside 50s, or contested possessions than its opponent.
- Winning the uncontested possession count is more heavily associated with success for Adelaide, Collingwood, Fremantle, Geelong, Richmond, the Sydney Swans, and the Western Bulldogs.
- Having more marks is more important to the winning percentage of Adelaide, Collingwood, Fremantle, Hawthorn, the Sydney Swans, and the Western Bulldogs.

Percentage of games won when a team led the count for a specified metric, 2015–2017

Metric	ADE	BL	CAR	COL	ESS	FRE	GEE	GC	GWS	HAW	MEL	NM	PA	RIC	STK	SYD	WC	WB
Overall win rate, 2015–2017	67.4%	18.2%	25.8%	43.2%	31.3%	44.1%	65.7%	25.0%	62.0%	64.6%	43.9%	47.1%	53.7%	58.6%	44.7%	67.6%	66.0%	62.0%
Kick	90.9%	50.0%	43.2%	65.3%	62.1%	75.0%	92.2%	65.0%	78.7%	82.2%	75.0%	78.8%	82.9%	78.0%	71.0%	94.7%	93.4%	91.7%
Inside 50	86.4%	44.4%	50.0%	61.4%	61.1%	69.0%	79.5%	62.5%	87.5%	77.0%	61.3%	63.3%	70.0%	77.8%	78.8%	83.3%	91.3%	70.6%
Uncontested possession	88.9%	28.0%	38.5%	65.2%	47.5%	74.1%	82.6%	55.0%	72.7%	74.4%	58.5%	63.3%	60.6%	74.3%	60.0%	82.9%	82.3%	84.6%
Contested possession	76.7%	46.2%	40.6%	61.3%	55.0%	72.4%	83.8%	52.6%	79.8%	78.6%	64.9%	56.5%	77.4%	73.8%	68.0%	83.7%	90.8%	72.0%
Mark	88.6%	31.0%	39.4%	65.0%	44.7%	69.2%	81.7%	44.2%	67.6%	83.3%	63.6%	60.6%	66.7%	65.8%	62.5%	85.7%	84.2%	95.7%
Gather	78.6%	31.8%	41.7%	54.5%	43.8%	71.4%	77.3%	46.7%	83.7%	73.0%	54.5%	63.9%	70.0%	63.3%	61.7%	87.8%	76.4%	88.9%
Loose-ball get	75.0%	25.8%	32.4%	58.3%	43.3%	58.1%	84.7%	36.4%	77.4%	75.0%	53.1%	57.1%	75.0%	75.8%	55.2%	80.6%	81.3%	73.3%
Contested mark from team	88.2%	35.7%	29.6%	48.7%	33.3%	64.5%	69.4%	29.0%	75.0%	81.0%	43.8%	56.3%	74.3%	67.7%	56.5%	85.4%	84.3%	83.3%
Clearance	75.0%	29.2%	27.6%	57.8%	43.5%	55.3%	77.3%	39.3%	78.8%	68.8%	62.5%	60.6%	67.7%	64.5%	56.5%	77.5%	85.5%	75.6%
Handball receive	77.4%	36.8%	35.0%	50.0%	40.5%	69.7%	69.3%	52.2%	67.4%	71.4%	54.5%	50.0%	56.7%	70.0%	44.0%	71.7%	81.0%	69.4%
Running bounce	69.7%	33.3%	24.1%	53.0%	68.8%	66.7%	69.4%	35.4%	68.5%	68.3%	48.0%	67.7%	57.5%	67.5%	56.8%	73.3%	88.0%	73.9%
Handball	79.3%	33.3%	33.3%	51.6%	40.5%	61.8%	71.3%	45.0%	65.5%	70.3%	55.6%	48.6%	56.7%	69.0%	42.9%	67.4%	80.4%	68.0%
First possession	74.2%	29.2%	19.2%	60.3%	35.7%	55.0%	80.9%	39.3%	75.6%	63.8%	56.8%	62.2%	63.6%	65.5%	56.0%	77.3%	80.9%	73.0%
Hard-ball get	72.2%	30.8%	28.1%	48.7%	45.5%	50.0%	81.4%	38.7%	67.6%	87.5%	48.6%	44.8%	59.0%	64.4%	39.1%	72.0%	79.7%	63.2%
Tackle	75.0%	17.2%	35.7%	44.0%	32.4%	40.0%	70.5%	35.0%	68.1%	65.0%	69.6%	64.7%	54.8%	73.9%	52.3%	66.7%	60.0%	65.5%
Contested mark from opposition	67.9%	20.8%	36.4%	43.8%	46.9%	54.2%	63.5%	25.9%	61.5%	72.2%	37.0%	48.5%	60.0%	56.3%	64.0%	78.9%	67.0%	79.2%
Hit-out to advantage	71.4%	22.2%	26.7%	44.4%	25.9%	61.9%	67.9%	37.5%	67.6%	66.1%	45.9%	53.3%	58.6%	58.6%	58.7%	73.0%	77.0%	63.6%
Smother	79.6%	16.0%	26.1%	46.9%	33.3%	37.9%	69.7%	30.9%	61.4%	69.7%	51.5%	50.0%	53.6%	65.0%	44.6%	66.7%	65.5%	61.0%
Free for	69.7%	21.4%	37.1%	44.9%	33.3%	59.1%	73.2%	26.6%	68.5%	75.0%	51.6%	54.5%	53.8%	55.9%	62.1%	66.7%	75.6%	67.4%
50 m penalty for	79.3%	13.6%	40.0%	44.4%	23.1%	52.0%	71.2%	32.5%	55.0%	64.6%	63.6%	48.0%	45.5%	56.3%	57.1%	80.0%	72.7%	71.0%
Hit-out	68.6%	13.3%	22.6%	43.1%	21.4%	58.7%	58.7%	30.4%	71.4%	64.3%	50.0%	50.0%	58.8%	56.3%	55.4%	70.6%	72.6%	64.7%
Spoil	67.7%	12.2%	30.6%	48.3%	27.0%	29.2%	63.6%	20.7%	55.4%	65.0%	46.7%	52.0%	48.9%	45.2%	26.2%	66.7%	66.7%	61.0%
Rebound 50	54.7%	19.6%	21.1%	25.9%	30.2%	34.4%	50.0%	17.7%	39.4%	60.0%	45.7%	45.0%	44.8%	53.8%	15.9%	60.0%	48.5%	52.9%
Turnover	37.1%	11.6%	24.2%	18.2%	35.7%	30.6%	35.7%	13.0%	36.2%	32.1%	35.1%	32.4%	40.0%	23.3%	17.3%	46.4%	36.0%	42.9%

- Having more loose-ball gets generally contributes to more wins for Geelong, Greater Western Sydney, Port Adelaide, and Richmond.
- The hard-ball get count is an especially good indicator for Geelong and Hawthorn.
- Winning the running bounce count has a noticeable effect on the win rates of Essendon, North Melbourne, and West Coast.
- Winning the tackle count is closely related to Melbourne and Richmond winning games.
- Committing fewer turnovers leads to better win rates for every team, but least of all for Adelaide, Geelong, Greater Western Sydney, Hawthorn, Port Adelaide, West Coast, and the Western Bulldogs.

As with any analysis, we need to be careful not to draw overly bold conclusions from this table, since some of the variability will solely be due to chance. Most of the teams only played about 70 games during our three-year sample period, and some might have won certain statistical counts only a handful of times. That means some of the percentage estimates in the table will have large sampling errors associated with them. To give us some idea of this, the table opposite shows what proportion of games each team won the head-to-head count for each statistic. We need to be particularly cautious about the conditional winning rates shown in the preceding table for those metrics that a team won infrequently.

We see opposite, for example, that Adelaide recorded more kicks, marks, gathers, clearances, inside 50s, and contested possessions than its opponent in about 60% of its games, regardless of whether it won or lost. We also find that Hawthorn ranked second-last for recording more contested possessions than its opponent, and last for winning the hard-ball get count. At the same time, it ranked first for winning the counts for inside 50s, marks, gathers, and spoils, and second for having more kicks. It has clearly been a unique brand of football that the Hawks have played in recent seasons. 'There are always elements of playing a threat versus playing possession and you've got to have both,' said Rath. 'I think if you look back at that

Percentage of games that each team won the head-to-head count for a specified metric, 2015–2017

Metric	ADE	BL	CAR	COL	ESS	FRE	GEE	GC	GWS	HAW	MEL	NM	PA	RIC	STK	SYD	WC	WB
Kick	61.1%	24.2%	56.1%	54.5%	43.3%	41.2%	45.7%	30.3%	66.2%	62.5%	42.4%	47.1%	52.2%	58.6%	47.0%	51.4%	52.8%	50.7%
Inside 50	61.1%	13.6%	30.3%	53.0%	26.9%	42.6%	62.9%	24.2%	56.3%	69.4%	47.0%	42.9%	59.7%	51.4%	50.0%	56.8%	55.6%	71.8%
Uncontested possession	50.0%	37.9%	39.4%	50.0%	59.7%	39.7%	61.4%	30.3%	62.0%	59.7%	62.1%	42.9%	49.3%	50.0%	45.5%	55.4%	43.1%	54.9%
Contested possession	59.7%	19.7%	48.5%	60.6%	29.9%	42.6%	57.1%	28.8%	59.2%	29.2%	56.1%	65.7%	46.3%	60.0%	37.9%	58.1%	52.8%	70.4%
Mark	61.1%	43.9%	50.0%	45.5%	56.7%	38.2%	58.6%	39.4%	52.1%	66.7%	50.0%	47.1%	49.3%	54.3%	48.5%	47.3%	52.8%	32.4%
Gather	58.3%	33.3%	36.4%	50.0%	47.8%	51.5%	47.1%	22.7%	60.6%	69.4%	50.0%	51.4%	44.8%	42.9%	45.5%	55.4%	50.0%	38.0%
Loose-ball get	55.6%	47.0%	51.5%	63.6%	44.8%	45.6%	51.4%	33.3%	59.2%	52.8%	48.5%	40.0%	35.8%	47.1%	43.9%	48.6%	33.3%	63.4%
Contested mark from team	47.2%	21.2%	40.9%	57.6%	31.3%	45.6%	70.0%	47.0%	39.4%	40.3%	48.5%	45.7%	52.2%	44.3%	34.8%	55.4%	48.6%	33.8%
Clearance	61.1%	36.4%	43.9%	48.5%	34.3%	55.9%	47.1%	42.4%	56.3%	44.4%	48.5%	47.1%	46.3%	44.3%	47.0%	54.1%	43.1%	57.7%
Handball receive	43.1%	28.8%	30.3%	53.0%	62.7%	48.5%	62.9%	34.8%	64.8%	48.6%	66.7%	45.7%	44.8%	42.9%	37.9%	62.2%	40.3%	69.0%
Running bounce	45.8%	18.2%	43.9%	50.0%	23.9%	26.5%	44.3%	62.1%	76.1%	56.9%	37.9%	44.3%	59.7%	57.1%	56.1%	20.3%	34.7%	64.8%
Handball	40.3%	36.4%	31.8%	48.5%	62.7%	50.0%	67.1%	30.3%	59.2%	44.4%	68.2%	50.0%	44.8%	41.4%	42.4%	62.2%	38.9%	70.4%
First possession	43.1%	36.4%	39.4%	51.5%	41.8%	58.8%	48.6%	42.4%	57.7%	40.3%	56.1%	52.9%	49.3%	41.4%	37.9%	59.5%	47.2%	52.1%
Hard-ball get	50.0%	19.7%	48.5%	57.6%	32.8%	35.3%	50.0%	47.0%	47.9%	16.7%	53.0%	41.4%	58.2%	64.3%	48.5%	67.6%	51.4%	80.3%
Tackle	50.0%	43.9%	42.4%	63.6%	55.2%	29.4%	55.7%	45.5%	66.2%	55.6%	34.8%	48.6%	62.7%	32.9%	66.7%	56.8%	27.8%	40.8%
Contested mark from opposition	38.9%	36.4%	33.3%	36.4%	47.8%	35.3%	52.9%	40.9%	54.9%	37.5%	40.9%	47.1%	52.2%	45.7%	37.9%	51.4%	65.3%	33.8%
Hit-out to advantage	48.6%	40.9%	45.5%	40.9%	40.3%	61.8%	40.0%	36.4%	71.8%	43.1%	56.1%	64.3%	43.3%	41.4%	34.8%	50.0%	51.4%	31.0%
Smother	37.5%	37.9%	34.8%	48.5%	26.9%	42.6%	54.3%	51.5%	49.3%	45.8%	50.0%	34.3%	41.8%	57.1%	42.4%	48.6%	40.3%	57.7%
Free for	45.8%	42.4%	53.0%	59.1%	44.8%	32.4%	40.0%	48.5%	38.0%	50.0%	47.0%	62.9%	38.8%	48.6%	43.9%	24.3%	56.9%	60.6%
50 m penalty for	40.3%	33.3%	37.9%	27.3%	38.8%	36.8%	37.1%	30.3%	28.2%	33.3%	16.7%	35.7%	32.8%	45.7%	31.8%	33.8%	45.8%	43.7%
Hit-out	48.6%	45.5%	47.0%	54.5%	41.8%	67.6%	32.9%	34.8%	59.2%	48.6%	57.6%	68.6%	50.7%	45.7%	42.4%	45.9%	58.3%	23.9%
Spoil	43.1%	62.1%	54.5%	45.5%	55.2%	35.3%	31.4%	62.1%	52.1%	69.4%	45.5%	35.7%	70.1%	44.3%	31.8%	36.5%	33.3%	57.7%
Rebound 50	44.4%	69.7%	57.6%	40.9%	64.2%	47.1%	40.0%	72.7%	46.5%	27.8%	53.0%	57.1%	43.3%	55.7%	33.3%	47.3%	45.8%	23.9%
Turnover	43.1%	65.2%	65.2%	50.0%	49.3%	72.1%	30.0%	75.8%	40.8%	38.9%	56.1%	52.9%	44.8%	42.9%	39.4%	37.8%	34.7%	39.4%

period, people talked about us being a kicking and possession team, but that wasn't all we did. We were also very good when we wanted to kick the ball long and create threat from that. You need to have a balance, otherwise you can get over-defended in one way.'

Consistency

'We need to get a much better consistency.' – Hawthorn coach Alastair Clarkson, 6 April 2017.

'The players who have been playing haven't been up to the level of consistency that we want.' – Sydney Swans coach John Longmire, 18 April 2017.

'I think the frustrating thing for our players and our coaches is that we can deliver good football, but then on occasions we don't. Our consistency is something we're looking at.' – West Coast coach Adam Simpson, 26 April 2017.

'Our aim is to build consistency in our week-to-week efforts.' – Essendon coach John Worsfold, 2 May 2017.

'We want to be more predictable in the way we play. For varying reasons, we haven't been able to get that consistency.' – Collingwood coach Nathan Buckley, 3 May 2017.

We could continue ad infinitum, but by now you probably get the picture. Coaches crave consistency. 'Footy is an effort game, so the coaches are always looking for consistency of effort,' said Read. 'If your team doesn't give its greatest effort possible, and your opponent does, you're going to get in trouble. It isn't a throwaway line. It's an important part of the game, because that's what footy is based on. It's a running, physical game, so if you don't give that effort, you can be quickly found out.'

It is possible to measure a team's game-to-game consistency by using statistics. We can do this by assessing the variability of its performance around some average. A consistent team will show little fluctuation or variability around its normal level from one match to the next, while an inconsistent team will fluctuate more widely around its normal level. To test the relationship between consistency and success, we have analysed the contested possession differentials for each team in every season from 2007 to 2017. Each of the dots in the following chart shows a team's season-long winning rate in relation to the variability of its contested possession differentials across all games that year.

To get an idea of how we have calculated the level of variability, consider a team that has recorded contested possession differentials of +6, +5, +5, +7, and +4 across a five-game sample. If it goes on to record similar differentials across an entire season, it will have shown a low level of variability for that metric. In this limited sense it might be considered a 'consistent' team, because it typically recorded similar contested possession numbers each week. A team that recorded differentials such as -6, -5, -5, -7, and -4 across a season would be considered equally consistent. Consistency relates to the variability of a team's performance, not its quality. In comparison, a team that returned a fluctuating sequence of contested possession differentials such as -7, +12, -4, -3, +10 would record a high level of variability. Such a team would be considered 'inconsistent' based on this measure.

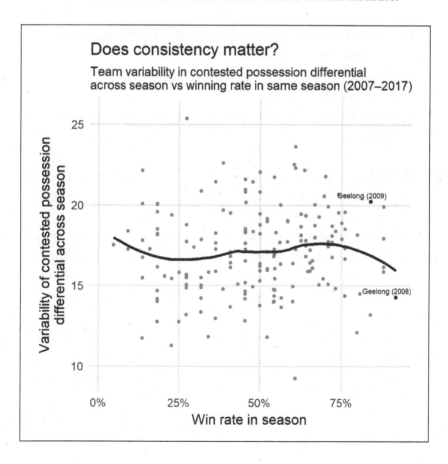

125

Our chart (previous page) reveals that there was basically no relationship between the consistency in a team's week-to-week contested possession differential across a season, and the rate at which it won games. Geelong's 2008 and 2009 teams, which are labelled, provide a useful example. Although both recorded roughly the same win rates (92% and 84% respectively), the 2008 side:

- lost the contested possession count three times, and only once by as much as 16
- drew or won the contested possession count by nine or fewer in eight games
- won the contested possession count by 20 or more in six games.

And the 2009 team:

- lost the contested possession count seven times, including four times by 15 or more
- drew or won the contested possession count by nine or fewer in only five games
- won the contested possession count by 27 or more in seven games.

Geelong's 2009 team was less consistent than its 2008 side in terms of winning the contested possession count, but both still managed to win about 85% to 90% of their games.

If consistent teams tended to win more regularly, we would expect the dots on our chart to follow a line starting at the top left, signifying high variability and low win rates, and falling to the bottom right, signifying low variability and high win rates. Clearly, they don't. We can quantify the extent to which they don't by calculating the correlation coefficient between variability in contested possessions and win rate. The closer this correlation is to -1, the more it supports the claim that the two measures are highly (negatively) associated.

Correlation between variability in team metric differential and season-long winning percentage, 2007–2017	
Metric	Correlation
Running bounce	−0.18
50 m penalty for	−0.15
Free for	−0.07
Handball receive	−0.06
Handball	−0.03
Uncontested possession	−0.03
Clearance	−0.01
First possession	0.00
Mark	0.00
Points	0.02
Smother	0.03
Spoil	0.04
Hit-out to advantage	0.04
Hit-out	0.05
Gather	0.05
Inside 50	0.08
Contested possession	**0.09**
Contested mark from team	0.10
Rebound 50	0.11
Loose-ball get	0.11
Hard-ball get	0.11
Tackle	0.12
Contested mark from opposition	0.13
Kick	0.15
Turnover	0.17

The correlation is +0.09, meaning there is essentially no relationship at all. A successful team's week-to-week contested possession differential is just as likely to be highly variable as it is constant. We performed the same analysis for other game stats and found this to be true of all of them. The largest correlation coefficient (in absolute terms) for any metric is just -0.18, which was for running bounces.

It is fair to assume, however, that when coaches call for greater consistency, they are really after consistently high performance. No coach would aspire to consistent mediocrity. But what if their team's average performance just isn't as good as their opponent's? Should they still be striving for consistency then, assuming they can't lift their side's performance? If they have the weaker team, a consistent performance by both their side and their opponent will almost guarantee that they lose. As the weaker team, wouldn't it make sense to trade off consistency for a higher chance of outscoring their opponent?

Consider a highly simplified example. Imagine you are the coach of a team that is preparing to face a stronger opponent. Not only is the other side better, but it is also incredibly consistent. In fact, you can guarantee that it will score 100 points no matter what you do. Your team, meanwhile, is less consistent. Each week, depending on how well it executes your game plan, it will record one of three scores with some probability. Using your standard plan, your team will have a 50% chance of scoring 82 points, a 25% chance of scoring 95 points, and a 25% chance of scoring 106 points. If we played the contest many times over, you could expect your team to score, on average, about 91 points for a loss of about 14 points. It will only have a one-in-four chance of winning (i.e. when it scores 106 points).

A bright young assistant coach has presented you with an alternative game plan, but it has a few drawbacks. It makes your team more likely to score 82 points, lowers your average score, and increases the size of your average loss. But it will also increase your team's probability of scoring 106 points to 30%, thereby lifting your chance of victory to this same higher figure. What the alternative game plan does, then, is trade a greater chance of victory for higher levels of variability in performance. It does not, however, increase the team's average performance. The 'MAD' figure in the table opposite reflects the 'mean absolute deviation', which is the average amount by which your team will deviate from its long-term average performance. In other words, it shows how inconsistent your team will be under each game plan. It shows that the second game plan leads to about 10% more variability than the first.

| | Team A
Always scores 100 | |
| | Team B | |
Possible scores	Probability under first game plan	Probability under second game plan
Score 82	50%	60%
Score 95	25%	10%
Score 106	25%	30%
Outcomes		
Average score	91.3	90.5
Average loss	13.7	16.1
MAD	9.3	10.2
Win	25%	30%

Under the alternative game plan, your team will underperform relative to its average score 60% of the time, compared to 50% under your original game plan. At the same time, however, your side will increase its chances of winning from 25% to 30%.

In the real world, of course, it is never this simple. For one thing, your opponent would be able to respond to the alternative game plan. But the principle still applies: variability, rather than consistency, could conceivably increase an underdog's chances of victory. At some level, coaches do understand this. It is why they employ riskier strategies when they trail late in games. Still, we probably shouldn't expect them to start using their pre-game media conferences to call for greater inconsistency any time soon.

Chapter Seven

Home and Away

Different roads

Round 19 of the 2016 AFL season was a bumper weekend for milestones. Corey Enright set a new games record for Geelong, playing his 326th match. At the same time, his Cats teammate Jimmy Bartel became the fourth player from the club to reach 300 games. The celebrations at Kardinia Park were overshadowed, though, by the fanfare surrounding North Melbourne veteran Brent Harvey at Docklands. The 38-year-old was breaking Michael Tuck's mark for the most matches in the AFL/VFL. Harvey's new record, 427, was boldly printed on the front of the Kangaroos' jumpers. His playing number, 29, was painted on the 50-metre arcs. His name and image were everywhere. 'He had done more interviews in a week than most players do in a lifetime, appeared on almost every footy show and received enough text messages to keep Telstra shareholders happy,' wrote Glenn McFarlane in the *Herald Sun*. 'Incredibly, he was still responding to messages on his way into the ground late Saturday.' One of those messages went to the other side of the country, where a fourth big milestone was about to take place. Fremantle captain Matthew Pavlich was preparing to play his 350th match. 'I texted Pav and said "Mate, what an extraordinary effort. That's bigger than my 423 games",' said Harvey. 'Nearly every second week you have to do what we do once or twice a year.' What he was referring to was travelling back and forth across the Nullarbor.

Not only was Pavlich the first Western Australian–based AFL player to reach 350 games, but he was still the only one to have played 300. West Coast's Dean Cox had retired on 290 games, 14 more than his

131

former teammate Glen Jakovich. 'I was aware of the great West Coast players who had fallen short of it,' said Pavlich in his autobiography, *Purple Heart*. 'It took most of the week for me to finally acknowledge the achievement and reflect upon the challenging times, mental torment, physical pain, constant application, and over 1,000 hours spent airborne travelling to and from games.' Pavlich and Harvey had played for a combined 38 seasons, but their experiences within the same competition had been vastly different. Harvey doubted he would have broken the league's games record if he had been drafted by the Dockers or Eagles. 'No, I don't think so,' he conceded. 'They fly to Melbourne about eight times a year and to other interstate venues probably three times a season. Matthew would have gotten used to it, no doubt, but his preparation must have been flawless.'

Pavlich was highly durable for a key position player. Since his debut in 2000, he had missed just 31 games on the way to his 350th, but the constant travel was catching up with him by his 17th season. 'The best way to describe the hindrance of travel is that it's the accumulative effect of a season, and the accumulative effect of a career,' he said. When Pavlich was younger, flying to games had been a novelty and the trips away were fun. The average flight time from Perth to Melbourne was about four hours. Unlike a lot of his teammates, who preferred to kill the time by watching TV shows or movies, Pavlich used it to complete two university degrees. Study was made more difficult on the flight home, as he was often strapped to an ice machine to aid his recovery from the match. His discomfort was at its worst in 2012, when he needed back surgery to relieve nerve pain and damage. 'I was able to play through it, but I had some significant problems with my back and hips towards the end of my career, which really started to curtail my performance,' he said. 'It's likely that I still would have had some level of back injury even if I was based interstate, but would it have made it easier if I wasn't travelling so much? The answer would probably be yes.'

A similar back injury had caused West Coast defender Guy McKenna to retire at the age of 31, having played 267 games. McKenna believed the fortnightly flights were the main reason his career had been cut short. 'If you were to give someone, say, 10 years playing for a Victorian club as opposed to a decade with a West Australian side and the impact on the player's body, I'm convinced their career could be longer,' he said. 'The impact of the travel, getting on a plane every second week and the effects of trying to recover from the travelling on players' bodies was an enormous burden.' The disparity between the burden of travel shouldered by Western Australian–based players and their Victorian counterparts is laid bare in a comparison of the round-19 milestone men. As it turned out, all four of them retired at the end of 2016. Harvey had taken the league's games record to 432 and Enright had set Geelong's at 332. Bartel ended on 305 matches, while Pavlich called time at 353. Remarkably, Pavlich had covered more kilometres during his career than the other three combined.

How big is the travel burden on teams?

We can figure out how far each team has had to travel for every game in AFL/VFL history by getting the latitude and longitude of each city or town that has hosted a match, from Shanghai to Yallourn. We can calculate the distance from the team's home city to the place that hosted the game, using a standard formula for geographical distance from point to point. When Harvey's North Melbourne team played in Melbourne, for example, it had a travel distance of zero. When Enright and Bartel's Geelong side played in Melbourne, it had a travel distance of 65 kilometres. When Pavlich's Fremantle team flew from Perth to Melbourne, it had a travel distance of 2,725 kilometres. We then need to double those figures to account for the return trip.

All clubs have had to deal with interstate travel to varying degrees since South Melbourne relocated to Sydney in 1982. These days, 10 of the AFL's 18 clubs are based in Victoria, with the remainder scattered around the continent. It is not surprising, then, that the travel burden is distributed unequally. The Western Australian sides cover the most kilometres, followed by the teams from Queensland. The Sydney- and Adelaide-based teams are next, while the Victorian clubs travel the least. However, there is quite a lot of variation among the Victorians. The distance covered by clubs such as Hawthorn, North Melbourne, Melbourne, and the Western Bulldogs is boosted by the fact they regularly play home games interstate. Collingwood is the competition's homebody, accumulating the fewest frequent flyer points over the past few years. Since the league expanded to its current 18-team format in

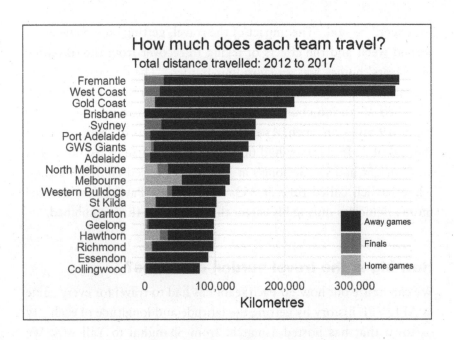

How much does each team travel?
Total distance travelled: 2012 to 2017

2012, the Magpies have travelled a leisurely 78,000 kilometres, which is less than a quarter of the Perth-based teams. Both the Eagles and Dockers flew more than 350,000 kilometres to and from their games in the period between 2012 and 2017.

Which players have had the biggest travel burdens?

The Western Australian teams fly across the Nullarbor and back nearly every second week during the regular season, which has resulted in some of their players posting truly impressive career travel totals. Pavlich holds the competition record at 855,128 kilometres, which is more than enough to make it to the moon and back. His total is more than 100,000 kilometres clear of that posted by the second most travelled player in AFL/VFL history, the Eagles' Glen Jakovich. Fremantle's David Mundy and Aaron Sandilands are both in the top 20 most travelled players, but it seems unlikely that either of them will challenge Pavlich for top spot.

Predictably, the list of well-travelled AFL footballers is a rollcall of West Coast and Fremantle players who have played a lot of games. Still, the extent of their travel burden compared to Victorian-based players is striking. For example, let's put Pavlich alongside Brad Johnson.

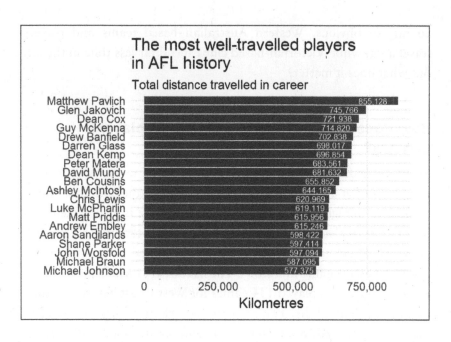

The most well-travelled players in AFL history

Total distance travelled in career

Player	Kilometres
Matthew Pavlich	855,128
Glen Jakovich	745,766
Dean Cox	721,938
Guy McKenna	714,820
Drew Banfield	702,838
Darren Glass	698,017
Dean Kemp	696,854
Peter Matera	683,561
David Mundy	681,632
Ben Cousins	655,852
Ashley McIntosh	644,165
Chris Lewis	620,969
Luke McPharlin	619,119
Matt Priddis	615,956
Andrew Embley	615,246
Aaron Sandilands	598,422
Shane Parker	597,414
John Worsfold	597,094
Michael Braun	587,095
Michael Johnson	577,375

Johnson travelled 263,495 kilometres during his 364-game career for the Western Bulldogs. Pavlich played nine fewer games, but covered almost 600,000 kilometres more. Or, how about this: West Coast's Jamie Cripps travelled further in his first 108 matches than Essendon's Dustin Fletcher did in his 400-match, 23-year career.

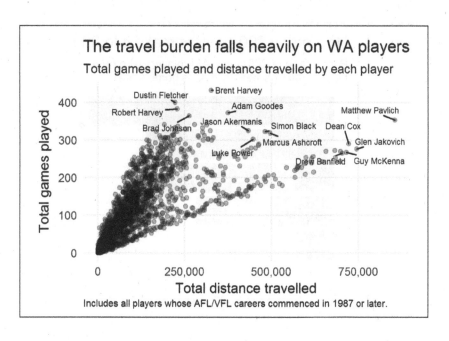

The travel burden falls heavily on WA players

Total games played and distance travelled by each player

Includes all players whose AFL/VFL careers commenced in 1987 or later.

So far, so obvious. Western Australian–based teams and players travel a lot, while Victorian-based clubs spend far less time in the air. But what does it matter?

How does travel affect the length of players' careers?

Most of the discussion about the effect of travel in the AFL focuses on its impact at a team level, and we will explore the notion of home-ground advantage later in this chapter. But there is also evidence of its influence on the individual, particularly in determining a player's longevity. There are 26 Western Australian–based players who have reached the 200-game milestone. The list doesn't include players such as Chris Judd, who played 134 games for West Coast before spending the second half of his career with the relatively lightly travelled Carlton. Of the 26, only Pavlich has gone on to notch 300 games. That represents a rate of just 3.8%. One in 26 is by far the lowest proportion of any state in the period since 1987, which is the year the Eagles and Brisbane Bears entered the competition.

In the post-1987 era, there have been 220 Victorian-based players who have reached 200 games, excluding the multi-state players

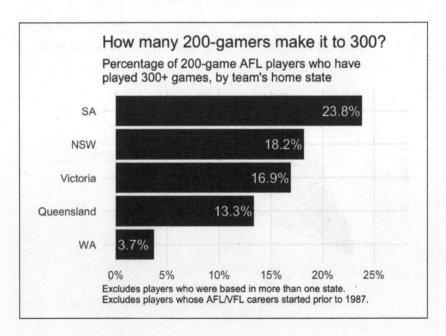

How many 200-gamers make it to 300?

Percentage of 200-game AFL players who have played 300+ games, by team's home state

SA	23.8%
NSW	18.2%
Victoria	16.9%
Queensland	13.3%
WA	3.7%

Excludes players who were based in more than one state.
Excludes players whose AFL/VFL careers started prior to 1987.

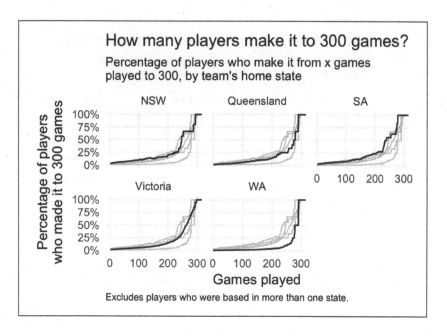

How many players make it to 300 games?

Percentage of players who make it from x games played to 300, by team's home state

Excludes players who were based in more than one state.

like Chris Judd. Of those 220, 38 have gone on to 300 games, at a healthy rate of 17%. A slightly lower percentage of 200-gamers from New South Wales (18.2%) and Queensland (13.3%) have made it to the 300-game mark than in Victoria, but still well above Western Australia's lowly figure. South Australia is something of a surprise, with five of the 21 players who made 200 appearances for the Crows or Power going on to reach 300 games (23.8%).

Of course, there is nothing especially significant about the 200-game mark beyond it being a nice round number. Perhaps the differing rates at which 200-gamers become 300-gamers could just be a weird quirk? To find out, we can test whether players from Western Australia are less likely to make it to 300 from other points in their career. Maybe 150-gamers from West Coast and Fremantle are just as likely to make it to 300 as their Victorian counterparts?

The answer is no, they are not. A smaller proportion of Western Australian–based players has made it to 300 games from any given number of games. Fewer 100-gamers, fewer 150-gamers, and fewer 250-gamers from Western Australia have ended up reaching the 300-match milestone than players from other states. Western Australia doesn't have fewer players who make it to the 150- or 200-game marks. About the same percentage of players hit those

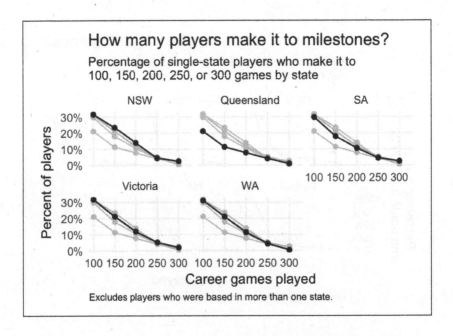

How many players make it to milestones?

Percentage of single-state players who make it to 100, 150, 200, 250, or 300 games by state

Excludes players who were based in more than one state.

milestones in the West as they do in South Australia and Victoria. But something seems to happen to players from the Eagles and Dockers once they have reached 200 matches. They retire between 200 and 250 games at a higher rate than players from anywhere else.

Why is this the case? McKenna's assertion that constant travel shortens their careers is plausible, but we can't be sure about it. To test whether Western Australian–based players fade faster after hitting 200 games, we will need to compare their output with footballers from other states. As a taster, let's begin by setting Pavlich side by side with Harvey. Pavlich reached his career peak, at least in terms of counting stats, shortly after his 200th game in 2009. He was averaging slightly more than 20 disposals per match at the time. His disposal output fell sharply over the next five years, and by his 300th match he was back to his career average of about 17 per game. In his final season, Pavlich was typically accruing only about 14 disposals per match, or about 75% of his career average. The story is similar if we look at AFL Fantasy points, which might be a more representative metric, because changes in disposal counts could be skewed by Pavlich's move from the midfield to the forward line in the latter stages of his career. In terms of both Fantasy points and disposals, Pavlich's decline from his peak at around the 200-game mark was reasonably steep.

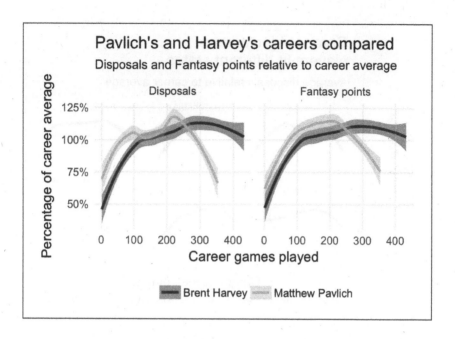

Pavlich's and Harvey's careers compared

Disposals and Fantasy points relative to career average

Harvey's career arc looks quite different. His output followed a broadly similar trajectory to Pavlich's up until about the 200-game mark. But Harvey peaked a little later, somewhere between his 250th and 300th games. At the end of his record-breaking career, he was still putting up disposal and Fantasy numbers that were higher than his career average. His decline was barely noticeable on the stats sheet.

In comparing Pavlich and Harvey, clearly the Western Australian–based player faded faster. This difference could be partly due to travel. 'No doubt it has an effect,' said Pavlich. 'As I mentioned, it's an accumulation. It's not necessarily just that you're travelling, it's that 850,000 kilometres is a lot.' But how much can we really learn by weighing up just two players? There are a lot of differences between them other than the number of kilometres they travelled, some of which could also have contributed to the relative steepness of Pavlich's decline. To get a more comprehensive picture, we can look at the career trajectories of all single-state players in the post-1987 era.

For every player, we will calculate how his disposal count in each game compared to his career average. For example, if a player had 30 disposals in a game and his career average was 20, we will give him a score of 150% for that match. We will exclude all players who started their careers before 1987, as well as those who spent time at clubs in

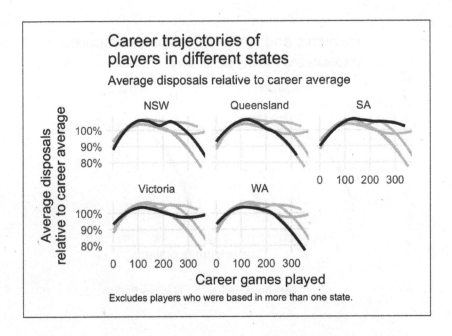

Career trajectories of players in different states

Average disposals relative to career average

more than one state. Finally, we will work out the overall disposal averages for each state's players at different stages of their careers.

The results are striking. Players' career trajectories are broadly similar across borderlines until they approach the 200-game mark. Western Australian and Victorian players, for example, follow a virtually identical arc up until that point. But beyond that, the average disposal counts for Western Australian– and Queensland-based players fall off a cliff, while those of their South Australian and Victorian counterparts barely decay at all. Players from New South Wales decline a little later and from a higher level than the Western Australians and Queenslanders. The picture looks much the same if we restrict the comparison only to those who played at least 200 games. The average output of Western Australian and Queensland players declines earlier and more rapidly than that of their counterparts from the other states, particularly Victoria and South Australia. 'I'm not surprised by it,' said Pavlich. 'Even with the advent of sports science and better recovery methodologies, and there being a much better emphasis on prolonging careers, the fact is that having to travel so much is still a burden on performance.'

It is possible that the tendency for Western Australian players to have shorter careers, and for their performance to decay more quickly, is just a quirk or statistical anomaly that will eventually work itself out. But with more than 30 seasons of interstate competition now in the AFL/VFL history books, it seems more likely that the late-career woe of Western Australian players is real, and that travel is the probable culprit. In 2017, his first year of retirement, Pavlich played a key role as president of the AFL Players' Association in negotiating a new six-year collective bargaining agreement with the league. Among the improved conditions he helped win for the players was a promise from the AFL to provide West Coast and Fremantle with a minimum of 12 business class seats on all flights to and from Perth. 'We wanted it recognised that the teams from the West have to travel so much more, and that it is a burden on performance,' said Pavlich. 'It's a competitive balance issue as much as anything else and we were steadfast in our negotiations to win that concession. Albeit, my career is over now and it's the next generation that will enjoy the fruits of our labour.'

Home-ground advantage in the AFL

There is a reason that teams fight so hard for the right to host a home final. Home-ground advantage matters. The home team in the AFL has a 58.3% winning percentage in regular-season matches, which puts the league's home-ground advantage around the middle of the

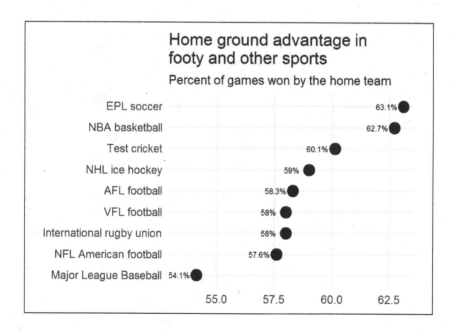

Home ground advantage in footy and other sports

Percent of games won by the home team

EPL soccer	63.1%
NBA basketball	62.7%
Test cricket	60.1%
NHL ice hockey	59%
AFL football	58.3%
VFL football	58%
International rugby union	58%
NFL American football	57.6%
Major League Baseball	54.1%

pack among major sports. It is not as pronounced as in American basketball's NBA or English soccer's Premier League, but more of a factor than in American football or baseball.

It is interesting that home teams win about as often in the AFL as they did in the VFL. After all, VFL teams had genuine home grounds with idiosyncratic shapes and facilities. Collingwood's Victoria Park was a scene of misery for many visiting teams. St Kilda, for example, won there just once in 58 attempts prior to 1962, and finished with a winning percentage of 8.3% (seven from 84) against the Magpies at the venue. The Saints' home record against the same opponent was markedly better, winning 36.2% (21 from 58) when Collingwood visited the Junction Oval through to 1964.

In the modern AFL, all the Melbourne-based teams share just two grounds: the antiseptic Docklands and hallowed MCG. A major reason for home-ground advantage remaining high during the AFL era has been the introduction of non-Victorian clubs. Teams flying to hostile territory are at a significant disadvantage. When both teams are playing in their home state (such as North Melbourne playing St Kilda at Docklands) the home team wins 54% of the time in the AFL. If the home team is playing in their home state, but their opponent has travelled from interstate (such as North hosting

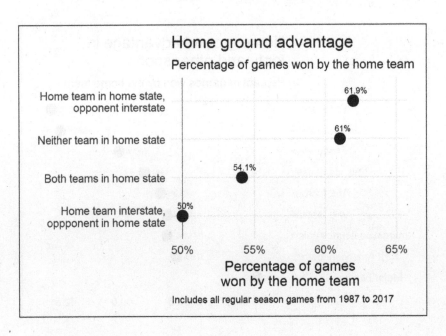

Home ground advantage

Percentage of games won by the home team

Home team in home state, opponent interstate — 61.9%

Neither team in home state — 61%

Both teams in home state — 54.1%

Home team interstate, oppponent in home state — 50%

Percentage of games won by the home team: 50%   55%   60%   65%

Percentage of games won by the home team

Includes all regular season games from 1987 to 2017

Brisbane at Docklands) then the home team wins 62% of the time. If neither team is in their home state (such as North facing Fremantle in Hobart) the home team wins 61% of the time.

The burden of travel is often cited as one of the reasons that teams playing interstate are less likely to win. Players from the home team can wake up in their own beds and drive to work, while the visitors must deal with the arduous slog of life on the road. 'It's multifaceted, it's not just one element,' said Pavlich. 'It is the physical element of flying, it is the mental drain waiting around a long time in airports and on planes, and it is certainly the time zone factor.' Pavlich's first coach at the Dockers, Damian Drum, agreed with the last point especially. 'The time in the plane is no great drama, but changing time zones is a problem,' he said. 'It can be worrying. I constantly had players struggling to get to sleep. Some of them used sleeping pills. Continually throwing your body back and forward can have a draining effect.' A traditional Saturday afternoon fixture in Melbourne can be an exhausting experience for a player from the West. 'For a game in Victoria that starts at 2 pm, you'd probably be up at about 8 am Melbourne time, which is 6 am Perth time,' said Pavlich. 'You get up, start the day and get moving, and then you play the game. Then you probably don't land home until sometime between 10 pm and midnight Perth time. So realistically it's a long, long day. You're on the go the whole time, both to the game and on the plane. It's very tough on you, physically.'

Ground familiarity is another potential factor in determining home advantage, particularly in a league such as the AFL, in which the playing surface is not a standard length or width. Geelong players know from training and playing at Kardinia Park that its pockets are deceptively deep, and the prevailing breeze means one flank is easier to score from than the other. Visiting sides might play there once every two years, and no amount of theory substitutes for the shock of being trapped in the unplayable zone. Players also speak of the difficulty adjusting to different types of soil and grass. This could affect their running gait, the bounce of the ball, or the length of their recovery from using unfamiliar muscles. Jakovich believes this was a big problem for West Coast when it first joined the competition. 'It was a new club and its players had been accustomed to Western Australia's fast-track decks,' he said. 'When you play on big grounds where you can play fast and attacking football, it's completely different to when you get to Windy Hill and Moorabbin and the slosh heaps that they were.'

Such were the Eagles' early struggles that they won just five out of 27 matches on Victorian soil in their first three seasons. During those years, they would travel to Melbourne the day before a game, but it would be late at night before they got to their hotel. To shake off any stiffness from the flight, coach John Todd would take the players to a nearby park to train, in darkness, with 'invisible' footballs. 'During one such session, forward Troy Ugle decided he'd had enough and kicked his imaginary footy away, at which point Todd ordered him to "go and get it",' reported the *Sunday Times*. 'Ugle did, but on returning told Todd he couldn't find it.' It wasn't until Mick Malthouse took over in 1990 that the Eagles won at the MCG. 'My change of tactics included travelling a day earlier and completing our final training session of the week on a bigger Melbourne ground in heavier Victorian weather conditions,' wrote Malthouse, in *The Ox Is Slow but the Earth Is Patient*. 'It was a big deal in Perth; the media celebrated the fact we were the first WA team to defeat a Victorian side at the MCG. It seemed that my theories had been correct. A few adjustments to our travel and training regime was all that had been needed to get the result we wanted.'

Yet, almost three decades later, West Coast is still searching for the right formula to win consistently on the road. During coach Adam Simpson's first four seasons in charge, the Eagles' record in Victoria was eight wins and 15 losses. 'We've had our ups and downs, but it probably gets overplayed a little bit, because a lot of teams struggle to play away from home,' said Simpson. 'You're always looking for that perfect mix where the players can do their own thing, and get them best prepared. And how do you judge that? Is it on the result? Is it on the first quarter? Is it on the warm-up? Over the last 20 years I think we've tried every single scenario. Every club is different. Everyone is trying to find a way that works.' That includes clubs visiting Perth to face the Eagles. In fact, some coaches and players argue that West Coast and Fremantle enjoy an even greater home-ground advantage because of the way umpires are (allegedly) subconsciously swayed by their partisan crowd support. 'I call it the noise of affirmation,' said St Kilda coach Alan Richardson after his side lost to the Eagles at Subiaco in 2017. 'There's this incredible noise that potentially gives the umpire some form of affirmation. Or, if you're an opposition player, there is no noise, and no affirmation for the umpire to receive.'

In researching their bestselling book *Scorecasting*, the American authors Tobias Moskowitz and Jon Wertheim investigated the roots of home-ground advantage by studying 19 competitions covering seven different sports. Their analysis led them to discount many of the commonly cited factors such as travel and crowd support. Instead, they found its leading cause was the type of umpiring bias described by Richardson. 'What we've found is that officials *are* biased, confirming years of fans' conspiracy theories,' they wrote. 'But they're biased not against the louts screaming unprintable epithets at them. They're biased for them, and the bigger the crowd, the worse the bias. In fact, "official's bias" is the most significant contributor to home field advantage.' We can test whether Moskowitz and Wertheim's hypothesis holds up in the AFL, but first we need a reliable method of quantifying home-ground advantage.

Measuring home-ground advantage

At face value, working out one team's home-ground advantage over another should be straightforward. As we learned earlier, St Kilda beat Collingwood more than four times more often at home than it did away in the years before its move to Moorabbin Oval in 1965. In absolute terms, there was a 28% gap between the Saints' winning percentage against the Magpies at Victoria Park (8%) and at the Junction Oval (36%). But to get a more accurate picture of home-ground advantage over time, we need to account for changes in the number of clubs, the length of the fixture, and the competition's geographical spread. To do this, Hawthorn analyst Darren O'Shaughnessy has created a metric he calls the Standardised Win Percentage Added by Home Ground (WPcA). At its core, WPcA says if two teams are equal in strength, and have a 50–50 chance of beating the other at a hypothetical neutral venue, then the same match on Team A's home ground will be won by Team A [50+WPcA]% of the time, and by Team B [50-WPcA]% of the time – ignoring draws. The difference between home and neutral, measured in WPcA, is the home-ground advantage. O'Shaughnessy has calibrated his formula so that it be used to compare teams in different eras with higher and lower scoring than today. As an example, if we apply his calculations to those historical St Kilda–Collingwood results, we find the Magpies' WPcA was a massive 19.7%. In real terms, that means that if Collingwood was to face an opponent of equal strength, against which it would be an even-money chance at a neutral venue, it would have beaten that team 69.7% of the time at Victoria Park ([50+19.7 WPcA]%).

By applying the measurement to all past results, we see that home-ground advantage remained remarkably stable during the VFL era. From 1897 until 1969, the league-average WPcA held steady at 11%. The only season in which away teams scored more points than the hosts was 1907, with a net -1% WPcA. The next year, in 1908, it was +21%, which was the second-highest in history after 1900's outlier at +32%. These early seasons only had 56 games, so the results could vary considerably. But each season saw an advantage to the home team that would reliably create an extra win per nine games. While the advantage as measured in scoreboard points grew slowly from about seven points to nine points as the scoring rate increased, the 11% WPcA held steady. Only two clubs extracted a little more than the average: Geelong (which was the only team outside metropolitan Melbourne) at 16%, and St Kilda at 15%.

From 1970 to 1986, the VFL used a double round robin schedule, with each side playing every other team twice. This could have been the ideal scenario in which to measure home-ground advantage, if not for the fact the VFL's neutral venue at Waverley also opened in 1970. The league's 12 clubs took turns to host games there. The nexus between a club's training base and its nominal home venue was also breaking. Richmond moved its home games to the MCG in 1965, but retained its training base at the adjacent Punt Road Oval. Hawthorn's supporters outgrew Glenferrie Oval in 1974, and the club's home games were moved across town to Carlton's Princes Park. By 1985, the MCG was too busy for its historical tenant Melbourne to train on, as North Melbourne became its third 'home' club. Win percentage added during this era was 10%. The slight drop from the previous seven decades was entirely attributable to two clubs. The Hawks were winning as easily at opposition venues as at their adopted home ground and had a WPcA of only 5%, while Richmond recorded just

4% WPcA after moving to the MCG. St Kilda, back at the foot of the ladder after a brief surge in the 1960s, was still seeing a decent 13% WPcA. Curiously, the other struggling clubs of this era also had larger-than-average home benefits: South Melbourne (13% before moving to Sydney and dropping to 10%), Footscray (12%), Melbourne (11%), and Geelong (11%). This was because it was probably more accurate to call the bias an 'away-ground disadvantage' during the 1970s and '80s, as the VFL's whipping boys endured crushing losses away from home.

The VFL expanded into New South Wales, Western Australia, and Queensland in the six years between 1981 and 1987. South Australia joined the party during the 1990s. If travel was a significant factor in home-ground advantage, we would expect to see the new clubs recording a higher WPcA than the Victorian teams. This is indeed the case. Topping the list with 22% Win Percentage Added at its home venue is the Gold Coast Suns, followed by West Coast, Adelaide, Fremantle, Brisbane, and Port Adelaide, which each have a WPcA of at least 15%. St Kilda and Geelong continue to have the highest WPcA of the Victorian clubs at around 13%, although that includes intra-Victorian games. If we only count matches between sides from different states, we find the league-average advantage for a team hosting an interstate visitor was a whopping 18% in the first 12 years of the national competition. This corresponded with a 32-point difference in average margin in one state compared to the other. WPcA has decreased to 12% in recent years, but still represents a 20-point shift depending on the venue. It means that if a Victorian team faces a non-Victorian side of similar quality, the bookmakers' line is likely to be 10 points in favour of the host.

Confined to this focus on matches against an interstate rival at the home team's base, West Coast has the largest difference in performance when not travelling. Its WPcA is 18%. St Kilda is second with 17% WPcA, followed by Gold Coast, Fremantle, the two Adelaide teams, and Brisbane, which are all slightly above the league average of 15.7%. The Saints are the Victorian anomaly in the top bracket, which tells us everything we need to know about their abysmal interstate record. Four teams have kept their home bias to 10% or less: Sydney (10%), Melbourne (9%), Collingwood (8%), and Richmond (7%). The most freakish bias shows up in the 14

147

Q-Clashes between Brisbane and Gold Coast. Measured against the rating difference for the two clubs, the host team has outperformed the expected result 13 times, and there have been several thrashings at both the Gabba and Carrara. This equates to a whopping 32% WPcA in these derbies. In intra-Victorian clashes, a WPcA of 6% is the norm when the home side is at its usual venue and the away side isn't. St Kilda (11%), Collingwood (10%), and Geelong (9%) head the list for this category, with Essendon (-1%) and Hawthorn (+2%) sitting close to zero. In recent years, a few clubs have created substantial advantages at secondary bases outside their home state. Hawthorn has recorded a 13% WPcA in Launceston, GWS 16% in Canberra, and North Melbourne an average 12% across several venues. For St Kilda, a diabolical -16% WPcA in Tasmania and New Zealand has given it cause to reconsider hosting matches outside Melbourne.

The South Australian and Western Australian clubs have always shared their venues in Adelaide and Perth respectively. Their season-ticket packages usually give fans access to all their home-ground matches, except the Showdowns or Western Derbies in which they are the visiting team. This can lead to lopsided crowd support in favour of the side on the left-hand side of the Showdown or Derby fixture, because the away fans – if they can find a ticket at all – must pay additional fees to attend. These matches, in which the teams meet at the same venue but with alternating hosting rights, can provide some insight into the effect of crowd support. A 2017 Harvard study of major European soccer leagues found a small boost to the home team's fortunes at shared grounds, such as when AC Milan and Internazionale host each other at the San Siro. The size of the boost was only 20% to 25% of their average home-ground advantage when playing other clubs in the league. Similar results are seen in the AFL. While the South Australian and Western Australian teams average 16% WPcA against interstate clubs, the 'home' bias drops to 11% when the Crows and Power meet in Adelaide, and 3% when the Eagles and Dockers clash in Perth. A change in home venue – say from Football Park to Adelaide Oval – does little to change a team's WPcA either. Ultimately, if a club's fans turn up, the advantage will appear.

How does home-ground advantage manifest in the stats?

Aside from the obvious detail that home teams score more points than away teams, how else do they gain their advantage on the field? To answer this question, we have looked back at every statistic recorded by Champion Data during the 2010 to 2017 home-and-away seasons, and compiled two dozen key performance indicators across three types of matches:

1. **HGA:** Matches with full home-ground advantage for a team hosting an interstate rival. These constituted just over half of the games in our sample, and the home team enjoyed an average boost of +11% points on the scoreboard compared to the away team.
2. **Small Win:** Close matches between teams from the same state. We used games with a final margin of under three goals as our 'control' group, because they had the same +11% average scoreboard advantage for the winning team over the losing team.
3. **Big Win:** Margins of more than 10 goals in games between teams from the same state. This type of match should show which statistics are dominated by teams when they beat up weaker opponents. On average, the winners of these games scored +145% more points than the losers.

By separating the matches in this way, we can tease out which statistics contribute to home-ground advantage by comparing the HGA games to the control group. A handful were broadly similar across the two:

Statistic – similar size	HGA	Small win	Big win
Scoreboard points	+11%	+11%	+145%
Total disposals	+4%	+2%	+21%
Uncontested possessions	+5%	+3%	+25%
Contested marks in forward 50	+14%	+14%	+120%
Clangers (errors)	−4%	−2%	−11%
Tackles	+1%	+3%	+9%
Intercept marks	+4%	+7%	+27%

The importance – or unimportance – of each statistic is emphasised in the rightmost column. For example, we see that the number of tackles or clangers that a team makes is only weakly correlated with winning. In contrast, taking contested marks in the forward 50 is a strong indicator of success.

Only two statistics were noticeably higher in the control group than the HGA matches:

Statistic – less in HGA	HGA	Small win	Big win
Clangers in defensive 50	−12%	−8%	−40%
Gathers in space	+1%	+7%	+30%

Both tell a story. Teams travelling interstate tend to make a lot more mistakes in their defensive zone, where the home team can make them pay on the scoreboard.

Meanwhile, the ability to find space and run onto a ball delivered by a teammate – a trait that is underrated by pundits but treasured by coaches – does not seem to be enhanced by the home venue. Instead, the home team generally derives its advantage through hard work and contested play:

Statistic – more in HGA	HGA	Small win	Big win
Marks on lead	+16%	+2%	+71%
Playing on after marking	+9%	−1%	+35%
Running bounces	+10%	+4%	+61%
Clanger kicks	+1%	−5%	−16%
Hard-ball gets	+2%	−3%	+9%
Clearances from stoppages	+3%	−1%	+14%
Contested possessions	+4%	0%	+15%
One percenters	+1%	−2%	+6%
Contested marks	+8%	+5%	+42%

The table above suggests that home teams work harder for their wins than those at neutral venues. That is reinforced when we look at some of the key performance indicators involving territory, and find that teams with home-ground advantage record substantially more of their statistics in the forward half:

Statistic – territory	HGA	Small win	Big win
Disposals in forward half	+10%	+3%	+58%
Inside 50s	+8%	+1%	+50%
Long kicks to advantage	+7%	+4%	+61%
Free kicks in forward half	+18%	+3%	+39%

Home sides set their own terms through repeat efforts, extra territory, and a bit more grunt in the 50–50 contests. Most conspicuously, though, they are also awarded more free kicks.

The free-kick count is the only statistic in the game that favours home teams more than even the most lopsided of winners. Over the eight seasons prior to 2018, two teams playing in front of a neutral crowd averaged 19 free kicks apiece. In matches between teams from different states, the visiting side averaged 17.5 free kicks per game compared to the home team's 19.5. In the following table, we have broken down the free-kick counts to provide some additional context:

Statistic – free kicks	HGA	Small win	Big win
Total free kicks	+11%	+1%	+9%
Free kicks in forward half	+18%	+3%	+39%
50 m frees	+4%	–2%	+25%
Free kicks for the ball carrier	+9%	+3%	+5%
Free kicks for holding the ball	+15%	+1%	+29%
Deliberate out of bounds or run too far	+49%	–12%	+12%

The massive discrepancy in forward-half free kicks is actually a red herring. We know that HGA teams play in front of centre 7% more than the control group, so the extra forward-half free kicks they receive is merely a consequence of that. The real evidence of umpire bias is seen in the decisions that might be affected by crowd noise, such as free kicks for holding the ball, deliberate out of bounds, or running too far. These are what Richardson alluded to when he spoke of the noise of affirmation. The call of 'BALL' is an iconic part of the footy soundscape, and sure enough we see 15% more free kicks for holding the ball awarded to the home team, despite the away team having fewer possessions on average. But that discrepancy pales in comparison to the one seen for deliberate out of bounds or running too far. It is no coincidence that the umpires have the most time to absorb the urgings of players and spectators before making these decisions. Of the 743 paid in different-state matches during our sample, the split fell 445 to 298 in favour of the home team.

It is an incontrovertible fact that umpires favour teams playing in front of their home crowd, but it is one the AFL seems unwilling to acknowledge. The league's head umpires coach, Hayden Kennedy, never discusses the impact of crowd noise with his officials. 'We haven't spoken about it,' said Kennedy. 'My philosophy is that we'll just continue to coach around what is a free kick and what's not, with a clear headspace around that. I think as soon as you start talking about crowd noise, I think there's just another element to their decision-making or their processing that they need to think about, which could possibly cause more problems than it's worth.' The AFL's former national umpiring director, Peter Schwab, was of the same mind. 'Fundamentally, you're just trying to make sure the umpires understand the interpretations that we're trying to apply to the game,' said Schwab. 'As you know, that happens in a pretty fast, complex game. Do they consider crowd noise when they're making a decision? I never ask them. I've never even broached the subject with them, to be honest.'

Few would dispute Kennedy and Schwab's assertion that umpires already have a lot on their minds. There is a lot riding on the calls they make or don't make. The AFL is serious business, and there are many thousands of people who are financially or emotionally invested in its results. On top of that, the umpires' job is made even more difficult by constant changes to Australian football's rules and interpretations. 'God, yeah,' said Kennedy. 'It takes time, too, because you can't replicate the pressure situations at training.' Since the AFL established its Laws of the Game Committee in 1994, the average number of annual rule changes has jumped from 0.8 to 2.5 per year. For most of the sport's history, a consensus among the various state governing bodies needed to be reached before a law could be altered. After becoming unencumbered of this requirement, the AFL was free to tinker as it pleased.

In 1996, for example, there was a major amendment to the holding-the-ball rule. Then in its third year, the Laws of the Game

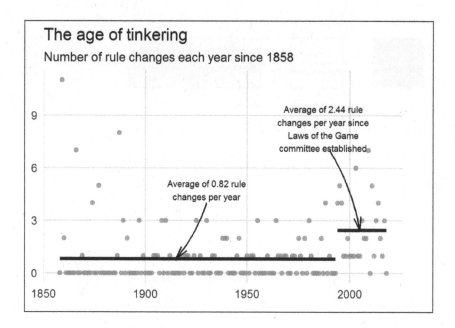

The age of tinkering
Number of rule changes each year since 1858

Average of 2.44 rule changes per year since Laws of the Game committee established

Average of 0.82 rule changes per year

Committee introduced the notion of 'prior opportunity'. It believed the tackler was too often going unrewarded, particularly when his opponent had spurned a chance to dispose of the ball. The rule relating to holding the ball is now part of Rule 15.2: Free Kicks Relating to Possession of the Football. It is defined in its most basic essence in Rule 15.2.3:

(a) Where the field Umpire is satisfied that a Player in possession of the football:

(i) has had a prior opportunity to dispose of the football, the field Umpire shall award a Free Kick against that Player if the Player does not Correctly Dispose of the football immediately when they are Correctly Tackled;

The rule requires an umpire to interpret the players' actions in three distinct ways: 1) whether the player being tackled had prior opportunity; 2) whether the player being tackled correctly disposed of the football; and 3) whether the player applying the tackle correctly tackled their opponent. We can map the rule using a decision tree framework:

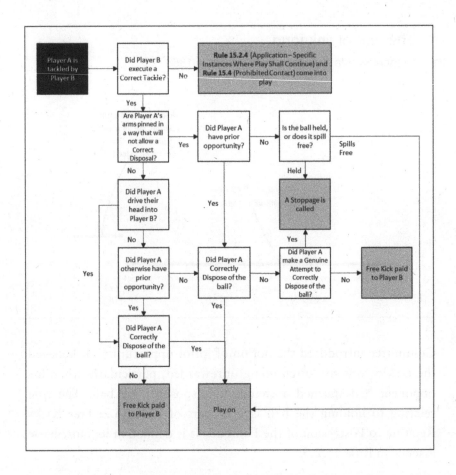

An umpire must contemplate these questions every time a player attempts or successfully executes a tackle. They have just seconds to decide whether to award a free kick, during which time they will be flooded with external stimuli. Is it any wonder there are perceived inconsistencies in the rule's application? 'When humans are faced with enormous pressure – say, making a crucial call with a rabid crowd yelling, taunting, and chanting a few feet away – it is natural to want to alleviate that pressure,' wrote Moskowitz and Wertheim in *Scorecasting*. 'By making snap-judgement calls in favour of the home team, referees, whether they consciously appreciate it or not, are relieving some of that stress. They may also be taking a cue from the crowd when trying to make the right call, especially in an uncertain situation.'

Every fan would have their own anecdotes of how their club has been 'cheated' by a one-eyed umpire late in a game at an interstate venue. A video of a forlorn Crows supporter lamenting a decisive free kick paid to Collingwood forward Jack Anthony in the dying moments of the 2009 semifinal has been viewed more than 150,000 times on YouTube. 'Absolutely, the Crows were robbed!' cried the fan. 'Right in front of me! Right ... in front ... of me!' In that instance, the free kick virtually decided the match, with Anthony's goal putting the Magpies in front with just seconds remaining. But how much is an extra couple of free kicks generally worth? Using a simple rule of thumb, possession of the ball in the middle of the ground is worth approximately one point on the scoreboard. That is what the average AFL team manages to convert a centre clearance into. Internally, teams refer to this as 'scoreboard equity'. It is the value of the team's current position and quality of possession in scoreboard terms.

The most influence an umpire's decision could exert would be to overturn a mark in the goal square, changing an expectation of six points into approximately zero. However, most interventions have much less impact than that. Our research has established that, on average, an extra free kick is worth about two points of scoreboard equity. The two extra free kicks enjoyed by a HGA team will benefit it to the tune of four points. This, then, is the answer we set out to find. It means that umpire bias accounts for approximately 40% of all home-ground advantage in the AFL. It is difficult to imagine any other single factor – whether that be the benefit of familiarity with the venue, or the rigours of travel faced by the visitors – could exceed an effect of that size. Moskowitz and Wertheim's hypothesis that umpire bias is the most significant contributor to home advantage therefore rings true for the Australian game. That is not to say, of course, that umpires in any way intend to favour home teams. But perhaps it is time for the league to at least acknowledge the noise of affirmation, so that it can train its officials to deal with it.

Chapter Eight
The Draft

Looking forward

A severe weather warning had been issued for Melbourne. The Bureau of Meteorology was forecasting winds averaging 40 to 60 kilometres per hour, and even stronger gusts. Planes were being diverted to Sydney. Hundreds of homes were without power, as the squalls brought down powerlines. 'We're predicting the worst winds of the year so far,' said senior forecaster Stuart Coombs. 'In some parts they may be so strong they could potentially dislodge or bring down trees.' That seemed a distinct possibility at the sprawling grounds of Carey Grammar's sports complex, where the melaleuca trees bordering the southern side of the main oval were heaving up and down. 'What do you think it's worth?' one uniformed student asked another, as two teams ran out. 'Dunno,' came the reply. 'Four goals, maybe five?'

The two students were among about 200 people braving the windy conditions to watch Carey's First XVIII take on the visitors from Geelong Grammar School. The teams were competing in the Associated Public Schools (APS) competition, which featured 11 of Victoria's top independent schools. Despite the schoolyard setting, there was an undeniable sense of professionalism, and an unmistakable smell of money. In the car park there was a Maserati, a few BMWs and Mercedes, and a handful of Range Rovers. The playing surface was immaculately manicured. There was a 450-seat grandstand, and a 10-metre-tall scoreboard. The field umpires wore fluoro yellow, the goal umpires wore butchers' coats, and about a dozen of the players wore Alice bands to keep their flowing locks in place. Perhaps most conspicuously, there were serious-looking men dotted around the ground clutching binoculars in one hand and clipboards in the other. They were AFL talent scouts, dispatched by their clubs to find the next generation of top-level players.

Adrian Caruso's clipboard was orange and charcoal, the colours of Greater Western Sydney. He was the Giants' national recruiting manager. He wore a New York Yankees cap, a black duffle coat, black skinny jeans, and black shoes. He had sharp eyes and a quiet intensity. He was focused. It was days like this that recruiters really earned their keep. 'We can get recorded vision of most games now, but what it doesn't show is what the players are doing off the ball,' said Caruso. 'It's also good to get a sense of the conditions, especially if it's windy. Being at the game gives you a better understanding of what happened, and it also allows you to put a player's performance in the right context, which you can't always do from watching a tape.'

Caruso was in his fourth season with the Giants in 2017. He had been lured to the club by coach Leon Cameron, with whom he had worked for two years at the Western Bulldogs. Prior to that, Caruso had spent eight years with Champion Data. 'As soon as I finished high school I wrote to Champion and said, "Look, I'm a young kid, I love footy, I love stats – how do I get into it?"' he said. 'I was lucky enough to start working for them part-time while I was at university for four years studying sports administration and business management. Once that finished, they put me on full-time. It was at the same time the *Moneyball* data movement was growing in the AFL. We started covering the Under-18 Championships and TAC Cup, and coding all the vision of underage footy. I took a real interest in that.'

After winning the toss, Carey took advantage of the wind in the opening quarter to kick four goals to one. But Caruso wasn't interested in the scoreboard. He was there to monitor five specific players: Geelong Grammar's Paddy Dow, Lochie O'Brien, Jarrod Brander, and Brent Daniels, and Carey's Ed Richards. Caruso rated Dow as the outstanding player of the 2017 draft class, but knew he had little chance of calling his name come November. GWS had lost its round-one pick for breaching anti-doping rules. Dow, O'Brien, and Brander were all being projected as first-round picks, but there was a possibility that Daniels and Richards would both still be available at the Giants' opening selection.

Caruso's clipboard held sheets of white paper with the names of his players of interest. As the match progressed, he carefully noted their individual contributions. He listed their strengths, as well as what he called 'RFIs', or their 'room for improvement'. When Dow gathered a contested ball with one hand during the third quarter, for example, Caruso was glowing in his praise. 'Clean ball handler,' he wrote. 'Rarely fumbles, no matter the situation.' At various other times, he noted when players missed tackles, over-ran the ball, or were too easily pushed out of a contest. 'Lack of intent to sit under high ball when numbers around,' he wrote of one player. 'Just throws one arm up, or avoids the contest altogether.'

About half-a-dozen coaching or support staff were attached to each of the school teams. The former AFL forward and NFL punter Sav Rocca was one of Carey's assistants. He stood a few metres behind the head coach, watching the game intently and muttering incantations to himself. 'Take your time, take your time, take your time,' he repeated. 'Defensive, defensive, defensive.' It wasn't unusual to see former stars like Rocca on the sidelines. 'The schools hire ex-players to add to the prestige of their programs,' said Caruso. 'It helps them when they're trying to attract players. These days the private schools identify the better kids when they're 14 or 15 and offer them scholarships. They see it as a great selling point to be able to show they've had a certain number of players drafted.'

Despite – or perhaps because of – the money that schools invest in their football programs, the quality of teams in the APS competition can be wildly uneven. On that same windy July day, there were five APS matches being played around Melbourne. The average winning margin was 51 points, with the largest being Carey's 67-point victory over Geelong Grammar. Caruso believed the art of scouting lay in the ability to separate the quality of the individual from that of the team. 'That's the hardest thing,' said Caruso, as the players shook hands and left the field. 'In this game we've just watched, the four most draftable players were on a team that lost by more than 10 goals. You need to be able to look beyond the score and see the players as individuals, define their strengths, and project how they will perform in the AFL. Even if they can't help their school win on the day, they might still have the best tools for the AFL, and for your club.'

After the match had ended, Caruso typed out his notes and entered them into the Giants' database. His scouting report for the game ran almost 2,000 words, but it was just one of 20 matches attended by GWS recruiting staff that weekend. Emma Quayle, the former *Age* football reporter who had joined the Giants a few months earlier, was sent to watch TAC Cup games in Oakleigh and Bendigo. 'It's been interesting for me, because even though I kind of knew what I was getting into, it's a very different way of watching footy,' she said. 'What I've found is that you're really breaking the players down into a series of qualities or attributes, whether it be that they're quick, or tough, or powerful, or have good hands. You end up seeing them so many times that you feel like you know exactly what they're going to do.'

That was how Caruso felt about Dow, whose performance in his side's thrashing at the hands of Carey had not tempered his admiration. 'Nothing has changed my mind on Paddy, I still believe he is the best player in the draft,' he wrote in his report. 'His ability to turn up to play every week, as well as his actual football ability, make him the standout midfielder in the pool.' Although the Giants would eventually trade their way back into the first round, Dow was gone well before their opening selection at number 11. Carlton snared Dow with pick three and fellow Geelong Grammarian Lochie O'Brien with pick 10. After strongly considering Carey's running defender Ed Richards, Caruso plumped for powerful utility Aiden Bonar from the APS premier, Haileybury College. With the Giants' second selection, at pick 27, he took Dow and O'Brien's schoolmate Brent Daniels. At just 171 centimetres and 70 kilograms, Daniels was the 2017 draft's smallest player, and the shortest to be selected inside the top 30 since Danny Craven in 1988. 'When I look back at historical drafts, I think height and athletic build have been the most overrated things,' said Caruso. 'Players were drafted earlier if they were tall and athletic and had a good build, but that didn't necessarily mean they made it. There was a push maybe 10 to 15 years ago to draft the athletes, but now it's probably come back to picking the footballers.'

Looking back

On the morning of Tuesday 6 October 1981, representatives of the league's then 12 clubs gathered at the old VFL House in Jolimont, near the MCG. They were there for the first player draft, which was being introduced to democratise the VFL's interstate recruitment process. 'It is a system that is a big deal in the United States,' explained the league's general manager, Jack Hamilton. Indeed, the major American sports had for decades used drafts to allocate players to their professional teams. The NFL held its first draft in 1936 in a bid to reduce the dominance of its continual contenders. The team with the worst record from the previous season, the Philadelphia Eagles, was given the first choice from the player pool, and the process continued in reverse order of the standings. Professional basketball adopted the system in 1947, followed by ice hockey and Major League Baseball in the 1960s.

Historically, Australian football had employed different methods of player distribution. In the sport's earliest years, footballers were free to play for the club of their choice. Although they were nominally amateur, it wasn't uncommon for them to be induced to join clubs by job offers or payment. Public interest in football dwindled when a small number of clubs began to dominate. The South Australian Football Association addressed this problem in the late 1890s by introducing 'electorate football', which assigned players to clubs based on where they lived. The VFL adopted a similar metropolitan zoning system during the First World War. In response, the VFL clubs placed a bigger emphasis on recruiting 'free agents' from country Victoria or other states. The wealthier clubs were rumoured to attract talent by offering illegal signing-on fees or other inducements, and by paying above the maximum player wage that had been set for the first time in 1930. Country zoning was eventually introduced in 1968, but the clubs were still able to recruit two interstate players per year.

The interstate players were handed what were known as 'Form Four' documents. Once a player signed, he was tied to that club if he ever chose to play in the VFL. Some SANFL and WAFL players signed and took the money even if they had no intention of moving. Those who wanted to play in the VFL could auction their services to the highest bidder. This contrasted with the Victorian players, who could

161

only negotiate with the club to which they were zoned. The transfer and signing-on fees for interstate players increased exponentially, and several VFL clubs were facing financial difficulties by the start of the 1980s. The league's solution was to hold a US-style draft, in which each club could select two interstate players. 'The scheme will help all clubs makes selections for key positions and will give the bottom clubs the best chance to gain the best players available,' said Hamilton.

Melbourne, the 1981 wooden spooner, took East Perth's Alan Johnson with the inaugural draft's number one pick, and Port Adelaide's Danny Hughes with pick 13. With selections 12 and 24, the premier, Carlton, selected Claremont's Ross Ditchburn and Glenelg's Chris Veide. 'Most clubs seemed happy with their results,' wrote Mike Sheahan in the afternoon edition of the *Herald*. 'Although Collingwood had the 11th and 23rd choices because it finished second on the premiership ladder, its nominated pair, Tasmanians Chris Carpenter and Scott Knight, were among its top five selections.' Carpenter never played for the Magpies, while Knight only managed five games. The Demons enjoyed a much greater return from Johnson and Hughes, who combined for 259 matches and three best-and-fairest medals. Footscray selected future Crows coach Neil Craig at pick two, but he chose to play out his career in Adelaide.

Of the 24 players selected in the VFL's first draft, 15 were from South Australia, seven from Western Australia, and two from Tasmania. The draft was only twice held in its initial format, after Melbourne and Geelong pushed for a moratorium on interstate transfers to allow SANFL and WAFL clubs to replenish their stocks. A revised, heavily compromised draft was reintroduced in 1986 to coincide with the league's expansion. The fledgling West Coast Eagles and Brisbane Bears were given exclusive access to players from their states, while the Sydney Swans had domain over most of New South Wales. That left only South Australia, Tasmania, the ACT, and the Northern Territory as potential recruiting grounds. The player pool expanded the following year after the abolition of Victoria's country zoning system, but it wasn't until the metropolitan zones were phased out in the early 1990s that the draft began to resemble what we know today. It marked the first time since the beginning of the century that clubs were given relatively equal access to new players, and it created the platform for what was arguably the first competitively balanced draft – as well as the first to be broadcast live on television – in 1993.

Talent identification was something of a hit-and-miss affair during the draft's early years. Of the 409 players taken in the six VFL drafts of the 1980s, 201 (49%) failed to play a single senior game. This was partly because clubs seldom even spoke to the players before calling their names. Martin Leslie was about to head to the dole office in Darwin when he read in a newspaper that Brisbane had selected him with pick one in the 1986 draft. 'You'd just draft them and then try to convince them to come across,' said Cameron Schwab, who was one of the decade's few full-time recruiters. The son of former Richmond secretary Alan Schwab, he had joined Melbourne as a teenage office boy in 1982. 'I was quite fortunate that the people who were involved in the club at the time, like the senior coach, Ron Barassi, allowed me to sit in on match committee and their other discussions about football,' he said. 'Surprisingly, from my perspective, they were prepared to listen to my opinions as to who I thought was a good player or not.' Schwab volunteered to spend his weekends scouting junior players that the Demons could select from their zones, and it didn't take long for the club to appreciate the value of his work. Within a couple of years, he was appointed recruiting manager. 'That was a period when a lot of clubs were struggling financially, and to allocate any sort of resource to a longer-term situation was a real battle,' he said. 'One of the reasons we were able to justify it at Melbourne was that I was very young and wasn't getting paid very much.'

Schwab supplemented his live scouting with rudimentary video and statistical analysis. 'By the time the first draft came around in '86, we were in a good position compared to a lot of the other clubs, which were trying to scratch together a recruiting network in any shape or form,' he said. Schwab's first two picks at the 1986 draft were the Tasmanian twins Steven and Matthew Febey, who would play a combined 401 games for the Demons. An incident the following year gave him an insight into how little attention some of his competitors were devoting to the task. 'We'd played the Swans in a final and beaten them, so they had the draft choice immediately before us,' said

Schwab. 'They drafted a fellow called Scott Salisbury from Glenelg. I leant over to their recruiting guy and said, "You know Salisbury is going on 30?" He looked at me and said, "No, he's not!" I couldn't believe it. He didn't even know his age.' In 1988, at just 24 years old, Schwab joined Richmond as the youngest general manager in VFL history. He maintained an active interest in recruiting, but believes it took the dissolution of the Victorian zones for the draft's significance to be fully realised. 'It wasn't until it became the clubs' only currency that most of them started to think, "Well, we better get this right",' he said.

A brief history of valuing players

Before a draft, each club needs to sort the pool of available players into its preferred order. The idea of rating players is almost as old as football itself. In 1875, the inaugural edition of *The Footballer*, a journal of the year's results, devoted eight pages to a section titled 'Notes on our chief players'. Carlton's William Lacey, for example, was described as 'an all-round player of undoubted excellence, unequalled for taking the ball into play from bounds', while his teammate Edward Williamson was 'courageous, but lacking judgment'. In 1898, the South Australian Football Association presented the inaugural Magarey Medal to the player judged by the umpires to have been the season's 'fairest and most brilliant player'. The WAFL followed suit with the Sandover Medal 1921, and the VFL struck the Brownlow Medal in 1924. Many clubs established their own best-and-fairest awards around the same time.

The weekly publication of match statistics in Harry Beitzel's *Footy Week* newspaper in the 1960s provided a new and more immediate way of comparing players' output. Beitzel's pioneering work was consolidated by Ray Young's APB Sports in 1980s, and then Ted Hopkins's Champion Data in the 1990s. Hopkins and Swinburne University's Stephen Clarke designed a formula to calculate the combined value of a player's statistics in a match. 'Ted understood that there was a need for a product that ranked players,' said Champion Data's former chief statistician Darren O'Shaughnessy. 'People love comparing players from different teams. Ted and Steve did a pretty good job of identifying what mattered in a game, and then scaling it to reflect an action's relative importance. If a player hit his target with a kick, that was worth about four points. If he turned it over, that was worth about minus six.' The formula was refined in 2002, and eventually became the basis of the popular online fantasy football game SuperCoach.

In 2013, the AFL began publishing what it billed as its 'Official Player Ratings'. The ratings were based on a system developed by Karl Jackson, who had succeeded O'Shaughnessy at Champion Data. 'The AFL asked us to create a rating system like the ones used in tennis and golf,' said Jackson, who happened to have already spent several years working on a prototype. Building on a paper O'Shaughnessy had written called 'Possession Versus Position: Strategic Evaluation in AFL', Jackson aimed to put a value on every action that a player made in a game. 'We threw five or six years of x, y coordinate data into a model and came up with a system that calculated the value of having possession at a certain part of the ground,' said Jackson. 'Players would either accrue or lose points every time they were involved in a passage of play, depending on the impact of their involvement. A player who moved the ball into a better position than when they took possession received a positive score, while anyone who put the ball into dispute from no pressure lost points.' Heading into 2018, Geelong's Patrick Dangerfield was the system's top-rated player (727.3), ahead of Richmond's Dustin Martin (666.6), and Collingwood's Scott Pendlebury (607.5).

While Jackson's system is now one of the most advanced player-rating algorithms used in any team sport in the world, the complexity of the data involved means that it can only be applied to matches played at AFL level. This restricts its utility as a recruiting tool. Over the past few years, most clubs have developed their own in-house methods of ranking players, but Caruso believes that football's intangibles – such as leadership and work ethic – make it all but impossible to draft players according to a mathematical formula. 'Yes, the sport is data-rich, but it's so complex and random, and there's so many factors and variables, that it will never get to a stage where you can just pick players based on data,' he said. 'You have to incorporate the athletic component, and you have to incorporate the psychological. We gather a lot of data from psych testing, because it's important to be able to identify the kids who are mentally equipped to make it.'

Although the media has little or no access to this aspect of the recruiting process, they are rarely shy of providing instant appraisals of each club's draft haul. In 2009, several outlets published draft 'report cards', marking the clubs with a letter grade for the group of players they had just selected. *Inside Football* gave an A+ to Melbourne, which had taken Tom Scully and Jack Trengove with picks one and two, Jordan Gysberts with pick 11, and Luke Tapscott with pick 18. The *Herald Sun* was also suitably impressed, awarding them an A-. Scully played 31 matches for the Demons before joining Greater Western Sydney, while injuries restricted Trengove to 86 games in eight seasons. Gysberts was traded to North Melbourne after three seasons, and Tapscott was delisted after five.

Emma Quayle, who for many years specialised in covering the draft for the *Age*, always thought it was folly to rush to immediate judgement. 'How can you mark a club on what they've just done when they know far more about why they've done it than you do?' she said. 'How can you say, "They had a lousy draft because these guys can't play"? I didn't like that. You can probably only do it in hindsight, a few years down the track.' Alas, it can even be difficult to make objective historical assessments. Rating points (i.e. SuperCoach scores) can only be calculated back to 2002, while the newer Official Player Ratings can't be retroactively applied to matches prior to 2010. 'That's when we started to record how much pressure a guy is under with the ball, and before then we've got no measure of that,' said Jackson.

Introducing 'Player Approximate Value' (PAV)

For this book, the football analysts Cody Atkinson and Sean Lawson have developed a new method of rating AFL players called 'Player Approximate Value', or PAV for short. In the spirit of the NBA player projection system CARMELO (a backronym based on the name of Oklahoma City forward Carmelo Anthony) and Major League Baseball's PECOTA (named for former MLB journeyman Bill Pecota), we have named our system in honour of Fremantle great

Matthew Pavlich. As we will soon see, the system rates Pavlich as one of its stars. PAV is a modernised version of the 'Approximate Value' measure originally outlined in 1982 by the famous baseball author and analyst Bill James, and later adapted by Doug Drinen in 2008 to evaluate American football players.

Unlike rating systems that are based on an individual's statistics, PAV has been designed to reflect a player's worth to their team. It uses a team's performance as the starting point, dividing it into three components: forward, midfield, and defence. Values are calculated for a team's output in each of the three areas, and then for how much each player contributed to that output. A player will therefore receive separate ratings for their attacking, midfield, and defensive prowess, providing an insight into how they add value around the ground. Their overall PAV is the sum of these three ratings.

We have tested the PAV formulas – which have been made publicly available on Atkinson and Lawson's website, hpnfooty.com – against the AFL's Official Player Ratings. We found a strong correlation between them, for all player types, between 2010 and 2017. The formulas have also been measured against Brownlow Medal votes and All-Australian selections. As the following graph shows, a higher season-long PAV will generally equate to more votes.

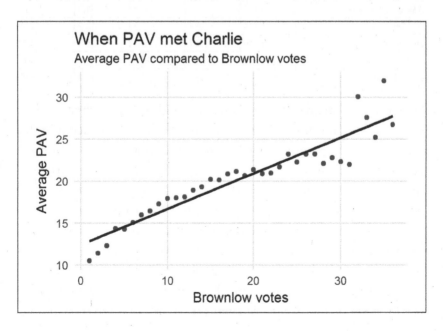

The real benefit of the system is that it can be retrospectively applied to past seasons. This means it can also be used to compare how teams have performed at the draft. Although we can't categorically claim that PAV will define the exact value of every footballer in relation to their peers, we believe it provides a better approximation, and can stretch further back, than any other method that uses publicly available data. We have calculated the PAV of every player in each season from 1988 to 2017. The following table shows the 15 players with the highest overall single-season ratings during our 30-year sample.

Highest single-season PAV, 1988–2017					
Player	Year	PAV Att	PAV Def	PAV Mid	PAV Total
Patrick Dangerfield	2016	9.6	4.3	18.1	32.0
Jim Stynes	1991	7.6	14.7	9.1	31.4
Robert Harvey	1998	7.0	9.4	13.7	30.1
Wayne Carey	1996	16.0	9.7	3.7	29.4
Nathan Buckley	2000	10.8	5.3	12.7	28.8
Wayne Carey	1993	15.2	9.8	3.3	28.3
Wayne Carey	1995	13.2	11.2	3.5	27.9
Nathan Buckley	2003	8.6	5.9	13.4	27.9
Patrick Dangerfield	2017	11.8	2.6	13.2	27.6
Andrew McLeod	2001	8.2	5.7	13.4	27.3
Wayne Campbell	1999	6.8	8.5	11.9	27.2
Joel Selwood	2014	8.4	5.6	13.2	27.2
Simon Goodwin	2006	6.7	5.2	15.3	27.2
Stewart Loewe	1990	9.8	15.5	1.8	27.1
Dustin Martin	2017	10.2	2.7	13.9	26.8

After Dustin Martin's 2017 season saw him become the first man to win a premiership, Brownlow Medal, and Norm Smith Medal in the same year, many pundits scrambled to proclaim it the best in history. 'No player has ever had as good a year as Dustin Martin, I suspect,' said Leigh Matthews. Sure enough, Martin's *annus mirabilis* appears in our table – but only just. According to PAV, it ranks as the 15th-best player season since 1988. Interestingly, though, it wasn't even the best of 2017. That honour went to Patrick Dangerfield, whose total of 27.6 PAV shaded Martin's 26.8. The Geelong superstar was coming off the highest-rated individual season, after his 2016 total of 32 PAV had taken that mantle from Jim Stynes's Brownlow-winning

168

year in 1991. A third of the top-15 single-season PAV totals coincide with Brownlow wins. A notable exception is North Melbourne great Wayne Carey, who appears on our list three times but never won the medal. The list validates the long-held belief that Adelaide's Andrew McLeod was robbed of the 2001 Brownlow. He finished two votes behind Jason Akermanis that year, after failing to poll in the final round despite having 37 disposals in a loss to Fremantle.

McLeod also appears 12th on the list of players with the highest career-long PAV totals. These players were not only highly successful, but also enjoyed remarkable longevity. The average number of games played by the top 15 during our sample was 340 matches. Seven of them won Brownlow medals, all made multiple All-Australian teams, and many were at some stage considered to be the finest player in the game. As such, we see that PAV recognises both quantity and quality. Appropriately, Pavlich himself owns the third-highest career PAV total, behind only Robert Harvey and Brent Harvey.

Highest career PAV, 1988–2017					
Player	PAV Att	PAV Def	PAV Mid	PAV Total	Games
Robert Harvey	98.6	82.8	171.5	352.9	383
Brent Harvey	147.9	64.7	117.8	330.4	432
Matthew Pavlich	177.5	52.1	85.5	315.1	353
Adam Goodes	131.7	75.1	107.8	314.6	372
Gary Ablett Jr	113.4	50.8	131.6	295.8	302
Nathan Buckley	105.5	73.7	116.4	295.6	280
Brad Johnson	142.9	64.0	86.6	293.5	364
Dustin Fletcher	24.8	231.3	30.6	286.7	400
Craig Bradley	84.7	77.7	122.1	284.5	328
Mark Ricciuto	88.6	78.4	114.0	281.0	312
Wayne Campbell	77.8	82.9	120.2	280.9	297
Andrew McLeod	86.3	80.2	113.3	279.8	340
Sam Mitchell	53.7	71.3	154.6	279.6	329
Simon Black	71.4	53.3	151.2	275.9	322
Stewart Loewe	124.6	111.2	38.0	273.8	291

Because PAV is fundamentally based on team ratings, it is harder for a player to draw a higher individual value from a bad side than a good one. The highest PAV totals are generally achieved by the best players in strong teams. As a rule of thumb, we would consider a season-long PAV of more than 20 to be a great season, and anything more than 25 to be exceptional. This varies slightly for different positions. An All-Australian key backman, for example, might have a lower overall PAV than a non-All-Australian midfielder, while having a significantly higher defensive rating.

To use the system to judge how teams have fared at the draft, we need to assign a value to each draft pick. We can do this by comparing the average PAV earned by players taken at each numbered selection. The following table has been created using a sample period starting in the year of the first relatively uncompromised draft in 1993, and ending in 2006. The aim was to make the sample size as

Draft Pick Value Chart					
Pick	Value	Pick	Value	Pick	Value
1	147.0	31	42.7	61	22.1
2	125.9	32	41.7	62	21.7
3	113.6	33	40.8	63	21.2
4	104.9	34	39.9	64	20.7
5	98.1	35	39.0	65	20.2
6	92.6	36	38.2	66	19.8
7	87.9	37	37.3	67	19.3
8	83.8	38	36.5	68	18.8
9	80.2	39	35.7	69	18.4
10	77.0	40	35.0	70	18.0
11	74.1	41	34.2	71	17.5
12	71.5	42	33.5	72	17.1
13	69.1	43	32.8	73	16.7
14	66.8	44	32.1	74	16.3
15	64.7	45	31.4	75	15.9
16	62.8	46	30.7	76	15.5
17	60.9	47	30.1	77	15.1
18	59.2	48	29.4	78	14.7
19	57.6	49	28.8	79	14.3
20	56.0	50	28.2	80	13.9
21	54.5	51	27.6	81	13.5
22	53.1	52	27.0	82	13.2
23	51.8	53	26.4	83	12.8
24	50.5	54	25.8	84	12.4
25	49.2	55	25.3	85	12.1
26	48.0	56	24.7	86	11.7
27	46.9	57	24.2	87	11.4
28	45.8	58	23.7	88	11.0
29	44.7	59	23.2	89	10.7
30	43.7	60	22.6	90	10.3

large as possible, while excluding most players who are still active. Once we had worked out the averages for each selection, we used a mathematical formula to smooth out the peaks and troughs. In short, the preceding table shows the average expected career-long PAV of players taken at each position in the draft, based on historical evidence. We will call this the 'Draft Pick Value Chart'.

By our estimates, the number one pick is worth about double the PAV of pick 11, which in turn is worth roughly twice that of pick 37. Our data confirms one of the great theories of drafting: there is a significant, real-world premium on holding early draft picks.

The AFL has a similar table called the 'Draft Value Index', which assigns a points value to every draft pick for the purposes of academy and father–son bidding. Clubs nominate their academy and father–son selections before a draft. If a rival selects any of these players, the club that has nominated them needs to have enough points from a combination of lower draft picks to match the bid. If it doesn't, the player will join the rival club. The value of the points the AFL attaches to each pick is based on confidential salary data from past seasons. The following graph compares our PAV-based Draft Pick Value Chart to the AFL's Draft Value Index. A similar index created with the average games played by players chosen at each pick is also presented as a comparison.

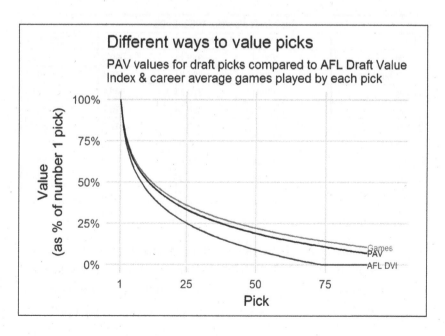

Clearly, our system values second-round picks significantly more highly than the AFL's index. This might suggest that second-round picks have traditionally been underpaid in relation to players taken in the first round. While the AFL's approach is statistically sound, it ignores historical on-field production as a method of valuation. A player's salary is sometimes set before they have demonstrated their true on-field value. Clubs might overpay certain players for a variety of reasons, including perceived potential, or the prestige associated with a high pick.

Winning (and losing) the draft

With our foundation in place, we can now begin to examine the draft performance of teams over time. To rate how well or poorly a club drafted in a certain year, we can use our Draft Pick Value Chart to calculate the combined expected PAV from the selections it held, and then compare that number with the combined career PAV of the players it drafted. Clubs with a high positive differential between their actual and expected PAV have drafted well, while the inverse is true for those with a negative differential. This next table shows the 10 best draft classes between 1993 and 2006, ranked according to how they outperformed expectation.

Best draft classes, 1993–2006				
Club	Year	Expected PAV	Actual PAV	Difference
Geelong	2001	348.1	1,060.3	712.2
Western Bulldogs	1999	263.3	772.4	509.1
Geelong	1999	370.5	848.1	477.6
Brisbane	1997	285.8	710.7	424.9
St Kilda	2001	413.7	812.2	398.5
Port Adelaide	2006	252.9	648.0	395.1
Sydney	1994	436.8	825.9	389.1
Hawthorn	2001	375.0	753.0	378.0
Port Adelaide	2000	194.7	547.9	353.2
Geelong	1995	207.4	509.3	301.9

Geelong's effort at the 1999 draft, ranked third on our table, shows that it is possible to achieve success without nailing every selection. The Cats, under the direction of their revered recruiting manager, Stephen Wells, used seven picks between eight and 47 that year.

Geelong's 1999 draft class				
Pick	Player	Expected PAV	Actual PAV	Difference
8	Joel Corey	83.8	211.9	128.1
15	David Spriggs	64.7	40.4	−24.3
17	Ezra Bray	60.9	0.0	−60.9
23	Daniel Foster	51.8	6.0	−45.8
31	Paul Chapman	42.7	223	180.3
38	Cameron Ling	36.5	154.9	118.4
47	Corey Enright	30.1	211.8	181.7

While Joel Corey ended up a dual All-Australian and club champion, the other three players who were taken in the top 30 – David Spriggs, Ezra Bray, and Daniel Foster – played a total of just 86 AFL games between them. Of course, Wells more than compensated for these slip-ups with his three remaining selections.

The Cats' 2001 alumni were even more impressive, recording the greatest return above expectation during our 14-season sample.

Geelong's 2001 draft class				
Pick	Player	Expected PAV	Actual PAV	Difference
8	Jimmy Bartel	83.8	239.6	155.8
17	James Kelly	60.9	199.6	138.7
23	Charlie Gardiner	51.8	23.0	−28.8
24	Steve Johnson	50.5	239.5	189
40 f–s	Gary Ablett Jr	35.0	295.8	260.8
41	Henry Playfair	34.2	23.7	−10.5
69	Matthew McCarthy	18.4	9.1	−9.3
81	David Johnson	13.5	30.0	16.5

Thus, we can see Geelong's 2007, 2009, and 2011 premierships were largely built on the back of two of the best single-season draft hauls in history. Corey, Chapman, Ling, Enright, Bartel, Kelly, and Steve Johnson played in all three flags, while Gary Ablett featured in two and won a Brownlow Medal before joining the Suns at the end of 2010. In fact, almost every player involved in those premiership sides had joined the club through the draft, with the exceptions of Tom Harley (traded from Port Adelaide), Cameron Mooney (traded from North Melbourne), and Brad Ottens (traded from Richmond).

The three biggest contributors to the Cats' premiership teams were the Geelong Falcons, the Calder Cannons, and the father–son rule. Wells claims he has no magic formula when it comes to selecting players, although he does follow a few basic principles. 'We pick the best kid, [but] if it's a close call we go for the local,' he told author James Button in *Comeback*. 'If they get family support, they won't want to go home.' Wells's focus on the Geelong Falcons has been a shrewd move. Since 1988, the Falcons have produced more draftees and PAV than any other TAC Cup, SANFL, or WAFL club.

PAV by club of origin, 1988–2017				
		Number of players	Sum of career PAV	Average PAV
TAC Cup	Geelong Falcons	95	3,890.0	40.9
	Northern Knights	78	3,608.2	46.3
	Calder Cannons	78	3,446.8	44.2
	Murray Bushrangers	82	3,007.1	36.7
	Eastern Ranges	74	2,722.3	36.8
	Bendigo Pioneers	54	2,660.8	49.3
	Dandenong Stingrays	81	2,611.9	32.2
	Oakleigh Chargers	73	2,324.3	31.8
	North Ballarat Rebels	67	2,310.8	34.5
	Gippsland Power	57	2,229.8	39.1
	Sandringham Dragons	73	2,002.1	27.4
	Western Jets	45	1,681.4	37.4
SANFL	Port Adelaide Magpies	34	2,275.9	66.9
	Woodville–West Torrens Eagles	46	2,024.5	44.0
	Glenelg Tigers	52	1,685.3	32.4
	Norwood Redlegs	45	1,486.9	33.0
	West Adelaide Bloods	37	1,227.0	33.2
	Central District Bulldogs	33	1,208.0	36.6
	North Adelaide Roosters	32	731.8	22.9
	Sturt Double Blues	31	712.1	23.0
	South Adelaide Panthers	20	611.7	30.6
	Woodville Warriors	3	151.6	50.5
	West Torrens Eagles	2	25.5	12.8

PAV by club of origin, 1988–2017			
	Number of players	Sum of career PAV	Average PAV
WAFL			
East Fremantle Sharks	63	3,264.4	51.8
Claremont Tigers	71	1,792.5	25.2
Perth Demons	34	1,331.8	39.2
Subiaco Lions	35	1,206.8	34.5
Swan Districts Swans	41	1,204.9	29.4
West Perth Falcons	35	1,193.1	34.1
East Perth Royals	30	1,060.6	35.4
South Fremantle Bulldogs	46	868.3	18.9
Peel Thunder	17	616.3	36.3
Other notable clubs			
Southport Sharks (SEQ)	12	841.9	70.2
St Mary's Saints (NT)	8	783.8	98.0
North Hobart Demons (Tas)	15	626.6	41.8
Devonport Magpies (Tas)	10	435.8	43.6
Glenorchy Magpies (Tas)	14	423.2	30.2
Zillmere Eagles (SEQ)	9	329.9	36.7
Tassie Mariners (Tas)	16	296.3	18.5
NSW/ACT Rams	9	281.0	31.2
Morningside Panthers (SEQ)	8	225.2	28.2
Clarence Kangaroos (Tas)	10	148.6	14.9

Caruso believes Geelong's dynasty proved, beyond doubt, the crucial importance of drafting well. 'The way you acquire players determines how successful you are,' he said. 'Coaching can have an impact, but at the heart of it you have to have talent, and you've got to be able to find a way to bring in that talent in a market where there's a salary cap and equalisation. It's all about utilising the picks you've got regardless of where they are.'

The Cats are not the only team to have assembled a strong side through astute drafting over a short period. Between 1999 and 2001, the Western Bulldogs put together consecutive above-average hauls. Its 1999 draft class was especially remarkable, with Bob Murphy, Daniel Giansiracusa, Mitch Hahn, Lindsay Gilbee, and Ryan Hargrave combining for 1,167 career games. The following year they added Daniel Cross at pick 56, and in 2001 they stole Brian Lake at pick 71. These players made up the core of the 'almost' teams that lost three consecutive preliminary finals between 2008 and 2010.

Best 3-year draft hauls, 1993–2006				
Club	Years	3-year Expected PAV	3-year Actual PAV	Difference
Geelong	1999–2001	782.5	2,027.7	1,245.2
Geelong	2000–2002	589.7	1,449.2	859.5
Geelong	2001–2003	736.8	1,400.9	664.1
Western Bulldogs	1999–2001	596.2	1,257.1	660.9
Geelong	1998–2000	600.3	1,153.4	553.1
Brisbane	1997–1999	673.2	1,184.7	511.5
St Kilda	2000–2002	967.1	1,473.7	506.6
Western Bulldogs	1998–2000	611.2	1,108.5	497.3
Hawthorn	1999–2001	771.9	1,260.2	488.3
St Kilda	2001–2003	773.8	1,248.9	475.1
Geelong	1997–1999	761.8	1,235.9	474.1

The Dogs' 1999 to 2001 period ranks fourth on the list of best three-year drafting bounties. The list is mostly dominated by the Cats, but St Kilda also appears twice. Between 2000 and 2003, the Saints were largely able to make the right decisions with their top draft picks, such as Nick Riewoldt, Luke Ball, and Brendon Goddard, while also unearthing talent at their later selections, such as Leigh Montagna at pick 37 and Sam Fisher at pick 55. Like Geelong, there were still busts, but they were outweighed by the success stories. Of the Saints' 17 selections made at those four drafts, eight ended up playing in their 2009 and 2010 Grand Final appearances.

Conversely, one of the least successful drafts of all time was Fremantle's effort in 1995. The Dockers had finished 13th out of 16 teams in their inaugural season, and had gaping holes to fill on their list. They were given permission to take several Western Australian players before the draft, and the right to sign up to five uncontracted players. They also held picks one, seven, 13, and 23 in the national draft. With this cache of assets at their disposal, the Dockers could have set themselves up for the next decade. Instead, they flubbed it.

Fremantle's 1995 draft class				
Pick	Player	Expected PAV	Actual PAV	Difference
1	Clive Waterhouse	147.0	65.8	−81.2
7	Ben Edwards	87.9	0.0	−87.9
13	Brad Rowe	69.1	3.7	−65.4
23	Jay Burton	51.8	1.2	−50.6

To be fair, the 1995 draft was particularly weak. Clubs that had lost uncontracted players to Fremantle the previous year had been compensated by being able to pre-list a 16-year-old. As a result, future stars such as Matthew Lloyd and Steven King were removed from the pool. But even taking this into account, Fremantle's performance was disastrous. With their first pick, the Dockers took Clive Waterhouse. He was a 21-year-old long-kicking forward, who had just starred in Port Adelaide's SANFL Grand Final victory over Central District. According to PAV, he is the least successful number one draft pick in the modern draft era. Somehow, things got even worse for the Dockers from there.

Next they selected Ben Edwards, a slightly built utility from Claremont. As he was a Western Australian, the Dockers could have taken Edwards before the draft. For reasons known only to them (former coach Gerard Neesham declined to tell us), they instead wasted their prized pick seven. Edwards has the rare distinction of being one of the few AFL draftees to be delisted by their club before the new season had even begun. We rate it as the worst draft selection made by any club in history. To cap things off, Fremantle took 25-year-old two-club veteran Brad Rowe at pick 13, and twice-delisted 23-year-old ruckman Jay Burton at pick 23. Rowe and Burton played a combined eight games in 1996 before being delisted at the end of the year. 'Anyone can pick over the bones of what we did right or wrong,' said Neesham. 'I do know a lot of other clubs back then selected blokes who totally missed as well.'

Worst draft classes, 1993–2006				
Club	Year	Expected PAV	Actual PAV	Difference
Fremantle	1995	355.7	65.8	−289.9
Sydney	1993	617.3	331.3	−286.0
West Coast	1995	300.1	42.8	−257.3
Carlton	2000	339.3	83.5	−255.8
Fitzroy	1995	419.5	203.3	−216.2
Port Adelaide	2004	238.2	23.2	−215.0
Sydney	1996	360.2	171.9	−188.3
Hawthorn	2005	421.8	234.1	−187.7
Fitzroy	1994	327.4	143.0	−184.4
Western Bulldogs	2002	330.4	147.4	−183.0

Coming of age

The four players Fremantle took in its disastrous 1995 draft had an average age of 22. While that might seem ancient compared to modern standards, at the time it wasn't a massive aberration. The mean age of that year's top 10 picks was 20.7. 'We had joined a men's competition and so we drafted out of other men's leagues instead of the under 18s,' said Neesham. 'We were drafting out of the WAFL and the SANFL. We were drafting guys who had senior experience.' Fremantle's philosophy was a carryover from the 1980s. The typical player selected in the first two drafts in 1981 and 1982 was 21 years old, or 22 if they were taken in the top 10. For the rest of the decade it was 19 overall, and about 20-and-a-half within the first 10 picks. 'There's a trend in the draft,' said Neesham. 'Initially, no-one was taking 17-year-olds. It took probably about 14 years to totally devastate the second-tier competitions around Australia, which then left only the teenagers coming out of colts or out of TAC Cup.'

In the book *Moneyball*, Oakland A's general manager Billy Beane punched the air in delight every time a rival club drafted a player out of high school. He was a firm subscriber to baseball analyst Bill James's theory that 'College players are a better investment than high

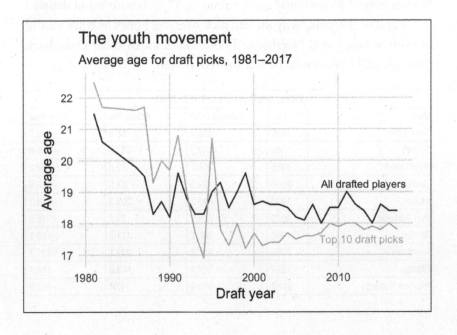

The youth movement

Average age for draft picks, 1981–2017

All drafted players

Top 10 draft picks

school players by a huge, huge, laughably huge margin.' Neesham also believed in this idea, even though it had little application in a system that was trending towards the identification and development of teenaged talent. 'The thing is, you don't know how good a player will be when they're 18,' he said. 'That's the stupidity of our whole system. In the United States, players can transfer through a second tier at college and get drafted at 22, but that doesn't happen here.' Nor is it likely to change. The average draft age has held firm at about 18-and-a-half since the year 2000. 'Unless the AFL increases the draft age, I can't imagine it rising naturally now at all,' said Caruso. 'We're always going to draft the kids coming out of high school the most.'

One aspect related to age that has changed significantly in the 21st century is the likelihood of an AFL draftee being born in a certain month. In recent years, books such as Malcolm Gladwell's *Outliers* and Steven Levitt and Stephen Dubner's *SuperFreakonomics* have highlighted how a disproportionate number of players in certain sporting competitions are born in the earlier months of the year. Known as the 'relative age effect', the bias is related to the cut-off dates used in junior sport. Gladwell pointed out that the cut-off for underage ice hockey in Canada was January 1, meaning that a player who turned 10 years old on January 1 could be playing against an opponent who didn't turn 10 until the end of the year. At that age, the players who were more physically developed were often identified as better athletes, and thus had a greater chance of being selected in representative teams. 'And what happens when a player gets chosen for a rep squad?' wrote Gladwell. 'He gets better coaching, and his teammates are better, and he plays fifty or seventy-five games a season instead of twenty games a season like those left behind in the "house" league, and he practises twice as much as, or even three times more than, he would have otherwise.' Gladwell found that in every level of elite Canadian ice hockey, 70% of players were born between January and June, and 30% between June and December.

A similar bias was visible in the AFL during the earlier years of the draft. Our data shows that from 1993 to 2003, recruiters tended to opt for more mature bodies. Players born between January and April made up 38% of the draft cohort, and 44% of the top 10 picks. In 2004, the draft age was lifted slightly, with only players

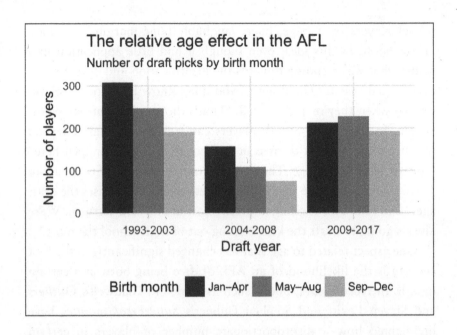

The relative age effect in the AFL

Number of draft picks by birth month

Number of players

Draft year

Birth month   Jan–Apr   May–Aug   Sep–Dec

who turned 17 by April 30 in the year of the draft eligible to be selected. The relative age effect remained evident for the next five years, with draftees being far more likely to have been born in the first four months of the year. It only seemed to vanish after 2009, when the eligibility rule was again changed so that players had to be 18 by December 31 in their draft year.

There are two plausible reasons for the effect's disappearance. The first is that the increase in draft age has diluted the physical advantages of the draftees born in the earlier months. The second is that the publication of the bestselling *Outliers* in late 2008 created a greater awareness of the bias among recruiters. Ironically, Caruso believes some clubs are now favouring players born towards the end of the calendar year. 'I know some prefer the kids born in the later months because they think they're younger and they've been up against it more,' he said. 'But really, you can never rule anyone out for something like their birthday.'

Not all drafts are equal

At least part of Geelong's success at the draft table was due to good timing. The Cats used a total of eight picks in the 2001 national draft, which has since unfailingly been referred to as the 'Superdraft'. It is easy to understand why it has earned that moniker when you scan its names and see Brownlow medallists like Ablett Jr, Bartel, Judd, Mitchell, and Swan, premiership captains such as Hodge, and All-Australians including Ball, Dal Santo, Johnson, Kelly, and Montagna. It was certainly a rare crop, but was it definitively the best? And will it remain so, compared to recent drafts?

There are several ways we can use Player Approximate Value to retrospectively measure a draft's strength. One is to take a simple summative approach, by looking at which drafts have produced the most output in raw terms. We need to be careful to qualify such comparisons, because some players taken in the 2001 draft are still playing in 2018. That means they are continuing to add to the draft's total PAV output. More recent drafts have even more players who are still active, but a quick scoreboard check won't hurt. The following table ranks the 1993 to 2006 drafts in order of how much PAV they had produced through to the end of 2017.

PAV by draft year				
Rank	Year	Total PAV output to 2017	Players	PAV Output per player
1	1999	5,307.1	87	61.0
2	2001	4,868.2	74	65.8
3	2000	4,510.8	73	61.8
4	2006	3,990.5	80	49.9
5	1997	3,740.4	83	45.1
6	1994	3,648.4	90	40.5
7	2005	3,345.0	66	50.7
8	1998	3,283.4	82	40.0
9	2002	3,241.9	69	47.0
10	1993	3,181.9	65	49.0
11	2004	3,047.6	71	42.9
12	1996	3,039.3	86	35.3
13	2003	3,016.9	70	43.1
14	1995	2,604.9	77	33.8

The 2001 draft ranked second to the 1999 edition, but players including Hodge and Ablett were still adding to its total output in 2018. It also had a smaller overall player pool. The average PAV per player taken in the 2001 draft was 65, which was the highest in

181

our sample. The three drafts immediately following 2001 were all relatively lean, but the 2006 version is already ranked fourth, with several of its players still in the prime of their careers.

Of course, there was a prior expectation that players such as Hodge and Ablett would prove to be successful. Hodge was taken at pick one, while Ablett was the son of one of the sport's all-time greats. Every draft has a top pick, and strong father–son candidates are not uncommon. But a draft also consists of dozens of other more garden-variety picks too. Clubs selecting in the third or fourth rounds won't expect to unearth superstars, but they will be hoping to find diligent role-players who can provide useful output. If a draft has few of these solid foot soldiers at later picks, it might be described as shallow regardless of its first-round quality.

So, was the 2001 draft 'super' all the way through? We can use our Draft Pick Value Chart to measure a draft's depth. Given we know what the average career looks like at each numbered selection, we can determine whether each pick met those expectations. The next table shows what percentage of each draft's live picks exceeded their expected career PAV. The results for the whole draft are listed on the left, and just the top 40 on the right.

PAV above expectation by draft year						
	Whole Draft			Top 40 Picks		
Year	Picks above expected PAV	Picks taken	% above expected PAV	Picks above expected PAV	Picks taken	% above expected PAV
1993	23	65	35%	15	40	38%
1994	30	90	33%	17	40	43%
1995	15	77	19%	9	40	23%
1996	25	86	29%	10	39	26%
1997	24	81	30%	15	39	38%
1998	24	78	31%	14	36	39%
1999	37	83	45%	22	37	59%
2000	36	71	51%	19	38	50%
2001	29	72	40%	19	39	49%
2002	18	64	28%	11	37	30%
2003	20	64	31%	8	36	22%
2004	20	66	30%	12	39	31%
2005	23	64	36%	15	38	39%
2006	28	78	36%	15	39	38%

On this measure, it is not the 2001 draft that comes out on top. Rather, it is the 2000 draft overall, and the 1999 edition within the first 40 picks. The 1999 draft produced fewer superstars than 2001, but at critical points it was deeper. For instance, it had more 150+ and 100+ PAV players, and 45% of its players exceeded their career expectations, compared to 2001's 40%. Following are the top 20 players from the 1999, 2000, and 2001 drafts, ranked on their career PAV to the end of 2017. It is left as an exercise for the reader to decide which crop is truly the 'Superdraft' of the turn of the millennium.

1999 Draft			
Pick	Player	Club	Career PAV
4	Matthew Pavlich	Fremantle	315.1
31	Paul Chapman	Geelong	223.0
8	Joel Corey	Geelong	211.9
47	Corey Enright	Geelong	211.8
56	Ryan O'Keefe	Sydney	196.4
13	Robert Murphy	Western Bulldogs	193.1
30 f–s*	Jonathan Brown	Brisbane	186.1
32	Daniel Giansiracusa	Western Bulldogs	173.8
19	Brad Green	Melbourne	169.6
2	Paul Hasleby	Fremantle	162.1
64	Cameron Bruce	Melbourne	161.5
1	Josh Fraser	Collingwood	155.4
38	Cameron Ling	Geelong	154.9
43	Lindsay Gilbee	Western Bulldogs	146.8
62	Ben Johnson	Collingwood	140.7
34	Leon Davis	Collingwood	139.4
10	Luke McPharlin	Hawthorn	134.5
28	Brent Guerra	Port Adelaide	134.3
40	David Hille	Essendon	128.6
18 f–s*	Rhyce Shaw	Collingwood	127.9

* f–s = father–son

2000 Draft

Pick	Player	Club	Career PAV
1	Nick Riewoldt	St Kilda	270.5
16	Scott Thompson	Melbourne	255.4
12	Shaun Burgoyne	Port Adelaide	245.1
23	Drew Petrie	North Melbourne	236.5
20	Kane Cornes	Port Adelaide	173.5
18	Daniel Kerr	West Coast	164.6
55	Chris Newman	Richmond	156.0
56	Daniel Cross	Western Bulldogs	148.0
67	Graham Johncock	Adelaide	143.4
27	Ted Richards	Essendon	137.3
3	Alan Didak	Collingwood	136.1
39	Adam McPhee	Fremantle	124.4
50	Domenic Cassisi	Port Adelaide	123.3
44	Josh Hunt	Geelong	119.1
2	Justin Koschitzke	St Kilda	113.3
13	Ashley McGrath	Brisbane	109.9
60	Corey Jones	North Melbourne	109.3
14	Daniel Harris	North Melbourne	98.6
10	Jordan McMahon	Western Bulldogs	87.6
8	Daniel Motlop	North Melbourne	81.2

2001 Draft

Pick	Player	Club	Career PAV
40 f–s	Gary Ablett Jr	Geelong	295.8
36	Sam Mitchell	Hawthorn	279.6
1	Luke Hodge	Hawthorn	269.5
3	Chris Judd	West Coast	263.1
13	Nick Dal Santo	St Kilda	262.7
8	Jimmy Bartel	Geelong	239.6
24	Steve Johnson	Geelong	239.5
37	Leigh Montagna	St Kilda	237.7
58	Dane Swan	Collingwood	222.2
17	James Kelly	Geelong	199.6
2	Luke Ball	St Kilda	169.7
46 f–s	Jarrad Waite	Carlton	149.9
60	Adam Schneider	Sydney	143.0
71	Brian Lake	Western Bulldogs	132.8
7	David Hale	North Melbourne	128.3
33	David Rodan	Richmond	117.2
19	Jason Gram	Brisbane	115.7
12	Brent Reilly	Adelaide	115.2
32	Campbell Brown	Hawthorn	113.0
56	Paul Medhurst	Fremantle	97.5

A lull in draft output took hold from 2002 to 2005. Although those drafts do have a few active players remaining, it is unlikely they will be able to significantly reduce the deficit in total PAV output in relation to the 1999 to 2001 cohorts. Some of the earlier drafts have valid excuses for their meagre returns. A lot of mid-1990s drafts were weakened by zone picks, concessions to new clubs Fremantle and Port Adelaide, and a variety of pre-draft compensation and pre-listing rules, including those for father–sons. The 1990s were a wild time.

If that is the past, what about the present? It would be misleading to analyse total outputs for drafts from 2007 onwards, because an increasing proportion of the players taken in those years are still writing their own football stories. However, we can compare how those drafts are tracking in relation to the trajectories of past editions. The following table shows the year-by-year average PAV recorded by the top 40 in each draft class between 1993 and 2016. The top row shows the age of the players in each corresponding column, starting with the fresh-faced 18-year-old draftees and ending with the grizzled 35-year-old veterans.

Average PAV for top-40 draft picks by age

Draft Year	18	19	20	21	22	23	24	25	26	27	28	29	30	31	32	33	34	35
1993	1.4	2.7	4.4	5.1	5.2	5.8	5.0	5.4	5.7	5.4	5.2	3.8	1.9	2.2	0.9	0.7	0.2	0.0
1994	1.6	3.2	5.4	5.2	5.1	7.6	7.1	5.8	5.4	5.0	4.6	4.4	3.5	1.4	0.6	0.0	0.0	0.0
1995	0.5	0.9	1.9	3.1	4.2	3.7	3.7	3.6	3.7	3.3	2.0	2.0	1.6	1.0	0.3	0.4	0.3	0.0
1996	0.5	1.5	2.9	3.2	4.5	5.0	5.2	3.7	4.2	3.5	2.3	2.2	1.9	0.9	0.2	0.0	0.0	0.0
1997	1.2	3.1	4.9	6.3	6.5	6.9	6.9	5.7	5.2	4.5	4.7	2.7	2.0	1.6	0.9	0.5	0.1	0.0
1998	0.2	1.4	4.1	5.7	6.7	7.0	6.9	6.1	5.4	5.3	3.9	3.3	2.3	0.9	1.0	0.6	0.4	0.0
1999	0.9	4.0	5.6	6.9	7.9	8.5	7.9	7.3	7.8	7.1	6.5	6.3	4.6	3.9	1.8	1.8	1.0	0.6
2000	0.8	2.5	5.0	7.1	6.9	6.9	7.3	6.8	6.2	4.5	3.1	3.8	3.4	2.5	2.2	1.5	1.2	1.0
2001	1.0	4.3	5.8	7.4	7.5	7.8	8.1	7.4	7.3	7.3	6.2	5.9	5.5	3.6	2.7	2.6	1.1	0.4
2002	0.8	1.6	2.6	4.3	3.7	6.4	5.3	5.2	5.1	4.6	5.0	4.2	3.3	2.2	1.9	0.5	0.0	0.0
2003	0.7	1.8	4.5	4.4	3.9	4.6	4.4	3.9	3.7	3.6	3.3	2.4	1.5	0.9	0.4	0.0	0.0	0.0
2004	1.1	2.8	5.1	5.8	6.4	6.9	6.4	6.1	5.0	4.9	4.4	3.3	2.9	0.9	0.0	0.0	0.0	0.0
2005	0.5	2.7	4.3	6.2	6.6	7.0	6.6	5.9	6.1	6.1	4.1	4.6	2.5	0.7	0.2	0.0	0.0	0.0
2006	0.4	1.9	3.9	5.7	7.5	7.6	7.4	7.7	6.5	6.4	6.8	4.1	0.1	0.0	0.0	0.0	0.0	0.0
2007	0.9	3.7	4.5	5.3	6.7	7.4	7.2	6.6	6.6	6.9	4.0	0.6	0.6	0.6	0.0	0.0	0.0	0.0
2008	0.4	3.7	6.8	8.7	9.6	8.9	9.3	9.9	8.5	5.5	0.3	0.3	0.1	0.0	0.0	0.0	0.0	0.0
2009	0.0	3.3	4.7	5.2	6.9	6.7	6.7	6.5	7.2	0.2	0.2	0.0	0.0	0.0	0.0	0.0	0.0	0.0
2010	0.0	3.3	5.8	6.0	8.4	7.4	6.9	6.3	0.8	0.8	0.4	0.4	0.0	0.0	0.0	0.0	0.0	0.0
2011	0.0	2.4	4.5	5.5	6.4	7.5	7.7	0.3	0.0	0.0	0.0	0.0	0.0	0.0	0.0	0.0	0.0	0.0
2012	0.0	2.4	4.0	5.1	4.7	5.9	0.0	0.1	0.2	0.3	0.0	0.0	0.0	0.0	0.0	0.0	0.0	0.0
2013	0.0	3.5	5.6	6.4	8.4	1.0	0.3	0.0	0.0	0.0	0.0	0.0	0.0	0.0	0.0	0.0	0.0	0.0
2014	0.0	2.3	4.5	5.0	0.7	0.1	0.1	0.0	0.0	0.0	0.0	0.0	0.0	0.0	0.0	0.0	0.0	0.0
2015	0.0	3.0	4.7	0.1	0.0	0.2	0.2	0.0	0.0	0.0	0.0	0.0	0.0	0.0	0.0	0.0	0.0	0.0
2016	0.0	2.8	0.1	0.0	0.0	0.0	0.0	0.0	0.0	0.0	0.0	0.0	0.0	0.0	0.0	0.0	0.0	0.0

Of the more recent editions, 2008 looks to be uniquely strong. Not only did it include some powerful first-round picks, such as Nic Naitanui and Jack Ziebell, it also had a smattering of later-round bargains, such as Dayne Beams (pick 29), Dan Hannebery (pick 30), and Rory Sloane (pick 44). The 2013 draft is also showing the potential to scale new heights, with players such as Josh Kelly, Marcus Bontempelli, Patrick Cripps, and Matt Crouch already establishing themselves as stars.

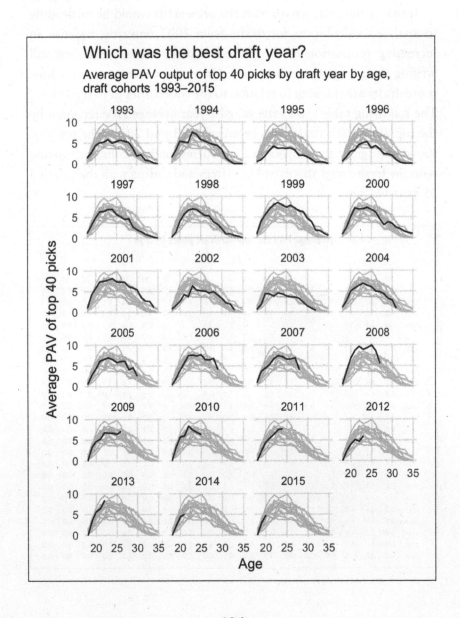

Which was the best draft year?

Average PAV output of top 40 picks by draft year by age, draft cohorts 1993–2015

We can see the downturn from 2002 to 2005 was partly characterised by the slower starts made by the draft classes of these years. These players took several seasons to start reaching the averages that the previous three intakes had achieved in their first two or three. This might simply have been because the players struggled to break into teams populated by the strong preceding drafts. The 2004 and 2005 drafts also appear to have suffered an early decline. Their players tailed off before the age of 30, whereas the best of the 1999 to 2001 group maintained a solid level of output. Although most of the 2004 draftees only turned 30 in 2017, just eight were still listed in 2018.

The rookie draft

The first AFL rookie draft was held in February 1997, three years after the size of each club's senior list had been reduced from 52 players to 42. The league decided to introduce supplementary rookie lists to provide greater recruitment opportunities for young players. The attraction of rookies to AFL clubs is that they are relatively low paid, don't count towards the salary cap, and don't take up room on the primary list. They are low-risk selections that can reap high rewards. Although the word 'rookie' suggests youth, it can be a misnomer in the AFL, as rookie-drafted players are often older than those taken in the main draft. Many players who have been overlooked as teenagers have subsequently found their way onto rookie lists after proving themselves in state-league football. Another function of the rookie draft has been to provide clubs with greater flexibility in their list management, such as through the delisting and redrafting of existing players. Fremantle was an innovator in this regard. The Dockers' Scott Gooch was the first player to be redrafted as a rookie in 1997. The common goal for rookies is to earn promotion to their club's primary list. It is a marginal existence in the AFL system, and until recently was poorly remunerated.

The rookie draft is held after the national draft, meaning the first rookie pick is essentially worth less than the last selection in the main draft. Our player-rating system places a rookie pick's expected value at zero. Thus, any rookie who plays a senior game has already outperformed expectation and is essentially a 'free hit' for recruiters. About 60% of rookie-drafted players never make it to the AFL. Nonetheless, some clubs have managed to obtain outstanding returns from the rookie draft. Since 1997, three clubs have seen more than 14% of their total PAV output generated by players who started on their rookie list.

Club	Percentage of PAV since 1997 obtained from rookie draft
Fremantle	16.5%
West Coast	14.9%
Melbourne	14.2%
Sydney	13.8%
Adelaide	12.4%
Carlton	12.3%
Collingwood	12.1%
Essendon	12.1%
North Melbourne	11.3%
Hawthorn	10.6%
Western Bulldogs	9.6%
St Kilda	7.8%
Richmond	7.8%
Brisbane	7.8%
Port Adelaide	6.5%
Geelong	5.7%
Gold Coast	5.5%
Greater Western Sydney	5.1%

The 2016 Grand Final illustrated the benefits of successful rookie drafting. An almost unprecedented share of the talent on the field that day had begun their AFL careers as rookies. During the 2016 season, Sydney obtained 32% of its total PAV from previous rookie selections, which was about the same as they received from players taken in trades or as free agents. The Western Bulldogs sourced 27% the same way, double what they received from their four father–son players, Lachie Hunter, Tom Liberatore, Mitch Wallis, and Zaine Cordy.

2016 PAV from rookie-drafted players			
Sydney	PAV	Western Bulldogs	PAV
Dane Rampe	21.2	Liam Picken	16.5
Kieren Jack	16.3	Matthew Boyd	14.7
Jake Lloyd	16.1	Luke Dahlhaus	13.0
Heath Grundy	13.3	Jason Johannisen	11.2
Nick Smith	12.2	Dale Morris	10.2
Tom Papley	8.5	Lin Jong	8.7
Harry Cunningham	6.3	Tom Campbell	5.5
Sam Naismith	6.1	Jack Redpath	4.7
Xavier Richards	4.5	Jed Adcock	2.5
Dan Robinson	2.6	Roarke Smith	0.4
Jordan Foote	0.1		
Rookie draft total	107.2	Rookie draft total	87.4
All sources	332.6	All sources	318.9

Sydney's 2016 rookie contribution was a league record, but the club set a new mark the following season with Nic Newman and Lewis Melican's elevation to regular senior football. The 2017 Swans gained over a third of their output – 111.6 PAV or 35% – from the rookie draft, which was much more than the 19% they received from traded-in players and free agents. The famous 'recyclers' had, for the moment, turned their focus to internal development.

Steals and busts

A major talking point each off-season is which clubs have landed the biggest steals of the draft. Despite the media's best efforts, however, this debate is impossible to settle until the players have been given sufficient time to show their wares at AFL level. Even looking back three or four years after the fact can be deceptive, because some players – particularly ruckmen and key forwards – are late bloomers. We have analysed every draft from 1993 to 2006, comparing the expected output of a given pick to what the chosen player generated during his career. Through this method, we have been able to establish each club's five best- and worst-value picks from those 14 drafts.

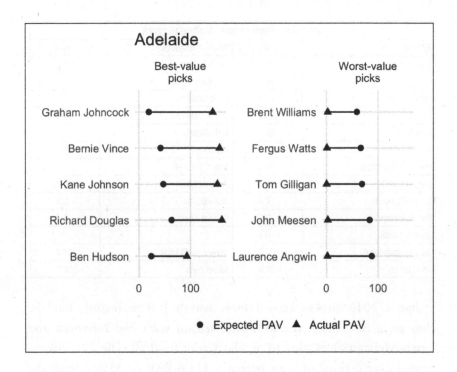

Adelaide

Best-value picks

Graham Johncock	
Bernie Vince	
Kane Johnson	
Richard Douglas	
Ben Hudson	

Worst-value picks

Brent Williams	
Fergus Watts	
Tom Gilligan	
John Meesen	
Laurence Angwin	

0   100   0   100

● Expected PAV   ▲ Actual PAV

Like Byron Pickett, Graham Johncock was a tough Indigenous player who played his junior football with Mallee Park in Port Lincoln. Like Pickett, Johncock was taken at pick 67 in the draft, and subsequently outperformed all expectations. Four of the Crows' other top-five best picks from the 1993 to 2006 drafts – Kane Johnson (pick 27, 1995), Bernie Vince (pick 32, 2005), and Ben Hudson (pick 58, 2003) – were all later traded to other clubs. That trend would continue later with Patrick Dangerfield (pick 10, 2007). Adelaide had a poor return from many of its top selections in the early 2000s, with Laurence Angwin (pick seven, 2000), Fergus Watts (pick 14, 2003), and John Meesen (pick eight, 2004) among the worst examples. All three ended up at second clubs, but they combined for just 16 career games between them.

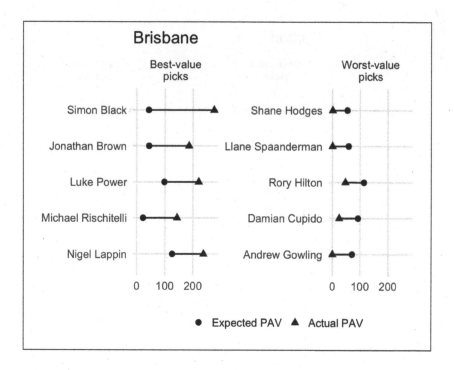

Brisbane

Best-value picks		Worst-value picks

Simon Black

Jonathan Brown

Luke Power

Michael Rischitelli

Nigel Lappin

Shane Hodges

Llane Spaanderman

Rory Hilton

Damian Cupido

Andrew Gowling

● Expected PAV   ▲ Actual PAV

Simon Black (pick 31, 1997), Jonathan Brown (pick 30 f–s, 1999), Luke Power (pick 5, 1997), and Nigel Lappin (pick 2, 1993) were all three-time premiership players for Brisbane. Power and Lappin more than justified their top-five status, while Brown's decision to commit himself to the Lions under the father–son rule paid great dividends for both parties. Black's late second-round selection was one of the great heists. He delivered a remarkable 233.2 PAV above his pick value of 42.7. Andrew Gowling failed to play a single game for Brisbane after joining the club at pick 12 in the notoriously weak 1995 draft, although Daniel Bradshaw's selection at pick 56 that same year helped mitigate the mistake.

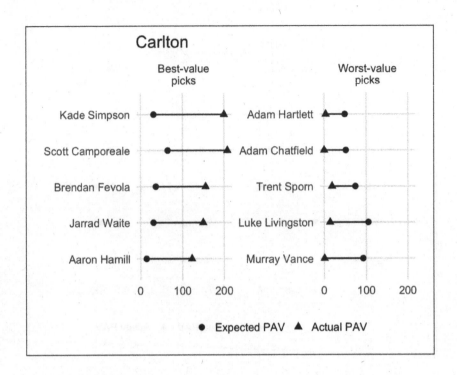

Carlton

Best-value picks

Kade Simpson	
Scott Camporeale	
Brendan Fevola	
Jarrad Waite	
Aaron Hamill	

0 100 200

Worst-value picks

Adam Hartlett	
Adam Chatfield	
Trent Sporn	
Luke Livingston	
Murray Vance	

0 100 200

● Expected PAV   ▲ Actual PAV

Of the 13 players that Carlton took from the 1995, 1996, and 1997 drafts, only Anthony Franchina (pick 81, 1996) played more than 100 matches for club. The rest combined for just 84 games. This left Carlton with a significant talent deficit, which was compounded by the penalties for salary cap breaches handed down by the AFL in 2002. It proved to be a significant factor in the club's struggles during the early part of the new millennium. Scott Camporeale (pick 15, 1994) and Brendan Fevola (pick 38, 1998) were rare early successes, while Kade Simpson (pick 45, 2002) provided the Blues with their greatest return on investment.

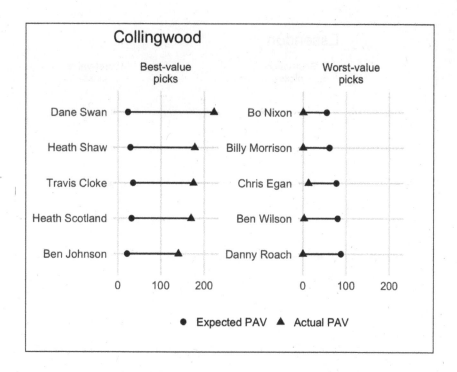

Collingwood

Best-value picks

| Dane Swan | Heath Shaw | Travis Cloke | Heath Scotland | Ben Johnson |

Worst-value picks

| Bo Nixon | Billy Morrison | Chris Egan | Ben Wilson | Danny Roach |

● Expected PAV ▲ Actual PAV

Father–son selections stand out as having delivered solid value for Collingwood. Four of the Magpies' 14 most valuable selections in our sample joined the club through their family ties. Scott Pendlebury (pick five, 2005) sat just outside the top five at the end of 2017, but is likely to work his way higher on the value list despite the high expected PAV associated with his lofty draft position. Pendlebury, Dane Swan (pick 58, 2001), Heath Shaw (pick 48 f–s, 2003), Travis Cloke (pick 39 f–s, 2004), and Ben Johnson (pick 62, 1999) all featured in the club's 2010 premiership side. Utility Danny Roach played just one game for the Magpies after being taken with pick seven in the strong 1999 draft, one selection before Geelong's Joel Corey. Roach had one tackle and no disposals in his sole appearance.

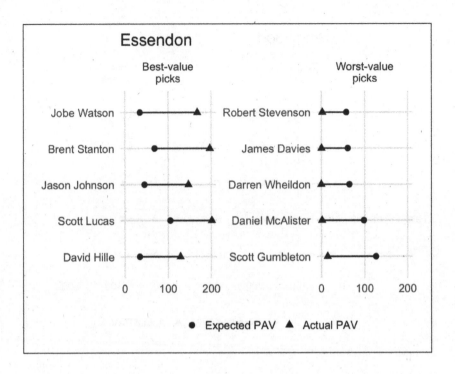

Essendon

Best-value picks | Worst-value picks

Best-value picks		Worst-value picks
Jobe Watson		Robert Stevenson
Brent Stanton		James Davies
Jason Johnson		Darren Wheildon
Scott Lucas		Daniel McAlister
David Hille		Scott Gumbleton

● Expected PAV ▲ Actual PAV

Although sometimes maligned by Essendon fans, Brent Stanton (pick 13, 2003) delivered the club a bang for its drafting buck that was only surpassed by father–son Jobe Watson (pick 40 f–s, 2002). Scott Lucas (pick 4, 1994) and Jason Johnson (pick 28, 1996) were both key cogs in Essendon's fabled team of 2000. Lucas managed to deliver almost 100 PAV above expectation. Injuries denied forward Scott Gumbleton the chance to reach his full potential. The 2006 number two pick managed just 35 games in seven seasons with the Bombers, before being traded to Fremantle at the end of 2013.

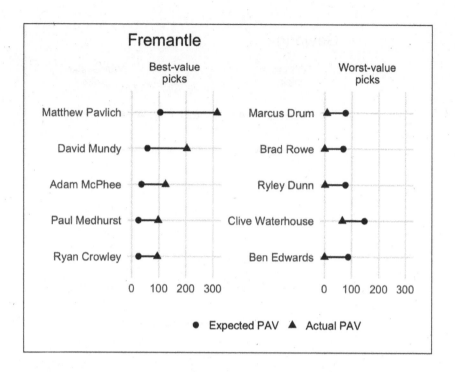

Fremantle

Best-value picks

Matthew Pavlich	
David Mundy	
Adam McPhee	
Paul Medhurst	
Ryan Crowley	

0 100 200 300

Worst-value picks

Marcus Drum	
Brad Rowe	
Ryley Dunn	
Clive Waterhouse	
Ben Edwards	

0 100 200 300

● Expected PAV ▲ Actual PAV

Fremantle's five most valuable picks prior to 2007 joined the club over five consecutive drafts. They represent both shrewd high-end selections, such as Matthew Pavlich (pick four, 1999), and later-round steals like Ryan Crowley (pick 55, 2002). This half-decade period absolved some of the draft crimes committed by the club during its foundation years. Three of the Dockers' four worst-value picks came from their calamitous 1995 draft, which we examined earlier. More recently the Dockers have shown a keen eye for a bargain, with Nat Fyfe (pick 20, 2009), Michael Walters (pick 53, 2008), and Lachie Neale (pick 58, 2011) all greatly outperforming expectations.

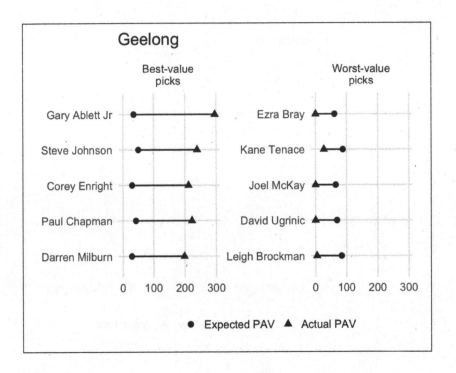

Geelong

Best-value picks

Gary Ablett Jr	●————▲
Steve Johnson	●———▲
Corey Enright	●——▲
Paul Chapman	●———▲
Darren Milburn	●—▲

0   100   200   300

Worst-value picks

Ezra Bray	▲—●
Kane Tenace	▲—●
Joel McKay	▲—●
David Ugrinic	▲—●
Leigh Brockman	▲—●

0   100   200   300

● Expected PAV   ▲ Actual PAV

No club was better than Geelong at nailing its top-10 picks between 1993 and 2006, with four of its six selections (Joel Corey, Jimmy Bartel, Andrew Mackie, and Joel Selwood) outperforming their expected PAV by more than 150%. Geelong made hay during the strong drafts of 1999 and 2001, but also plucked a diamond from the detritus of the 1995 edition. Defender Darren Milburn was selected at pick 48, with only the man taken immediately before him, Brent Harvey, finishing with more than his 292 career games. He was a rare success during a lean period for the Cats in the mid-1990s, which featured failures such as Leigh Brockman (pick 8, 1996), David Ugrinic (pick 13, 1993), and Joel McKay (pick 15, 1997). In fact, Geelong's drafting record was generally poor until the stellar 1998 to 2002 period that set up their three premierships.

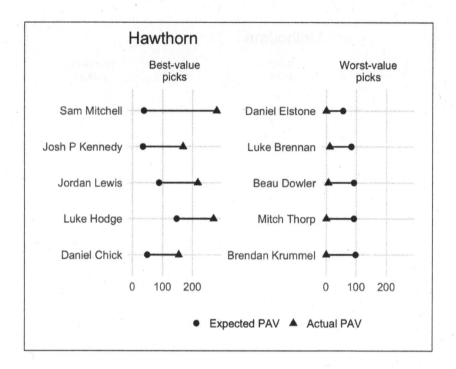

Like they do for Brisbane and Geelong, premiership players dominate Hawthorn's best-value list, although Josh Kennedy and Daniel Chick earned that title at other clubs. Another player no longer in the brown-and-gold, Lance Franklin, sits just on the cusp. Franklin (pick five, 2004), Luke Hodge (pick one, 2001), and Jordan Lewis (pick seven, 2004) were all worthy first-round draftees, but the Hawks did not always capitalise with their early selections. Mitch Thorp (pick six, 2006), Beau Dowler (pick six, 2005), and Luke Brennan (pick eight, 2002) were among their high-profile busts.

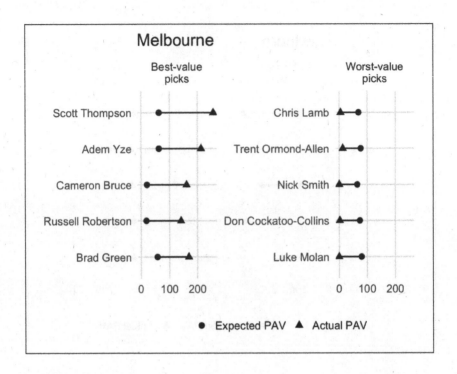

Melbourne

Best-value picks | Worst-value picks

Best-value picks		Worst-value picks
Scott Thompson		Chris Lamb
Adem Yze		Trent Ormond-Allen
Cameron Bruce		Nick Smith
Russell Robertson		Don Cockatoo-Collins
Brad Green		Luke Molan

0   100   200   0   100   200

● Expected PAV   ▲ Actual PAV

It is perhaps emblematic of Melbourne's years of woe that its greatest draft success ended up spending most of his career at another club. The Demons took Scott Thompson with pick 16 in 2000, but he played just 39 games for them before being traded to the Adelaide Crows, where he won two best-and-fairest awards and earned All-Australian selection. An earlier pick 16, Adem Yze (1994), gave the club longer service, and according to PAV was one of the most underrated players of his era. Of the Demons' misses, Luke Molan stands out as a particularly egregious example. He was surprisingly taken at pick nine in the 2001 'Superdraft', but failed to make a senior appearance for the Demons. The only other player in that year's top 10 who didn't reach 100 games was Ashley Sampi, who played 78 for West Coast.

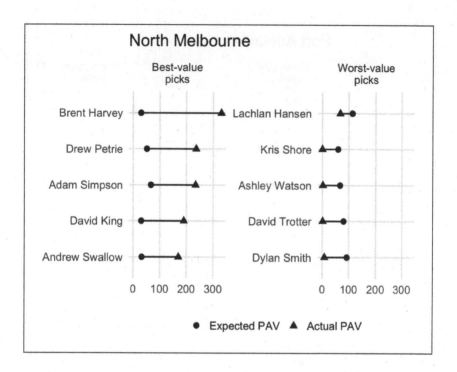

North Melbourne

Best-value picks | Worst-value picks

Best-value picks		Worst-value picks
Brent Harvey		Lachlan Hansen
Drew Petrie		Kris Shore
Adam Simpson		Ashley Watson
David King		David Trotter
Andrew Swallow		Dylan Smith

0 100 200 300   0 100 200 300

● Expected PAV   ▲ Actual PAV

In his final year of junior football, Brent Harvey made the Vic Metro under-18 squad, starred for the Northern Knights in their premiership-winning season, and was named best on ground in the TAC Cup Grand Final. Yet, despite his outstanding résumé, six of his Knights teammates were selected ahead of him. The Kangaroos didn't call Harvey's name until pick 47, with other clubs seemingly put off by his lack of height. He went on to become the greatest draft steal in AFL history, with his near-record career PAV total of 330.4 outperforming expectation by more than 300. Drew Petrie (pick 23, 2000), Adam Simpson (pick 14, 1993), and David King (pick 46, 1993) were also notable for their outstanding longevity. However, when other clubs were cashing in between 1999 and 2003, the Kangaroos missed with several of their high selections, including Dylan Smith (pick 6, 2000) and David Trotter (pick 9, 2003).

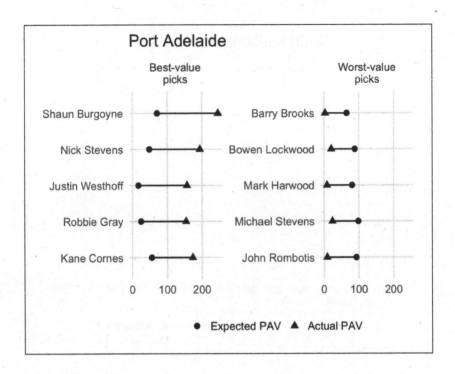

Port Adelaide

Best-value picks		Worst-value picks	
Shaun Burgoyne		Barry Brooks	
Nick Stevens		Bowen Lockwood	
Justin Westhoff		Mark Harwood	
Robbie Gray		Michael Stevens	
Kane Cornes		John Rombotis	

● Expected PAV ▲ Actual PAV

Port Adelaide's history at the draft has been highlighted by two outstanding hauls, six years apart. The Power's class of 2000 featured premiership players Shaun Burgoyne (pick 12), Kane Cornes (pick 20), and Domenic Cassisi (pick 50), who were critical to the club's successes between 2003 and 2007. Its 2006 draft class included Travis Boak (pick five), Robbie Gray (pick 55), and Justin Westhoff (pick 71), who were still core players at Alberton more than a decade later. These rich bounties were in stark contrast to the Power's inaugural national draft intake in 1996, where it struck out three times in the top 10 with John Rombotis (pick six), Bowen Lockwood (pick seven), and Mark Harwood (pick nine).

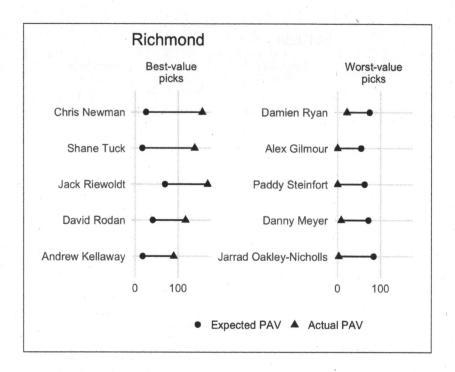

Richmond

Best-value picks
- Chris Newman
- Shane Tuck
- Jack Riewoldt
- David Rodan
- Andrew Kellaway

Worst-value picks
- Damien Ryan
- Alex Gilmour
- Paddy Steinfort
- Danny Meyer
- Jarrad Oakley-Nicholls

● Expected PAV ▲ Actual PAV

Richmond has proven adept at finding value in the draft's later rounds, with Chris Newman (pick 55, 2000), Andrew Kellaway (pick 71, 1997), and Shane Tuck (pick 73, 2003) among their many bargain buys. Premiership forward Jack Riewoldt somehow fell into the Tigers' lap at 13 in 2006. The year before, the club took Jarrad Oakley-Nicholls at pick eight. Oakley-Nicholls spent four seasons on Richmond's list for just 13 games. Shaun Higgins, Nathan Jones, Shannon Hurn, Grant Birchall, and Richard Douglas had been among the players selected with the eight picks after him.

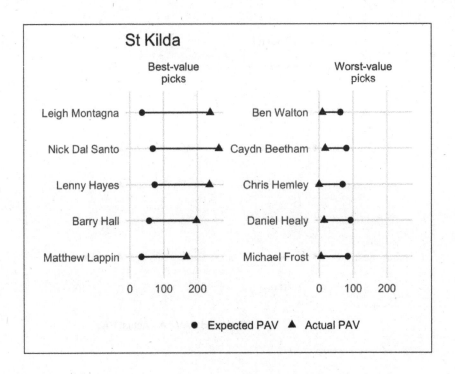

St Kilda

Best-value picks — Worst-value picks

Best-value picks	Worst-value picks
Leigh Montagna	Ben Walton
Nick Dal Santo	Caydn Beetham
Lenny Hayes	Chris Hemley
Barry Hall	Daniel Healy
Matthew Lappin	Michael Frost

● Expected PAV ▲ Actual PAV

St Kilda was one of the most successful clubs at the draft table during our 14-year sample period, even though it failed to win a flag. Nick Dal Santo (pick 13, 2001), Leigh Montagna (pick 37, 2001), and Lenny Hayes (pick 11, 1998) were all great servants of the club during their prime; however, both Barry Hall (pick 19, 1995) and Matthew Lappin (pick 40, 1993) enjoyed greater success elsewhere. The Saints' five biggest blunders were all relatively early picks from the 1990s. Michael Frost (pick eight, 1993) and Daniel Healy (pick six, 1995) enjoyed excellent state-league careers, but were unable to make their mark at the top level.

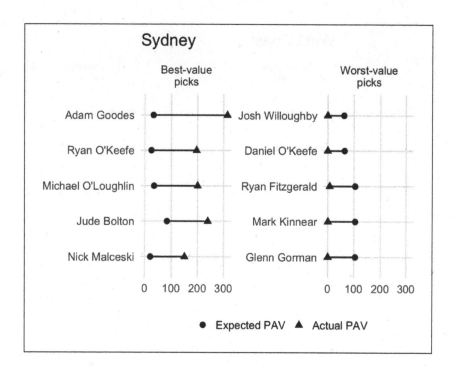

Sydney

Best-value picks | Worst-value picks

Adam Goodes — Josh Willoughby
Ryan O'Keefe — Daniel O'Keefe
Michael O'Loughlin — Ryan Fitzgerald
Jude Bolton — Mark Kinnear
Nick Malceski — Glenn Gorman

0 100 200 300   0 100 200 300

● Expected PAV   ▲ Actual PAV

The third and fourth rounds of the draft proved a happy hunting ground for the Sydney Swans during the 1990s. Adam Goodes (pick 43, 1997), Ryan O'Keefe (pick 56, 1999), and Michael O'Loughlin (pick 40, 1994) played a huge role in the club's rise to the top in the mid-2000s. At the same time, however, the Swans whiffed on pick four three times in six years. Glenn Gorman (pick four, 1993), Mark Kinnear (pick four, 1996), and now–radio announcer Ryan Fitzgerald (pick four, 1998) played a combined 16 games in the red-and-white, leaving the club with a combined PAV deficit of -305.8. Sydney has also largely struggled at the national draft since 2003, instead relying on its acumen with rookies and re-treads.

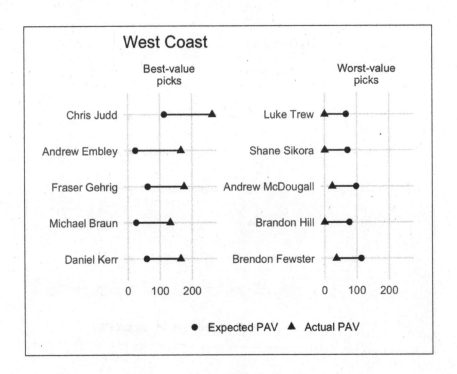

West Coast

Best-value picks / Worst-value picks

Best-value picks		Worst-value picks
Chris Judd		Luke Trew
Andrew Embley		Shane Sikora
Fraser Gehrig		Andrew McDougall
Michael Braun		Brandon Hill
Daniel Kerr		Brendon Fewster

● Expected PAV ▲ Actual PAV

Such was the quality of Chris Judd's career that he rates as West Coast's best-value pick even though he was taken at the pointy end of the 2001 'Superdraft'. His 263.1 total PAV was almost 150 more than the typical pick three's production. Judd helped the Eagles win a flag in 2007, but ended up playing 145 of his 279 games at Carlton. Likewise, Fraser Gehrig (pick 16, 1993) spent most of his career at St Kilda. Brendon Fewster (pick three, 1995), Brandon Hill (pick 10, 1998), and Andrew McDougall (pick five, 2000) were among the Eagles' most costly misses. Fewster and McDougall were later traded without cause for additional regret. Unlike many other clubs, West Coast found good value in some of the weaker drafts of the mid-2000s.

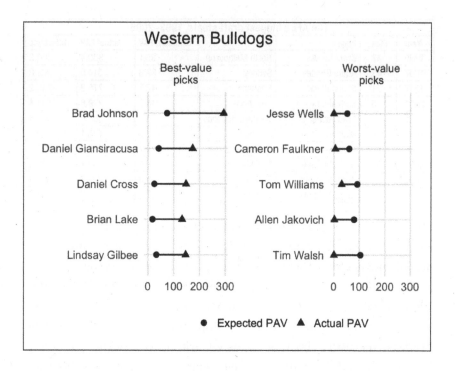

Western Bulldogs

Best-value picks	Worst-value picks
Brad Johnson	Jesse Wells
Daniel Giansiracusa	Cameron Faulkner
Daniel Cross	Tom Williams
Brian Lake	Allen Jakovich
Lindsay Gilbee	Tim Walsh

● Expected PAV ▲ Actual PAV

The Bulldogs' stellar 1999 draft class accounted for half of their eight biggest bargains. By also stealing Daniel Cross (pick 56, 2000) and Brian Lake (pick 71, 2001) over the following two years, the club assembled a core that would serve it well for the next decade. Allen Jakovich's selection at pick nine in 1995, however, remains baffling more than two decades on. The enigmatic full-forward was a 27-year-old at the time, and had just spent a year out of the game because of a chronic back injury. Perhaps unsurprisingly, he managed just seven games before his comeback was unceremoniously aborted.

The Dogs' best drafting decision was to take Brad Johnson with the 11th pick in the 1993 draft. The 'Smiling Assassin' played 364 games, earned six All-Australian selections, and won three club champion awards. His 293.5 career PAV was 219.4 above his pick value, placing him fifth on our list of the AFL's biggest steals between 1993 and 2006.

The AFL's biggest draft steals, 1993–2006						
Year	Pick	Player	Club	Expected PAV	Actual PAV	Difference
1995	47	Brent Harvey	North Melbourne	30.1	330.4	300.3
1997	43	Adam Goodes	Sydney	32.8	314.6	281.8
1997	31	Simon Black	Brisbane	42.7	275.9	233.2
2001	36	Sam Mitchell	Hawthorn	38.2	279.6	241.4
1993	11	Brad Johnson	Western Bulldogs	74.1	293.5	219.4
1999	4	Matthew Pavlich	Fremantle	104.9	315.1	210.2
2001	58	Dane Swan	Collingwood	23.7	222.2	198.5
2001	13	Nick Dal Santo	St Kilda	69.1	262.7	193.6
2001	37	Leigh Montagna	St Kilda	37.3	237.7	200.4
1999	47	Corey Enright	Geelong	30.1	211.8	181.7

Overall, Geelong's drafting performance stands far above that of its rivals during our sample period. In second place is Hawthorn. It is no coincidence that these two clubs have also enjoyed the most on-field success during the current century. Five of the top six drafting sides – Geelong, Hawthorn, North Melbourne, Sydney, and Brisbane – have won a combined 14 premierships since 1995. In contrast, the five least successful drafting teams – Carlton, Melbourne, Essendon, Richmond, and Fremantle – have won only three flags between them during the same period. 'I think it's definitely connected,' said Caruso. 'The clubs that have really nailed their drafting are the ones who have had success, and the clubs which have struggled are the ones that have been unable to bring in the best players.'

Return from drafting, 1993–2006			
Club	Expected PAV	Actual PAV	PAV Above Expectation
Geelong	2,838.5	4,222.9	1,384.4
Hawthorn	3,425.8	4,060.4	634.6
St Kilda	3,161.4	3,768.0	606.5
Brisbane	2,854.1	3,401.3	547.2
Port Adelaide	2,291.9	2,771.2	479.3
Sydney	3,266.7	3,687.1	420.4
North Melbourne	2,882.0	3,207.8	325.8
Western Bulldogs	2,949.3	3,237.7	288.4
Collingwood	3,223.5	3,448.9	225.4
Melbourne	2,674.1	2,713.9	39.8
Adelaide	2,210.8	2,154.5	−56.3
West Coast	2,973.1	2,913.1	−60.0
Carlton	2,539.6	2,425.3	−114.3
Richmond	2,819.2	2,674.8	−144.4
Fremantle	2,626.9	2,449.5	−177.4
Essendon	3,385.3	3,056.0	−329.3
Fitzroy	1,134.3	634.1	−500.2

Chapter Nine

Trading

On the block

An alternative approach to team building is acquiring players through the trade period. Trading has become vital in supplementing existing talent, or in hastening a rebuilding project. When the league started developing a formalised trade framework in 1988, initially only pick-for-player deals were allowed. The first such trade set a cracking pace, involving as it did the number one pick of the 1988 draft. St Kilda handed over the prized currency to Hawthorn in return for wingman Robert Handley, ruckman Paul Harding, and ruck-rover Peter Russo. The Hawks used the pick to select midfielder Alex McDonald. We can use PAV to judge which club 'won' the trade by adding up the total career value each player accrued in the wake of the deal.

Hawthorn		St Kilda	
In	PAV	In	PAV
Pick 1 (Alex McDonald)	61.4	Robert Handley	1.1
		Paul Harding	81.1
		Peter Russo	22.9
Total	61.4	Total	105.1
Difference	−43.7	Difference	+43.7

In this case, Harding's 62 games for St Kilda ended up being the most valuable commodity that either side gained from the trade. He was later on-traded to West Coast for pick 12 in 1991, and played in its premiership side the following year. Handley could only manage four senior appearances for the Saints, while Russo made 33. McDonald, who was a scrawny 69 kilograms when he joined the Hawks, struggled to cement a place in their powerful side. He played 46 matches in the brown-and-gold before being traded, along with Scott Crow, to Collingwood in exchange for the 54th selection in the 1995 national draft. He played a further 61 games for the Magpies before retiring because of a hip injury at the end of 1999.

The first pick changed hands two more times in the draft's early years. In 1990, Brisbane sent the first call to Geelong in return for forwards Shane Hamilton and David Cameron. Again, it was the club trading out the prime selection that got the better of the deal. The Cats' choice at number one, Stephen Hooper, played just 21 games before returning to his native Western Australia. He is perhaps best remembered now for seriously injuring West Perth's Basil Zempilas in a WAFL ruck contest, for which he was handed a four-match ban. While neither Hamilton (47 games) nor Cameron (15 games) made much of an impression at the Bears, their combined PAV of 38.2 outstripped Hooper's 9.4. The Sydney Swans and West Coast Eagles struck a similar deal two years later, but this time the draft choice returned considerably more value. The Swans gave up pick one in exchange for West Coast's Scott Watters and Tony Begovich, who combined for a further 68 career games and 48.9 PAV. The Eagles laughed all the way to the bank, taking local boy Drew Banfield with the initial selection in the 1992 draft. He earned 158.9 PAV in 265 games for the club, exceeding his expectations as a number one pick by 11.9 PAV.

With that cautionary tale in mind, it would be almost a decade before a club would again pluck up the courage to trade out the first draft choice. It was 2001, and the ramifications of Fremantle's disastrous early drafting were being fully felt. The club finished bottom that year with just two wins, after coach Damian Drum had been sacked following a round-nine loss to Sydney. The poor season at least had a silver lining, with the AFL handing the club a priority pick because of its poor performance. That meant it held a strong hand for the impending Superdraft, which included picks one, four, 20, and 36. Yet the Dockers were nervous. They were worried that if they took one of the draft's three highly touted young Victorians – Luke Hodge, Luke Ball, or Chris Judd – the player would either return home at the first chance or never move west to begin with.

The situation really was that dire. 'We'd had Jeff White, who'd been drafted at pick one and gone back, and we were also really concerned that we were going to lose Matthew Pavlich,' said Cameron Schwab, who had just become Fremantle's chief executive.

With doubts over Hodge's, Ball's, and Judd's willingness to commit to the club's long-term future, and anxiety rising over Pavlich's position, the Dockers identified a key position prospect called Graham Polak as their best bet at pick one. He was a similar size to Pavlich and was a local boy from East Fremantle, nullifying the go-home factor. The thing was, though, they knew Polak was a near certainty to still be available at their second call at pick four. As a result, the Dockers began to field interest from rival clubs interested in dealing for pick one. Schwab soon found a willing trade partner in his cousin, Hawthorn coach Peter Schwab. 'Our recruiting manager, John Turnbull, said that we had to get in early in the draft because there were some outstanding players,' said Peter Schwab. 'In the end you look at your list and you look at who's expendable and who will get you the pick. Trent Croad was that player.' It was a bold decision. The 21-year-old was already a fan favourite at the Hawks, just four years after they had taken him with pick three in the 1997 draft. In a blockbuster trade, Croad and fellow key defender Luke McPharlin were sent to the Dockers in return for picks one, 20, and 36.

To Fremantle, the deal seemed logical. 'We worked out that we were going to get the player that we would have otherwise drafted first at number four, so effectively we felt we were giving up our pick four for Croad and McPharlin,' explained Cameron Schwab. 'Pavlich had a year left on his contract but had effectively indicated he wanted to go home, so if you're going to lose the only quality tall player on your list, and you have the chance to bring in Croad, McPharlin, and Polak, that seemed like a good deal.' Sadly, for the Dockers, it wasn't.

Hawthorn spent the first pick of the Superdraft wisely, choosing Hodge over Ball and Judd. According to PAV, Hodge had the most productive career of the three. His 269.5 PAV to the end of 2017 was surpassed by that of only two of his other fellow 2001 draftees: Gary Ablett Jr (295.8), who was unavailable to Hawthorn as a Geelong father–son; and Sam Mitchell (279.6), who the Hawks took with the late second-round pick they also had obtained from the Dockers. The table below shows the total PAV each player earned for the rest of their careers after the transaction, with only Hodge still adding to his tally in 2018. The figures look even worse for Fremantle if we factor in a subsequent deal that sent the homesick Croad back to Hawthorn for pick 10 in the 2003 draft. With that pick, the Dockers selected eight-gamer Ryley Dunn. Of the 79 PAV that Croad earned after the initial 2001 trade, 52 came only when he had returned to the Hawks. If we consider both trades together, we find that Hawthorn gleaned 575 PAV overall and Fremantle just 160.

Hawthorn		Fremantle	
In	PAV	In	PAV
Pick 1 (Luke Hodge)	269.5	Trent Croad	79.0
Pick 20 (Daniel Elstone)	0.0	Luke McPharlin	131.9
Pick 36 (Sam Mitchell)	279.6		
Total	549.1	Total	210.9
Difference	+338.2	Difference	−338.2

For his part, Cameron Schwab argues that such evaluations can be misleading. 'People always talk about how the Hawks took Sam Mitchell with pick 36 and all that, but the fact is that every club had the chance to draft him before then,' he said. 'In fact, I think he'd gone through the whole 2000 draft without being picked up.' It is a fair point. Drafting is an imprecise science, and clubs that acquire picks through trades need to use them judiciously for the deals to be worthwhile. Of the trades that have been made since 1988, 93% have involved a draft pick, either as a deal's central component or as a makeweight. If a club consistently drafts above expectations with the picks it trades in, it will generate more value than might be apparent at the time the deals are struck.

The table opposite shows the net value that clubs either gained or lost via trades between 1993 and 2009. We have used a slightly broader sample period than for our earlier draft analysis because of the smaller number of selections involved. The 'Expected PAV' column includes the predicted value of the picks traded in or out by a club, based on the average output of those draft selections. The 'Actual PAV' column shows the value realised by the players chosen with those picks. For trades that involved established players, we have included the total PAV the player accrued in the wake of the deal in both columns. During our research, we discovered that the historical record of early trades is surprisingly patchy. Even the AFL itself is not in possession of a full list of the precise number and nature of every exchange. We have primarily relied on the resource compiled by the excellent Draftguru website (draftguru.com.au), and have cross-checked its data against contemporary newspaper reports, as well as the trade summaries printed in the annual AFL guide books.

Return from trades, 1993–2009			
Club	Expected PAV	Actual PAV	PAV above expectation
Hawthorn	−33.9	569.0	602.9
St Kilda	247.0	804.5	557.5
Geelong	473.3	848.4	375.1
Essendon	408.8	688.8	280.0
West Coast	317.8	586.9	269.1
Port Adelaide	66.6	261.3	194.7
Carlton	−231.6	−145.3	86.3
Brisbane	−372	−312.2	59.8
Fitzroy	−95.4	−108.9	−13.5
Richmond	53.1	19.0	−34.1
North Melbourne	40.7	−89.1	−129.8
Western Bulldogs	131.1	−8.7	−139.8
Collingwood	26.3	−282.8	−309.1
Sydney	239.3	−105.9	−345.2
Melbourne	−377.7	−810.6	−432.9
Fremantle	−1,281.3	−1,750.9	−469.6
Adelaide	387.9	−163.3	−551.2

The clubs in the table with a high expected PAV were the ones that struck the best deals on paper, whereas those with a large actual PAV were the ones that received a tangible benefit from their trades. Some, such as Geelong, St Kilda, Essendon, and West Coast, achieved both. Others, such as Fremantle, Melbourne, and Carlton, accomplished neither. Hawthorn finished with a much higher actual PAV than what was expected of the picks it traded, which underlines the strength of its drafting. At the other end of the table, Adelaide failed to capitalise on a theoretically sound performance at the trade table, to record a substantially lower-than-expected overall PAV.

While much of Hawthorn's 'PAV Above Expectation' can be attributed to trading out Croad in 2001 and taking him back in 2003, Adelaide's poor result was largely due to an unfortunate deal in the intervening year. Curiously, it was not completely unconnected with the Croad trade. When Pavlich had expressed interest in returning to his hometown, the Crows had appeared to be his natural destination. Adelaide had a strong midfield core that included Andrew McLeod, Mark Ricciuto, Simon Goodwin, and Tyson Edwards, but had been lacking an attacking focal point since Tony Modra's departure three years early. After initially showing interest in the young Docker, the Crows had their heads turned by the unexpected availability of superstar forward Wayne Carey. The North Melbourne captain sensationally quit the Kangaroos in March 2002 when it emerged he was having an affair with Kelli Stevens, the wife of his vice-captain and close friend Anthony Stevens. Four months later, the Crows' football manager, John Reid, wrote to Pavlich to tell him that while they were still keen to recruit him, the situation had been complicated by their pursuit of Carey. 'I appreciated their honesty, but it rubbed me the wrong way,' Pavlich wrote in his autobiography. 'After all that Carey had achieved in the game it was obvious why the Crows wanted him, but I kept thinking, Are you sure you'd rather a 31-year-old legend but a potential distraction?'

Although in hindsight it is probably a question the Crows wish they had considered more closely, at the time they were far from the only ones willing to take a chance on the veteran. Given that few clubs had ruled themselves out of the bidding for the still-contracted Carey, Adelaide entered its negotiations with North Melbourne at a significant disadvantage. The Kangaroos had publicly declared they would accept no less than a first-round draft pick for their fallen star, but they ended up getting even more. When it went through, the Carey trade was reported as being a 'complicated three-club deal'. In fact, it was two discrete trades made on consecutive days. 'North wanted a top-10 pick and we didn't have one,' remembered Reid. 'We had Kane Johnson, who was keen to go back to Melbourne, so we traded him to Richmond.' That exchange saw the Crows send Johnson and their top three draft picks at 14, 30 and 45 to the Tigers, in return for defender Jason Torney and picks four, 20 and 36. 'We did that deal the night before and North said, "Yeah, that's okay, see you in the morning",' said Reid. 'But then the next morning they turned up and said they wanted both first-round draft picks, so we gave them number 20 as well.' The deals were reported as being a 'win-win-win' situation for the three clubs, although within weeks their entire complexion had changed.

On the eve of the 2002 draft, the AFL Commission stripped Carlton of picks 1, 2, 31, and 34 after finding it guilty of deliberate salary cap cheating. As a result, the fourth and 20th picks that Adelaide had traded to North for Carey became the draft's second and 18th selections. The Tigers, from whom the picks originated, were not happy. 'Had we known we'd have the number two rather than the number four pick in the draft, we would not have given up our second-round draft choice,' said Richmond's football director, Greg Miller. The Crows might have made the same complaint. The draft reshuffle meant that instead of giving up an expected 160.9 PAV for Carey – still an extraordinary price for an injury-plagued forward on the wrong side of 30 – they were now giving up a predicted 185.1. Yet the die had been cast. The Kangaroos used their newly elevated selection to swoop on the smooth-moving Western Australian midfielder Daniel Wells.

Adelaide		North Melbourne	
In	PAV	In	PAV
Wayne Carey	18.0	Pick 2 (Daniel Wells)	196.4
		Pick 18 (Kris Shore)	0.0
Total	18.0	Total	196.4
Difference	−178.4	Difference	+178.4

It was perhaps fortunate for Adelaide that North's second-round pick, Kris Shore, failed to play a senior game, because the enduring comparisons between Wells's and Carey's post-trade output caused it quite enough anguish. Carey played 28 matches for the Crows before retiring because of a neck injury midway through 2004. The Kangaroos got 243 games in 14 seasons from Wells, but it took nowhere near that long to realise they had comprehensively won the trade. Just a few months after Carey's retirement, the Adelaide *Advertiser* described 20-year-old Wells as second to only Chris Judd as the AFL's most 'exhilarating entity'. 'Wells should be the top-drawer paratrooper reviving Adelaide's ageing midfield battalion,' wrote *Advertiser* reporter

Richard Earle. Although it can be pointless to wallow in such what-ifs and hypotheticals, the Carey trade does at least teach a few important lessons. Firstly, undervaluing draft picks is fraught with risk. Secondly, clubs that base their decisions on past rather than future performance tend to overpay for ageing stars, especially when they believe they are just 'one player away'. Modern teams are still willing to gamble in this way. In 2016, for instance, Greater Western Sydney traded future first- and third-round picks for Richmond's Brett Deledio. The veteran turned 30 years old early in his debut season with the Giants, during which a lingering calf injury restricted him to only seven games. 'Now, if he wins us a premiership then it's a success, but if he doesn't then it's kind of like, well, why did you do it?' concedes Adrian Caruso. 'We think we've got enough talent on our list that one player is not going to make a big difference between us winning or not, but with that one it was definitely a case of let's give up a future pick to bring in a good player.'

The longest thread

The Carey deal is also useful in illustrating how trades can be interconnected, and how their legacies can linger for years after they are struck. Wells is arguably still delivering value to North Melbourne even after his move to Collingwood. His free agency switch in 2016 saw the Kangaroos compensated with pick 36 in that year's draft, which they used to select wingman Josh Williams. The compensation pick had an expected PAV of 38.2, which was more than double what Carey had earned at the Crows a decade-and-a-half earlier. After digging through hundreds of trades and thousands of draft picks, we found many similar examples. We have called these 'trade strings'. They involve a series of consecutive moves that weave in and out of footballing eras.

The longest trade string that we have uncovered ran for three decades, and started when West Coast took Port Adelaide utility David Hynes with the 24th selection in the 1988 draft. Hynes initially chose to remain in South Australia, and played in the Magpies' 1989 and 1990 SANFL premiership sides before moving west. He made his debut for the Eagles in the opening round of 1991, and later played in their 1994 AFL Grand Final victory over Geelong. At the end of 1995, Hynes was traded to cross-town rival Fremantle in return for pick three and future All-Australian forward Phillip Matera. The Eagles used the top-three selection on Brendon Fewster, a full-forward from West Perth. Fewster struggled to find a regular place in the Eagles' line-up after suffering a serious knee injury early in his debut season, but the Dockers saw something they liked. In return for Fewster, they gave West Coast the 1999 draft's 16th pick, which became half-forward David Haynes.

It had taken just two trades for the Eagles to turn David Hynes into David Haynes, but they were not finished there. When the Geelong Falcons product also failed to nail down a place in the

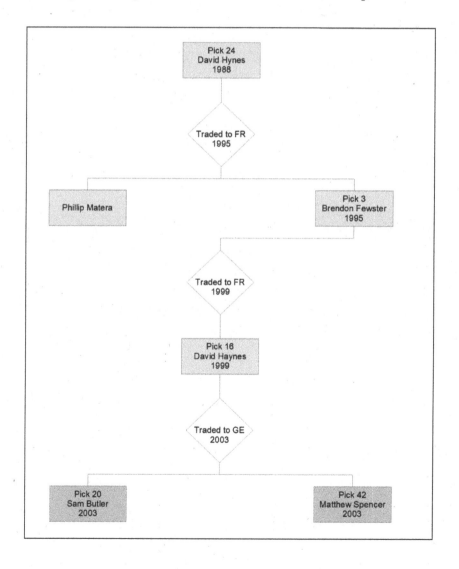

Eagles' senior side, West Coast put him on the trade table at the end of 2003. Haynes's hometown Cats came knocking, and offered pick 20 in return for him and pick 42. With the 20th selection of the 2003 draft, the Eagles snared Central District's Sam Butler. The defender played 166 games over 14 years for the Eagles, including their 2006 premiership. He retired at the end of 2017. The Hynes–Butler trade string reaped 206 PAV for the Eagles, who won every single deal along its 30-year course.

Another long string that started in 1988 involved Essendon. The

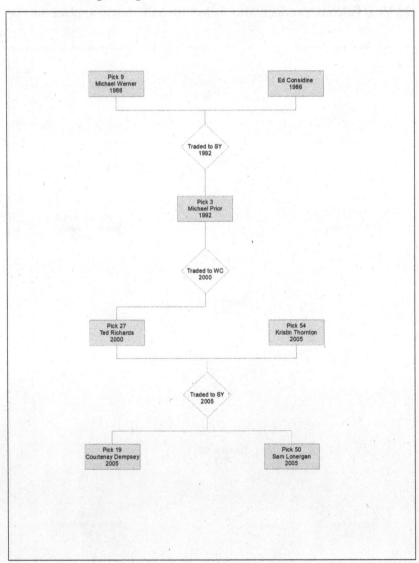

Bombers took Canberra-raised full-forward Michael Werner with the ninth pick in that year's draft. He kicked 60 goals from 40 games over four seasons, before being traded along with former zone player Ed Considine to the Sydney Swans for pick three in 1992. With that selection, the Bombers picked up wingman Michael Prior from East Perth. The man labelled 'Prior Conviction' by commentator Rex Hunt represented the Bombers 81 times, before being sent back to his native Western Australia at the end of 2000. In return, Essendon got West Coast's pick 27, which it promptly spent on Ted Richards. Five years later, Richards and pick 54 were sent to the Swans in exchange for the 19th and 50th choices in the draft of 2005. Essendon called the names of Courtenay Dempsey and Sam Lonergan. Dempsey wore the red-and-black 133 times before being delisted at the end of 2016, while Lonergan made 79 senior appearances and was cut at the end of 2012. Unlike the Eagles' string, not all these trades were wins for Essendon, with Sydney getting the better of the Richards–Dempsey deal. Overall, however, the Bombers ended up well ahead, gaining 141.9 PAV by the time the last two players, Dempsey and Richards, retired in 2016.

Heists and howlers

According to our research, there were 637 trades completed between 1988 and the end of 2017. The single-season record was set in 2016, with 39 deals. We have analysed a 17-season sample of 315 trades between 1993 and 2009 and judged each club's best and worst transactions, based on the future PAV output of each player or pick involved. Some may argue that it is unfair to hold a club accountable for the performance of players selected with picks that it has traded away. After all, who is to say they would have selected those same players had they kept the picks? However, this method does give us an objective starting point from which to measure all clubs the same way.

Adelaide

Best Trade – 1994
In: Andrew McLeod and pick 38 (Matthew Collins) from Fremantle
Out: Chris Groom to Fremantle
Total PAV Gain: 292

Worst Trade – 2000
In: Evan Hewitt from North Melbourne
Out: pick 23 (Drew Petrie) to North Melbourne
Total PAV Loss: 232

Adelaide had one of the finest trading years on record in 1994, setting the scene for its back-to-back premierships in 1997 and 1998. The centrepiece was unquestionably the one-sided deal that delivered it dual Norm Smith medallist Andrew McLeod. Fremantle had the rights to take McLeod because he had been overlooked in the previous year's draft, but traded them away without first watching him play. The earringed 18-year-old had failed to impress Dockers coach Gerard Neesham at a brief meeting. 'Gerard came up and said to me, "He thinks he's Viv Richards",' the club's then recruiting manager, Phil Smart, later recalled. The young key forward that Adelaide sent in exchange, Chris Groom, failed to fulfil his promise because of injuries.

Although the Wayne Carey deal was calamitous for the Crows, an earlier trade they made with North Melbourne was even worse. In 2000, they went after a young ruck-forward called Evan Hewitt, who had struggled for game time at the Kangaroos behind Carey, Corey McKernan, and John Longmire. He played 15 games in two seasons with Adelaide before being delisted at the end of 2002. With the second-round pick it received for Hewitt, North selected 332-gamer Drew Petrie.

Brisbane

Best Trade – 1997
In: pick 31 (Simon Black) from Sydney
Out: Simon Hawking and Brent Green to Sydney
Total PAV Gain: 274

Worst Trade – 1999
In: Michael Martin from Western Bulldogs
Out: Trent Bartlett and pick 32 (Daniel Giansiracusa) to Western Bulldogs
Total PAV Loss: 183

Brisbane's best win at the trade table was directly connected to its greatest drafting triumph. It picked up three-time premiership player and 2002 Brownlow medallist Simon Black with the 31st selection in the 1997 draft, which it had secured from Sydney in exchange for Brent Green and Simon Hawking. Both Green and Hawking retired after just one season at the Swans because of persistent injuries.

The Lions incurred their heaviest loss a couple of years later. It started when they traded David Calthorpe to North Melbourne for pick 32 in the draft of 1999. Viewed in isolation, this deal was a clear win for Brisbane, as Calthorpe only managed 13 games in his only season with the Kangaroos. Unfortunately, it didn't stop there. The Lions packaged their newly acquired pick with forward Trent Bartlett to prise Michael Martin from the Bulldogs. Martin played 10 games early in the 2000 season before being diagnosed with career-ending osteitis pubis. Bartlett kicked 34 goals in 42 matches in the tricolours, but Brisbane's biggest regret was giving up the draft pick that became Daniel Giansiracusa.

Carlton

Best Trade – 2003

In: Heath Scotland from Collingwood
Out: pick 35 (Brent Hall) to Collingwood
Total PAV Gain: 148

Worst Trade – 1999

In: Michael Mansfield from Geelong
Out: pick 31 (Paul Chapman) to Geelong
Total PAV Loss: 199

Heath Scotland crossed the Collingwood–Carlton divide two hours before the 2003 trade deadline. He was 23 years old and had played in two losing Grand Final sides with the Magpies. 'People might ask how could you leave when you have a really good chance of playing more finals,' he said. 'But I knew where I stood at Collingwood, and I wasn't going to make any more inroads or be a more important player.' He had made just 10 appearances during the previous season, and had spent 44.4% of those games on the bench. The Blues sensed an opportunity, and secured his services in return for pick 35. The Pies spent the pick on ruckman Brent Hall, who had three disposals in his only AFL game. Scotland, meanwhile, thrived with greater opportunity. He played all 22 matches in his first season with Carlton. By 2006, he was averaging 27.2 disposals per game, and spending 95.5% of each match on the field.

Michael Mansfield signed a lucrative long-term contract with Geelong in 1994, shortly after being named an All-Australian for the first of two times. The Cats had been keen to ward off interest from Fremantle. As the deal was ending, however, the Cats' new chief executive, Brian Cook, was reluctant to pay the final year. He traded the 28-year-old halfback to Carlton in exchange for pick 31 in the 1999 draft. 'I just couldn't conceive how a born-and-bred Geelong person who'd given blood, sweat, and tears for the club could be treated like that by a CEO who'd only been there for three months,' Mansfield told the AFL website. Cook's hard-nosed decision was ultimately vindicated after the Cats used the pick to secure three-time premiership player Paul Chapman.

Collingwood

Best Trade – 1998
In: Paul Licuria, Mark Orchard, pick 12 (Adam Ramanauskas), and
pick 44 (Heath Scotland) from Sydney
Out: pick 3 (Nic Fosdike) to Sydney
Total PAV Gain: 295

Worst Trade – 2003
In: pick 35 (Brent Hall) from Carlton
Out: Heath Scotland to Carlton
Total PAV Loss: 148

Nic Fosdike was a solid soldier for Sydney, with which he won a premiership in 2005, but it took a king's ransom to get him there. Paul Licuria had played 10 games in three years with the Swans, and would go on to play a further 182 for Collingwood. The other ready-made midfielder in the deal, Mark Orchard, was returning to the Magpies after being sent the other way three years earlier in a trade for Anthony Rocca. He made another 32 appearances in the black-and-white before being delisted at the end of 2000. Collingwood on-traded pick 12, which became Adam Ramanauskas, for Essendon's Ricky Olarenshaw and pick 41. With 41 the Magpies took former Vic Metro captain Craig Jacotine, and three picks later they took Scotland. The Scotland trade to Carlton in 2003 ranks as Collingwood's worst.

Essendon

Best Trade – 1994
In: pick 4 (Scott Lucas) from Fremantle
Out: Tony Delaney to Fremantle
Total PAV Gain: 164

Worst Trade – 1994
In: pick 39 (Stephen Carter) from Fremantle
Out: Dale Kickett
Total PAV Loss: 86

It is generally held that these two trades, along with Fremantle's recruitment of Essendon's Todd Ridley, were a package deal. The Dockers had been given permission to recruit several uncontracted players ahead of their inaugural season. The clubs that lost players to the competition newcomers were given compensation in the form of special access to a pool of 16-year-old talent, which would be drafted in reverse-ladder order. In the years since, it has been alleged that an agreement was struck that saw Essendon approve Ridley's, Delaney's, and Kickett's return to Western Australia in return for an assurance from Fremantle that it would not take any uncontracted players from clubs below it on the ladder. That essentially gave the Bombers first pick in the compensation draft, which it used to take future three-time Coleman medallist Matthew Lloyd. With pick four in the national draft, which it received for Delaney, it selected Lloyd's long-time forward partner Scott Lucas. Lloyd and Lucas each played 270 matches and kicked a combined 1,397 goals. Kickett's 135 quality games for Fremantle were the only redeeming feature in the deal for the Dockers.

Fremantle

Best Trade – 2003

In: pick 19 (David Mundy) from Western Bulldogs
Out: Steven Koops to Western Bulldogs
Total PAV Gain: 199

Worst Trade – 2001

In: Trent Croad and Luke McPharlin from Hawthorn
Out: pick 1 (Luke Hodge), pick 20 (Daniel Elstone), and
pick 36 (Sam Mitchell) to Hawthorn
Total PAV Loss: 338

A lot of ink has been spilled on Fremantle's stumbles and bumbles, so it is refreshing to be able to report at least one tale of success. A combination of injuries and inconsistent form had restricted Steven Koops to 78 games in eight seasons for the Dockers. In 2003, his former teammate Chris Bond became an assistant coach at the Western Bulldogs, and convinced them to take a chance on the talented flanker. 'I'm sure that did help out, playing with Bondy at Fremantle,' said Koops. 'He's certainly a great character and he's always believed in me.' However, Koops's injury troubles persisted in Melbourne, and he took to the field only 11 times for the Dogs before retiring at the age of 26. The pick that Fremantle received for him, number 19 in the shallow 2003 draft, became club stalwart David Mundy. The midfielder had played 271 games for the Dockers to the end of 2017.

Geelong

Best Trade – 1999

In: Cameron Mooney, pick 15 (David Spriggs), pick 17 (Ezra Bray), and pick 47 (Corey Enright) from North Melbourne

Out: Leigh Colbert, pick 53 (Clayton Lasscock), and pick 67 (Robert Shirley) to North Melbourne

Total PAV Gain: 257

Worst Trade – 1998

In: Jason Mooney from Sydney

Out: pick 8 (Jude Bolton) to Sydney

Total PAV Loss: 217

Almost two decades on, it is sometimes hard to fathom the shockwaves caused by Leigh Colbert's demand to be traded from Geelong at the end of 1999. The 24-year-old club captain had just missed the entire season after suffering a serious knee injury before round one. The Cats won their first five games without him, but then lost their next nine in a row. They finished 11th, and Colbert was worried about their on- and off-field future. That he asked to be sent to the newly crowned premier, North Melbourne, however, did not exactly endear him to Geelong's fans. A convoluted five-club deal fell apart on the eve of the deadline, leaving the Kangaroos and Cats to scrabble together a last-minute compromise. The prospect of losing Colbert for nothing in the preseason draft motivated Geelong to get the deal done, but it never could have imagined the scale of its recompense. Even though it failed to capitalise on either of the first-round picks it received, it struck gold at pick 47 with Corey Enright, and picked up another three-time premiership player in Cameron Mooney. The Cats had traded for Mooney's brother Jason the year before, although that deal rates at the other end of value spectrum. The eighth draft choice of 1998, which they sent to Sydney in return for the utility, became the 325-game star Jude Bolton.

Hawthorn

Best Trade – 2001

In: pick 1 (Luke Hodge), pick 20 (Daniel Elstone), and pick 36 (Sam Mitchell)
from Fremantle

Out: Trent Croad and Luke McPharlin to Fremantle

Total PAV Gain: 338

Worst Trade – 2000

In: Shaun Rehn from Adelaide

Out: pick 12 (Shaun Burgoyne) to Adelaide

Total PAV Loss: 227

Dual All-Australian and two-time Adelaide Crows premiership player Shaun Rehn was still an excellent ruckman in 2000. The problem was that he was 29 years old and had already undergone three knee reconstructions. He was also falling out of love with the game. In a bid to recapture his passion, Rehn asked to be traded. He said he wanted a fresh start in a new environment. Hawthorn, which had just lost its 35-year-old ruckman Paul Salmon to retirement, seemed the perfect fit. The Hawks agreed to give Adelaide its first-round pick for the veteran. He retired just two years and 33 games later. Serendipitously for the Hawks, the player taken with their traded pick, Shaun Burgoyne, would eventually join them anyway.

Melbourne

Jeff Farmer was the central player in two of Melbourne's three biggest trade wins. Farmer was initially dealt to the Demons from Fremantle as a 17-year-old in 1994, in return for former Claremont defender Phil Gilbert. 'The Wiz' played 118 games for Melbourne and was three times its leading goal kicker. The Dockers delisted Gilbert after he had played 14 games in two seasons. At the end of 2001, Farmer asked to be traded back to his native Western Australia. After initially trying to convince him to stay, the Demons agreed to let him go in return for pick 17 in the 2001 Superdraft. It was future All-Australian midfielder James Kelly whose name was read out at that selection, but it was Geelong, not Melbourne, making the call. The Demons had on-traded the draft choice with pick 41 (Henry Playfair) to the Cats, in return for defender Clint Bizzell. It is another example of a significant trade win that was squandered by parlaying a high pick into a player, although occasionally the strategy does pay off. We have already gone over the unfortunate ramifications of the Scott Thompson deal for the Demons, but they did attenuate some of the damage by sending on pick 12 to Geelong in exchange for hard-bodied midfielder Brent Moloney.

North Melbourne

Best Trade – 2000
In: pick 23 (Drew Petrie) from Adelaide
Out: Evan Hewitt to Adelaide
Total PAV Gain: 221

Worst Trade – 1999
In: Leigh Colbert, pick 53 (Clayton Lasscock), and pick 67 (Robert Shirley) from Geelong
Out: Cameron Mooney, pick 15 (David Spriggs), pick 17 (Ezra Bray), and pick 47 (Corey Enright) to Geelong
Total PAV Loss: 257

The Kangaroos' two most significant trade wins were the transactions with the Crows that netted them Drew Petrie and Daniel Wells for Evan Hewitt and the 31-year-old Wayne Carey. Their third best was an unusual deal that secured future club captain Andrew Swallow. Jade Rawlings had been desperate to join his brother Brady Rawlings at Arden Street during the 2003 trade period, but Hawthorn had rejected North's offer of picks nine and 24. Instead, he was forced into the preseason draft and claimed by the Western Bulldogs. The Hawks had allowed him to walk for 'nothing' after a Machiavellian three-club trade with the Dogs and Essendon that became known as the 'Veale Deal'. The deal saw the Bulldogs part with pick six and Mark Alvey in exchange for untried Hawks youngster Lochlan Veale, and the understanding that Rawlings would be sent to the preseason draft, where they held the first pick. It was devious but not illegal, and the Dogs were extremely pleased with themselves until Rawlings proved to be a bust. Two years later, in 2005, they were so desperate to off-load him that they accepted a three-pick downgrade to send him to North. The Kangaroos received Rawlings and pick 43 in return for pick 46. While Rawlings was unable to reboot his career alongside his brother, pick 43 was used to select Swallow. Swallow played 224 games for North, won its best-and-fairest award three times, and captained the club from 2012 to 2016. At pick 46, the Dogs took Brisbane Lions rookie Travis Baird, who was delisted with three games to his name.

Port Adelaide

Best Trade – 2000
In: pick 12 (Shaun Burgoyne) from Adelaide
Out: Matthew Bode and pick 48 (Matthew Smith) to Adelaide
Total PAV Gain: 197

Worst Trade – 2003
In: pick 39 (Robert Forster-Knight) from St Kilda
Out: Brent Guerra to St Kilda
Total PAV Loss: 108

Shortly after the Crows had won the Shaun Rehn trade by extracting the 12th call of the 2000 draft from the Hawks, they undid their good work by passing it on to their local rival. The Power sent midfielder-cum-small forward Matthew Bode and pick 48 across town in exchange. Bode was serviceable for the Crows, kicking 71 goals in 79 games. Matthew Smith, taken at 48, spent five seasons with them without making his AFL debut. Port used pick 12 to recruit Shaun Burgoyne, who was the younger brother of their midfielder Peter Burgoyne. The brothers played together in the Power's 2004 premiership, as well as the 2007 Grand Final thrashing at the hands of Geelong. Shaun was traded to Hawthorn at the end of 2009, where he went on to win three more flags.

Another player to have represented both Port and Hawthorn, Brent Guerra, was the focal point of the Power's worst trade. Guerra played 65 games in four seasons with Port, without ever fully establishing himself. 'Port Adelaide was a great team and it was just hard to break in,' said Guerra. 'I didn't know where I stood and I thought if I came back home, I hopefully could make an impact.' Port allowed the 21-year-old to join St Kilda in return for pick 39, which it used on discarded Bomber Robert Forster-Knight. Forster-Knight failed to play a senior game for the Power, while Guerra made 31 appearances for the Saints before being delisted at the end of 2005. Guerra was handed a third chance at an AFL career by Hawthorn coach Alastair Clarkson, who had worked with him at both the Power and SANFL club Central District. 'Clarko contacted me and told me I needed to pull my head in because he'd heard about me in the past,' he said. Guerra played 159 games for the Hawks, winning two premierships.

Richmond

Best Trade – 1993
In: Paul Broderick, Matthew Dundas, and Michael Gale from Fitzroy
Out: pick 6 (Trent Cummings) to Fitzroy
Total PAV Gain: 196

Worst Trade – 1998
In: Craig Biddiscombe from Geelong
Out: pick 8 (Jude Bolton) to Geelong
Total PAV Loss: 219

At the trade table 1993 was a reasonably busy year, with 19 deals made and several high-profile names changing clubs. Brisbane traded Nathan Buckley to Collingwood for pick 12, which became Chris Scott. Adelaide picked up Tony Hall from Hawthorn for pick 17, which the Hawks used on Angelo Lekkas. And Brisbane signed forward Alastair Lynch to a 10-year contract after securing him from Fitzroy for pick seven, with which Chris Johnson was selected. But it was Fitzroy's decision to trade for Richmond's pick six that was the year's most substantial deal in terms of both the value of the selection, and the number of players involved. The Tigers were the clear winners. In return for the pick, they received Paul Broderick, Matthew Dundas, and Michael Gale. The trio played a combined 274 games for the Tigers. Broderick, a left-footed midfielder, played 169 and was the winner of the club's best-and-fairest award in 1996.

St Kilda

Best Trade – 2001

In: pick 13 (Nick Dal Santo), pick 17 (James Kelly), and
pick 45 (Nathan Clarke) from Sydney
Out: Barry Hall and Pick 53 (Daniel Hunt) to Sydney
Total PAV Gain: 314

Worst Trade – 1998

In: pick 22 (James Begley) and pick 53 (Troy Schwarze) from Carlton
Out: Matthew Lappin and pick 58 (Ian Prendergast) to Carlton
Total PAV Loss: 110

Although St Kilda notionally won the deal that sent Barry Hall to Sydney, its decision to on-trade one of the draft picks meant that it failed to reap the full rewards. Pick 17 in 2001 was one of the most journeyed selections in the history of the draft. Originally held by Richmond, which had finished that season in fourth place, it was first sent with Nick Daffy to Sydney in return for mature-aged ruckman Greg Stafford. The Swans included it in their package for Hall, but the Saints immediately flipped it for Fremantle's Heath Black. The Dockers then used it in their previously discussed deal to lure Jeff Farmer home from Melbourne, which in turn on-traded it to Geelong in the deal for Clint Bizzell. By keeping the pick and using it to select James Kelly, the Cats extracted more value out of it than any of the other five clubs through which it had passed.

To date, only two trades have caused the Saints to lose more than 70 PAV. One was the deal that delivered the Dockers pick 17 for Black. He ended up being sent back the other way three years later in a three-club swap that saw Aaron Fiora join St Kilda. The other involved the Saints giving up Matthew Lappin and the 1998 draft's 58th pick, which became Ian Prendergast, in return for picks 22 (James Begley) and 53 (Troy Schwarze). Lappin kicked 221 goals in 196 matches for the Blues, and was named an All-Australian in 2004.

Sydney

Best Trade – 1998
In: pick 8 (Jude Bolton) from Geelong
Out: Jason Mooney to Geelong
Total PAV Gain: 217

Worst Trade – 2001
In: Barry Hall and pick 53 (Daniel Hunt) from St Kilda
Out: pick 13 (Nick Dal Santo), pick 17 (James Kelly), and
pick 45 (Nathan Clarke) to St Kilda
Total PAV Loss: 314

In many respects, it seems ridiculous and jarring to see Barry Hall's name listed as part of Sydney's worst trade. Everyone knows he enjoyed immense success at the Swans. He won All-Australian selection in 2004, 2005, and 2006, and he captained the club to its drought-breaking premiership in 2005. On top of that, he was a key forward, which is arguably the most difficult type of player to acquire. He was seven times the Swans' leading goal kicker, booting 467 goals from 162 games in the red-and-white. However, to get him, Sydney had to relinquish two high picks in the strongest draft on record. Those picks became Nick Dal Santo and James Kelly, who together played 635 games, earned four All-Australian selections, and won three premierships. Even if we ignore Dal Santo's and Kelly's personal achievements and consider just the average PAV of the two picks they were selected at, the Saints still end up ahead on the deal. So, would Sydney make the trade again? It is difficult to believe they wouldn't, even if they had the benefit of hindsight.

West Coast

Best Trade – 2000

In: pick 27 (Ted Richards), pick 45 (Trent Carroll), and pick 57 (Steven Sziller) from Geelong

Out: Mitchell White

Total PAV Gain: 156

Worst Trade – 2000

In: Michael Prior

Out: pick 27 (Ted Richards) to Essendon

Total PAV Loss: 132

West Coast's 'best' trade is yet another example of how it is often more prudent to hold on to draft picks than to flip them for fringe players from other clubs. At the end of 2000, the Eagles traded forward Mitchell White to Geelong in return for picks 27, 45, and 57. Pick 27 was on-traded to Essendon for Michael Prior, and the Bombers used it to take Ted Richards. The resulting loss of 132 PAV made it West Coast's worst trade. The Eagles also dealt pick 57 to Richmond for Mark Merenda, who only managed another 26 games after the switch. Of the 30 most lopsided trades between 1993 and 2009, the side receiving the greater number of draft selections won the trade 27 times. This seems to indicate that picks were traditionally undervalued, although there has been a correction in recent years. West Coast has generally done well at exchanging fringe players for medium-range picks, with the departures of David Hynes, Daniel McConnell, Chad Morrison, Paul Johnson, and David Haynes all providing the club with solid returns.

Western Bulldogs

Best Trade – 1999
In: Trent Bartlett and pick 32 (Daniel Giansiracusa) from Brisbane
Out: Michael Martin
Total PAV Gain: 188

Worst Trade – 1997
In: Simon Garlick from Sydney
Out: pick 31 (Simon Black) to Sydney
Total PAV Loss: 192

The Western Bulldogs indirectly let Simon Black slip through their fingers in 1997, when they traded pick 31 to Sydney for Simon Garlick. It feels unfair that the numbers show this as the Dogs' worst trade, for Garlick did play 137 games in seven sturdy seasons at the Whitten Oval before becoming their well-regarded CEO for five years. We also know the Swans were guilty of passing on the pick too. The Bulldogs did somewhat atone for missing Black when they snagged club stalwart Daniel Giansiracusa in the 1999 draft, after they had traded out Michael Martin to Brisbane for pick 32. In the same year, the Dogs sent Leon Cameron to Richmond for picks 37 and 66, which they used on long-term contributors Mitch Hahn and Ryan Hargrave respectively.

Free agency

There is a third way that players can move from one club to another in the AFL. Free agency was reintroduced to top-level Australian football at the end of 2012, after an absence of many years. In contrast to drafting and trading, free agency gives players the power to themselves decide where to ply their trade. It is the primary form of player movement in global sport, although in other football codes it is sometimes accompanied by a 'transfer fee' paid from the player's new club to their old one. The AFL has two forms of free agency: restricted (RFA) and unrestricted (UFA). Restricted free agency is granted to players who have served at least eight years, are coming out of contract, and are in the top 25% pay bracket at their club. A club has the right to match any offer made to an RFA from a rival. If it does, the player can choose to stay, seek a trade, or enter the draft. Unrestricted free agency applies to a club's top-quarter earners coming out of contract after serving at least 10 years, and to any other player whose contract is expiring after at least eight years' service. An unrestricted free agent can automatically move to the club of their choice.

In the first six years following its reintroduction, free agency has been a relatively minor factor in the league's overall player movement. Excluding delisted free agents, there has been an average of five-and-a-half free agency moves per off-season, and never more than 10 in a single year. The high-water mark was set in 2012, and there has been a noticeable year-on-year decline since then. In 2017, more players found new clubs through delisted free agency (five) or redrafting (also five) than via restricted or unrestricted free agency (three). However, players who choose to pursue free agency generally have a higher PAV per-season average than standard players. They are also more likely to produce at an elite level, which we classify as being a season-long PAV of at least 17. The right-hand column in the following table shows the percentage of all player seasons that were of an elite standard between 2013 and 2017.

	Average PAV per season	Elite seasons
All players	8.28	8.8%
Free agents	8.51	11.1%

Although the sample size is small, the early indications are that restricted free agents provide the best value. On average, they produce about 50% more PAV per season than unrestricted free agents, and 100% more than the average delisted free agent.

Type of free agent	Average PAV per season	Elite seasons
Restricted	12.0	34
Unrestricted	8.0	10
Delisted	6.1	2

Because of the length of time required to attain RFA or UFA status, free agency flings can be short-lived. Of the 10 players who changed clubs via restricted or unrestricted free agency in 2012, only Brendon Goddard and Danyle Pearce were still on an AFL list in 2018. Troy Chaplin was alone among the other eight in playing more than 50 games after moving. That year's crop of delisted free agents didn't fare any better, with Dylan Roberton the only of the four to last more than three years at his new team. In the five years to the end 2017, only 45% of restricted and unrestricted free agents spent at least four seasons at their new club, and only 32% of delisted free agents managed the same feat. In general, clubs sign free agents for a good time rather than a long time, although there have been some notable exceptions.

Chapter Ten

Shared Experience

A blessing in disguise

Confetti was still being cleared from the MCG after Hawthorn's 2013 Grand Final victory over Fremantle when the football industry turned its collective attention to the all-important question: what would Buddy do? Lance Franklin, the left-footed forward powerhouse, was out of contract with the newly crowned premiers, and had put off negotiations until the end of the season. It had been widely reported that he was bound for the cashed-up expansion side Greater Western Sydney, in an echo of how the Gold Coast Suns had poached Gary Ablett Jr a few seasons earlier. As it turned out, Franklin did end up in Sydney, but in the red and white of the Swans rather than the Giants' orange and charcoal. His nine-year, $10 million deal caused much gnashing of teeth, and not just among jilted Hawks fans. Coming only a season after Kurt Tippett's controversial move to the same club, the Franklin deal prompted allegations that the Swans were exploiting an unfair advantage in the form of their 'cost of living allowance' (COLA). Under the allowance, the Swans' players were paid an additional 9.8% to compensate for the expense of living in the harbour city. The AFL eventually reacted to the grumblings by announcing that the allowance would be phased out, and that Sydney would be banned from trading in players for two years. The Swans were furious. 'We believe that the trade ban and restrictions are unconstitutional and a serious restraint of trade,' said the club's chairman, Andrew Pridham. 'It has no justification. We have broken no rules. It is a senseless sanction.'

It is often thought that trading is important because good teams are created by signing good players. The theory goes that if a club can collect enough talented individuals, success will surely follow. However, history is littered with examples of star-studded sides that could never quite put it together. In large-sided sports, such as Australian football, especially, the skill of individual players can be negated if they don't gel as a team. It is for this reason that sports analyst Simon Strachan believes the AFL may have inadvertently done Sydney a favour. 'The trading ban might have been beneficial, because it created stability,' he said. 'It might have had the opposite of the league's intended effect.' Strachan belongs to an emerging school of thought that posits that stability and cohesion contribute more to sporting success than talent. He runs a prominent analytics consultancy, GAIN LINE, with the former Australian rugby union player Ben Darwin. For the past few years, they have been preaching the message that talent is overrated and that the role of coaches is overstated. 'We think the evidence shows that the skill and talent of the individual is overestimated as a driver of success, and that cohesion is grossly underestimated,' said Strachan.

Although Hawthorn's Alastair Clarkson might wince at the suggestion his role is overplayed, he is one of several AFL coaches who agree on the importance of cohesion. 'It's about knowing what you're doing, a real togetherness, a real mission that you're on,' he said before the 2017 season. 'Passion comes about with cohesion.' Many players, too, have acknowledged the benefits of stability. Former Geelong and Essendon player James Kelly experienced both sides of the coin. He built up a lot of shared experience with his teammates in 273 games with the Cats, before swinging to the other end of the spectrum with a cobbled-together Essendon squad in 2016. 'The teams that have played together for a long time just bounce off each other really well and there's a real harmony and synergy about them,' said Kelly. 'That's something that can't be manufactured. You can only give it little pushes along here and there.'

GAIN LINE calculates team cohesion in the AFL, and a range of other sports, using a measure it calls the 'Team Work Index'. It is a proprietary metric that is based on what it describes as the quantity and intensity of linkages in a team. Recent experience is weighted more heavily than games in the distant past. 'We have found that the

TWI algorithm is a very strong indicator of success,' said Strachan. 'Teams that have a naturally high TWI are successful over the long term. They might have a couple of down seasons, but they can rebound quickly. Likewise, teams with a low TWI are generally unsuccessful. They can have a couple of good seasons, but they are usually very volatile over the long term, and even volatile within seasons.'

The importance of team cohesion, according to GAIN LINE, isn't necessarily the feeling of camaraderie and esprit de corps it might generate. Instead, GAIN LINE believes that cohesion contributes to a group of players being able to correctly anticipate each other's next move. This is particularly important in the defensive aspects of 'invasion' sports, such as Australian football and rugby, where a team's structure and positioning can be the difference between success and failure. 'It doesn't matter if two guys don't like each other or talk to each other outside of training and game time, so long as they know what the other can do on the field and that they can work together,' said Strachan. 'It almost gets down to the minutiae of things like if you're handballing to a teammate and he steps off his left leg, you know how far he is going to step. Essentially our measurements are a proxy for how well teammates can play with each other.' Kelly believes the great Geelong sides of 2007 to 2011 developed the sort of intuitive understanding described by Strachan. 'A lot of teams talk about being predictable to each other, and while part of that comes down to your game plan, it's also getting to know your teammates,' he said. 'For example, we knew that Steve Johnson was going to be predictably unpredictable. When he had the ball and you were around him, you just had to be ready for anything. We also knew that if Cameron Ling had the ball, he was probably going to kick it short most of the time. It is things like that which you can only learn from playing and training with each other, and spending time together.'

Measuring team cohesion

In a way, it is a motherhood statement to say that team cohesion is important. Few would dispute that a team with a lot of shared experience would likely beat an equally talented side that had been thrown together yesterday. But just how important is it? Does it matter a little bit, or does it matter a lot? Is shared experience the sort of thing that can make a great team into a slightly greater team, or can it turn a mediocre side into a great one? To try to answer those questions, we will need a measure of shared experience. The formula for GAIN LINE'S 'Team Work Index' (which includes more than just shared experience) is closely guarded, so we are unable to simply reproduce it. Instead, we have developed a metric based on the sum of all the senior games that a team's players have played together during their careers. The method is straightforward. When two players play a game together on the same team, they add a game of shared experience to their total. A team's shared experience is the sum of its players' shared experience. Our measure only accounts for VFL games from 1969 to 1989, and the AFL matches from 1990 to 2017. It doesn't include any experience built up during the preseason, the reserves, junior football, or any other level. This might not matter, because a game of shared experience in the reserves clearly isn't the same as one in the seniors. 'I think it's important to learn the AFL system at the AFL level,' said Kelly. 'I won a reserves premiership in my first year and played alongside a few of those guys for a long time, which was certainly important from a relationship point of view, but I don't think the experience made us better teammates in the AFL. It was a different standard.'

We have calculated the shared experience of each team before and after every AFL/VFL match since 1969. Although we are only interested in the effect of shared experience in the AFL era from 1990 onwards, we started our calculations two decades earlier so that games shared in the pre-national competition still counted towards their total. There were no active senior players in 1990 who began their careers prior to 1969, so we are sure that we have accounted for every relevant game. If players who had played together at one club later reunited at a different team, we carried over the shared experience they had already built up. Our measure doesn't involve any kind of 'decay', meaning that a game played together last week is worth no more and no less than shared experience from 10 years ago. To clear up any confusion, let's look at an example of how a team might build or lose shared experience over time. In this stylised, fictional example, the team only has three players on the field at one time.

Game	Player A	Player B	Player C	Shared experience before the game	Shared experience after the game
1	Jordan Lewis	Sam Mitchell	Luke Hodge	0	3
2	Jordan Lewis	Sam Mitchell	Luke Hodge	3	6
3	Cyril Rioli	Sam Mitchell	Luke Hodge	2	5
4	Cyril Rioli	Sam Mitchell	Luke Hodge	5	8
5	Cyril Rioli	Ty Vickery	Luke Hodge	2	5

In the first game, the three players have never played together before, so they start with no shared experience. At the end of the match, their collective shared experience is three games. Lewis has played with Mitchell, Mitchell with Hodge, and Lewis with Hodge. You will notice that we don't 'double count'. When Mitchell and Hodge have played one game together, their shared experience is one, not two. The trio then starts the second game with three games of shared experience and ends it with six. In the third game, however, Cyril Rioli replaces Jordan Lewis in the line-up. The team is therefore left with just two games of shared experience, being the two games Mitchell and Hodge have played together. Shared experience rises every time players play together, but is temporarily reduced every time new players are introduced.

We have calculated the shared experience of real players in the same way as this made-up example, but instead of the 15 player-games shown above, our real data draws on all 343,970 player-games from the start of the 1969 season until the end of 2017. AFL teams typically have many thousands of games of shared experience. For example, Richmond's 2017 premiership side went into the Grand Final with 9,905 games of shared experience. Bachar Houli had played with Alex Rance 133 times, Brandon Ellis and Rance had lined up alongside each other 127 times, Houli and Ellis had 118 games together, and so on. The table overleaf shows the team's shared experience, broken down into each player's experience with each of his teammates. Although calculating shared experience for real teams is a bit more complicated than our three-a-side example, the process is fundamentally the same.

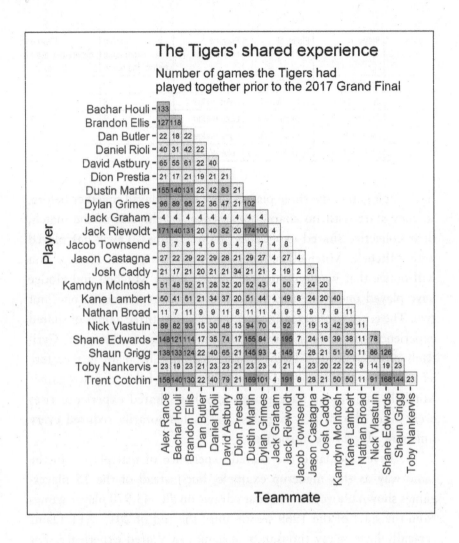

The Tigers' shared experience

Number of games the Tigers had played together prior to the 2017 Grand Final

Band of brothers

If you add together the shared experience of each of Richmond's 22 premiership players, you get the Tigers' pre-game total of 9,905. That put them slightly below the typical Grand Finalist, which averages 11,856. Interestingly, the team that boasts the most shared experience in AFL history failed to make the Grand Final in the season it reached the mark. At its zenith, Geelong's class of 2010 had played together a combined 22,000 times. The Cats teams that won flags in the preceding and following years, 2009 and 2011, are second and fourth on the list for the most shared experience. Only the Brisbane Lions' side from 2004, which was the season after the third of their

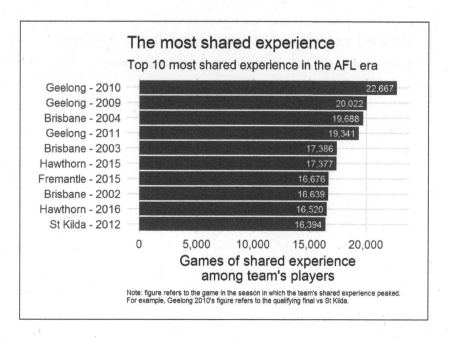

The most shared experience

Top 10 most shared experience in the AFL era

Team - Year	Games of shared experience
Geelong - 2010	22,667
Geelong - 2009	20,022
Brisbane - 2004	19,688
Geelong - 2011	19,341
Brisbane - 2003	17,386
Hawthorn - 2015	17,377
Fremantle - 2015	16,676
Brisbane - 2002	16,639
Hawthorn - 2016	16,520
St Kilda - 2012	16,394

Games of shared experience among team's players

Note: figure refers to the game in the season in which the team's shared experience peaked. For example, Geelong 2010's figure refers to the qualifying final vs St Kilda.

three straight flags under Leigh Matthews, prevented Geelong from making a clean sweep of the top three.

James Kelly points out that the core of the Geelong team during that period was composed of players of a similar vintage. 'The majority were drafted within a few years of each other, so we sort of all came up together,' said Kelly. 'The group wasn't pulled together from all different parts. The bulk were from the 1999, 2000, 2001 draft years, so I think that really helped. We sort of grew up together and had time to build relationships.' Kelly believed that the strong bond between the Cats' players was important, because it enabled them to give frank and fearless feedback. 'You understand that you're friends first, and that creates a platform to be able to provide really strong, constructive criticism,' he said. 'Giving feedback to someone you know really well is always a lot easier because you know how to give it, and they understand you're not giving it from a personal point of view. You're giving the footballer feedback, not the person. We had players who were best mates and inseparable off the field, but they were as hard as anyone on each other on the field. I think that plays a big part in building a successful culture.'

The truly freakish nature of Geelong's level of 'cohesion' in 2010 can be seen in this next chart, which shows the shared experience

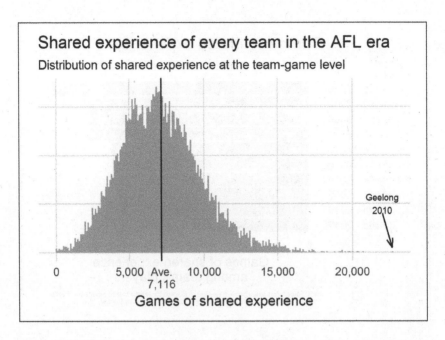

Shared experience of every team in the AFL era
Distribution of shared experience at the team-game level

0   5,000 Ave. 10,000   15,000   20,000
            7,116

Geelong
2010

Games of shared experience

for each team in every game during the AFL era. The average amount of shared experience across all teams during the era is 7,116 games, which is less than a third of what the Cats had during Mark Thompson's final year as coach.

The Cats reached their shared experience peak of 22,667 games in the 2010 qualifying final against St Kilda. The match wasn't an aberration, because the same team also holds the highest season-long average for shared experience. Across its 25 matches that season, Geelong averaged a record 16,293 shared games. The late-dynasty Brisbane Lions are the only other team to come close to that average, at 14,997 games of shared experience across the 2004 season. Every club's average shared experience for each season of the AFL era is shown in the graph opposite.

The profiles provide an interesting insight into the history of each club. For example, Brisbane's shared experience soared during its premiership years and plummeted thereafter, without ever recovering. The Suns' and Giants' shared experience profiles began similarly, starting from around zero and climbing sharply in their first four seasons. The Suns' then started to taper off, while the Giants' steadily grew. Essendon has maintained a remarkably consistent level of shared experience from year to year, with the glaring exception of 2016, when a dozen of its senior players were serving doping bans. However, the Bombers aren't alone in experiencing a big year-on-year decline in games shared. In fact, that season's team only comes in at number three on the following list of the biggest falls in shared experience. North Melbourne's 2017 side had the biggest single-season decrease. Its average shared experience dropped by about 6,000 games after the departures of veterans Drew Petrie, Nick Dal Santo, Michael Firrito, and the AFL's games record-holder, Brent Harvey.

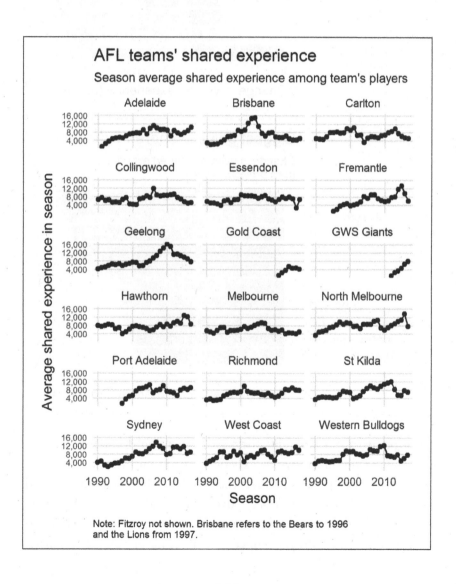

AFL teams' shared experience
Season average shared experience among team's players

Note: Fitzroy not shown. Brisbane refers to the Bears to 1996 and the Lions from 1997.

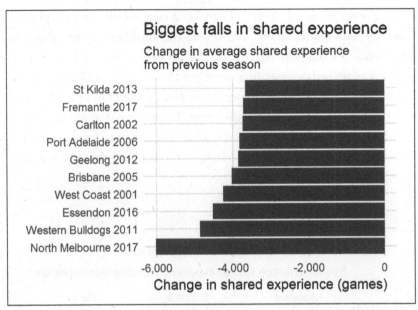

Biggest falls in shared experience

Change in average shared experience from previous season

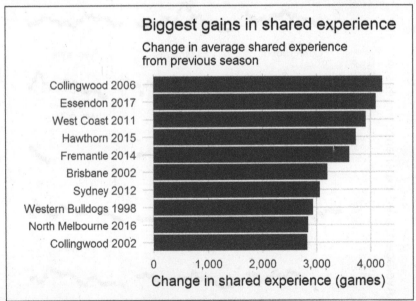

Biggest gains in shared experience

Change in average shared experience from previous season

Unsurprisingly, the 2017 Bombers rate a mention in the list of teams that gained the most shared experience from one year to the next. After its banned players had returned to the club, Essendon averaged more than 4,000 shared games above what it had when they had been missing the previous season. At number one of the list is the 2006 Collingwood side, which regained several senior players from injury.

The chicken or the egg?

Teams with a lot of shared experience might be more likely to win, but successful sides are also less likely to tinker with their line-ups – enabling them to accrue more shared games. This makes it difficult to determine whether it is cohesion that leads to success, or whether success leads to cohesion. It could be both. That is the statistical problem of 'endogeneity', which really is just a fancy way of saying that the effect runs in both directions. GAIN LINE insists that shared experience is the starting point. 'Stability is the key to the start of sustained success in basically all the evidence we've seen,' said Strachan. 'From all the teams we've looked at, only very rarely have we encountered teams that have become successful searching for the result.' Without access to the company's data and metrics, however, the assertion is difficult to assess.

There is another statistical problem we must face when trying to measure the importance of teams' shared experience. It also has a complicated-sounding name: collinearity. This problem arises because shared experience is connected to other factors that influence teams' success, such as plain old experience. If a team has a group of experienced players in the 150- to 250-game bracket, for example, then those players have probably amassed a lot of shared experience together. This is especially true for a competition such as the AFL, where there is still relatively little movement between clubs. Such players will usually be in their late 20s, which is when the performance of AFL footballers typically peaks. How, then, can we separate the effect of players' individual experience and age from their experience of playing together? Because they are so closely related to each other, it is hard for us to isolate them.

Neither of these problems should discourage us from trying to determine the effect of shared experience on team success, but they should cause us to tread carefully when measuring the relationship, and to be somewhat humble about the results.

			Team 1 shared experience	Team 2 shared experience	Difference in shared exp.	Margin	Did the team with more shared exp. win?
Season	Team 1	Team 2					
1990	Collingwood	Essendon	9,142	7,942	1,200	48	Yes
1991	Hawthorn	West Coast	10,213	6,838	3,375	53	Yes
1992	Geelong	West Coast	6,703	8,015	−1,312	−28	Yes
1993	Carlton	Essendon	7,350	5,989	1,361	−44	No
1994	Geelong	West Coast	8,364	11,882	−3,518	−80	Yes
1995	Carlton	Geelong	10,529	9,206	1,323	61	Yes
1996	North Melbourne	Sydney	11,650	6,177	5,473	43	Yes
1997	St Kilda	Adelaide	7,029	5,404	1,625	−31	No
1998	North Melbourne	Adelaide	12,861	8,588	4,273	−35	No
1999	Carlton	North Melbourne	13,321	12,963	358	−35	No
2000	Melbourne	Essendon	8,548	12,222	−3,674	−60	Yes
2001	Essendon	Brisbane	13,315	12,988	327	−26	No
2002	Collingwood	Brisbane	9,708	16,639	−6,931	−9	Yes
2003	Collingwood	Brisbane	8,672	16,705	−8,033	−50	Yes
2004	Port Adelaide	Brisbane	13,369	19,237	−5,868	40	No
2005	Sydney	West Coast	13,587	9,203	4,384	4	Yes
2006	Sydney	West Coast	14,217	13,117	1,100	−1	No
2007	Geelong	Port Adelaide	14,836	9,699	5,137	119	Yes
2008	Hawthorn	Geelong	11,348	16,166	−4,818	26	No
2009	St Kilda	Geelong	12,789	20,022	−7,233	−12	Yes
2010	St Kilda	Collingwood	14,823	9,065	5,758	−56	No
2011	Collingwood	Geelong	12,643	18,298	−5,655	−38	Yes
2012	Hawthorn	Sydney	11,545	14,253	−2,708	−10	Yes
2013	Hawthorn	Fremantle	13,474	11,830	1,644	15	Yes
2014	Hawthorn	Sydney	12,538	14,436	−1,898	63	No
2015	Hawthorn	West Coast	17,377	12,007	5,370	46	Yes
2016	Western Bulldogs	Sydney	8,088	10,868	−2,780	22	No
2017	Richmond	Adelaide	9,905	12,511	−2,606	48	No

Grand finalists' shared experience and results in the AFL era

How much does shared experience matter?

Let's return to the 2017 Richmond Tigers. We have established that the group of players who ran out onto the MCG for the Grand Final had 9,905 games of shared experience between them. That is a respectable total, but it was well short of their opponents'. The Adelaide Crows went into the match with 12,511 shared games. If players' shared experience was all that mattered, the Crows should have won the flag. It was a similar story the previous year, with the Western Bulldogs' premiership team having fewer games of shared experience (8,088) than the losing Sydney Swans side (10,868). In fact, in the AFL era, the Grand Finalist with more shared experience has taken home the cup only 16 times in 28 seasons, for a success rate of 57.1%.

The relationship between shared experience and Grand Final success seems, at the very least, to be unstable. That holds true if we extend our analysis to other matches as well. Out of all the games in the AFL era, from 1990 to 2017, the team with more shared experience won 62.5% of the time.

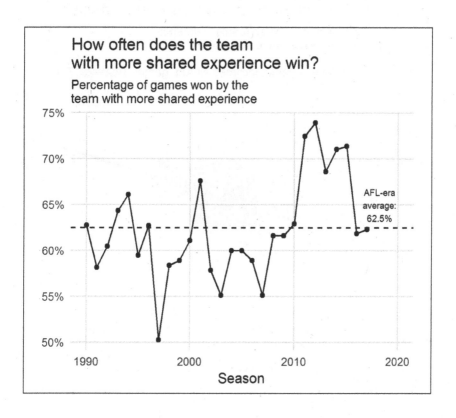

A team with more experience will tend to beat a less experienced team, but the correlation is far from perfect. To get a better picture of the strength of the relationship we can run a regression analysis. Regression is a common statistical technique for measuring the correlation between variables. If we just look at the relationship between shared experience and game margins, we do find a statistically significant correlation. On average, the team with more shared experience has a greater likelihood of winning. The following scatterplot shows the relationship between these two variables for every game in the AFL era. Each dot is a game, and the black line shows the average relationship between a game's margin and the difference in the shared experience of the two competing teams. If a team has 1,000 more games of shared experience than its opponent, it can expect about a five-point boost on the scoreboard. That is nothing to sneeze at. However, as the scatterplot shows, the relationship is noisy.

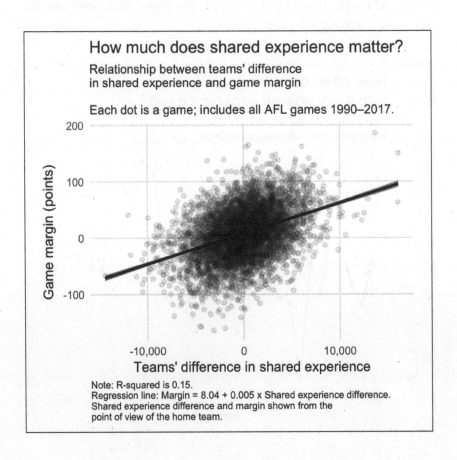

How much does shared experience matter?

Relationship between teams' difference
in shared experience and game margin

Each dot is a game; includes all AFL games 1990–2017.

Game margin (points)

Teams' difference in shared experience

Note: R-squared is 0.15.
Regression line: Margin = 8.04 + 0.005 x Shared experience difference.
Shared experience difference and margin shown from the
point of view of the home team.

Only about 15% of the variation in game margins can be explained by shared experience. Clearly, a club can't just stick with a squad of middling veterans who have played a lot of games together and expect to win a flag. Even GAIN LINE acknowledges this fact. 'A team can only play to a certain capacity,' conceded Strachan. 'If you have a lot of money and low skill, you can buy talent and still perform well. That would be a team like Manchester City in the English Premier League.' To get some idea of the relative importance of shared experience, then, we need to consider the other factors that contribute to team success. The talent of a team's players is one. In other sports, measuring talent might be more straightforward. In the NBA, for example, a player's salary will be a reasonably good first approximation of his expected level of skill or talent. In the AFL, where players' salaries are capped and usually undisclosed, our task is more difficult.

If 1,000 games more shared experience than an opponent is worth an extra five points on the scoreboard, one additional shared game equates to just five one-thousandths of a point (0.005). However, that estimate doesn't account for the overall quality of the two teams. We can factor in team quality by using Elo ratings. We will discuss Elo ratings in more detail later in the book, but basically they are a mathematical measure of a team's true strength relative to that of its competitors. If we run a regression analysis to predict game margins by using teams' Elo ratings, the difference in their shared experience, and home-ground advantage, we find that the effect of cohesion shrinks. After the regression, one additional game of shared experience is associated with just fifteen ten-thousandths of a point (0.0015). That means a team with 1,000 more shared games could expect a one-and-a-half-point bump on the scoreboard. The effect is small but statistically significant, meaning we can be confident that it is not just noise.

So, shared experience does matter, but only to an extent. To be fair, our analysis has only looked at the results of individual games. It is possible that stability and cohesion have more of an effect on long-term success, but there, too, the jury is out. Richmond won a flag with a group that had only a middling level of experience playing together. The 2016 premiers, the Western Bulldogs, had spent even

251

less time together as a group. By the same token, North Melbourne had high and steady levels of shared experience for several seasons without making a Grand Final. Many coaches and analysts agree that all else being equal, it is better to have players who are familiar with each other. But is it more important than talent, or even home-ground advantage, in determining which teams win and lose? On our figures the answer seems to be no, but GAIN LINE insists the picture is more complicated. 'Shared experience is just one of many factors that contribute to the way people understand each other,' said Strachan. 'Understanding between players is important, but it's the lack of it that will really hurt you.'

Chapter Eleven
The Brownlow Medal

44 Disposals, 0 Votes

As the strains of 'We Are the Navy Blues' rang out over Princes Park in celebration of another handsome Carlton victory, the teenaged Glenn Luff was huddled over his statistics sheet. Luff was just 18 years old, but already in his third season with the league's pioneering stats provider APB Sports, the pre-electronic forerunner to Champion Data. The art of the flashing pen had been passed down to him from his father, Peter, who had been Fitzroy's numbers man. 'Everyone at APB was assigned to a particular club,' said Luff. 'Mine was Carlton, so as a kid in 1993 I'm sitting there doing Williams, Kernahan, Bradley and all those great players every week, which was just sensational.'

It was Williams who had kept him especially busy that day. Luff's working sheet had a row of boxes alongside each player's name, which he would cross off with each kick or handball they completed. When the full-time siren blew, he was almost running out of room for the man whose slow pace but impressive engine had earned him the nickname 'Diesel'. 'How many did Williams have?' yelled one of the dozen or so journalists craning for a glimpse over the young statto's shoulders. Luff would not be hurried, though, for accuracy was everything. He methodically went over his figures, line by line, to make sure they balanced. When he came to 'Williams, Greg' he checked and then double-checked every box before carefully inscribing a number that would be talked about for years to come. The reporters scurried back to the press area, their deadlines rapidly approaching. 'It was a fairly ordinary effort from Melbourne, which could have gone down by more than its 54-point losing margin,' dashed off one of the newspaper men. 'Greg Williams dominated the game with 44 possessions.'

Below the grandstand, John Russo and Murray Bird were in the umpires' room filling in the voting slip for the Brownlow Medal. Luff's figures were unavailable to the men in white. Both quickly agreed that Mil Hanna, the Blues' tall, athletic wingman, had been best afield. Hanna, who Luff had recorded as having 19 disposals, was awarded the maximum three votes. 'What about Diesel, didn't he get it a bit today?' asked Bird, as discussion turned to who they should mark down next. Russo looked at his less experienced colleague. 'Did he make your job any easier today?' he queried. 'No, he didn't. He was a prick,' said Bird. They gave two votes to ruckman Justin Madden, who'd had 14 disposals and 12 hit-outs. 'Just one for Diesel, then?' said Bird. 'Did he make your job any easier?' repeated Russo. 'No, you're right – stuff him. We won't give him a vote.' Fullback Stephen Silvagni, whose 11 disposals were a quarter of what Williams had gathered, was the final name added to the ballot.

Four months later, Williams was beaten to the Brownlow Medal by a single vote by Essendon back pocket Gavin Wanganeen. It sparked a bitter and seemingly endless cycle of recrimination. Williams grew hugely resentful that history would not record him as a three-time winner of the Brownlow alongside Haydn Bunton Sr, Dick Reynolds, Bob Skilton and Ian Stewart. He even contemplated legal action, at one stage asking the AFL Players' Association to pressure the AFL Commission into reviewing the result. His indignation was fuelled by the belief that Russo had snubbed him because of a personal grudge. 'He never gave me a free kick in his life and so I gave him buggery,' Williams said. 'He didn't like me and I didn't like him, and he got me back.'

Russo retired from umpiring the following year, having overseen 222 senior games. But frequent media retellings and ongoing public harassment from Carlton fans meant he was never allowed to forget the matter. After later reviewing Luff's statistics in the newspaper reports of the match, he was keen to point to the fact that 26 of Williams's 44 disposals had been handballs. 'It was pretty hard for an umpire to see the handballs the way Diesel used to get them,' he tried to explain. He always steadfastly denied that Williams had been overlooked for the way he treated the officials, claiming that backchat or insulting language was never considered when completing a ballot. 'I was called a prick a thousand times, but it was a bit like sticks and stones stuff.'

Bird had a different view, insisting Williams's abuse had been vicious, foul-mouthed, and incessant. 'He was a shocker, the worst,' said Bird. 'And in those days, it was a completely different environment because you didn't pay a free kick, you didn't pay a 50-metre penalty – while you were on the field you either ignored the abuse or you reported them.' He said Williams's reckoning came during the voting process. 'It was an unwritten thing that if a bloke gave you a hard time, you didn't give him a vote,' he said. 'The prevailing ethos was you couldn't call someone the best and fairest if they were abusing the umpire all day.' His point comes into even sharper relief when it is remembered that the Brownlow's official descriptor is, in fact, 'fairest and best'. The premium on sportsmanship partly explains why the medal has been left in the stewardship of the umpires. The fairness criterion is met in at least one transparent way, which is to rule ineligible any player who is suspended during the regular season. But what else constitutes fair play is largely at the umpires' discretion. 'There's no coaching or no direction on that,' said the AFL's umpires head coach, Hayden Kennedy. 'I don't think it would be ethical for me or anyone else within the department to come in and say these are the guidelines as to how you should be voting.'

On one level, it is understandable that Russo should be defensive to the claim that he had penalised Williams because of a personal feud, for there are few more damaging accusations against an umpire than bias. It is curious, though, that he insisted, 'Nothing serious enough was ever done to me to preclude a bloke from votes.' If there really was an unwritten code not to reward abusive players, clearly Russo believed it should also remain unspoken. Bird's contrasting candour was gleefully seized upon by several past and present players, including North Melbourne great Wayne Carey, whose own testy relationship with the umpiring fraternity was viewed as a major reason he had never won the medal. 'I'm glad that we've finally found out that umpires do hold grudges if you give them a spray,' Carey said. 'It's good that it's been brought forward so we know that these little germs have done it.' Bird, however, was nonplussed at the suggestion he had broken some sort of omertà. 'I just thought it was how things were,' he said. 'It wasn't a bias.'

Whatever the case, it seems unlikely that the Williams–Russo imbroglio will soon be repeated. Even Carey concedes that relations between players and umpires have improved markedly in recent times. 'It's definitely changed,' he said. 'These days they're much more professional.' The officials, too, are optimistic. 'The amount of respect out on the field for an umpire is really positive,' said Kennedy. 'The game has become so quick over the past 20 years that there's just no time for a player to stand there and continually berate the umpires.' Yet ironically, the sport's faster pace might also have presented a new set of challenges to the Brownlow's integrity. While the prospect of voting being influenced by real or perceived conscious bias has diminished, the grounds for unconscious bias may have been made more fertile.

The midfielders' medal

Compared to many of Australian football's laws and traditions, there have been relatively few changes to the rules governing the Brownlow Medal since Geelong's Edward 'Carji' Greeves Jr became its inaugural recipient in 1924. For the first seven years, the sole officiating umpire would award a single vote at the end of each home-and-away match. The procedure was modified to the current 3–2–1 voting method in 1931. When a second field umpire was introduced in 1976, initially they were both expected to fill in separate voting slips, until two seasons later the league reverted to a single ballot from each match. The system remained unchanged following the introduction of a third umpire in 1994.

While it is difficult to deny that the umpires' on-field presence gives them a unique perspective from which to assess the Brownlow's fairest component, there has long been debate about whether they are the most appropriate arbiters of the best. Comparable player-of-the-season awards in other sports are more commonly adjudged by the media, a panel of experts, or the players themselves. A key piece of evidence in the argument against the umpires' suitability is the rollcall of greats who were never bestowed the honour. In 2008, the *Herald Sun*'s long-time chief football writer and list-making doyen,

Mike Sheahan, was asked to name his top 50 players of the sport's first 150 years. His top five of Wayne Carey, Leigh Matthews, Ted Whitten, Gary Ablett Sr and Jason Dunstall were unable to boast a single Brownlow Medal between them.

Carey, who dominated football in the '90s from centre half-forward, has been one of the leading proponents of changing the voting system. He does not believe the umpires should be completely excluded, instead suggesting they be represented on a panel like those assembled annually to decide the Norm Smith Medal for the Grand Final's best afield. Implicit in Carey's argument is that, left to their own devices, the umpires are too heavily swayed by the players who are constantly under their nose. 'We put Brownlow medallists up on a pedestal, but ultimately only a select group of players can actually win the award because of the flaws in the current model,' Carey said. 'More than ever the game's highest individual honour has become exclusively a midfielder's award.' Carey is far from alone in this assertion, which we will attempt to test here.

From Carji Greeves's victory through to Dustin Martin's win in 2017, factoring in the dozen occasions that two or three players tied for the most votes, the medal was awarded 104 times from 90 counts. In the table overleaf, we have sorted the 86 different winners into their playing positions. This task was not so straightforward as it might seem, not least because of modern football's positional fluidity and the difficulty in making comparisons over time. In the end, we settled on five broad categories: midfielders, ruckmen, backmen, forwards and utilities. A variety of sources were consulted during the sorting process, including the *Football Record*, newspaper reports, player biographies, club historians and official statistics.

Care was taken to ensure each assigned position reflected the player's most regular role during their Brownlow-winning season, which led to some widely held beliefs being challenged. For example, although Footscray's 1980 Brownlow medallist, Kelvin Templeton, is often cited as the first player to have won as a forward, we believe Malcolm Blight beat him to the punch two years earlier. Blight was equally at home as a backman, ruck-rover or forward, so when his career is viewed in totality he might rightly be classified as a utility. In 1978, though, Kangaroos coach Ron Barassi had decided to make full use of Blight's talents in attack. 'I was position-less for the majority of my career, but I played a fair bit forward when I won the Brownlow,' said Blight, upon being elevated to Legend status in the Australian Football Hall of Fame. 'I kicked 77 goals that year, by the way.'

Sydney's Adam Goodes is the only player to be included in two categories. After spending his twilight years as a forward, it is sometimes forgotten that Goodes had primarily been sharing the Swans' rucking duties with Jason Ball when he first won the medal in 2003, and that he had switched to a predominantly midfield role by the time he claimed his second in 2006. The genuine within-season utilities were perhaps the hardest to pigeonhole. Essendon's James

Brownlow Medal winners by playing position, 1924–2017					
Forwards	Utilities	Backmen	Ruckmen	Midfielders	
Malcolm Blight (1978)	Colin Watson (1925)	Albert Collier (1929)	Syd Coventry (1927)	Edward 'Carji' Greeves Jr (1924)	Paul Couch (1989)
Kevin Templeton (1980)	Ivor Warne-Smith (1926, '28)	Denis Ryan (1936)	Norman Ware (1941)	Harry Collier (1930)	Tony Liberatore (1990)
Bernie Quinlan (1981)	Des Fothergill (1940)	Bert Deacon (1947)	Don Cordner (1946)	Allan Hopkins (1930)	Paul Kelly (1995)
Tony Lockett (1987)	Ross Glendinning (1983)	Col Austen (1949)	Bill Morris (1948)	Stan Judkins (1930)	Michael Voss (1996)
	James Hird (1996)	Ron Clegg (1949)	Roy Wright (1952, '54)	Haydn Bunton Sr (1931, '32, '35)	Robert Harvey (1997, '98)
		Bernie Smith (1951)	Brian Gleeson (1957)	Wilfred 'Chicken' Smallhorn (1933)	Shane Crawford (1999)
		Fred Goldsmith (1955)	John Schulz (1960)	Dick Reynolds (1934, '37, '38)	Shane Woewodin (2000)
		Neil Roberts (1958)	Noel Teasdale (1965)	Marcus Whelan (1939)	Jason Akermanis (2001)
		Verdun Howell (1959)	Len Thompson (1972)	Herbie Matthews (1940)	Simon Black (2002)
		John James (1961)	Gary Dempsey (1975)	Allan Ruthven (1950)	Mark Ricciuto (2003)
		Gordon Collis (1964)	Graham Moss (1976)	Bill Hutchison (1952, '53)	Nathan Buckley (2003)

Hird and Collingwood's Des Fothergill were their club's leading goal kickers during their respective Brownlow years of 1996 and 1940, but were just as damaging during their frequent stints on the ball. North's Ross Glendinning was a swingman, able to hold down key posts at either end of the ground, while the 1920s stars Ivor Warne-Smith and Colin Watson tended to play wherever they were most needed by their Melbourne and St Kilda teams.

With Goodes listed twice, 48 of the 87 names in our table are midfielders, or a rounded 55%. Seventeen are ruckmen, or 20%. Backmen account for 15%, with the last of the 13 specialist defenders being Wanganeen when he controversially edged out Williams. Hird

Brownlow Medal winners by playing position, 1924–2017					
Forwards	Utilities	Backmen	Ruckmen	Midfielders	
		Brad Hardie (1985)	Graham Teasdale (1977)	Peter Box (1956)	Chris Judd (2004, '10)
		Gavin Wanganeen (1993)	Peter Moore (1979, '84)	Bob Skilton (1959, '63, '68)	Ben Cousins (2005)
			Barry Round (1981)	Alistair Lord (1962)	Adam Goodes (2006)
			Jim Stynes (1991)	Ian Stewart (1965, '66, '71)	Jimmy Bartel (2007)
			Scott Wynd (1992)	Ross Smith (1967)	Adam Cooney (2008)
			Adam Goodes (2003)	Kevin Murray (1969)	Gary Ablett Jr (2009, '13)
				Peter Bedford (1970)	Dane Swan (2011)
				Keith Greig (1973, '74)	Trent Cotchin (2012)
				Brian Wilson (1982)	Sam Mitchell (2012)
				Robert DiPierdomenico (1986)	Matt Priddis (2014)
				Greg Williams (1986, '94)	Nathan Fyfe (2015)
				John Platten (1987)	Patrick Dangerfield (2016)
				Gerard Healy (1988)	Dustin Martin (2017)

and the other four utilities make up 6%, leaving the forwards Blight, Templeton, Bernie Quinlan and Tony Lockett as the smallest group at 5%. Viewed in aggregate, these figures make it plain to see how the 'midfielder's medal' epithet has taken root.

A decade-by-decade analysis, however, reveals it hasn't always been the case. Midfielders were in the minority with four out of 10 medals (40%) in the 1970s, when half the winners were ruckmen. The following decade they won six of 13 medals (46%) and in the '90s they won seven of 11 (64%). It wasn't until the 21st century that near absolute midfield domination was reached. In the 2000s, on-ballers won 11 of 12 (92%), with Goodes's '03 victory the lone outlier, while from 2010 to 2017 they took home all nine (100%).

Professor Michael Bailey is one of the foremost authorities on the Brownlow Medal. As a biostatistician, his day-to-day focus is on saving lives by analysing data related to hospital admissions. He has seen the ICU mortality rate almost halve during his time with the Australian and New Zealand Intensive Care Research Centre. 'I can't tell you it's been me that's directly responsible, but somewhere along the line some of the things that are happening are improving the chances of living,' he said. 'That's pretty satisfying.' Given his vocation, one suspects Professor Bailey might not subscribe to the oft-

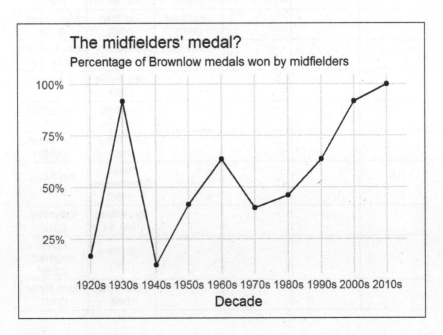

The midfielders' medal?
Percentage of Brownlow medals won by midfielders

quoted observation that football isn't a matter of life and death, but is much more important. Yet his passion for sport, and particularly the AFL, was a driving force behind his 2005 PhD, which outlined a statistical approach to predicting sporting outcomes. His dissertation included a chapter dedicated to Brownlow Medal voting, and he has since described himself as the only person known to have been awarded a PhD for the prediction of the award's winner.

As part of his thesis, Professor Bailey developed a model that used past results to identify specific match and player data to aid in forecasting who would be awarded votes. He found, for example, that umpires had a strong tendency to vote for players from the team that had won. In the 16 seasons prior to 2018, 90% of all three-votes, 79% of all two-votes and 72% of all one-votes had gone to players from winning sides. Similarly, Professor Bailey discovered the margin of victory had a bearing, that club captains were more likely to poll than the men they led, and that statistics such as hit-outs, marks, and goals were significant predictors. By far the strongest correlation to votes, however, was seen in the number of disposals a player accumulated during a match. The leading possession winner had a 61% chance of polling votes, with that probability jumping to 76% if they had also been on the winning side.

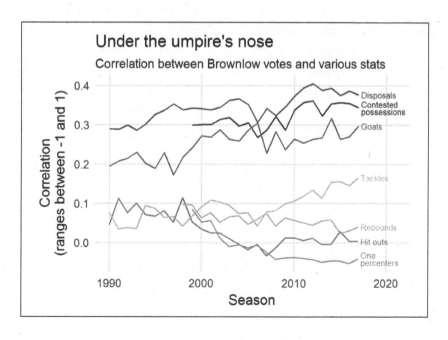

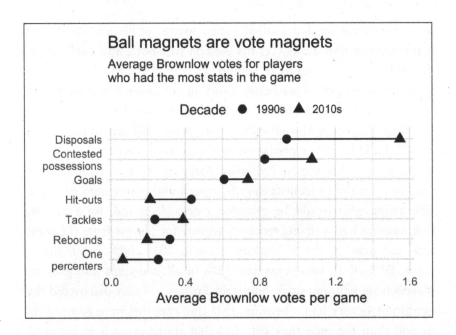

Ball magnets are vote magnets

Average Brownlow votes for players
who had the most stats in the game

We have crunched the numbers ourselves, picking out the winners of each statistical category from every home-and-away match since 1990. As the above graph shows, players who recorded the most disposals during a game in the '90s received, on average, 0.94 Brownlow votes per match. That number jumped to 1.54 votes per game between 2010 and 2017. Put simply, the league's ball magnets are now being more rewarded by the umpires than in the past. Some of the other statistics have lessened in importance when it comes to voting. For example, the player who had the most hit-outs in a match has received an average of 0.21 votes per game since 2010, which is down from 0.43 per game during the '90s. Recording the most one percenters or rebounds has also become a far less reliable way to clinch votes than it once was.

Having reviewed all the variables, Professor Bailey has been unsurprised by the recent trend in Brownlow winners. If disposal totals are the key predictor of success, logic follows that the group that has greatest access to the ball is favoured. 'I suspect the fact that the Brownlow is now predominantly a midfielders' medal is a consequence of the changing style of play over the past 20 years,' he said. 'The importance of key forwards and backs has been diminished due to the increased emphasis on retaining possession.' This, of

262

course, would be little solace to Greg Williams, whose feeling of disaffection at missing those votes against Melbourne is perhaps even more understandable in hindsight. In the AFL era, there have been 63 instances of a player gathering 44 or more disposals in a game. On just 14 occasions was this feat deemed unworthy of votes, although eight of those occurred between 1991 and 1995. As both Bailey and Hayden Kennedy have observed, football was different in the '90s. The slower pace not only enabled Williams to maintain a steady stream of invective towards Russo and Bird, but also granted the umpires time to appreciate the contribution of all players more fully.

As the speed of play has increased, the umpires have found themselves under greater pressure to remain in the moment. Their focus is concentrated on the ball, who has the ball, and who is trying to get it. When it comes time for them to vote, therefore, it is only natural that the on-ballers would spring to mind. Professor Lionel Page, the head of the Queensland Behavioural Economics Group, is another academic who has considered the vagaries of Brownlow voting. 'There is a term we use in behavioural economics called "salience",' he said. 'With more than 40 players in a game, AFL umpires have a lot to remember. If a player is, for any reason, more likely to be remembered, they're more likely to be in the final pool of players to be considered for votes.' According to Professor Page, spending time in the midfield is a sure-fire way for a player to increase their salience, but it is not the only one.

Umpires prefer blonds (and baldies)

Crows wingman Rory Atkins turned heads as he arrived at Adelaide Airport for a flight to an interstate match in early 2017. Television cameramen jostled with press photographers for the best shot as Atkins made his way through the security queue. Michelangelo Rucci, the *Advertiser*'s chief football writer, could barely supress his smile. He fired up his ageing laptop to pump out the breaking news. 'Atkins has surprised all as the 23-man Crows squad flew to the Gold Coast this morning, with his dark hair completely bleached,' he wrote. At a media conference held near the group check-in area, Crows coach Don Pyke was asked for his opinion on his player's new look. 'If he is happy, I'm happy,' Pyke said, diplomatically. 'I'm sure there is a method in his madness.' It was one of Pyke's assistants, James Podsiadly, who had the inside scoop. 'He told me it was the fact that he's never had a Brownlow vote, and he thought it might get him one!'

If true, Atkins was far from the first player to reach for the bleach in the quest for votes. In 1972, Melbourne's Peter 'Crackers' Keenan defied warnings from MCC president Sir Albert Chadwick – the inaugural Brownlow runner-up – to go bottle blond prior to the Demons' season opener against Hawthorn. 'I got the peroxide and did the eyebrows and all – I looked like an albino,' Keenan said. Although he finished with only two votes for the year, the colourful ruckman felt he had been a trendsetter. 'I turned football on its head,' he claimed. 'All these blokes with blond hair at the Brownlow – I started all that.'

The idea that umpires somehow favoured blond-haired players really gained traction around the turn of the century. Heading into the 2001 season, the *Herald Sun* suggested the AFL should enforce a new rule, 13.7.7, decreeing that every field umpire be made to write 100 times: 'When allocating Brownlow votes, I must not be lulled into thinking the player with peroxide hair is necessarily better than the one whose hair is naturally coloured.' The tongue-in-cheek recommendation was ignored, and later that year Brisbane's Jason Akermanis became the third blond midfielder in succession to win the medal, following Hawthorn's Shane Crawford and Melbourne's Shane Woewodin. 'One obvious conclusion can be drawn from Monday night's Brownlow Medal result,' reported the *Australian*. 'Any player who covets the prestigious award had better get his hair bleached.'

It was around this time that Professor Bailey was making his first strides into the world of Brownlow prediction. He decided to dabble with the widely discussed hair colour theory by roughly sorting players into two groups: distinctive and non-distinctive. 'I went through the team photos and just noted down any blokes who stood out to me,' he said. 'It was really anyone who stood apart from everyone else, whether that was because they were a blond or redhead, or because of their skin tone.' Heavily tattooed players, such as the more recent winners Dustin Martin and Dane Swan, also fit the bill. Professor Bailey discovered that the players he had classified as being of distinctive appearance averaged twice as many votes as everyone else. 'It was very subjective, though,' he conceded. 'At the end of the day the two groups were really just based on my opinion. It was difficult to make it completely objective.'

Notably, Professor Bailey's 'distinctive' group included the league's Indigenous players. A sports economist from Melbourne's La Trobe University, Dr Liam Lenten, would later build on this work by examining whether Indigenousness itself influenced voting. Like Professor Bailey, Dr Lenten used the mathematical technique called regression. Rather than simply calculating the average number of votes polled by Indigenous and non-Indigenous players, this type of analysis enabled him to examine the relationship between Indigenousness and votes while holding constant the influence of other statistical factors, such as kicks, marks and goals. This may sound complicated, but the wonders of modern computing have made it a relatively straightforward exercise. For each match in his sample size, Dr Lenten entered into a spreadsheet the names of the participating players, how many votes they had been awarded (0, 1, 2 or 3), an indication of whether they were Indigenous, a variety of individual statistical information, and whether their team had won or lost. Once all the data was entered, at the click of a mouse he could find out how sensitive voting was to each factor. His readout showed him that all else being equal, umpires were significantly more likely to award votes to Indigenous players than to their non-Indigenous peers.

The biggest hurdle in conducting such research is often collecting the huge amount of data required for meaningful results. The AFL's own website does provide access to many of the counting statistics collected by Champion Data, but its archives only date back to 2001. Fortunately, there are also a few publicly curated databases, the best of which is the brilliant AFL Tables maintained by Paul Jeffs. Jeffs's database includes, among other information, results from every AFL/VFL match since 1897, detailed player statistics dating back to 1965, and round-by-round Brownlow voting records from 1984 onwards. 'It's a nice dataset, I can say that,' said Dr Lenten. 'It gives me good bang for my buck because it's possible to look at a number of problems.' Apart from Indigenousness, Dr Lenten has also used the data to show that players who have a lower number on their jumper are more likely to attract votes than those with higher numbers, and that veterans poll better than rookies even if they have delivered the same standard of on-field production.

Conducting a deeper evaluation of the effect of hair colour beyond Professor Bailey's rudimentary classifications, however, would prove a more complex challenge. While variables such as jumper numbers and career games totals are easily accessible, and a list of every known Indigenous AFL/VFL player is published annually in the *AFL Record*'s season guide, there is simply nowhere to go if you want a list of, say, all blond-haired players from 1998. To that end, we decided to make our own. We have used the AFL's online image database (aflphotos.com.au) to create an index of players' hair colour, year by year, from 1998 to 2017. For each year of their career, the players were sorted into one of seven categories: black hair, blond hair, brown hair, light brown hair, red hair, shaved hair or bald, and helmet.

As might be expected, this was a laborious and tedious task that took several weeks to complete. Unfortunately, as with Professor Bailey's distinctive and non-distinctive groupings, it was also unavoidably subjective. What shade, for example, should separate blond from light brown, and light brown from brown? How close-cropped should the hair be for it to be regarded as 'shaved'? And how should one classify Jack Riewoldt? The Richmond forward has reportedly bristled at being called a redhead, although his former teammate Daniel Jackson claimed his complexion betrayed him. 'He's quite pasty,' said Jackson, himself a proud ginger. 'He burns more than all of us and he has red freckles.' Riewoldt would be pleased to learn, however, that we erred on his side, listing his hair colour variously as brown or light brown, even if we strongly suspected the presence of dye. Players who changed colour within a season also presented a problem. The amount of work that would have been required for a game-by-game index made that option impractical, so we instead settled on listing the colour the player had sported for most of a season. Thus, despite his brief flirtation as a blond, we recorded Rory Atkins's hair as being brown for the 2017 season, because that was his colour for 14 of his 22 home-and-away appearances.

Once we had completed our tally, we found that brown was by far the AFL's most common hair colour, accounting for 60% of the total number of games played. Next was black hair at 19%, followed by light brown and blond at 7% each, and red at 4%. Players in the bald/shaved hair category only accounted for 3% of matches played, while those who wore a helmet, such as Western Bulldogs midfielder Caleb Daniel and St Kilda's Nathan Burke, contributed a measly 0.2%. A superficial look at the basic vote-polling averages of each group would appear to support the supposition that blond hair makes players more noticeable to umpires. At an average of 0.187 votes per game, blond-haired players easily outperformed both their brown-haired (0.128) and black-haired (0.129) counterparts, although it seemed no hair was even more preferable. Bald players, or those who favoured a close shave, managed to poll an average of about one vote for every four games played.

AFL games played and Brownlow votes by hair colour, 1998–2017			
Hair colour	Games	Votes	Average
Black	30,213	3,892	0.129
Blond	10,647	1,986	0.187
Brown	97,404	12,439	0.128
Light brown	11,480	1,661	0.145
Red	6,414	808	0.126
Bald/shaved	4,675	1,140	0.244
Helmet	296	46	0.155
Total	161,129	21,972	0.1364

There can be little doubt, though, that the overall success of the relatively small bald grouping has been inflated by the presence of the dual medallists Gary Ablett Jr and Chris Judd, who both happen to be among the top five vote-getters in the award's history. This is a prime example of why relying on averages can be deceiving. 'If you just look at averages, that's not telling you the full story,' explained Dr Lenten. 'It could just be that the players who are bald or blond within your sample are better or more talented than the others.' To counter this possibility, we asked Dr Lenten to conduct a regression analysis on our dataset. By running the hair colour data against more than 150,000 statistical observations from AFL Tables, each corresponding to a single player in a single match, Dr Lenten could confirm that being bald or blond did increase the likelihood of a player receiving votes when compared to others who had delivered the same level of performance. Professor Bailey, while insisting that he would be hesitant to insinuate that the umpires were biased in any way, believed that the results were to be expected. 'It makes intuitive sense,' he said. 'If someone has blond hair or in some way stands out, they're just more likely to be noticed.'

Psychology calls this phenomenon the 'pop-out effect'. It happens when there is a visual display that consists largely of similar-looking objects (in this case, dark-haired players in uniform), with a few different-looking objects that 'pop out' from the rest (such as the 7% of blond-haired players or 3% of bald players). 'Brownlow voting is very retrospective, in that the umpires need to reflect upon and essentially rate all the players within a game,' said Professor David Neumann from the School of Applied Psychology at Griffith University. 'From a cognitive perspective, that's a lot of overload. Umpires can't go through a minute-by-minute recall of the game, so what they're going to do instead is make their job a little bit easier by picking out the most salient players and events.' Professor Neumann said it would be highly unlikely that the umpires knew they were doing it. 'I'd be very surprised if they were consciously aware of it,' he said. 'These types of things happen to everybody in different types of context, but what we're looking at is one specific type of instance where this is happening, and you really have to bring it to consciousness for them to then start to discount it.'

The invisible men

There is one other source of potential voting bias that is difficult to ascribe to either the conscious or unconscious. Do umpires treat players differently once they have been ruled ineligible through suspension? The spectre of such prejudice was raised after the 2017 count, when Geelong's Patrick Dangerfield failed to poll in his side's late-season win over Collingwood despite widely being judged best afield. In his second match back from a one-game suspension, Dangerfield had gathered 32 disposals and kicked two goals. 'I was pretty happy with that game,' he later admitted. 'But really it was inconsequential because Dusty [Martin] was the deserved winner.' The fact remains, however, that had Dangerfield been awarded the three votes, he would have finished level with Martin at the top of the leaderboard, making him just the third ineligible player to be denied the medal in such circumstances.

The results of some casual statistical modelling conducted by Dr Lenten add some weight to the whispers of conspiracy that surrounded Dangerfield's round-22 snubbing. Once he had accounted for the possibility of selection bias, he found some weak evidence that previously suspended players received fewer votes than their eligible counterparts. 'One explanation might be a belief [among umpires] that votes to ineligible players have less meaning, since the player cannot win the medal,' he said. 'Another might simply be the possibility of a tainted view of such a player post-suspension.' Professor Lionel Page said that while it was impossible to determine whether the umpires were consciously deciding to ignore ineligible players, Dr Lenten's findings were still interesting from a behavioural standpoint. 'We don't know what they're thinking because we're not in their head,' he said. 'But regardless, the allocation of votes should be independent of whether a player has a chance of winning the medal or not. We found that wasn't the case, so there was a difference between how the rules were explicitly stated and how they were applied.'

Of course, the fact that Dangerfield was suspended at all went a long way towards disproving another conspiracy theory: that Brownlow contenders were a protected species in the eyes of the Match Review Panel. Wayne Carey had again voiced the theory just two weeks before Dangerfield's ban was issued, when Martin had escaped with two fines for separate incidents in a match against the Brisbane Lions. 'I tell you what the MRP don't want – they don't want Dustin Martin, or Patrick Dangerfield, or any of the other Brownlow favourites to miss a game for an incident like that,' said Carey. 'I can tell you firsthand, even before the MRP was the MRP – I'm talking about tribunal days – it has always been lenient towards the better players in the competition and those who are favourites for the Brownlow Medal.'

The VFL had first formed an independent tribunal to hear charges against players in 1913. The inaugural hearing was held on 7 May that year, when it was alleged that Melbourne's Michael Maguire, who was also a welterweight boxer, twice punched University's Stan Neale after a marking contest, and subsequently fought one of

269

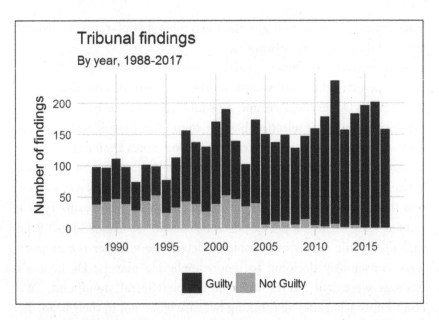

Tribunal findings
By year, 1988-2017

Number of findings

Guilty Not Guilty

Neale's teammates who had told him to pick on someone his own size. Despite several differing accounts, Maguire was found guilty and suspended for four matches.

There were few changes to the way the tribunal operated until 2005, when the AFL overhauled the system in a bid to reduce the number of hearings. It introduced a publicly available table of offences, as well as a three-person Match Review Panel. The panel reviewed all the weekend's matches to decide which players had committed offences according to the table's predetermined criteria. Those players were then able to accept set penalties to avoid a hearing. Until 2018, the players could receive a reduced penalty if they entered an early guilty plea. The change did meet its stated aim of cutting the number of tribunal appearances, but it also led to a dramatic increase in the number of charges being laid, as well as a significantly higher rate of guilty verdicts.

To test Carey's claim that star players are treated more leniently, we will use two measures of player quality: Brownlow Medal votes (BVs) and our own Player Approximate Value (PAV) metric that we outlined earlier in the book. We have categorised a player's season as 'elite' if they received at least 17 PAV or seven Brownlow votes. Those totals represented the top 10% of players in our 30-season sample, from 1988 to 2017. We have also split our sample into two eras: pre-MRP (1988–2004) and post-MRP (2005–2017).

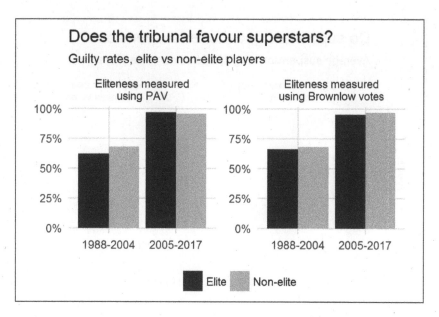

At first glance, any difference in the rate at which elite players were found guilty of offences appears negligible. This is particularly true for the post-MRP period, which is because the incentive to enter early guilty pleas reduced the number of players pleading not guilty.

When we look at the length of the suspensions handed to the two groups, however, a clear split emerges. Elite players have traditionally received shorter bans than everyone else, both before and after the introduction of the MRP.

While we might be tempted to conclude that elite players are getting charged more often with lesser offences, such as wrestling, the pattern remains when we narrow our analysis to more serious offences, such as striking.

It should be noted that we only have data for the incidents in which players were charged. We have no way of testing the other common complaint that the MRP and tribunal have sometimes simply ignored offences committed by stars that would have normally resulted in a player being suspended. 'They [the MRP] want the good players out there playing,' argued Carey, after Brownlow medallist Nat Fyfe avoided suspension for elbowing an opponent in 2017. 'The stars of the competition get more leeway than other players.' To be fair, Carey was speaking from a position of personal experience. As one of the AFL's biggest stars, he was found guilty only seven of the 12 times

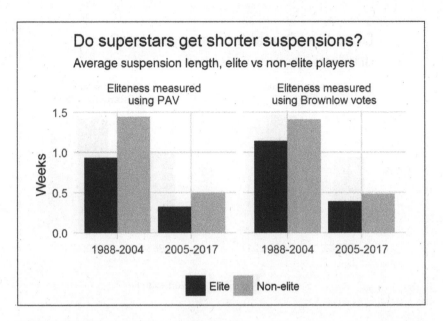

Do superstars get shorter suspensions?

Average suspension length, elite vs non-elite players

Eliteness measured using PAV

Eliteness measured using Brownlow votes

Weeks

1.5

1.0

0.5

0.0

1988-2004   2005-2017   1988-2004   2005-2017

■ Elite   ■ Non-elite

he was cited during his career, resulting in suspensions totalling just eight games. During the same period, his less glamorous teammate Mick Martyn was found guilty on five out of seven occasions, leading to a total of nine games suspended. Who said 'the King' got a rough ride from the officials?

Chapter Twelve
The Hall of Fame

Legends in their lifetime

Tom Leahy and Sam 'Shine' Hosking were born a week apart, on opposite sides of Adelaide, in January 1888. They made an odd pair. Leahy grew to be a giant for his day, at about 193 centimetres and 95 kilograms. He had huge hands and muscular shoulders. Hosking stood at just 167 centimetres, and weighed 57 kilograms wringing wet. They first met as football-mad teenagers in 1906, when they were working together at the Government Workshops at Glanville. At the time, Leahy was already forging a name as one of the state's most promising ruckmen. He had made his senior debut for West Adelaide the previous year, when he was still a 17-year-old schoolboy at Christian Brothers' College. Hosking, meanwhile, was secretly playing for Semaphore Centrals in the Adelaide and Suburban Association. He was doing so under the assumed name of 'Sampson', so that his father wouldn't find out. The elder Hosking had banned his son from taking up the sport after he had fallen out of a baker's cart as a child, leaving him with an elbow prone to dislocation. Hosking got around this edict by sneaking out for training and games, and asking his teammates to launder his uniform. He successfully hid his football career from his parents for three years, until his precocious talent began to attract the attention of league clubs. Hosking was a Port Adelaide supporter, but Leahy tried his best to recruit him to West. 'He kept asking me when I was going to try for league football,' said Hosking. 'Day after day, Tom would ask me, "Well, little 'un, have you made up your mind yet – West or Port?" I was invited to

Alberton, and from that day on my football anonymity had to be abandoned.'

The two workmates were as different in style and temperament as they were in size. Leahy prided himself on being a scrupulously clean footballer, and was said to have 'few rivals in the matter of fair tactics'. 'He has earned that reputation, and it rests on a solid foundation,' wrote the *Mail*. 'Tom Leahy plays the game fair, even against the very dirtiest opposition.' Hosking was one of those to whom the label 'dirtiest' applied. He was a mischievous rover, and well versed in football's dark arts of trickery and deceit. 'When I saw the play coming towards me, I would bend down and idly take up a handful of grass, or perhaps a twig or a pebble, and throw it in the opposite direction,' he said. 'Nine times out of 10 my man would turn his head to see what I'd thrown, and as soon as he did, I'd make a break.' He was never shy of dishing out a 'quick backhander' to the solar plexus of an unsuspecting opponent. 'I had the reputation of being one of the dirtiest players who ever stripped, but I always took the crowd's hoots as a compliment,' said Hosking. 'It reminded me of the villain in a play.' There was one occasion, however, when Leahy turned the tables on his cunning little friend. 'We were still working together and during the week before the Port–West match Tom beamed at me one day and said, "Now look here, little 'un, you keep out of my way on Saturday and I'll keep out of yours."' Hosking agreed to do so, and so was caught off guard by a heavy hip-and-shoulder from Leahy that bumped him halfway up the asphalt cycling track that then encircled Adelaide Oval. 'When I picked myself up, there was Big Tom, chuckling,' remembered Hosking. 'So much for our "understanding".'

Hosking was nothing if not courageous. Despite always using tight strapping, his troublesome elbow was dislocated more than a dozen times during his league career. He missed part of the 1909 season because of a workplace accident, in which a ladle of molten metal spilled into one of his boots and severely burned his leg and foot. He made a triumphant return in 1910, winning the first of two Magarey medals, the first of four flags as a Magpies player, and the first of three Championships of Australia. The last was decided in a challenge match between the SAFL and VFL premiers. Hosking's team beat its black-and-white counterpart Collingwood in 1910,

Fitzroy in 1913, and Carlton in 1914. Leahy also twice contested the Australian club championship with West Adelaide, after it claimed back-to-back SAFL premierships in 1908 and 1909. His team clinched the national title against Jack Worrall's great Carlton side, but was unable to defend it against South Melbourne. Because of a rift at West, Leahy then transferred to North Adelaide in 1910, and three years later joined Hosking in becoming a Magarey medallist. When the league resumed after the First World War, he captained the club to victory in the 1920 SAFL Grand Final against Norwood.

For many years, Leahy and Hosking formed a lethal one-two punch for South Australia's state side. 'I remember one match against Victoria, played on the North Melbourne ground, which we used to call the "gluepot",' said Hosking. 'My opponent volunteered the news that it was his first interstate game, so I had a quick conference with Tom. I said to him, "This bird I'm on is playing his first state game. We'll trap him. When you go for the ball, I'll run him right up to you, then drop back smartly, and you can hook it back over his head".' Their plan worked to perfection. 'I ran the youngster almost into Tom's arms every time the ball was in the air, and Tom would pat it back,' he said. Hosking kicked two goals, and South Australia beat the VFA by nine points. Two months later Leahy and Hosking were again prominent as the Croweaters won the 1911 interstate carnival in Adelaide, making a clean sweep of their four matches against the VFL, Western Australia, Tasmania and New South Wales. 'That team was, in my opinion, the best South Australian 18 to have competed in carnival football,' declared Leahy. 'Individually and collectively, the players who formed that all-conquering combination excelled in every branch of the game.'

There was no-one better qualified than Leahy to make such a judgement. Along with Victoria's Dick Lee and Western Australia's William 'Nipper' Truscott, he was one of only three men to play in every national carnival between 1908 and 1921. It was on this stage that he cemented himself as one of Australia's best players of the first quarter of the 20th century. 'He held his own with any ruckman in Australia,' said Truscott, while Worrall described him as 'perhaps the greatest ruckman the game has produced'. Such was his dominance that Victoria's ruckmen at the 1921 carnival in Perth, Roy Cazaly and Con McCarthy, resorted to deliberately and maliciously kicking his shins in an attempt to stop him. 'At half-time a doctor operated on my shins and cut away a handful of flesh – yes, flesh not skin,' said Leahy. It would be his last representative match. When he retired shortly before the beginning of the following season, the *Mail* wrote that he was leaving the game 'as probably its most conspicuous figure, and best-known player in the Commonwealth'.

Fresh from leading Port to the 1921 flag, Hosking also decided the time was right to hang up his boots. He and his former colleague went straight into coaching. Hosking took charge of West Adelaide, while Leahy joined Norwood. Neither club had won a premiership for a decade, but under their new mentors both immediately reached the Grand Final. In a match billed as the 'Battle of the Giants', it was Leahy's side that prevailed over Hosking's wildly inaccurate West: 9–7 (61) to 2–16 (28). Leahy repeated the dose the following year with another Grand Final victory over Sturt, but Hosking's time would come soon enough. In 1927 he rejoined the Magpies and coached them to three premierships. He also led West Torrens to a flag in 1933, and a combined Port–Torrens side to a premiership during the Second World War.

In all, Leahy and Hosking combined for three Magarey medals, seven premierships as players, seven premierships as non-playing coaches, four Championships of Australia, and a national title with South Australia. Both left an indelible mark on the sport. Yet more than two decades after its establishment, neither man had been inducted to the Australian Football Hall of Fame. How could that be? Well, unfortunately for them, our data suggests they might simply have been born in the wrong place, at the wrong time.

A troubled beginning

The seed for the Australian Football Hall of Fame was planted in the early 1990s, when the AFL's then chief executive, Ross Oakley, travelled to the United States. 'We visited Cooperstown, the ancestral home of American baseball, and were captivated by Doubleday Field, where the first game of baseball had been played, and the Hall of Fame museum that had been built to honour baseball's greats,' he wrote in his autobiography *The Phoenix Rises*. 'To walk into that

276

Hall of Fame ... instilled in me a reverence I had never experienced in a sporting sense. It was an almost spiritual feeling. I knew we had to replicate the experience in Australia.' Oakley had decided he would step down at the end of 1996, which he deemed to be the league's centenary season. Many events and celebrations were planned to mark the year. 'It seemed to be the right time to celebrate our great game, our survival, our development, and the success that this 100-year-old code – the oldest codified sporting competition in the world – had achieved in its time,' said Oakley. It was an odd pronouncement, for it betrayed an almost wilful ignorance of the sport's history. Australian football had first been codified in 1859, which meant it was 137 years old, not 100. Oakley's 'centenary' was in fact the remembrance of the VFL's formation in 1896 and its inaugural season in 1897, which caused some discontent outside Victoria. 'As far as the AFL's centenary is concerned, it isn't,' insisted the South Australian football historian Bernard Whimpress. 'The AFL is six years old.'

This inconvenient point did nothing to deter Oakley from pursuing his grand plans. The jewel in the crown of his celebrations would be the inauguration of the Hall of Fame. A selection committee was hastily convened, and met for the first time in June 1995. It included the former players and coaches Kevin Bartlett, John Kennedy, Lou Richards, and Percy Beames, administrators Peter Allen, Max Basheer, and Mark Patterson, the journalists Geoff Christian, Mike Sheahan, Harry Gordon, and Caroline Wilson, and the politicians Joan Kirner and Tom Reynolds. Notably, only two of the 13-strong committee – Basheer (the long-serving president of the SANFL) and Christian (a Perth-based journalist and broadcaster) – were not Victorians. To try to allay fears of home-state bias, the committee wrote to the various state leagues and associations to assure them that their nominations for induction would be given full consideration. It said the candidates could be former players, coaches, umpires, administrators, or members of the media.

When Basheer returned to Adelaide, he put together a subcommittee to help him draw up a list of South Australian nominees. The subcommittee was made up of himself, Whimpress, dual Magarey medallist Bob Hank, former player and administrator Bob Lee, and SANFL general manager Leigh Whicker. After long and careful deliberation, they settled on 29 names to put forward, although Basheer remained unconvinced that he would receive a fair hearing. 'It was very much Victorian dominated, and I knew I would need to fight pretty hard to get the South Australians recognised,' he said. To avert some of the prejudice he had already detected bubbling to the surface in Melbourne, Basheer craftily proposed, and had accepted, a resolution that all three-time Brownlow medallists be automatically inducted. 'I felt that if I pushed for that, then the Victorians couldn't very well turn around and block our own three-time medallists,' he said. Basheer's gambit worked, and the triple Magarey winners Tom MacKenzie, Walter Scott, Dan Moriarty, Len Fitzgerald, Lindsay Head and Barrie Robran, and four-time winner Russell Ebert, were all ushered in during the inaugural intake.

Of the 29 candidates that had been nominated by South Australia, 18 were immediately inducted by the national panel. Thirteen were players, although a third of them had spent a considerable portion of their careers in other states. They included Fitzgerald (96 games for Collingwood), Vic Cumberland (126 games for St Kilda and 50 for Melbourne), Bernie Smith (183 games for Geelong), and Malcolm Blight (178 games for North Melbourne). Thus, aside from the dual-state stars and the triple Magarey winners, the only other South Australian players to make the cut were Norwood's colonial-era star John 'Bunny' Daly, nine-time premiership winner Jack Reedman, and Port Adelaide's dual Magarey medallist Bob Quinn. 'The Victorians thought their players and league were so superior to ours,' said Basheer. 'To give you an example of what I was up against, I can quite clearly remember that some of the selectors were even questioning Barrie Robran's credentials, because he'd never played outside of the SANFL. I told them, "What does that matter? It's not the AFL Hall of Fame, it's the Australian Football Hall of Fame." It was such rubbish.'

Robran's place was secured by virtue of Basheer's Magarey–Brownlow horsetrading, but there were other southern sons who were not so fortunate. 'What particularly sticks in my craw are some of those who missed out,' wrote Whimpress, shortly after the first wave of inductees was announced. 'Leaving out Leahy, [Ken] Farmer and [Neil] Kerley strikes me as ludicrous.' We have already outlined Leahy's credentials, but it was the last two's omission that dealt perhaps the biggest blow to the new Hall's credibility west of Bordertown. Farmer's exploits were so legendary in Adelaide that he was known as the 'Bradman of goal kicking'. He had booted more than a century of goals in 11 consecutive seasons between 1930 and 1940, finishing his SANFL career with 1,417 majors from 224 games. Kerley, meanwhile, was regarded as the 'King' of South Australian football. He played for or coached half the clubs in the league across a period of four decades, leading three of them to premierships. He was also synonymous with the state team, which he had represented on 32 occasions. 'By leaving him off the list, not only Kerley but South Australian football has been kicked squarely in the guts,' wrote Whimpress. 'Our only consolation is that we have done better than Western Australia and Tasmania, who probably didn't have any historian pushing their claims.'

Indeed, only three of the first 100 players to be inducted had spent their whole careers in the WAFL, and none had played solely in Tasmania. The Western Australian football historian Brian Atkinson joined the Hall of Fame committee shortly after Geoff Christian's death in 1998, and his early memories closely accorded with Basheer's. 'The bias was extraordinary, and just so unfair it wasn't funny,' said Atkinson. 'The thing that really annoyed me was that they would ask Max and I to prepare detailed information about our nominees, which we did, but they would then be overlooked for Victorian players who were put forward on a whim without any background information at all. Someone at the table would just ask, "What about Joe Blow, is he in?" and if he wasn't he soon would be. That sort of thing happened all the time.'

At the heart of the tension lay two fundamentally different readings of football history. The Melbourne-based reporter and commentator Stephen Quartermain unwittingly summarised one of them when he declared, 'Prior to 1987, big time football was played in Victoria, and Victoria only.' South Australia and Western Australia, of course, begged to differ. For every Malcolm Blight, Barry Cable, and Graham Farmer who had been lured east, there had been countless other stars, such as Tom Leahy, Barrie Robran, and Stephen Michael, who had been quite content to confine their careers to Adelaide or Perth. According to the respected football historian John Devaney, these players could do so 'comfortable in the knowledge that they were playing football of an elite standard in the company of some of the finest players in the land'. 'People often asked me why I didn't play in Melbourne,' said Neil Kerley. 'It was pretty simple. I just didn't like Melbourne.' He was far from alone. 'Several times has Mr Leahy been tempted to transfer to Victoria,' reported the *Mail* in 1922. 'But he always resisted the invitations, dazzlingly attractive as some of them were.' Robran, who is often described as South Australia's greatest ever footballer, grew so tired of being hounded by VFL recruiters that he signed a Form Four with Carlton just to make them stop.

Nor was it necessarily always a one-way street. Haydn Bunton Sr, for example, represented Fitzroy in the VFL, before moving west to play for Subiaco in the WAFL, and ending his playing career with Port Adelaide in the SANFL. Famously, he won three Brownlow medals in Victoria and three Sandover medals in Western Australia. The following table shows a league-by-league breakdown of Bunton's career.

Haydn Bunton Sr, 1931–1945			
League	Clubs	Games	Proportion of games
VFL	Fitzroy	119	57.2%
WAFL	Subiaco	72	34.6%
SANFL	Port Adelaide	17	8.2%
Total		208	100.0%

To test Atkinson and Basheer's claims of Victorian bias in the Hall of Fame, we have similarly analysed the careers of every inaugural player inductee. By aggregating the results, we can see that three-quarters of all games accumulated by them were played in the VFL. In contrast, just 10% were played in the SANFL, and 7% in the WAFL.

Therefore, in the selectors' eyes at least, football played on Victorian soil was more than four times more significant than that played in South Australia and Western Australia combined. The skew continued during the Hall's first decade, when Victorian inductees outnumbered their non-Victorian counterparts by a multiple of about 3.5. During one particularly stark stretch between 2003 and 2005, each one of the 15 players who were inducted had spent all or a significant part of their career in the VFL or AFL. By 2009, Atkinson

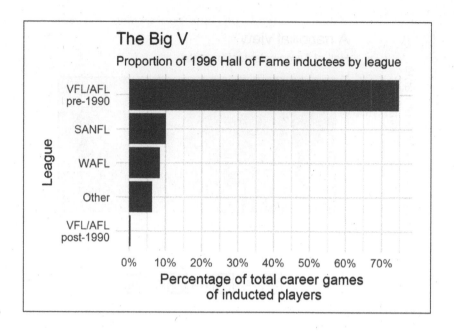

The Big V

Proportion of 1996 Hall of Fame inductees by league

League (y-axis, top to bottom): VFL/AFL pre-1990, SANFL, WAFL, Other, VFL/AFL post-1990

Percentage of total career games of inducted players (x-axis): 0%, 10%, 20%, 30%, 40%, 50%, 60%, 70%

was at the end of his tether. 'At that stage I'd just had enough,' he said. 'A local radio station in Perth used to ring me every year to talk about the latest inductees. I hadn't revealed much during the nine years I'd been on the committee, but on this occasion, I just let it all out about the bias I'd faced, and about some of the deserving Western Australian players who couldn't get a look-in. It wasn't very long afterwards that I got a phone call from the chairman, Mike Fitzpatrick. He was a Western Australian, too, so he was somewhat sympathetic, but he said that I'd angered most of the other members and that it might be best if I pulled the plug. I agreed with him.'

Correcting the record

Atkinson's departure coincided with sweeping changes to the selection panel. Following him out the door were the cadre of Victorian journalists with whom he had constantly butted heads – Patrick Smith, Mike Sheahan, and Caroline Wilson – as well as Kevin Bartlett. Fitzpatrick announced a review of the Hall of Fame's charter to be led by the historian and former journalist Harry Gordon. In February 2010, the AFL Commission approved the review committee's recommendations. Key among them were to increase the

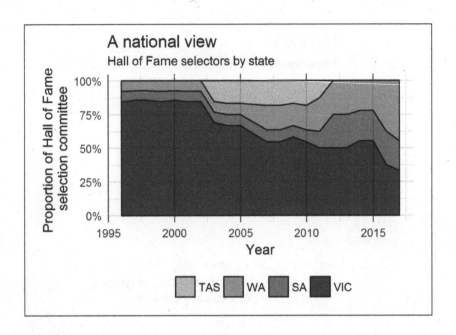

A national view

Hall of Fame selectors by state

Proportion of Hall of Fame selection committee — TAS / WA / SA / VIC

Hall's exclusivity by restricting the number of inductees to six per year, and to prescribe that at least 25% of the selectors were to reside outside Victoria. Western Australian native Dennis Cometti replaced Atkinson on the panel, and within a couple of years he was joined by his South Australian co-commentator Bruce McAvaney, and Adelaide *Advertiser* journalist Michelangelo Rucci.

Rucci had previously been one of the foremost critics of the selection committee's short-sightedness, but he sensed there was a genuine appetite for change. 'Fitzpatrick was very strong in emphasising that it wasn't the AFL's Hall of Fame, it was Australian football's,' said Rucci. 'We decided to put it back to every competition in the land, and ask them to renominate those players they believed should have been in from the start.' There was a prompt uplift in the number of inductees who had played their entire careers outside the VFL/AFL system. Western Australian great Stan 'Pops' Heal, whose case Atkinson had advocated for years, was finally selected in 2010. The following year Horrie Gorringe became the first inductee to have played exclusively in Tasmania.

In the eight years immediately following the review, the WAFL (13% of the share of games of inducted players) and SANFL (10%) were on near-equal footing to the pre-1990 VFL (16%). 'Due to us

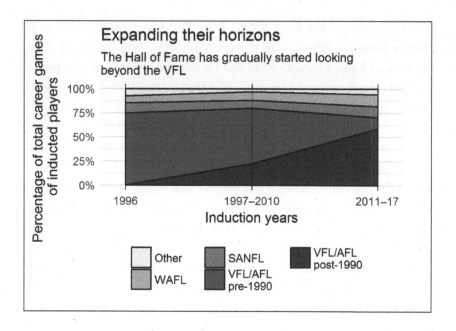

Expanding their horizons

The Hall of Fame has gradually started looking beyond the VFL

Percentage of total career games of inducted players

100%
75%
50%
25%
0%

1996   1997–2010   2011–17

Induction years

Other   SANFL   VFL/AFL post-1990

WAFL   VFL/AFL pre-1990

taking a calmer, more pragmatic view, a lot of the guys who were nominated but overlooked in the late '90s were eventually inducted,' said Rucci. 'We couldn't go back and clear the slate and start again, but we could try to bring about some sort of correction or catch-up.' Of the 45 players to earn selection during this period, those who either exclusively or predominantly made their names beyond Victoria's borders were Gorringe (Tasmania); Heal, Brian Peake, Austin Robertson, and Ray Sorrell (Western Australia); and Graham Cornes, Rick Davies, Paul Bagshaw, and John Halbert (South Australia). Added to them were genuine dual-league stars, such as Bob Johnson (VFL/WAFL), Ern Henfry (WAFL/VFL), Hassa Mann (VFL/WAFL), Maurice Rioli (WAFL/VFL) and Verdun Howell (Northern Tasmanian Football Association/VFL). Never before had such a geographically diverse spread of players been inducted at such a rate.

The time that time forgot

Two names that have so far been excluded from the post-2009 correction are Tom Leahy and 'Shine' Hosking, although the disregard shown to them might have more to do with when, rather than where, they played. Specifically, they made their senior debut on the wrong side of the First World War. The under-representation of players from the first half of the sport's history was ingrained from the Hall of Fame's inception. In the foundation document sent to the various state bodies, it was suggested that 2 to 10 of the inaugural inductees should have been active during the years 1858 to 1900, 10 to 30 between 1901 and 1930, 15 to 30 between 1931 and 1960, and 15 to 30 between 1961 and 1992. It is unclear why there was a lower quota for the sport's colonial era. 'Perhaps the architects of the guidelines believed there just weren't that many champions before 1901, or they were somehow less significant than their twentieth century counterparts,' wrote Adam Cardosi in a 2014 essay on the subject. 'Whatever the reasoning, it portrayed a condescending attitude towards the pioneers of the distant past, and betrayed a lack of understanding as to how rich in history the game already was by the time of Federation, not to mention how many champions it had produced.'

One thing to be said for the initial quota system is that it at least compelled the selectors to give some consideration to players they hadn't personally seen. Of the initial inductees, 11 of the 100 players had debuted during the 19th century. They were George Coulthard (Carlton Imperial/Carlton, 1874–1882), Peter Burns (Geelong/ South Melbourne, 1885–1902), Jack Worrall (Fitzroy, 1884–1893), Jack Reedman (South Adelaide/North Adelaide, 1884–1906), John 'Bunny' Daly (Norwood/West Adelaide, 1887–1904), Albert Thurgood (Essendon/Fremantle, 1892–1906), David 'Dolly' Christy (Melbourne/Fremantle/WA Imperials/East Fremantle, 1891–1912), Henry 'Tracker' Young (Geelong, 1892–1910), Charlie Pannam (Collingwood/Richmond, 1894–1908), Vic Cumberland (Melbourne/ St Kilda/Sturt, 1898–1920), and Tom MacKenzie (West Torrens/ North Adelaide, 1900–1913). Despite their outstanding on-field feats, two of the sport's founding fathers, Tom Wills and his cousin Henry Harrison, were inducted as administrators rather than players.

The inaugural player intake also included 10 men who debuted between 1901 and the beginning of the First World War, and whose careers roughly overlapped those of Leahy and Hosking. This group included Rod McGregor (Carlton, 1905–1920), Dave McNamara (St Kilda/Essendon Association, 1905–1923), Dick Lee (Collingwood,

1906–1922), Vic Belcher (South Melbourne, 1907–1920), Wels Eicke (St Kilda, 1909–1926), Vic Thorp (Richmond, 1910–1925), Roy Cazaly (St Kilda/South Melbourne, 1911–1927), Mark Tandy (South Melbourne, 1911–1926), and Dan Minogue (Collingwood/ Richmond/Hawthorn, 1911–1926). The only non-Victorian in the cohort was the previously mentioned William 'Nipper' Truscott (East Fremantle, 1913–1927).

In all, 21% of the initial wave of inductees played their first senior game before Archduke Franz Ferdinand was assassinated in June 1914. However, once the selectors were given free rein after the abrogation of the quota in 1997, they added just one more pre–World War I debutant to the Hall's player category through to the end of 2017. Gorringe (Cananore, 1914–1930) was bestowed the honour in 2011, making him the sole pre-WWI representative among the 121 players inducted during those two decades. As a result, heading into 2018, just 10% of the 221 Hall of Fame players had played in the first 56 years of Australian football's 159-year history. In contrast, 17% (37 of the 221-strong cohort) made their senior debut during the 1960s alone.

There are other techniques that we can use to illustrate the distorted distribution of inductees across time. One is to measure the number of Hall of Fame players who were active in a particular decade. Using this method, Barrie Robran's career, which began in 1967 and ended in 1980, would count towards the tallies for the 1960s, 1970s, and 1980s. Another way is to count the combined number of seasons played by the entire Hall of Fame cohort in a particular decade. In this instance, Robran's career would contribute three seasons to the tally for the 1960s, ten to the 1970s, and one to the 1980s. The graph overleaf shows the results from each method.

Both lines trend steadily upwards from the 1870s until reaching a peak during the 1970s. From there they drop steeply to the present day. More than a third (34%) of all inducted players were active at some point during the 1970s, and 15% of the seasons played by the entire pool took place during this decade. The latter number is comparable to the combined proportion of player seasons from the six decades between the 1870s and 1920s. Although a similar number of inductees were active in the 1960s (32%) and 1980s (34%), those

285

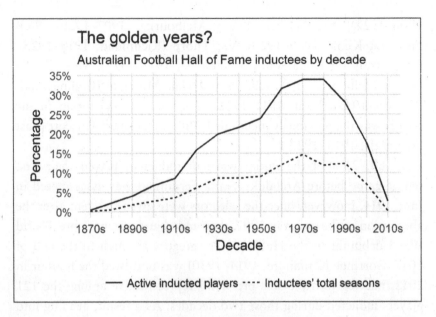

The golden years?

Australian Football Hall of Fame inductees by decade

— Active inducted players ···· Inductees' total seasons

decades fall on either side of the pinnacle because they share a slightly lower proportion of combined player seasons at 12% each.

Curiously, in the initial intake there were fewer player seasons from the 1960s to 1980s (31%) than there were from the 1930s to 1950s (37%). It was only from 1997 onwards that the skew towards the televised era took hold, which can be seen in the next graph. For this exercise we have broken down the Hall of Fame's roughly two-decade history into five distinct periods: 1996, 1997 to 2001, 2002 to 2006, 2007 to 2011, and 2012 to 2017.

As the graph shows, the proportion of inductees from the 1990s to 2010s has risen dramatically, from almost none in the Hall's inaugural cohort (when few were eligible), to 62% in the seven years to 2018. This has been partly driven by a clause in the charter stipulating that at least two of each year's inductees must be players who have retired in the previous decade. The stipulation was inserted to raise the appeal of the Hall of Fame ceremony as a televised event. 'The clause was created to give the event greater currency after a year when most of the then eight inductees were from the distant past, a couple of them deceased,' said former selector Mike Sheahan. In other words, it was considered preferable that the host of the ceremony was able to interview the players being inducted. That might also explain why the rate of 'baby boomer' inductees has remained consistently high. Of

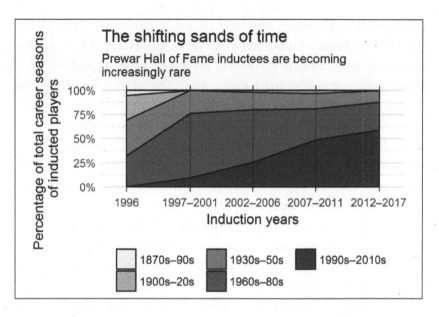

The shifting sands of time

Prewar Hall of Fame inductees are becoming increasingly rare

Percentage of total career seasons of inducted players

Induction years

- 1870s–90s
- 1900s–20s
- 1930s–50s
- 1960s–80s
- 1990s–2010s

the 121 players inducted since 1997, almost half (45%) of the seasons in which they participated were in the 1960s, 1970s, or 1980s. At the same time, the decades prior to 1930 have been all but forgotten. 'The Hall of Fame has eschewed the onerous task of inducting pre-modern candidates to concentrate instead on the more straightforward task of evaluating recently retired candidates and, more broadly, those of the modern era,' argued Cardosi in 2014. 'While satisfying the demand of the wider footy-loving public for recognisable heroes, the upshot is that the Hall has become absurdly skewed in favour of the TV age at the expense of the forgotten greats who developed and shaped the Australian game.'

Apples and oranges

But what if modern players are simply more deserving than their forebears? And what if the overwhelming number of Victorian inductees is justified? Perhaps the great Tom Leahy's achievements just don't stack up to the 10 (no exaggeration) VFL ruckmen of the 1970s who have made the Hall of Fame ahead of him. If all the major leagues and eras genuinely merit equal consideration – as the committee now insists – one way of testing whether the skews are defensible would be to benchmark the players' achievements. However, this task is made extremely difficult by the Hall of Fame's rather fuzzy selection guidelines. There are no minimum requirements for games played or goals kicked, nor for premierships or individual awards won. The official line from the AFL is that candidates are judged on their 'record, ability, integrity, sportsmanship, and character'. Apart from the first, these criteria are nebulous and near impossible to quantify. Meanwhile, factors that are easier to benchmark, such as games played or years served, have been deemed by the league to be of 'consideration only', and not a determinant of eligibility.

In truth, there are certain measurable touchstones that do seem to influence the selectors in their deliberations. Of the inductees for whom complete playing records are available, it is notable that almost all of them played 100 or more games at an elite level in Victoria, South Australia, or Western Australia. The anomalies are few, and their achievements truly exceptional: Dan Moriarty (three consecutive Magarey medals in a 92-game SANFL career limited by the First World War); Laurie Nash (99 VFL matches but another 119 in Tasmania and the VFA, in addition to being a Test cricketer); Colin Watson (93 games in the VFL, eight appearances for Victoria, and a Brownlow Medal); Jack Worrall (another Test cricketer who played 95 games in the VFA before the VFL split, and was later a five-time VFL premiership coach); and John Coleman (only 98 VFL games, but two premierships, 537 goals, and the second-highest goal-per-game average in VFL/AFL history). These five men aside, we can tentatively set a baseline of 100 games in the VFL/AFL, or the pre-1990 SANFL and WAFL, as an assumed eligibility mark.

The graph opposite shows that the number of players who met the 100-match benchmark in each decade since the 1890s closely matches the corresponding number of Hall of Fame inductees. At first thought, one might assume that this vindicates the high proportion of inductees from the 1960s to the 1980s. Games played can be a marker of quality, for it is rare for below-average players to enjoy career longevity. If the pool of 100-game players in a certain decade is larger, then why shouldn't it contribute more candidates? However, this line of thinking fails to account for the differing lengths of seasons over time. One-hundred games was a significant tally for

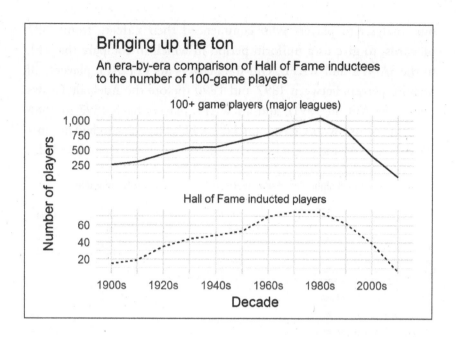

Bringing up the ton

An era-by-era comparison of Hall of Fame inductees to the number of 100-game players

100+ game players (major leagues)

Hall of Fame inducted players

Number of players

1,000
750
500
250

60
40
20

1900s   1920s   1940s   1960s   1980s   2000s

Decade

pre-1950s players, many of whose careers were either interrupted by war or ended by injuries that would have been treatable in later eras. Contrastingly, of all inductees who debuted in the 1960s or later, only the master full-forward Peter Hudson (129 games) featured in fewer than 180 senior games in the three major states (although he did take to the field on another 159 occasions in Tasmania). None of the inductees who debuted in the 1970s onwards played fewer than 200 games.

If matches played is an impractical yardstick on its own, are there any other tacit benchmarks that a candidate needs to achieve in those games? The biographical information about each inductee that is published annually in the AFL's season guide provides some insight into what the selection committee considers important. These brief profiles typically include statistics such as goals kicked, state appearances, seasons captained, All-Australian selections, Grand Final best-on-ground awards, league and club leading goal-kicker awards, league and club best-and-fairest awards, and selection in league and club teams of the century. By bringing together some of these datasets from the VFL/AFL, SANFL and WAFL, we can use a regression model to statistically test which factors have been consistently deemed valuable in the eyes of selectors. We will restrict our analysis to players who commenced their careers from 1897 onwards, to give us a uniform period in which to compare the VFL to the SANFL and WAFL. Our data covers all VFL/AFL players, all SANFL players between 1897 and 1990 (before the Adelaide Crows joined the AFL in 1991), and all WAFL players from 1897 to 1986 (the year before West Coast joined the VFL). Players who had not met the five-year-retired eligibility criterion in 2017 have been excluded.

Statistical significance of player achievements towards induction in the Australian Football Hall of Fame				
	VFL/AFL (1897–1989)	SANFL (1897–1990)	WAFL (1897–1986)	VFL/AFL (1990–2011)
Career games	Yes	Yes	Yes	Yes
Career goals	Yes	–	–	Yes
League leading goal-kicker awards	Yes	Yes	Yes	–
League best-and-fairest awards	Yes	Yes	Yes	–
Club leading goal-kicker awards	–	–	–	–
Club best-and-fairest awards	Yes	Yes	–	Yes
Premierships	Yes	–	–	Yes
All-Australian selections	Yes (National carnival era)	–	Yes (National carnival era)	Yes (AFL era)

Considering our earlier findings regarding the selectors' predisposition towards Victorians, it is unsurprising that VFL/AFL premierships and goals have been more statistically significant to Hall of Fame selection than those won or kicked in the SANFL or WAFL. League best-and-fairest awards have been rated as significant to the chances of induction across all the major states, which was partly a result of Basheer's deal to have all three-time winners of the Brownlow, Magarey, and Sandover medals included as inaugural inductees. The leagues' leading goal-kicker awards – the VFL's Coleman Medal, SANFL's Ken Farmer Medal, and WAFL's Bernie Naylor Medal – have also all been strong contributors to a player's chances of induction, although the Coleman has lessened in importance during the AFL era. This is perhaps linked to the trend towards a more team-based scoring approach. Again, it is important to note that this table only shows the aspects of a player's 'record' that have been most significant to induction so far. It does not account for the intangibles of 'ability, integrity, sportsmanship, and character', and so cannot be used as a guide to future selection.

The Legend and Leahy

There is no better example of the Hall of Fame's skewed nature than its 'Legends' category. This exclusive group is reserved for those deemed to have changed the game significantly for the better. Membership is restricted to 10% of the total pool of inductees. As of the start of 2018, 25 of the Hall's 221 player inductees had been elevated to Legend status, 24 of whom had spent all or a significant part of their career in Victoria. Barrie Robran was the sole exception, having played exclusively in the SANFL. However, Robran did have an important point in his favour. He was one of the nine Legends who had entered senior football during a seven-year period between 1962 and 1969. Remarkably, 16 of the 25 Legends were active in the final season of that stretch. In contrast, just five had debuted in the 81 years of Australian football prior to the Second World War, and just one in the 56 years before the First World War.

The only pre-WWI Legend was Roy Cazaly, who made his debut for St Kilda in 1911. He was worthy of the honour, having played and coached in more than 400 games in Victoria and Tasmania. He claimed St Kilda's best-and-fairest award in 1918, and South Melbourne's in 1926. At South, he formed a famous ruck combination with Fred Fleiter. Fleiter played as a 'ruck shepherd', and it was his job to clear space for Cazaly to jump for the ball. Once he had done this he would yell, 'Up there, Cazaly.' The phrase became a battle cry for Australian troops during World War II, and was later immortalised in a 1979 song by Mike Brady that became the sport's unofficial anthem. Cazaly also represented Victoria on more than a dozen occasions, a few of them against South Australia's Tom Leahy.

Considering Cazaly's position as a Legend of Australian football, it is instructive to reflect on the fact that he was regarded as the inferior ruckman to Leahy by many of his contemporaries. Even Cazaly himself described Leahy as 'the best follower' he ever met. As we discussed at the start of this chapter, Leahy was forced into retirement by Cazaly's brutal and somewhat desperate decision to kick his shins at every opportunity during their clash in the 1921 carnival in Perth. But Cazaly had not had it all his own way during that match. 'How well I remember bumping up against that fine old

South Australian,' Cazaly said several years later. 'I came out of the collision with a split eye. That was an accident. I was hurt but I can still hear the big fellow say to me as he left the pack, "I can't tell you how sorry I am: I never like anything like that to happen." It took half the sting out of the crack.'

At the final bell, the hobbling Leahy approached Cazaly and invited him back to South Australia's rooms. Considering his side's painful loss and the viciousness he had just endured, it was a gesture of good sportsmanship of a kind rarely seen. 'After the match he took me in hand and taught me a few of the finer points of ruck play,' said Cazaly. 'In that talk I learned more about ruck work than I could have done in years of actual play. That was typical of the big fellow. He towered over us by three inches and had about two stone advantage in weight, but I never saw Tom take a mean advantage of his weight. He played the game hard but fairly, and was always there with his hand out to help up a fellow who had got a crack in a scrimmage.' To say that nice guys finish last and that the winners write history is to draw on clichés, but in Leahy's case they both ring all too true. He was a legitimate giant of Australian Rules football, and his long absence from the Hall of Fame has been one of the sport's greatest injustices.

Chapter Thirteen
Team Ratings

The eternal question

Eddie McGuire was mad as hell and he wasn't going to take it any more. All weekend, the Collingwood president had been stewing over comments made by Alastair Clarkson after Hawthorn had lost its 2016 semifinal to the Western Bulldogs. The Hawks had been aiming to become only the second club in AFL/VFL history to win four straight premierships, following Jock McHale's Magpies of 1927 to 1930. Although Clarkson hadn't explicitly stated that his side's modern-day accomplishments were more meritorious than those of the Collingwood teams known collectively as 'The Machine', the insinuation was there. 'We've marvelled at the achievement of our players over the last three years, to win three in a row,' the Hawthorn coach had said. 'They talk about Collingwood and four in a row, and it was a fantastic achievement, but honestly, they won two of those after losing a preliminary final.'

To many fans, Clarkson's comments might have sounded nonsensical. In today's AFL, preliminary finals are knockout affairs, with no second chances for the loser. But Clarkson was a student of history. Between 1907 and 1930 the VFL had used what was called the 'Argus' finals system, which gave an inordinate advantage to the team that had finished the regular season on top of the ladder. If the minor premier won its first two finals, it would claim the flag. If it lost either of them, it had the right to 'challenge' the team that had advanced. Collingwood had taken the former route to its premierships in 1927 and 1928, and the latter to its 1929 and 1930 flags. To McGuire, though, the method didn't matter as much as the result. Furious at the perceived slight from Clarkson, he used his radio show to return fire on Monday morning. 'It's laughable. It's been the record since 1930. Everyone has accepted it and everyone understands it,' said McGuire. 'It is just ridiculous. Jock McHale is a legend of the game, and Gordon Coventry and Syd Coventry. If you want to line them up side by side on achievements, fair dinkum, they [The Machine] are miles ahead of what has happened in the last period of time.'

The argument was, in many respects, just a higher-profile version of the debate that has engaged fans and the media for more than a century: which is the greatest of all Australian football teams? Many would argue the debate is futile, because it is impossible to objectively rank teams across anything but the shortest expanse of time. The tactics, skills, and rules of today are vastly different from those used during the interwar and other periods. In 1924, the former long-time Collingwood secretary Ern Copeland was responsible for helping implement a radical change to football's out-of-bounds law. As the Victorian delegate to the Australasian Football Council, he betrayed the VFL's wishes to cast the deciding vote in favour of abolishing the boundary throw-in and replacing it with a free kick against the last team to have touched the ball. The rule change led to a spike in the scoring rate, after it had stagnated during the First World War.

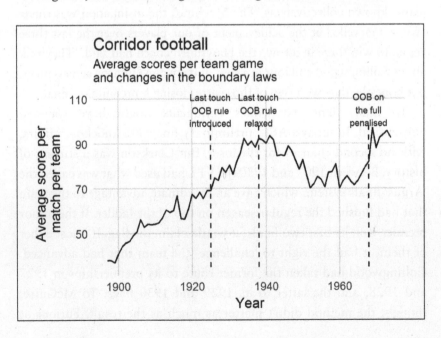

Copeland's club was the chief beneficiary of the new law, as the resulting corridor-focused play suited the strengths of Collingwood's key forward Gordon Coventry. In 1929, Coventry became the VFL's first single-season century goal kicker. Four other players would achieve the feat over the next decade. The following graph shows the number of players in each season who have averaged at least 4.5 goals per game, which is the rough benchmark for a 100-goal return in a 22-match season.

As we can see, there was a noticeable increase in the number of prolific goal kickers during the period the last touch out-of-bounds rule was in force, and again after the introduction of the out-on-the-full rule in 1969. The former rule was in use during all The Machine's premierships, meaning it was effectively playing a different version of the game to Hawthorn's premiers of 2013 to 2015. Such drastic evolution and change are huge obstacles to our ability to compare sides from different eras, but it doesn't stop us from trying. Nostalgia is a powerful emotion. There is a tendency to romanticise the great teams of the past, even if the level of professionalism and athleticism has increased many times over. This happens in all sports. During Golden State's rise to the top of the NBA, a procession of former basketball stars insisted the Warriors would have been no match for their own

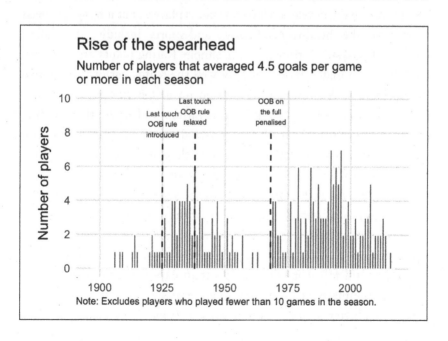

Rise of the spearhead

Number of players that averaged 4.5 goals per game or more in each season

Note: Excludes players who played fewer than 10 games in the season.

teams in their heyday. Scottie Pippen claimed he and Michael Jordan's Chicago Bulls sides of the 1990s would have swept the Warriors had they ever met in the finals. It prompted a sarcastic response from Golden State's coach, Steve Kerr, who was himself a member of those Bulls teams. 'They're all right. They would kill us,' Kerr joked. 'The game gets worse as time moves on. Players are less talented than they used to be. The guys in the '50s would've destroyed everybody. It's weird how human evolution goes in reverse in sports. Players get weaker, smaller, less skilled. I don't know, I can't explain it.'

In fact, even comparing teams in the same season can be trickier than it looks. Coaches and the media are fond of telling us that the ladder doesn't lie, but rarely does it tell the whole story. Although North Melbourne was undefeated and two games clear on top of the ladder after nine rounds of the 2016 AFL season, seven of the teams it had beaten would fail to make that year's finals. The Kangaroos' easy fixture had given an unrealistic impression of their ability. They fell to eighth after losing 10 of their last 13 games, and were thrashed by 10 goals in an elimination final against the Crows.

One method of measuring a team's relative ability is by using a mathematical ratings system. Among the most popular is the Elo system, which was devised by the Hungarian-American physics professor Arpad Elo. He originally developed it to rate chess players, but it has since been applied to other head-to-head games and sports, including Australian football. The system's principles are simple. Rating points are won and lost after each match based on how well the teams performed relative to expectation. A team's rating will go up if it performs better than predicted, given both teams' pre-game ratings and where the match is played. If it performs worse than expected, its rating goes down. The change in the two teams' ratings after they've played sum to zero, meaning that the increase in one side's rating is equal to the decline in the other's. An important feature of the system is that it adjusts the final margin to account for the quality of the opposition, which allows it to differentiate between a narrow win over a poor team and a similar result against a stronger line-up. Consequently, a victorious team's rating can still fall if it wins by less than expected against a weaker opponent. Similarly, a losing team can actually gain rating points by performing better than expected against a stronger opponent.

Rating teams in this way allows us to look beyond the ladder to get a more accurate reading of a side's true strength. The traditional four points for a win and two for a draw are nowhere near as nuanced. The ratings provide a useful, if still imperfect, starting point for comparing teams over time. We can also use them to predict the results of upcoming games, or even to simulate entire seasons. Of course, they are far from foolproof in this respect. The ratings are good at accounting for a team's past results, the margins by which it won or lost, and where its games were played – but they don't factor in other information that would be used by your friendly neighbourhood bookmaker. For example, the ratings didn't 'know' that Geelong was missing its best player, Patrick Dangerfield, through suspension when it was soundly beaten at home by the Sydney Swans in 2017. If a player is out for an extended period, a team's rating will adjust over time as its on-field results reflect that player's absence, but it will not do so immediately.

Attack versus defence

Tony Corke is a freelance data scientist who specialises in statistical modelling and analysis. Businesses and corporations employ him to analyse their data and create predictive and other statistical models that will help them understand, attract, and keep customers. In his spare time, he spends hours each week running the cult football analytics blog Matter of Stats. It started in 2008 as a newsletter he sent to friends, but it has since evolved into an online treasure-trove of statistical information about football. Corke uses several different ratings systems, many of them Elo variants, to proffer predictions and probabilities for upcoming games. Some provide not only a single rating for each team, but, like our Player Approximate Value metric outlined in chapter eight, separate ratings for a side's attacking and defensive capabilities.

The specifics of Corke's equations and how he optimises them are too technical for our purposes here, but basically a team's attacking rating will hinge on its record of scoring points relative to the quality of the defences it faces. A team's defensive rating will accord with its record of preventing its opponents from scoring, relative to the quality of the attacks that it meets. Both ratings will be adjusted for the venues at which the games were played, and the teams' accuracy in front of goal. Clubs start with attacking and defensive ratings of zero in their first game, and both are adjusted each week based on their performances relative to expectation. A fixed proportion of a team's end-of-year ratings are then carried into the following season. This reflects that playing lists, and therefore abilities, are at least somewhat stable from one season to the next.

The numerical value of each rating has a practical interpretation, as a team with a +10 attacking rating would be expected to score 10 more points than an average team when facing an average opponent at a neutral venue. A team with a -10 defensive rating would be expected to concede 10 more points than an average team under the same circumstances.

Highest-rated historical attacks		Highest-rated historical defences	
Team and year	Rating	Team and year	Rating
Richmond 1967	+29.6	St Kilda 2009	+27.9
Geelong 1989	+29.2	West Coast 1994	+26.7
Essendon 2000	+27.4	West Coast 1992	+23.8
Hawthorn 1991	+27.2	Carlton 1981	+23.4
Hawthorn 2012	+27.2	Sydney 2006	+23.3
Geelong 2011	+25.7	Adelaide 2005	+22.9
Carlton 1932	+24.2	Sydney 2005	+22.3
Adelaide 2016	+23.8	West Coast 1993	+22.0
North Melbourne 1998	+23.3	Essendon 1981	+21.9
South Melbourne 1934	+23.2	Geelong 1981	+21.6

The above table shows the 10 highest-rated attacks and defences in the history of the AFL/VFL, as measured by Corke's raw end-of-season ratings. At the top of the attacking pile is Richmond's 1967 side, which was the first of four Tigers teams to win premierships under coach Tom Hafey. It narrowly edged out Geelong's 1989 team, which was the first of three to lose Grand Finals under coach Malcolm Blight. Hafey's Tigers are one of four premiers on the list, and Blight's Cats are one of five runners-up. The other is the 2016 Adelaide Crows team, which, despite its attacking proficiency, failed to reach a preliminary final.

Number one on the list of highest-rated defences is Ross Lyon's 2009 St Kilda side, which lost that year's Grand Final to Geelong by 12 points. Lyon's Saints defended from the front, using a forward press that changed the way AFL teams played when they didn't have

298

the ball. The next two spots are held by Mick Malthouse's West Coast premiership teams of 1994 and 1992, while the 1993 Eagles team had the eighth-highest-rated defence. The list includes four premiers, two runners-up, and four non–Grand Finalists. Notably, there are three teams from the 1981 season. Carlton, Essendon, and Geelong were the most miserly sides in what was a high-scoring year.

Whether we can consider these teams also to be the 'best' historical attacks and defences is a matter of contention. As noted earlier, ratings are measured in points, but the league's scoring rate has varied significantly throughout history depending on the prevailing rules, playing conditions, and equity of the competition. Being a certain number of points better than an average opponent has implied different odds of victory in different eras. For example, a 20-point-better team would be more likely to win in an era where average total scores were around 120 points per game than in an era where average totals are nearer 180 points per game. Seasons have also varied in length, which provides stronger teams with more opportunities to accumulate rating points, and weaker teams with more chances to lose them. That tends to spread out the ratings across all the teams in the more recent, longer seasons. In 1927, for example, end-of-season attacking ratings spanned almost 22 points, and defensive ratings about 33 points. In 2013, the spans were about 42 and 56 points respectively. To get a truer sense of a team's attacking or defensive prowess, we can standardise its ratings by subtracting the mean rating and dividing by the standard deviation of all teams' end-of-season ratings for the relevant era.

Highest-rated historical attacks			Highest-rated historical defences		
Team and year	Rating	Standardised rating	Team and year	Rating	Standardised rating
Richmond 1967	+29.6	+3.41	Geelong 1931	+20.3	+2.53
Geelong 1989	+29.2	+2.98	St Kilda 2009	+27.9	+2.42
Melbourne 1940	+22.5	+2.98	West Coast 1994	+26.7	+2.40
Essendon 2000	+27.4	+2.84	Footscray 1931	+18.9	+2.37
Hawthorn 2012	+27.2	+2.82	West Coast 1992	+23.8	+2.14
Carlton 1932	+24.2	+2.79	Carlton 1981	+23.4	+2.10
Hawthorn 1991	+27.2	+2.78	Geelong 1951	+17.7	+2.06
South Melbourne 1934	+23.2	+2.67	Collingwood 1927	+16.3	+2.04
Geelong 2011	+25.7	+2.66	Sydney 2006	+23.3	+2.02
Collingwood 1902	+18.0	+2.63	St Kilda 1971	+18.8	+2.01

Standardising the ratings sees Hafey's 1967 Tigers retain their mantle as the top attacking side, but Lyon's Saints dethroned by Geelong's 1931 premiers as the top defensive team. Charlie Clymo's side conceded an average of only 60 points per game during its 21 matches that year. Standardisation also allows teams such as Collingwood's 1902 side to appear in the attacking list, even though its raw attacking rating of +18.0 is well below many others throughout history. That Magpies team played in an era when scoring was much lower and seasons much shorter, which made for significantly less variability in team attacking ratings. As such, its +18.0 rating is historically comparable to Geelong's +25.7 rating in 2011, which was earned across a longer season and in an era with higher average scores and larger variability in team ratings.

Lowest-rated historical attacks			Lowest-rated historical defences		
Team and year	Rating	Standardised rating	Team and Year	Rating	Standardised rating
Greater Western Sydney 2012	−28.9	−2.96	St Kilda 1899	−35.2	−3.81
St Kilda 1948	−20.9	−2.71	Brisbane Lions 2016	−37.6	−3.30
St Kilda 1955	−19.1	−2.47	Greater Western Sydney 2013	−36.1	−3.16
Melbourne 2014	−24.0	−2.45	Hawthorn 1928	−26.3	−3.14
St Kilda 1945	−18.4	−2.38	St Kilda 1901	−28.0	−3.02
North Melbourne 1943	−18.0	−2.33	Fitzroy 1996	−32.3	−2.99
North Melbourne 1930	−19.2	−2.33	Hawthorn 1950	−24.9	−2.96
Melbourne 2013	−22.6	−2.31	Fitzroy 1995	−32.1	−2.96
Greater Western Sydney 2013	−22.3	−2.27	Geelong 1945	−24.9	−2.96
Melbourne 2008	−21.7	−2.21	Geelong 1944	−24.2	−2.87

We can also use standardisation to quantify which of the roughly 1,500 AFL/VFL teams have finished with the lowest ratings, adjusted for the era in which they played. Through this method, Greater Western Sydney's inaugural team rates as the worst attacking side in the competition's history. The newcomers won only two of their 22 matches, and averaged just 58 points per game. The Giants' 2013 side also makes the bottom 10 for both attack and defence. St Kilda's 1899 team was historically woeful. In a season where the average team conceded 32 points per game, it let in an average of 82 per match.

Era-by-era overall ratings

One of the reasons that great teams are not inducted into the Australian Football Hall of Fame is the difficulty in objectively ranking their achievements. Using Corke's rating system, not only can we separately assess a team's attacking and defensive abilities, we can also obtain a team's combined or 'overall' rating by adding together its attacking and defensive ratings. Again, however, context is indispensable. A team can only beat what is in front of it, and its rating reflects only how much better or worse it was than its cohorts. In attempting to compare NBA teams from different eras in his book *Basketball on Paper*, Dean Oliver made a good analogy for this type of change in basic assumptions. 'If kids are learning in high school now what Isaac Newton was the first to figure out three hundred years ago, does that mean that Isaac Newton wasn't very smart?' he wrote. 'In two hundred years, when they're teaching Einstein's general theory of relativity to high school kids, won't we look dumb? Noooo. We're smart!'

Given the varying levels of average scoring and different season lengths across eras, we think it makes sense to look firstly at teams' overall ratings on an era-by-era basis, rather than on an all-time basis. A lack of reliable data has sadly forced us to overlook nearly four decades of colonial football (1858–1896), but we will divide the rest of football history into six distinct eras, each defined broadly by the similarity of total scoring in that era:

- Era 1: 1897 to 1919
- Era 2: 1920 to 1939
- Era 3: 1940 to 1959
- Era 4: 1960 to 1979
- Era 5: 1980 to 1999
- Era 6: 2000 to 2017

Applying Corke's rating methodology to the AFL/VFL's week-by-week results generates the data for the chart overleaf, which shows the five highest-rated teams at the end of seasons in each of our six eras. Again, we have used end-of-year ratings as the measure of a side's ability

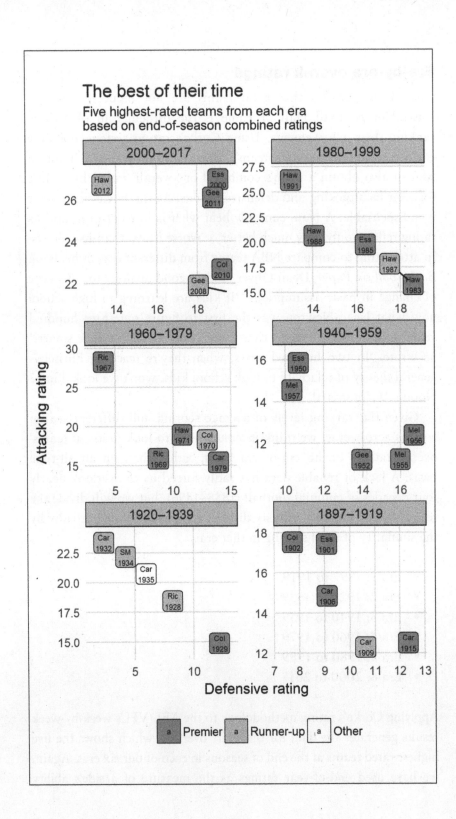

The best of their time

Five highest-rated teams from each era
based on end-of-season combined ratings

2000–2017

Haw 2012 · Ess 2000 · Gee 2011 · Col 2010 · Gee 2008

1980–1999

Haw 1991 · Haw 1988 · Ess 1985 · Haw 1987 · Haw 1983

1960–1979

Ric 1967 · Haw 1971 · Col 1970 · Ric 1969 · Car 1979

1940–1959

Ess 1950 · Mel 1957 · Mel 1956 · Gee 1952 · Mel 1955

1920–1939

Car 1932 · SM 1934 · Car 1935 · Ric 1928 · Col 1929

1897–1919

Col 1902 · Ess 1901 · Car 1906 · Car 1909 · Car 1915

Attacking rating

Defensive rating

Premier   Runner-up   Other

because we believe they best reflect the efforts of an entire season. Teams that enjoyed a late-season surge will undoubtedly benefit from this decision, while those that endured an end-of-year slump will suffer. 'Every decision you make as a data scientist has some influence on the outcome of your analysis,' said Corke. 'Your duty is to highlight these decisions, argue the case for them, understand their impact, and make an honest assessment of whether you think their effects are excessively distortionary. There is "science" and objectivity in data science, but there is also subjectivity, choice, and bias.'

On the charts opposite, the teams that won a flag in the same season as recording a top-five rating in their era appear in labels with a dark-grey background. Those that finished as runner-up have labels with a light-grey background, and those that failed to make the Grand Final are labelled with a white background.

There is no premiership weighting built into the ratings. 'Rating systems are designed to measure underlying talent and that isn't always reflected on that one day in September,' said Corke. 'To some extent, ratings are about demonstrated class over time and, quite often, Grand Final wins are about on-the-day form. Single-game results are subject to considerable random variation, but building a rating above 30 is far less so.'

Still, given the choice between finishing a season with a trophy and finishing it with a high rating, every fan, player, and coach would undoubtedly take the silverware. Some may argue that the ratings' ignorance of premiership success diminishes their ability to arbitrate the 'greatest teams' debate. After all, it was presumably just the one extra flag that made McGuire so adamant that The Machine's four straight premierships were more noteworthy than the Hawks' three-peat under Clarkson. But was its streak as significant as Melbourne's five flags in six years under Norm Smith, divided as they were into runs of three straight and two straight? For that matter, how exactly do we define a 'team'? Less than half the players who were in the Demons' 1955 premiership side featured in the team that won the 1960 Grand Final. Is wearing the same colours and having the same coach enough for them to be grouped together?

We will try to assuage some of these issues by separating the following era-by-era analysis into two parts. For each two-decade period, we will begin by discussing its top-five rated single-season teams. We will then overlay each club's season-by-season ratings with the era's Grand Final results. Through this method, we will anoint a 'champion club' for each of our six eras. Before we start, though, it is interesting to make some comparisons of the spread of ratings across the eras.

Era	Variability in teams' end-of-season attacking ratings	Variability in teams' end-of-season defensive ratings	Variability in teams' end-of-season combined ratings
1897–1919	6.5	9.1	14.4
1920–1939	8.5	8.2	13.9
1940–1959	7.6	8.5	14.0
1960–1979	8.5	9.7	15.0
1980–1999	10.0	11.0	17.1
2000–2017	9.7	11.5	18.7

The first thing to note in the above table is that the variability of combined ratings in each era has tended to grow over time, from 14.4 points in the earliest era to 18.7 points now. That mostly reflects higher levels of scoring in the modern era. Also conspicuous is the fact that the variability in attacking ratings has been smaller than the variability in defensive ratings for every era except 1920 to 1939, which suggests that the gap between the best and worst teams' defences has tended to be wider than the gap between the best and worst teams' attacks in a typical season.

Era 1: 1897–1919

Team	Year	Combined rating	Attacking rating	Defensive rating
Essendon	1901	+25.5	+16.9	+8.6
Collingwood	1902	+25.3	+18.0	+7.3
Carlton	1915	+24.8	+12.0	+12.8
Carlton	1909	+23.5	+12.4	+11.1
Carlton	1906	+22.9	+14.3	+8.6

The single-season dominance of Essendon's and Collingwood's premiership teams of 1901 and 1902 was reflected in their percentage. Essendon finished the 1901 season on 186.43%, while Collingwood ended the 1902 season on 199.47% – ranking them fifth and first on

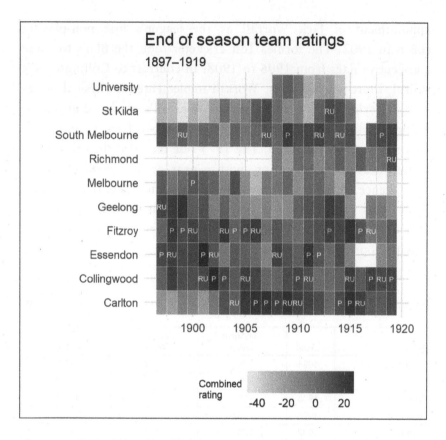

End of season team ratings
1897–1919

the AFL/VFL's all-time list for the best percentage in a home-and-away season. They were also our highest-rated sides of the VFL's first two decades.

Essendon, then nicknamed 'the Same Olds', was spearheaded by Hall of Fame centre half-forward Albert Thurgood. He was nearing the end of his career by 1901, but still starred with three of his side's six goals in that year's Grand Final win against Collingwood. One of his goals was reportedly scored with an 85-metre place kick. The Magpies turned the tables on Essendon in the 1902 decider, with a new, fast-paced passing strategy based on the stab kick.

Champion club: Carlton

Carlton made a slow start to life in the VFL. The Blues finished second-last in every one of the league's first five seasons, winning just 17 of their 82 games. The club's fortunes improved with the appointment of Jack Worrall as the league's first non-playing coach in 1902. The former Test cricketer took the Blues to three consecutive flags from 1906 to 1908. In contrast to Collingwood's skilful, short-passing sides, Worrall implemented a physical, long-kicking style. One of the players in Worrall's premiership teams, Norm Clark, later coached the club to back-to-back Grand Final victories in 1914 and 1915. The 1915 side recorded the era's third-highest season-ending rating, with a near perfect blend of attack and defence. Although Fitzroy claimed one more flag than Carlton during this period, the Blues' combination of premiership success and sustained high ratings after 1903 was enough for them to be crowned our first champion club.

Era 2: 1920–1939

Team	Year	Combined rating	Attacking rating	Defensive rating
South Melbourne	1934	+28.3	+23.2	+5.1
Collingwood	1929	+27.2	+14.0	+13.2
Carlton	1935	+26.8	+19.9	+7.0
Richmond	1928	+26.5	+19.3	+7.2
Carlton	1932	+25.6	+24.2	+1.4

The previously mentioned abolition of the boundary throw-in from 1925 to 1938 led to a league-wide rise in scoring, as well as increased attacking ratings. South Melbourne's Bob Pratt kicked 150 goals in 1934, which still stands as an equal record for the AFL/VFL. His output contributed to South's era-high rating of +28.3. It lost the 1934 Grand Final to Richmond, having defeated it the season before. Carlton's 1935 and 1932 sides both made the top five almost entirely on their attacking abilities. The 1935 team was eliminated in the semifinals, while the 1932 side lost that year's Grand Final to the Tigers.

Champion club: Collingwood

Collingwood ruled the interwar period under the stewardship of legendary coach Jock McHale. It claimed six premierships from

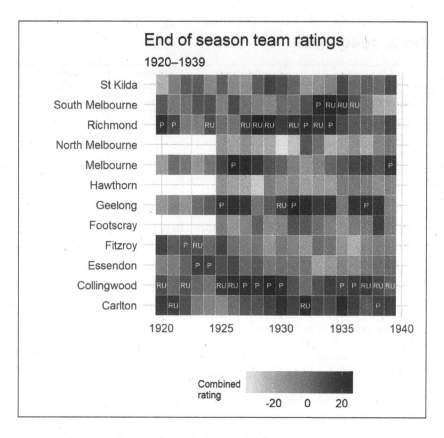

End of season team ratings
1920–1939

Combined rating

-20 0 20

13 Grand Final appearances, including its famous four in a row. The Machine was so named because of its machine-like teamwork and efficiency. Its game plan was geared around moving the ball quickly down the central corridor to its strong-marking forward Gordon Coventry. He kicked a century of goals four times during the period, and his career tally of 1,299 stood as a league record for six decades, until being broken by Tony Lockett in 1999. His older brother, Syd Coventry, was a champion ruckman, and one of The Machine's three Brownlow medallists, along with Albert and Harry Collier. The 1929 team went through the home-and-away season undefeated, finishing with 18 wins, no losses, and a percentage of 171%. It also would have been the era's top-rated side if not for a surprise 10-goal semifinal loss to Richmond, which cost it about 3.5 rating points.

Era 3: 1940–1959

Team	Year	Combined rating	Attacking rating	Defensive rating
Melbourne	1956	+28.7	+11.8	+17.0
Melbourne	1955	+28.3	+11.7	+16.6
Essendon	1950	+27.1	+16.4	+10.7
Geelong	1952	+24.6	+10.6	+14.0
Melbourne	1957	+24.3	+14.5	+9.7

Defensive ability became more important in this era, and the highest-rated team had a defensive rating more than five points higher than its attacking one. That team, Melbourne's 1956 premiership side, successfully defended the flag it had won the previous year. It had finished 1955 rated +28.3, placing it second on our list. The Demons completed a hat-trick of Grand Final victories in 1957, with that side rounding out the top five at +24.3.

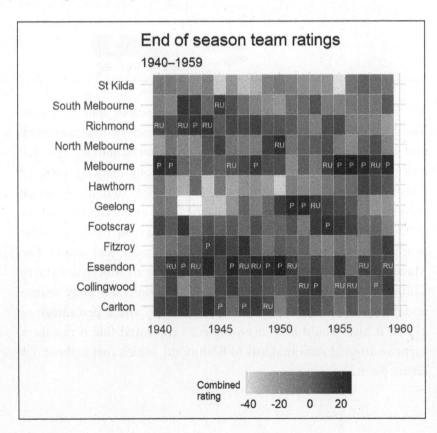

The 1950 and 1952 premiers, Essendon and Geelong, also recorded high combined ratings. Both sides claimed the second of back-to-back flags for their clubs. The 1950 Bombers featured the great full-forward John Coleman in his prime. He finished the season with a career-best 120 goals. Reg Hickey's 1952 Cats were thought to be the VFL's fastest team to that point, and were also renowned for the speed and efficiency of their ball movement.

Champion club: Melbourne

Having won four premierships with Melbourne as a player, Norm Smith returned as coach in 1952 and became the architect of the greatest period in the club's history. It was he who pushed the increased emphasis on defence. 'I believe football is a two-part game, and that defence is equally important as attack,' he said. Smith instructed his defenders to kick wide to the boundary. At the time, there was no out-on-the-full rule and players were rarely penalised for deliberately kicking the ball out of bounds. Once they had cleared the ball from their backline, the Demons played a direct, long-kicking style. They used what was known as a 'decoy' forward system, with the full-forward leading high up the ground to create space near the goal square for a resting ruckman and smaller, crumbing players. Melbourne had a different leading goal kicker in each of its premiership seasons while Smith was coach.

Era 4: 1960–1979

Team	Year	Combined rating	Attacking rating	Defensive rating
Richmond	1967	+32.6	+29.6	+3.0
Hawthorn	1971	+31.5	+19.6	+11.9
Carlton	1979	+29.0	+14.1	+15.0
Collingwood	1970	+28.3	+16.0	+12.3
Richmond	1969	+27.1	+17.3	+9.8

The attacking game received a fillip with the introduction of the out-on-the-full rule in 1969, which removed the boundary as a sanctuary for defenders. Four of the era's five highest-rated teams came after the rule change, although the top-rated side preceded it. Richmond's 1967 premiership team was all about attack. The Tigers averaged 106 points per game across the entire season, which was more than four goals better than the average team. It was also more than two goals per game better than the next best team, Geelong, which they beat by nine points in the Grand Final.

The 1971 Hawks were built around full-forward Peter Hudson, who equalled Pratt's single-season record of 150 goals. 'We'd just kick the ball as far as we could,' said captain David Parkin. 'We'd then start a brawl, win the ball, kick the ball as far as we could again, start another brawl, and then kick it to Peter Hudson.'

Champion club: Richmond

Tom Hafey succeeded Len Smith as Richmond coach in 1966, but borrowed heavily from the directness and physicality that Len's

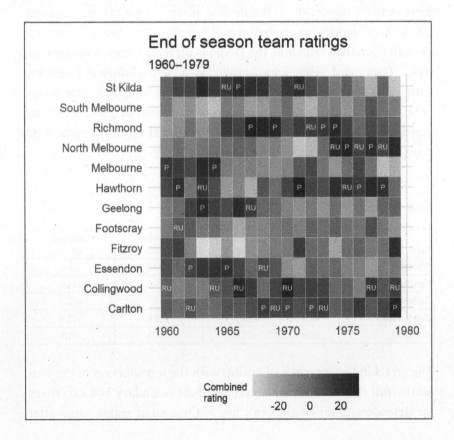

brother Norm Smith had used to such effect at Melbourne. 'He was the one I copied and loved. He was the role model,' said Hafey. 'No nonsense, no frills, no finessin' – very, very direct.' The Tigers' philosophy was to move the ball forward at all costs. They took relatively few marks because of Hafey's belief that most goals were scored from crumbs or handballs received. Their frenetic, play-on style was underpinned by their superior fitness, developed through Hafey's uncommonly tough training regimen. During his reign, they won premierships in 1967, 1969, 1973 and 1974. In 1972 they lost to Carlton in the highest-scoring Grand Final in history, 28.9 (177) to 22.18 (150).

Era 5: 1980–1999

Team	Year	Combined rating	Attacking rating	Defensive rating
Hawthorn	1991	+39.7	+27.2	+12.5
Hawthorn	1988	+36.3	+21.7	+14.6
Essendon	1985	+35.0	+18.5	+16.5
Hawthorn	1987	+34.6	+16.2	+18.4
Hawthorn	1983	+33.9	+15.1	+18.8

A typical team of the 1980s or 1990s scored and conceded 99.6 points per game, which is comfortably the highest of any era. The average margin of victory was 37.4 points. Hawthorn's 1991 side was the era's highest-rated team. It averaged a remarkable 126.3 points per game, while conceding 93.4 per match, on its way to claiming the Hawks' fifth flag in nine years. Hawthorn's 1988 and 1983 premiership sides also made the top five, as did the 1987 team, which lost to Robert Walls's Carlton in that year's Grand Final.

The only non-Hawthorn team on the list is Kevin Sheedy's Essendon side of 1985. It finished the home-and-away season on top of the ladder, three wins clear of Footscray. It had the highest percentage of any team (138.4), the highest points-scored total (2,755 from 22 games), and the highest scoring-shot conversion rate (58%). The Bombers defended the premiership they had won the previous year, thrashing the Hawks by 78 points in the Grand Final.

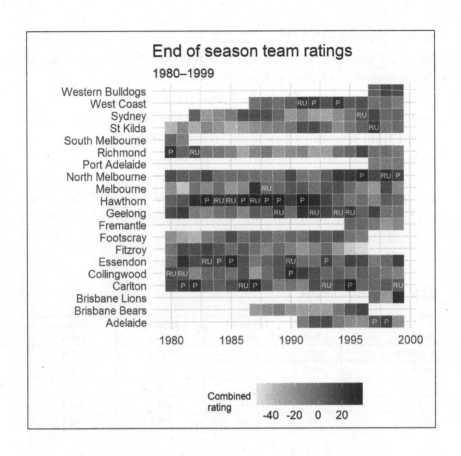

Champion club: Hawthorn

Allan Jeans described his side's style as 'the classical running game'. The Hawks' backmen were encouraged to run with the ball and join the team's midfielders on their attacking raids. They were also one of the first clubs to consistently use a switch in play coming out of defence. 'If you're going to change direction in the backline and swing it around and come back down the other side, you've got to be very skilful,' said Jeans. Up forward, Jason Dunstall and Dermott Brereton provided strong focal points. Dunstall became a three-time Coleman medallist. His career total of 1,254 goals places him third on the all-time list behind Lockett and Coventry. Between 1983 and 1991, Hawthorn claimed five premierships from a remarkable eight Grand Final appearances. Its average combined rating over this nine-year period was +31.0.

Era 6: 2000–2017

Team	Year	Combined rating	Attacking rating	Defensive rating
Essendon	2000	+47.0	+27.4	+19.6
Geelong	2011	+43.9	+25.7	+18.3
Collingwood	2010	+41.6	+22.1	+19.6
Geelong	2008	+41.0	+21.6	+19.4
Hawthorn	2012	+39.9	+27.2	+12.7

Although Brisbane, Geelong, and Hawthorn have all put together dynastic streaks during the modern era, Essendon owns the best single-season performance. It swept all before it in 2000, winning 20 games in a row. It was denied a perfect record only by the radical 'ultra flood' tactics used by the Western Bulldogs to snap their streak in round 21. Sheedy's side thrashed Melbourne by 10 goals in the Grand Final.

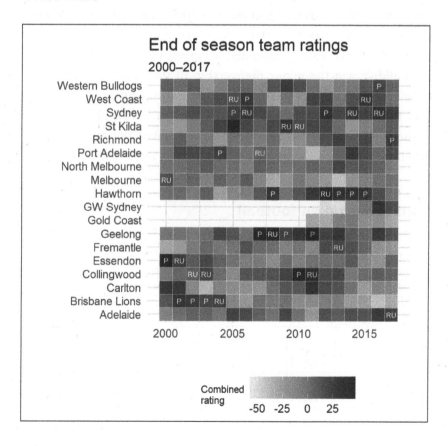

Geelong features twice on this list, with its 2011 premiership side and the 2008 team that finished runner-up to Hawthorn. Despite the Hawks claiming four flags between 2008 and 2015, the only one of their teams to finish among the era's top five highest-rated sides was the one that lost the 2012 Grand Final to the Sydney Swans.

Champion club: Geelong

Brisbane's and Hawthorn's three-in-a-row premierships are perhaps more regularly nominated in any discussion about history's best teams, but in our opinion, they are both shaded by the great Geelong sides of 2007 to 2011. Geelong's average combined rating across this five-year period was a truly impressive +34.7. Mark Thompson and skills coach David Wheadon devised a system of play they called 'run and carry'. 'It was big on risk-taking, using a lot of handball, and carrying the ball more,' said Cats defender Matthew Scarlett. They won premierships under Thompson in 2007 and 2009, and another under Chris Scott in 2011. The Lions' premiership sides coached by Leigh Matthews never dominated a season in quite the same way. They didn't win the minor premiership in the same year as any of their flags, and none of their Grand Final–winning teams were in the era's top-10 highest-rated sides. Hawthorn, meanwhile, beat Geelong in the 2008 Grand Final and finished the era with one more flag, but never quite reached the rating peaks scaled by the Cats.

South Australian football

Era 1: 1897–1919	Year	Combined rating	Attacking rating	Defensive rating
Port Adelaide	1914	+33.5	+23.3	+10.3
South Adelaide	1898	+28.5	+19.2	+9.3
Port Adelaide	1897	+22.1	+6.4	+15.7

Era 2: 1920–1939	Year	Combined rating	Attacking rating	Defensive rating
Port Adelaide	1937	+30.6	+17.4	+13.2
South Adelaide	1938	+29.4	+23.3	+6.1
Norwood	1922	+23.7	+14.1	+9.7

Era 3: 1940–1959	Year	Combined rating	Attacking rating	Defensive rating
Port Adelaide	1957	+37.2	+26.6	+10.6
Port Adelaide	1959	+30.5	+13.9	+16.6
Port Adelaide	1956	+29.3	+9.5	+19.7

Era 4: 1960–1979	Year	Combined rating	Attacking rating	Defensive rating
Glenelg	1975	+45.9	+36.8	+9.1
Sturt	1966	+39.4	+27.1	+12.3
Sturt	1974	+38.6	+6.6	+32.0

Era 5: 1980–1999	Year	Combined rating	Attacking rating	Defensive rating
Port Adelaide	1980	+45.8	+27.6	+18.2
WWT Eagles	1993	+42.5	+17.5	+25.0
Port Adelaide	1990	+38.2	+31.5	+6.7

Era 6: 2000–2017	Year	Combined rating	Attacking rating	Defensive rating
Central District	2004	+44.0	+18.9	+25.00
Central District	2000	+34.9	+23.4	+11.5
Central District	2005	+34.7	+15.9	+18.8

Port Adelaide won 34 South Australian premierships in the 121 seasons between 1897 and 2017, or more than one every four years. The 1940s was the only decade in which it failed to add to its tally. At the end of 1949, Fos Williams was poached from West Adelaide and appointed Port's captain-coach. The Magpies won nine flags with Williams at the helm, playing a tough, Victorian-inspired brand of football that vastly differed from the gentler, skilful style usually seen in South Australia. Williams's supremacy was ended by Jack Oatey's Sturt teams of the 1960s, which used handball as an attacking weapon. A new period of Magpies domination began in the late 1970s under John Cahill, who eventually became the inaugural coach of Port's AFL team in 1997. During the AFL era, the SANFL's most successful club has been Central District. The Bulldogs played in every Grand Final between 2000 and 2011, winning nine flags. Interestingly, the highest-rated team in SANFL history was the Neil Kerley–coached Glenelg side, which lost by two goals to Norwood in the 1975 Grand Final. Its +45.9 end-of-season rating included an astonishing attacking rating of +36.8. Two weeks before the finals it had kicked a record 49 goals 23, to annihilate Central by 238 points.

Western Australian football

1897–1919	Year	Combined rating	Attacking rating	Defensive rating
East Fremantle	1917	+35.6	+19.6	+16.0
East Fremantle	1911	+28.3	+20.5	+7.8
East Fremantle	1909	+27.7	+14.8	+12.9

1920–1939	Year	Combined rating	Attacking rating	Defensive rating
East Fremantle	1934	+26.8	+5.7	+21.0
East Fremantle	1931	+26.7	+14.1	+12.6
East Perth	1926	+23.8	+15.1	+8.7

1940–1959	Year	Combined rating	Attacking rating	Defensive rating
East Perth	1944	+45.1	+22.1	+23.0
South Fremantle	1953	+43.0	+23.9	+19.1
South Fremantle	1952	+43.0	+22.3	+20.7

1960–1979	Year	Combined rating	Attacking rating	Defensive rating
Perth	1968	+33.6	+15.4	+18.2
West Perth	1969	+29.9	+8.1	+21.8
Perth	1977	+27.4	+17.3	+10.1

1980–1999	Year	Combined rating	Attacking rating	Defensive rating
Claremont	1991	+54.9	+25.8	+29.0
Claremont	1981	+49.9	+31.3	+18.7
Claremont	1987	+47.0	+16.5	+30.5

2000–2017	Year	Combined rating	Attacking rating	Defensive rating
Claremont	2012	+46.9	+22.4	+24.5
Subiaco	2008	+46.9	+27.9	+18.9
South Fremantle	2005	+42.0	+22.7	+19.2

East Fremantle was by far Western Australia's most successful side during the first half of the 20th century, winning 21 premierships from 1900 to 1946. East Perth enjoyed a period of dominance under the master coach Phil Matson at the end of World War I, claiming seven flags in nine years between 1919 and 1927. Jack Sheedy and Graham 'Polly' Farmer helped revolutionise the sport with their handball-happy East Perth sides of the 1950s. Hall of Fame Legend Barry Cable joined Perth in 1962, and won the Simpson Medal for best on ground in all three of its Grand Final victories from 1966 to 1968. The 1968 team was the highest rated of its era. The highest-rated team in WAFL history was Claremont's 1991 side, which included six of the top seven players selected in that year's AFL draft. It was one of four Claremont premiership teams coached by Gerard Neesham, who later took his water-polo inspired tactics to the AFL as the inaugural coach of the Fremantle Dockers.

The best of the best

As we discussed earlier, one method for comparing ratings across time is to standardise them, using the average and standard deviation of ratings for each era. This adjusts for the effects of lower average scoring and shorter seasons in some eras, and affords teams from those eras a fairer shot at finishing on all-time lists. So, for example, the year The Machine's domination began in 1927, the standard deviation in end-of-season combined ratings was 15.8 points. For the entire 1920 to 1939 era it was 13.9 points. In comparison, when the Hawks embarked on their streak in 2013, the standard deviation of combined ratings was 23.1 points, or almost 50% higher. For the 2000 to 2017 era it was 18.7 points, or about 35% higher than the era in which The Machine played. As such, the 2013 Hawks' combined rating would need to be about 35% larger than that of the 1927 Magpies for their standardised ratings to be equal. As it happens, that is almost exactly what we find.

The Hawks versus The Machine: raw ratings				
Team	Year	Combined rating	Attacking rating	Defensive rating
Hawthorn	2013	+29.7	+19.2	+10.5
Hawthorn	2014	+29.2	+16.8	+12.4
Hawthorn	2015	+27.6	+15.1	+12.5
Collingwood	1927	+21.2	+5.0	+16.3
Collingwood	1928	+17.9	+7.5	+10.4
Collingwood	1929	+27.2	+14.0	+13.2
Collingwood	1930	+20.2	+19.5	+0.7

The Hawks versus The Machine: standardised ratings				
Team	Year	Combined rating	Attacking rating	Defensive rating
Hawthorn	2013	+1.59	+2.00	+0.90
Hawthorn	2014	+1.57	+1.75	+1.07
Hawthorn	2015	+1.48	+1.58	+1.08
Average		+1.55	+1.77	+1.01
Collingwood	1927	+1.52	+0.52	+2.04
Collingwood	1928	+1.29	+0.82	+1.33
Collingwood	1929	+1.95	+1.58	+1.67
Collingwood	1930	+1.45	+2.24	+0.15
Average		+1.56	+1.55	+1.05

Accounting for the eras in which they played, Clarkson's three-peat Hawks and The Machine are only a rounding error away from having an identical average overall rating during their premiership streaks. McHale's side gets the nod by a mere 0.01 of a rating point. Although Eddie McGuire would probably see that as enough to claim vindication, we would be inclined to call it a draw. Whatever the case, they were certainly not 'miles ahead', as McGuire had insisted. None of the individual teams in either streak, however, come close to the three highest overall standardised ratings in AFL/VFL history.

3rd: Hawthorn, 1991. Standardised combined rating: +2.32

After standardisation, Hawthorn's 1991 premiership team comes out, perhaps surprisingly, as the competition's third-highest-rated side of all time. Although the Hawks had dominated the 1980s under Allan Jeans and Alan Joyce, by 1991 they had largely been written off as being 'too old and too slow'. This perception was enhanced when they suffered an 86-point thrashing at the hands of the newly formed Adelaide Crows in round one. By the end of round 12 they had six wins and five losses, and were facing a fight to make the finals. From there, however, they played like a side possessed. The Hawks lost only once for the rest of the season, to the eventual minor premier, West Coast, in round 22. They beat the Eagles in Perth and Melbourne during the finals, including a 53-point Grand Final victory. West Coast under Malthouse may have been one of the greatest defensive units of all time, but Joyce's Hawks were an attacking juggernaut. They scored more than 100 points in 17 of their 25 games, including seven scores above 150.

Hawthorn's 1991 premiership team

B: James Morrissey, Chris Langford, Gary Ayres
HB: Michael Tuck, Chris Mew, Ray Jencke
C: Darrin Pritchard, Ben Allan, Andrew Gowers
HF: Paul Hudson, Dermott Brereton, Tony Hall
F: Darren Jarman, Jason Dunstall, Paul Dear
R: Stephen Lawrence, Anthony Condon, John Platten
Int: Dean Anderson, Andrew Collins
Coach: Alan Joyce

2nd: Geelong, 2011. Standardised combined rating: +2.36

Geelong came into 2011 with a new coach, Chris Scott, after Mark Thompson had resigned in the wake of a preliminary final loss to Collingwood. It had also lost its superstar midfielder Gary Ablett Jr, who had joined expansion team the Gold Coast Suns on a multimillion dollar contract. The Cats shrugged off the turmoil to win their first 13 games of the season. They suffered a brief midyear wobble with consecutive losses to Essendon and West Coast, before going on another five-game winning streak. In round 19 they had a 186-point win over Melbourne, kicking 37.11 (233) to the hapless Demons' 7.5 (47). They followed that up with a 150-point win over the Suns, who were missing Ablett through injury. Geelong finished the home-and-away season in second place, one win behind reigning premiers the Magpies, but having thrashed them by 96 points in the final round. They met again in the Grand Final, with Geelong prevailing by 38 points. For a dozen of the Cats' players, it was their third premiership in five years. 35-year-old Scott became the first man since Joyce in 1988 to win an AFL/VFL flag in his first year as a senior coach.

Geelong's 2011 premiership team

B: Josh Hunt, Matthew Scarlett, Tom Lonergan

HB: Corey Enright, Harry Taylor, David Wojcinski

C: Joel Selwood, Jimmy Bartel, Andrew Mackie

HF: Steve Johnson, Tom Hawkins, Travis Varcoe

F: Trent West, James Podsiadly, Paul Chapman

R: Brad Ottens, Cameron Ling (c), Joel Corey

Int: James Kelly, Mathew Stokes, Allen Christensen, Mitch Duncan (sub)

Coach: Chris Scott

1st: Essendon, 2000: Standardised combined rating: +2.52

Has there ever been a season quite like Essendon's in 2000? According to Corke's standardised overall ratings, Sheedy's Bombers are in a class of their own. The Bombers had won the previous year's minor premiership, but suffered a shock one-point preliminary final loss to Carlton. Determined to make amends, Kevin Sheedy's side ran roughshod over the rest of the competition. It recorded 20 consecutive victories and finished the home-and-away season five games clear of the second-placed Blues. Its percentage was 159.1, which was almost 25 percentage points better than any other team. The Bombers had a potent mix of goal-scoring firepower and miserly defence. Across their 22 regular-season games, they scored almost 150 points more and conceded 200 points fewer than any other side. Including their three finals victories, their average winning margin was 54 points. Matthew

Lloyd kicked 109 goals for the year and won the Coleman Medal, while captain James Hird returned to his match-winning best after three injury-plagued seasons. Hird claimed the Norm Smith Medal for best afield in his side's 60-point Grand Final win over Melbourne.

Essendon's 2000 premiership team

B: Mark Johnson, Dustin Fletcher, Sean Wellman

HB: Damien Hardwick, Dean Wallis, Dean Solomon

C: Chris Heffernan, Joe Misiti, Blake Caracella

HF: Mark Mercuri, Scott Lucas, James Hird (c)

F: Adam Ramanauskas, Matthew Lloyd, Michael Long

R: John Barnes, Justin Blumfield, Jason Johnson

Int: Darren Bewick, Paul Barnard, Steven Alessio, Gary Moorcroft

Coach: Kevin Sheedy

The best of the best: highest combined ratings (standardised)		
Team and year	Rating	Standardised rating
Essendon 2000	+47.0	+2.52
Geelong 2011	+43.9	+2.36
Hawthorn 1991	+39.7	+2.32
Collingwood 2010	+41.6	+2.23
Geelong 2008	+41.0	+2.20
Richmond 1967	+32.6	+2.18
Hawthorn 2012	+39.9	+2.14
Geelong 2007	+39.6	+2.13
Hawthorn 1988	+36.3	+2.12
Hawthorn 1971	+31.5	+2.11

In all, six of the top 10 highest overall ratings after standardisation come from the AFL's most recent era. In contrast, the 2000 to 2017 period boasted just two of the top 10 historical defences and three of the top 10 historical attacks. What this seems to suggest is that we are now in an era where the best teams are strong all over the ground, rather than at just one end of the field.

Chapter Fourteen
Fandom

The two Australias

A strange pall hung over Melbourne in the lead-up to the 2004 Grand Final between Port Adelaide and the Brisbane Lions. For the first time in 108 seasons of AFL/VFL competition, Victoria had no skin in the game. The state's inhabitants were warned to brace for the onset of 'GAS': Grand (Final) Absence Syndrome. Sufferers would experience symptoms including melancholy and detachment, and a 'pining for a bygone era when Victorian teams dominated'. 'It will be a more cerebral, intellectual exercise rather than a passionate exercise,' Deakin University psychology professor Boris Crassini told the *Herald Sun*. 'We are going to have a lot of people who couldn't care less.' Radio host Neil Mitchell labelled it an atrocity. 'Football is Victorian,' he howled. 'We understand football because it started here and because we had Ron Barassi, Lou Richards and Jack Dyer to tell us what it all meant.' Mitchell implored the league to enshrine laws that would protect Melbourne as the 'home of football', but his calls were ignored. Over the next two years, as the Sydney Swans and West Coast locked horns in successive deciders, the locals grew ever restless. When even the two preliminary finals became Victorian-free zones in 2006, the situation was seen to have reached crisis point. The great Barassi urged for an inquiry to be held. 'Of course, it worries me,' he said. 'It is not good for the game to have any one section dominating.'

It was curious that Barassi would view one section of the AFL as a mishmash of teams from not only Queensland and New South Wales, but also the traditional football states South Australia and Western Australia. It appeared typical of the myopic us-and-them attitude that prevailed throughout much of Victoria, although, ironically, Barassi had long been one of the most zealous preachers of the need for a national competition. He had coached Sydney for three seasons during the mid-1990s, helping to raise the sport's profile on the other side of the line that separated Australia's footballing tastes. This imaginary border between the native game and the rugby codes had always felt perfectly natural to Australians, but still had the capacity to surprise foreigners. It is rare for a country to be geographically divided by allegiances to different codes. Apart from climate-driven games like ice hockey, the concept is alien in sports-mad North America. It is certainly absent throughout most of soccer-obsessed Europe. The north–south split between rugby union and league in England is probably the most analogous comparison, although neither is that country's most popular code.

It was the late 1960s when the historian Ian Turner coined the term 'the Barassi Line' to describe the Australian sporting frontier. His reasoning was that anyone on the other side would be unlikely to know much about Australian Rules beyond its then best-known identity. 'Australia is divided by a deep cultural rift between the north and the south, known as the Barassi Line,' explained Turner. 'It runs between Canberra, Broken Hill, Birdsville and Maningrida, and it divides Australia between rugby and rules.' As his description implies, there is a portion of New South Wales in which Australian football is the predominant sport, because otherwise the River Murray would serve as a simpler demarcation. Over the years a few people have tried to chart exactly where the line runs.

According to ABS data, the geographical regions that fall south of the Barassi Line in New South Wales contain about 420,000 people. That is only slightly less than the population of Tasmania. The border is not a precise delineation, as both codes are played in the areas immediately surrounding it. Wagga Wagga is perhaps the best example of a mixed-code town, having produced AFL greats such as Wayne Carey and Paul Kelly, as well as rugby league legends like Peter Stirling and Steve Mortimer. Any iteration of the line, then, represents the midpoint in the gradient between the Victorian-style

The Barassi Line: four definitions

Ian Turner: the original

Ian Turner's line running between Canberra, Broken Hill, Birdsville in western Queensland, and Maningrida in Arnhem Land would look like this. It is unclear in what direction the line should run from Canberra to the coast, or whether Turner thought that rugby league was popular in East Arnhem Land.

Neil Pollock: the Jim Keys Line

Neil Pollock divided New South Wales by analysing local newspapers to determine how frequently they mentioned Australian Rules and rugby league. He named his resulting 'Jim Keys Line' for a country footballer who excelled in both codes. The towns on the Australian Rules side included Albury, Wagga Wagga, Griffith, Hay, Holbrook, and Leeton.

Colin Ross: the BaRossi Line

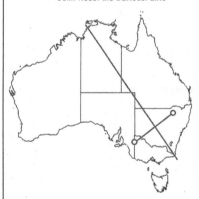

Colin Ross plotted the addresses of every local Australian Rules and rugby league club listed online to identify the geographical midpoint – or 'centre of gravity' – of each code. Australian football's was located south of Renmark on the South Australian–Victorian border. League's was near Moree in northern New South Wales. Bisecting the two points gave Ross a demarcation he labelled 'the BaRossi Line'. While it resembled other definitions, it put Darwin on the wrong side.

Our approach: ABS Statistical Areas

To estimate a population for New South Wales's 'Australian Rules country', we used the Australian Bureau of Statistics' geographical regions to define the portion of the state belonging on the southern side of the Barassi Line. The regions shaded here are the ABS's 'Statistical Area 4' regions of Murray and Riverina, as well as the smaller 'Statistical Area 3' of Broken Hill and Far West.

Australian Rules dominance seen in Albury or Broken Hill, and rugby league's equivalent supremacy in towns to the north and east, such as Gundagai and Cootamundra.

Interestingly, about a million more Australians live above the Barassi Line than below it. Despite the AFL's status as the country's most attended, most popular, and richest football league, 'Australian Rules Australia' is a minority nation in the Commonwealth. If we discount everyone north of the line, Victoria is by far the most populous Australian Rules state. In 2017, its population of 6.3 million outweighed that of South Australia, Western Australia, Tasmania, the Northern Territory, and sub-Barassi New South Wales put together.

Australian Rules Australia	
Location	Population
Victoria	6,300,000
Western Australia	2,600,000
South Australia	1,700,000
Tasmania	500,000
Northern Territory	200,000
Australian Rules NSW	400,000
	11,800,000

Rugby League Australia	
New South Wales	7,900,000
Queensland	4,900,000
ACT	400,000
	12,800,000

This fact, combined with fond memories of the AFL's former guise as the VFL, is often used to assert that Victorians are also the most fervent supporters. 'We invented football, we play it best, and we support it with numbers and passion the rest of the country can only imagine,' said Mitchell. One should always be wary of devoting too much thought to the ravings of shock jocks, but in this case the effort is actually worthwhile. To prove or disprove Mitchell's claim that Victorian fans barrack with an incomparable intensity, we need to disentangle fanaticism from size. While the scale of a packed MCG and the sheer number of cross-town rivalries undoubtedly make Melbourne a footballing mecca, we would argue the sport's true heartland is the place with the highest per capita fandom. In other words, it is the place you would be most likely to meet a fellow footy-head if you just picked a random person on the street. We will begin, therefore, from the premise that total volume needs to be considered alongside population-adjusted rates. Let's dig into some key figures measuring football obsessiveness, and tailor them to size where we can. Once we are done, we will tally up our numbers to find out which state loves Australian football the most.

Attendance

The most obvious way that a fan can show their support for their club, and by extension the code that it plays, is to buy a ticket and go to a game. So, which states have the most impressive attendance figures? Presented below are the state-by-state-by-territory figures for regular-season attendance during the 2017 AFL season.

State/Territory	Attendance	Games	Average
Victoria	4,085,120	100	40,851
South Australia	932,645	22	42,393
Western Australia	760,380	22	34,563
Queensland	330,545	22	15,025
New South Wales	475,021	19	25,001
Tasmania	85,550	7	12,221
ACT	37,507	3	12,502
Northern Territory	17,176	2	8,588
Shanghai	10,118	1	10,118

Victoria hosted more than half the season's home-and-away games, and, as befits its vast population, drew the majority of the total crowd numbers. However, it was South Australia that had the highest per-game average. The graph overleaf shows the average per-match attendance in each state since 2000. These figures include finals, although that barely affects the differences between states.

Western Australia's AFL crowds in 2017 reflected the state's long-term average of about 35,000 per game, but they were set to rise dramatically in 2018 with the opening of the new 60,000-capacity Perth Stadium. In South Australia, the shift to Adelaide Oval in 2014

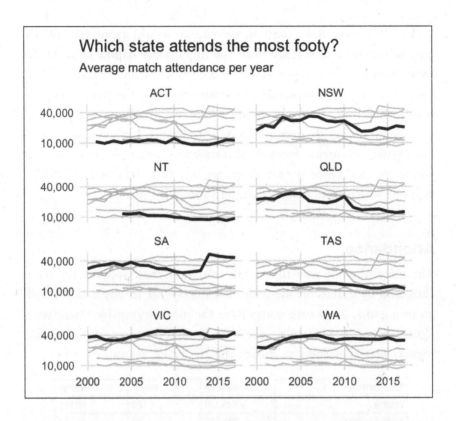

Which state attends the most footy?

Average match attendance per year

saw an immediate increase from a near-record low of 30,000 to a new high of 46,000. Its crowds have held firm at an average of more than 43,000 since then.

Per-game attendances dropped dramatically in Queensland and New South Wales after the introduction of the Gold Coast Suns in 2011 and the Greater Western Sydney Giants in 2012. Queensland's crowds have roughly halved since the Suns were established. This is partly as a result of the dilution of the state's AFL fanbase, with some of the Brisbane Lions' Gold Coast–based supporters switching allegiance to the Suns. It is also a reflection of both teams' poor on-field results. In the ACT, it took a while for the Giants' appeal and performance to bring crowds back to the levels seen when Melbourne-based clubs, such as the Kangaroos and Bulldogs, hosted games there during the 2000s.

If we want to use attendances to gauge a state's passion for the AFL, we also need to consider population size. In the next table we have converted the average attendance figures into a percentage of each state or territory's resident population.

Average match attendance as a percentage of population								
Year	NT	TAS	ACT	SA	WA	VIC	QLD	NSW
2017	3.5%	2.3%	3.1%	2.5%	1.3%	0.7%	0.3%	0.3%
2016	2.7%	2.9%	3.2%	2.5%	1.3%	0.6%	0.3%	0.3%
2015	3.4%	2.8%	2.6%	2.6%	1.5%	0.6%	0.3%	0.3%
2014	3.1%	2.5%	2.1%	2.8%	1.4%	0.7%	0.4%	0.3%
2013	3.2%	2.5%	2.2%	1.8%	1.4%	0.7%	0.4%	0.3%
2012	3.3%	2.9%	2.3%	1.8%	1.5%	0.7%	0.4%	0.3%
2011	4.1%	3.1%	2.8%	1.7%	1.5%	0.8%	0.4%	0.4%
2010	4.4%	3.2%	4.0%	1.8%	1.6%	0.8%	0.7%	0.4%
2009	5.0%	3.5%	2.8%	2.0%	1.6%	0.8%	0.6%	0.4%
2008	5.2%	3.5%	3.6%	2.1%	1.7%	0.8%	0.6%	0.5%
2007	5.4%	3.5%	3.8%	2.3%	1.9%	0.8%	0.6%	0.5%
2006	6.8%	3.5%	3.4%	2.3%	1.9%	0.8%	0.6%	0.5%
2005	6.4%	3.2%	3.7%	2.5%	1.9%	0.8%	0.8%	0.5%
2004	6.6%	3.4%	3.1%	2.3%	1.9%	0.7%	0.9%	0.5%
2003		3.5%	3.7%	2.5%	1.8%	0.7%	0.8%	0.5%
2002		3.5%	2.9%	2.4%	1.6%	0.7%	0.8%	0.4%
2001		3.7%	3.5%	2.3%	1.4%	0.8%	0.8%	0.4%
2000				2.2%	1.5%	0.8%	0.8%	0.3%
Avg	4.5%	3.1%	3.1%	2.2%	1.6%	0.7%	0.6%	0.4%

As much as 6.8% of the Northern Territory's entire population attended the Western Bulldogs' match against Port Adelaide in Darwin in 2006, which would be the equivalent of more than 300,000 Victorians attending a single game in Melbourne. Marrara Oval also once held 17,500 for an Indigenous All-Stars match, even though it has an official capacity of 12,500. Are Territorians the country's most avid football fans? Perhaps! However, it should be noted that this measurement shows Australia's three smallest jurisdictions as having the biggest crowds relative to population, when each host only a limited number of games per year. Four to seven are played annually in Tasmania, no more than three in the ACT, and a couple in the Northern Territory. This maintains a certain novelty factor that attracts not only the locals, but also a solid contingent of travelling fans who fly in to make a weekend of it. In contrast, the fans of the 10 Victorian clubs tend to frequent only their own team's games in Victoria, which suppresses the state's average turnout per match. Even if it was not a logistic impossibility, it would be financially prohibitive to attend all of Victoria's 100 regular-season games.

Of the three major AFL states, we can say with confidence that South Australians were attending games at a higher rate than Western Australians prior to 2018. Their crowds have been consistently bigger than or close to those seen in the West, even though Perth has about 50% more people than Adelaide. We can also comfortably declare that South Australians have been more avid AFL-goers than Victorians in recent years. The Crows have been a top-four side for home crowds since their move to Adelaide Oval, while the Power have fluctuated between fourth and sixth. These high rankings have been achieved despite neither side attracting many away fans to their games, unlike well-supported Victorian clubs, such as Essendon, Collingwood, and Richmond.

To rank the states, we have decided to use a composite measure that accounts for both the share of the population that attends an average game, and the total numbers through the gates. When we do so, South Australia comes out marginally ahead of Victoria.

Rank	State/territory	2017 per-game population percentage	Sub-rank	2017 attendances total	Sub-rank	Average rank
1	South Australia	2.2%	4	932,645	2	3.0
2	Victoria	0.7%	6	4,085,120	1	3.5
3	Western Australia	1.6%	5	760,380	3	4.0
4	Tasmania	3.1%	2	85,550	6	4.0
5	ACT	3.1%	2	37,507	7	4.5
6	Northern Territory	4.5%	1	17,176	8	4.5
7	New South Wales	0.4%	8	475,021	4	6.0
8	Queensland	0.6%	7	330,545	5	6.0

Club memberships

Another element we can consider when judging a state's affinity for football is its uptake in club memberships. Although precise regional breakdowns were generally not released in 2017, we do know that a) Hawthorn had a reported 9,000 Tasmanian members; b) North Melbourne had 7,000 Tasmanian members; c) the Brisbane Lions had an estimated 5,000 Victorian members; d) the Sydney Swans had a reported 12,000 Victorian members; and e) Greater Western Sydney had 4,258 Canberra-based members. These exceptions aside, we will assume most members are based in their club's home city. Only the Northern Territory is a complete mystery to us, but considering it only hosts a couple of games each year its population is unlikely to include a high proportion of card-carrying members. Here is our estimation of club memberships by state in 2017:

Rank	State/territory	Members	Share of population
1	Victoria	477,446	7.6%
2	South Australia	108,994	6.3%
3	Western Australia	116,318	4.5%
4	Tasmania	16,000	3.1%
5	New South Wales	63,524	1.3%
6	ACT	4,258	1.0%
7	Queensland	28,027	0.6%
8	Northern Territory	?	?

Victoria's strong membership culture stands out, even when accounting for its advantage in population and number of clubs. At 7.6% of the populace, a Victorian resident was more likely to be a member of an AFL club in 2017 than someone living in any other state or territory. South Australia again edged out Western Australia on a per capita basis. West Coast and Fremantle collectively had more members than Adelaide and Port Adelaide, but drew them from a larger population base.

The membership rate in Tasmania was substantial for a state that hosted only seven games during the season and had no hope of hosting a final. Together, the Hawks and Kangaroos boasted more members in the Apple Isle than the Gold Coast Suns had overall, and a similar number in Tasmania to both the Lions and Giants in their home states. Queensland lagged badly in terms of avidity demonstrated through memberships, sitting well behind New South Wales. The Sydney Swans had more members than the Lions, Suns, and Giants combined, albeit with about a quarter of their 58,000 based in Victoria. Their sustained success in recent seasons has obviously given their fans a strong incentive to sign up.

Registered participants

Football is woven into the fabric of life not just by passive observance of the elite competition, but also through active participation at the grassroots level. Part of a state's passion for the game is reflected by how many people play it. The following table has been compiled using the AFL's registration data for 2017. It shows state and territory participation numbers for both competitions and programs. The competition component includes club football, school football, and the 25,000 registered AFL9s players. This means there will be some double-counting of children who play both school and club football, and adult footballers who play AFL9s in the off-season. The amount of double-counting, however, should be similar throughout different regions. We should note that New South Wales and the ACT are reported together in AFL statistics, but we have estimated our own independent competition figures for the ACT.

Rank	Location	Population	Competitions	Competition participants as percentage of population	Programs	Program participants as percentage of population
1	Victoria	6,323,600	316,174	5.0%	145,506	2.3%
2	Northern Territory	246,100	12,292	5.0%	32,437	13.2%
3	Western Australia	2,580,400	112,116	4.3%	217,885	8.4%
4	Tasmania	520,900	21,838	4.2%	19,829	3.8%
5	South Australia	1,723,500	61,306	3.6%	112,742	6.5%
6	ACT	410,300	8,200	2.0%	?	?
7	Queensland	4,928,500	75,214	1.5%	165,764	3.4%
8	NSW/ACT	8,271,400	98,344	1.2%	156,468	1.9%
	Australia	24,594,400	697,284	2.8%	850,631	3.5%

We decided to rank the states and territories only by their competition participation numbers. This was because the program figures varied widely, and were probably more closely related to AFL and government investment than genuine community interest. The Northern Territory, for example, reported a huge percentage of its population as participating in football programs. This was especially marked in non-metropolitan areas, with the 22,000 registered participants seeming to account for every child outside of Darwin and Alice Springs. There are only 80,000 Territorians who don't live in those two cities, and roughly a quarter of them are under the age of 15. The rugby league states were also the beneficiaries of significant AFL investment, to the extent that Queensland had wider program participation than Victoria.

Surveyed participation rates

To corroborate the AFL's official figures, we can also consult public surveys about sports participation. The most recent relevant data we could find were the Australian Sports Commission's AusPlay surveys, but they didn't have enough state-by-state detail for our purposes. Instead, in the name of completeness, we have used the findings from slightly older surveys conducted by the Australian Bureau of Statistics. One of their advantages is that they avoid the double-counting inherent in the governing body's registration data. To account for variability in the sample-based surveys, we have ranked the states and territories by their average from three different years. We should bear in mind that these figures are based on self-reported survey responses. People were asked about their participation in organised sport over a 12-month period, so we must trust that they had a good memory and answered the questions honestly and accurately.

Rank	State/Territory	Average adult Australian rules participation rate, 2006, 2009, 2012	Average children's Australian rules participation rate, 2006, 2009, 2012	Combined Australian rules participation rate, accounting for demographic data
1	Victoria	2.7%	15.9%	4.3%
2	South Australia	2.7%	15.0%	4.2%
3	Northern Territory	3.2%	9.2%	4.1%
4	Western Australia	2.6%	12.9%	4.0%
5	Tasmania	2.9%	10.7%	3.9%
6	ACT	1.0%	4.9%	1.5%
7	Queensland	0.7%	3.5%	1.1%
8	New South Wales	0.3%	2.2%	0.5%

The Northern Territory comes out on top for adult participation, followed by Tasmania. However, there is a caveat. The sample sizes for the territories and smaller states were limited, and we were advised that they should be 'used with caution'. For children's participation, which excluded activities during school hours, Victoria and South Australia were decisively ahead of the rest. North of the Barassi Line, Queensland had notably higher rates than New South Wales. We suspect this is largely due to the strength of women's football in Queensland, where 40% of its participants in 2017 were female.

Elite player production

Included in Neil Mitchell's extended rant about the historic 2004 AFL Grand Final was a claim that Victoria is the centre of the football universe because 'We play it best.' While this appeared to be puerile trolling when set in its original context, an argument can be mounted that a fanatical heartland should indeed include a strong production line. Unsurprisingly, a large disparity still exists between the traditional football states and the rest of the country in terms of how much talent they contribute to the AFL.

Rank	Location	Population	Current AFL players	Share of all players	Current AFL players per million people	Average games by player
1	Victoria	6,323,600	432	54.2%	68.3	62.2
2	South Australia	1,723,500	102	12.8%	59.2	66.2
3	Northern Territory	246,100	14	1.8%	56.9	49.7
4	Tasmania	520,900	25	3.1%	48.0	62.7
5	Western Australia	2,580,400	116	14.6%	45.0	70.9
6	ACT	410,300	7	0.9%	17.1	44.1
7	Queensland	4,928,500	49	6.1%	9.9	49.1
8	New South Wales	7,861,100	41	5.1%	5.2	54.8
	Ireland (all)	6,638,560	10	1.3%	1.5	34.3

In general, players are listed as being drafted from the club for which they most recently played before joining the AFL. This has the potential to skew state of origin data. Some northerners who show an aptitude for football move south to board in their late teenage years, while older draftees often get their break only after crossing borders to prove themselves at state-league level. To ensure our findings were as accurate as possible, we manually altered our 'drafted from' dataset to attribute several players to their true home states. For example, we reassigned Tom Hawkins, Isaac Smith and Taylor Duryea to New South Wales, Charlie Cameron, Lee Spurr and Aliir Aliir to Queensland, and Cyril Rioli to the Northern Territory.

Despite our corrections, the data still showed Victoria had the most AFL-listed players in 2018 on both a total and per capita basis. Next in line was South Australia, which produced only 14 fewer than Western Australia despite its substantially smaller population base. The Northern Territory and Tasmania also contributed a respectable share relative to their size. Looking further afield, we have included Ireland as a comparison for the rugby league states. It is striking that New South Wales produced only about four times as much AFL talent as the Emerald Isle, half a world away.

One intriguing wrinkle was that the AFL's South Australian and Western Australian players had played more games on average than their Victorian counterparts. This might suggest that the Victorian talent pool is being more thoroughly scouted and drafted than the other states, leading to a slightly higher bust rate. Although we have awarded the Big V full points for this category, South Australia and Western Australia might justly feel that the talent identification scales are tilted in its favour.

'Soft' or casual fandom

How many footy fans are out there? Annual surveys by the Melbourne-based market research company Roy Morgan show that about 42.5% of Australians over the age of 15 identify as supporting an AFL club. That's about 8.3 million people. However, the surveys also reveal that in any given year about 5.8 million of those did not attend a match, and that nearly two million did not even watch a game on TV. These supporters are what we might call casual or latent fans, and they vastly outnumber the roughly 900,000 hardcore fans.

We know how many hardcore fans there are from the membership figures we ranked earlier, but the casual fans are a more statistically elusive bunch. They could be former hardcore fans whose commitment has lapsed because they have young children or work weekends. These people still follow their team's fortunes to some extent, even though they find it hard to get to games. But the casual fanbase also includes people who tell the survey-takers they support a club they rarely think about. You might have a workmate from Brisbane who claims they are a Lions fan, even though they believe Jonathan Brown is still playing. Or you might have a friend who doesn't usually discuss football, but who suddenly revealed themselves as a 'lifelong' Richmond or Western Bulldogs supporter around the time of their drought-breaking premierships. The AFL and its clubs spend a lot of time and energy trying to find ways to convert these casual fans into bigger devotees. Below are the club-by-club figures from Roy Morgan, which illustrate the difference between total fandom and the portion of fans who actively engage with their team.

Roy Morgan supporter survey results (2016–17)			
	Total fandom	Attended a game	Watched on TV
Adelaide	541,000	170,000	447,000
Brisbane	489,000	101,000	284,000
Carlton	464,000	145,000	346,000
Collingwood	663,000	190,000	510,000
Essendon	671,000	219,000	535,000
Fremantle	459,000	125,000	369,000
Geelong	515,000	174,000	404,000
Gold Coast	106,000	23,000	63,000
GWS	175,000	58,000	138,000
Hawthorn	528,000	167,000	422,000
Melbourne	229,000	103,000	178,000
North Melbourne	263,000	101,000	229,000
Port Adelaide	298,000	124,000	244,000
Richmond	442,000	153,000	337,000
St Kilda	294,000	85,000	231,000
Sydney	1,204,000	248,000	857,000
West Coast	669,000	169,000	573,000
Western Bulldogs	247,000	98,000	186,000
All clubs	8,257,000	2,453,000	6,353,000
No club	12,171,000	289,000	1,924,000
Total	20,428,000	2,742,000	8,277,000

In recent years, Roy Morgan has consistently found the Sydney Swans have had the AFL's largest fanbase. The Swans wrested the mantle from the three-peat Brisbane Lions in the mid-2000s. However, their base might fairly be described as a mile wide and an inch deep. If you have lived in Sydney, you will know that many of these fans only really pay attention to the AFL when the Swans make a Grand Final. Of the average 1.2 million people who identified as being Swans fans, only about a fifth attended a game in any given year. Essendon's total fanbase is about half the size of Sydney's, but it had almost as many attendees. The Swans are the most extreme example of a club with a lot of 'soft' support, but what about the states and territories?

One way that we can gauge an area's interest in football is by studying Google search data. A feature called 'Google Trends' cleverly aggregates search terms into topics. For example, searches for 'footy', 'afl scores' and 'afl fixture' will all be grouped under the topic 'Australian Football League'. The tool displays how much interest there is in topics over time and in different places. It also measures how commonly a topic was searched relative to all others, and shows where those searches originated. It can help us identify casual fans, because many more people keep tabs on a team online than attend games.

Data from Google Trends shows there was a higher proportion of footy-related searches made in Tasmania than anywhere else in Australia, with a relative interest level of 100. In Victoria, the data shows relative interest was 89% as high as in Tasmania. We have used this information from Google Trends to estimate the total footy fanbase in each state and territory. We can do this because we have two knowns: 1) the total Australian fanbase is 42.5% of the population; and 2) the relative interest level in each state and territory. Only one possible number of fans in each state and territory will satisfy both data points.

Rank	State/ Territory	Relative interest level (Google Trends)	Population over 15	Estimated fandom	Share of population
1	Tasmania	100	424,991	335,195	78.9%
2	South Australia	96	1,408,082	1,066,147	75.7%
3	Victoria	89	4,951,596	3,475,788	70.2%
4	Western Australia	79	2,113,924	1,317,148	62.3%
5	Northern Territory	63	191,319	95,064	49.7%
6	ACT	36	321,019	91,149	28.4%
7	Queensland	26	3,890,775	797,862	20.5%
8	NSW	23	6,285,152	1,140,149	18.1%
	Australia		19,586,858	8,318,503	42.5%

According to our calculations, there are about 335,000 Tasmanian football fans, which equates to a greater share of its total population than the fandom of the major football states. Does this mean it could support its own team? Well, we can say that if all of them could all be united behind a single Tasmanian side, it would have a supporter base larger than Roy Morgan's estimates for St Kilda, Port Adelaide, North Melbourne, the Western Bulldogs, and Melbourne.

The final scoreboard

When we tally up all our categories and adjust for population, it becomes apparent that Victoria really is Australian football's true heartland. It has more registered participants, a higher surveyed participation rate, a superior rate of elite player production, and more AFL club members than all the other football states. It sits second on our composite attendance measure because of South Australia's healthy crowds at Adelaide Oval, but, to quote the great Ted Whitten, the Big V 'sticks it up 'em' overall.

	State/ territory	Crowds	Members	Registration	Surveyed participation	Elite players	Soft support	Average rank
1	Victoria	2	1	1	1	1	3	1.5
2	South Australia	1	2	5	2	2	2	2.3
3	Tasmania	4	4	4	5	4	1	3.7
4	Western Australia	3	3	3	4	5	4	3.7
5	Northern Territory	6	8	2	3	3	5	4.5
6	ACT	5	6	6	6	6	6	5.8
7	Queensland	8	7	7	7	7	7	7.2
8	New South Wales	7	5	8	8	8	8	7.3

South Australia is the clear 'best of the rest'. In addition to its strong attendances, it placed second on every measure except official player registrations. Western Australia, Tasmania and the Northern Territory were all dragged down by a poor result in at least one category. For the West, it was its sluggish production of elite players. North of the Barassi Line, the ACT outperformed Queensland and New South Wales on every measure, even without an AFL club to call its own. Queensland, meanwhile, generally beat New South Wales on the grassroots measures, but had fewer members and smaller crowds.

This reflects the Swans' recent on-field success, and the struggles of the Lions and the Suns.

For all that, we concede our verdict should be taken with a grain of salt. To a certain extent, we have ourselves been guilty of equating the Australian Football League with the sport as a whole. Our measure of soft fandom, for example, focused only on the AFL, while ignoring latent support for state leagues, such as the SANFL and WAFL. The history and heritage of those leagues stretches back to the 19th century, and is a huge part of the lifeblood and culture of South Australian and Western Australian football. The AFL-centric data we used failed to paint that part of the picture. So, Croweaters and Sandgropers, you can hang your hats on that, and lament the hegemonic nature of Victorian bias, such that it extends even into ostensibly hard data.

Chapter Fifteen

Finances

Small business, big profile

If you have just landed at Coolangatta Airport and are looking for a good feed, it is hard to go past the Twin Towns Services Club. Its bistro serves pub-style meals, and for $17 you can have your choice of a rump steak, chicken parmigiana, fish and chips, an Aussie beef burger, or bangers and mash. Better yet, you will be given a complimentary beer, wine, or soft drink with which to wash it down. TripAdvisor ranks Twin Towns second out of the 85 dining options in Tweed Heads. 'The sports bar for dinner is absolutely great value,' wrote Louise from Melbourne, in a five-star review. 'The meals are huge and the variety of the menu is outstanding.' After eating you can try your luck at bingo, or have a flutter on the pokies. If gambling is not your thing, you might be able to catch some live music or watch a movie. The club also boasts a wide range of hotel rooms and apartments if you are looking for somewhere to stay.

Every September, the *Financial Review* publishes a list of the top 500 private companies in Australia. It ranks companies and associations that are not publicly listed on the stock market according to their estimated revenue. Twin Towns ranked 488th in 2017, with a revenue of $73.2 million and 311 employees. Two spots later came a club of a different kind. The Collingwood Football Club scraped in at 490th, with an estimated $71.5 million in revenue and 255 employees. To many readers, that might have seemed incongruous. How could the self-proclaimed 'biggest sporting club in Australia' be smaller than a regional RSL? Well, that is because despite how often they might have been told otherwise, the AFL is not big business. 'If you're talking about individual AFL clubs, they're small businesses really,' said *Financial Review* journalist John Stensholt. 'They're almost like a small emerging tech company in a way, in terms of turnover and staff numbers.'

The AFL's total operating revenue across all 18 of its clubs was $862 million in 2016, which was about the same as Ritchies IGA, a chain of independent supermarkets that ranked 45th on that year's top 500. In contrast, the Melbourne-based paper, packaging, and recycling company Visy was about seven times that size. Visy ranked number one on the list with a revenue of $5.7 billion in 2016 and $6.5 billion in 2017, but even it was dwarfed by Australia's two biggest listed companies. The Wesfarmers and Woolworths groups each turn over more $50 billion per year, or about 1,000 times more than the typical AFL club. 'If AFL clubs were listed on the stock exchange they'd be a microcap or a small cap maybe,' said Stensholt. 'They're pretty small fry.'

The paradox is that most AFL clubs will, on average, attract more media attention annually than Wesfarmers, Woolworths, and Visy combined. 'We have a turnover of $50 million and 120 staff, so we are relatively small in that sense, but we are a very big business when you look at our community impact and footprint,' said Adelaide Crows chief executive Andrew Fagan. 'The scrutiny the club receives is extraordinary. In Adelaide, it's more than perhaps any other entity – probably more than the government receives.' Indeed, the AFL has spawned an entire parallel industry devoted to covering it in minute detail – from newspapers and websites, to radio sports talkback and television panel shows. In recent years, the clubs have set up their own media departments to produce a steady stream of online content, to address what economists refer to as the problem of appropriability. 'Football clubs can't make money out of (can't appropriate) more than a tiny share of our love of football,' observed Simon Kuper and Stefan Szymanski in their 2009 book *Soccernomics*. To paraphrase them, Collingwood cannot charge us for talking or reading or thinking about Collingwood.

To that end, Kuper and Szymanski make the point that football arguably isn't even business at all. Clubs, especially the AFL's member-owned ones, exist to win premierships ahead of turning a buck. Their win–loss count matters more to them than their bottom line, and as not-for-profit entities they are exempt from paying income tax. 'It's sort of a blend of strict financial business and not-for-profit,' said Richmond president Peggy O'Neal. 'It's about a mission, it's about emotion, it's about a platform to do good things in the community. If we wanted to just make money, our model would be quite different.' So, if that is the case, why should we care about their finances at all? The answer probably lies in the vague notion that having more money will make a club more successful. 'I always like to think that on-field success is a product of off-field success,' said O'Neal. 'You need to have some money to invest in football before football comes good.'

Seeing through the spin

Even if AFL clubs are not officially out to make a profit, they certainly like trumpeting when they do. Only one club can win the premiership each year, but the others need to at least provide their supporters with the hope of future success. Fortunately for them, footy fans are naturally a hopeful bunch. A 2015 study found that fans 'were overly optimistic about their team's prospects relative to others'. Clubs know that supporters will take hope wherever they can find it, even if that's on an accounting balance sheet. 'That's certainly part of it,' said Stensholt. 'If North Melbourne can announce a small profit, then people will feel better about the club and it looks like the administration is doing a great job.' Thus, there is always an incentive for clubs to put a positive spin on their financial reporting. They can do this in numerous ways. 'When you're talking about profits, there are all sorts of different methods of carving it up,' explained Stensholt. 'There's net profit, operating profit, underlying profit – all that sort of stuff. Often it's just a case of choosing the one that paints the best outlook.'

A headline in the *Age* in November 2017 proclaimed that Essendon had posted a 'massive $5 million profit'. It prompted an on-air discussion between SEN breakfast radio hosts Garry Lyon and Tim Watson about whether Essendon was the AFL's biggest club. The result had been foreshadowed in an earlier article by *Age* and

SEN reporter Sam McClure. 'To put the Bombers' expected financial position into context, Hawthorn, during their mesmerising three-peat, recorded successive profits of $3.1 million, $3.4 million, and $3.3 million, but never broke the $4 million mark,' he wrote. 'Given what has transpired at Tullamarine in the past five years, the fresh air of positivity is rejuvenating almost every aspect of Essendon.' We have chosen this example because it shows how ambiguous club finances can be. While the Bombers had highlighted a $5 million net profit at the top of their media release, the full story could be gleaned only by a closer reading of their annual report. It revealed that most of the profit ($4.4 million) had come from grants and donations. Some of it had been raised through a successful fundraising campaign asking the club's wealthier supporters to donate to building works. If these 'one-off' donations were excluded, Essendon was closer to break-even than a massive profit.

Each year, the AFL produces a standardised review of its clubs' financial performance, but it is not publicly released. We have attempted to conduct our own analysis using a decade's worth of annual reports. It has not been a straightforward task. Comparing the health of clubs is made difficult by the inherent differences in their operations and reporting. These inconsistencies are caused by mundane variation in accounting practices rather than some elaborate conspiracy to obfuscate journalists and fans. The disparities in how clubs report profits or losses arise largely through how they account for non-recurring income (such as grants and donations) and expenses (such as building new training facilities). If we strip these from the equation, we can compare clubs by their operating profit, which is basically the balance of income and costs from their regular day-to-day and year-to-year activities. The graph opposite shows the average AFL club's operating revenue and operating expenditure. We have separated each into three components. These allow us to deduct expenses from their matching revenues and derive net measures of income, which are important when considering questions like profitability and sustainability.

A club's **core income** is its football-related commercial revenue. It is the money a club makes through ordinary football activities like selling tickets and getting sponsored. **Core expenses** are the

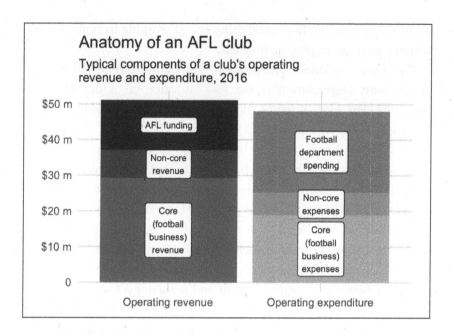

Anatomy of an AFL club

Typical components of a club's operating revenue and expenditure, 2016

administration and commercial costs associated with running the club. Deducting core expenses from core revenue will give us a measure of the amount of money actually made by a club from its commercial football activities, called **net core income**, which is a key measure we will discuss throughout this chapter.

Net non-core income covers the revenue and expenses from a club's side businesses. These are usually social venues with gaming facilities, although some clubs have started to explore other ventures such as fitness centres or even eSports teams. We will discuss these later in the chapter.

In addition to core and non-core income, there is also **AFL funding**. This includes fixed distributions, extra financial support, travel subsidies, and prize money. Isolating this part of a club's revenue reveals a club's profitability and sustainability independent of the AFL. It also helps us understand the effects of the league's equalisation policies.

The third component of operating expenditure is **football department spending**, which includes the money that clubs pay their players, coaches, trainers, and medical staff. This amounted to an average of $23.2 million per club in 2016, of which $10.3 million was salary-capped player payments. By segregating this portion of spending, we can see how everything else is working to fund a club's primary purpose of playing football.

We have excluded **depreciation** and **amortisation** from our calculations. Depreciation is the loss of value on a durable item over time. For football clubs, durable assets that depreciate include buildings, vehicles, equipment, and computers. Writing down their value is recorded as an expense by clubs, because it is assumed that at some point new investment will be needed to replace or refurbish them. Amortisation is another accounting term, which refers to allocating the cost of an asset over a period of time. For example, if a club spends $15 million on building a new training facility, it can amortise the cost by recording $1 million each year for 15 years as an expense on its annual statement. Many clubs do this, and it can sometimes be the difference between reporting a profit and reporting a loss.

If we were accountants, removing depreciation and amortisation from operating profit would be bad practice. We are not, however, and we have done so because it helps us to better compare the clubs. A recent example involving St Kilda illustrates our reasoning. The Saints moved headquarters to Seaford Oval in 2011, but just seven years later they returned to Moorabbin and moved into another newly built facility. After the club decided to return, its accountants altered the assumed useful lifespan of the relatively new Linen House Centre training facility at Seaford. The shorter lifespan raised the Saints' amortisation expenses from $0.5 million per year to about $3.5 million a year. Nothing really changed for their core operations, but amortisation tanked their operating profit. It would be unfair and artificial for us to make cross-club comparisons that treated this change as part of the fundamental expense and revenue situation at the St Kilda Football Club. After all, it was merely recording the replacement of one heavily subsidised facility with another.

Using our six key components of gross income and expenditure, we have broken down and standardised each club's 2016 annual report. These were the most recently available reports at the time of writing. Although we had to estimate some figures that were not explicitly presented, we are confident our numbers are broadly accurate. The graph opposite shows the operating revenue for each club. We have divided revenue into the three revenue components

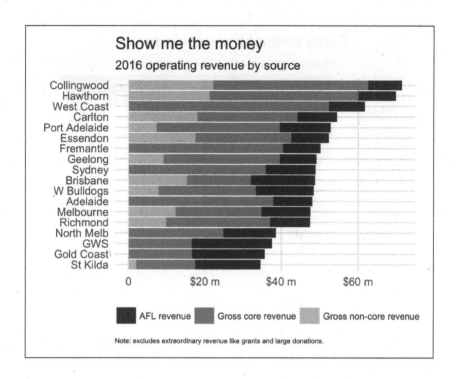

Show me the money

2016 operating revenue by source

Collingwood
Hawthorn
West Coast
Carlton
Port Adelaide
Essendon
Fremantle
Geelong
Sydney
Brisbane
W Bulldogs
Adelaide
Melbourne
Richmond
North Melb
GWS
Gold Coast
St Kilda

0        $20 m $40 m $60 m

■ AFL revenue   ■ Gross core revenue   ■ Gross non-core revenue

Note: excludes extraordinary revenue like grants and large donations.

we discussed above. Those were AFL funding, core revenue (from football business), and non-core revenue (from side businesses). Each item represents the money made by clubs before any expenses are deducted and can also be described as their turnover.

Collingwood recorded the highest gross income ahead of Hawthorn and West Coast. While all three clubs received similar levels of AFL funding, the Magpies had the largest source of non-core revenue. However, running their side businesses came at a cost, as can be seen in the chart overleaf showing each club's net income or profit. We have split these totals into core and non-core income, and excluded AFL revenue and football department spending.

Remember, core income is commercial football revenue minus administration costs. Net non-core relates mostly to social clubs and pokies. Although West Coast had no gaming operations, it booked the largest operating profit in 2016 as a result of the strength of its football business. The Eagles boast a huge, highly engaged fanbase, and the club has traditionally benefited from a favourable stadium deal. It made $18.9 million in net membership revenue, ranking first on that measure ahead of its cross-town rival Fremantle ($15.3 million) and

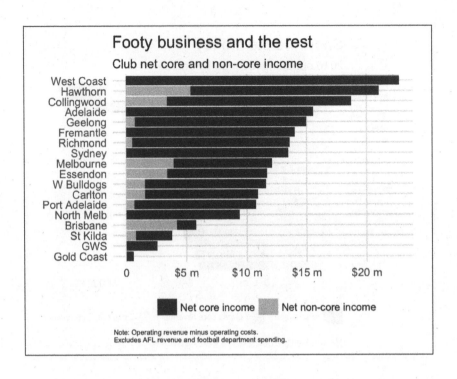

Footy business and the rest

Club net core and non-core income

West Coast
Hawthorn
Collingwood
Adelaide
Geelong
Fremantle
Richmond
Sydney
Melbourne
Essendon
W Bulldogs
Carlton
Port Adelaide
North Melb
Brisbane
St Kilda
GWS
Gold Coast

0   \$5 m   \$10 m   \$15 m   \$20 m

■ Net core income   ■ Net non-core income

Note: Operating revenue minus operating costs.
Excludes AFL revenue and football department spending.

the Adelaide Crows (\$11.6 million). Collingwood ranked fourth, but its membership earnings after costs were deducted (\$9.2 million) were less than half those of West Coast. It is more instructive to look at the revenue that clubs derive from membership, rather than the number of members they have. For example, Hawthorn's 75,351 members in 2016 were the most in the AFL, but its net membership revenue was \$3 million less than the Crows' with 54,307 members. That was partly because the Hawks' family memberships included up to four children, while the Crows' – restricted by a smaller stadium – included two.

The money generated by the two Perth-based clubs and Adelaide through membership and season-ticket sales can be largely attributed to the fact that demand in those cities exceeded supply. 'We are privileged to have a passionate supporter base who love attending our games at Adelaide Oval, which manifests itself into a largely sold-out venue across our season,' said Crows boss Andrew Fagan. 'In essence, it's fully subscribed as a venue.' The same went for the Eagles and Dockers at Subiaco, although they made an even bigger profit because of the higher cost of their reserved tickets. The price gap was also reflected in their corporate support. West Coast's net return from corporate hospitality of $9.2 million was more than four times the league average of $2.1 million. Fremantle made $6.1 million from that sector, well ahead of third-placed Geelong ($4 million) and Adelaide ($2.9 million).

Another key plank in the Eagles' business model was their sponsorship arrangements. They brought in a net $7.5 million from their sponsors in 2016, placing them fourth in the AFL behind Sydney ($9.4 million), Geelong ($8.5 million), and Fremantle ($8.1 million). Care needs to be taken in using sponsorship as a yardstick of a club's financial health, however, because of the differences between the markets in which they operate. As the established club in the country's biggest market, the Swans hold a clear advantage in this regard. Smaller sources of revenue, such as merchandising, can also be tricky to benchmark. Some clubs take a volume-driven approach that aims to put their colours on as many people as possible, but which makes little money in the process. Others try to spin a profit through more moderate programs.

A bit on the side

Although Collingwood had the highest gross income in 2016, its net profit took a hit from the costs associated with its non-core businesses. For the Magpies, this was primarily the expense of running their two gaming venues: The Coach in Ringwood and The Club in Caroline Springs. Together, the two venues had more than 150 poker machines. Collingwood was one of nine Victorian AFL clubs that owned and operated pokies. The only one that didn't was North Melbourne, which is an interesting quirk considering its pioneering role in developing non-traditional revenue streams.

Club football department spending started to spiral during the 1970s, driven by the advent of television deals and corporate sponsorship. According to the book *A National Game*, the average wage bill for VFL clubs rose from $89,000 to $269,000 between 1974 and 1978. The Kangaroos were a major factor in the spike. Ron Barassi had been appointed their coach in 1973, which was the same year the star players Doug Wade, John Rantall, and Barry Davis joined the club in free agency. Each of the trio was paid a $10,000 sign-on fee and $5,000 per year. The following year the club splashed out on the interstate stars Malcolm Blight and Barry Cable. It funded its extravagant spending through aggressively pursuing non-core revenue. North president Allen Aylett hired his former teammate Barry Cheatley as marketing manager. Cheatley expanded the Kangaroos' social club and branched out into other ventures. 'In that time, we started all new things like club sponsorships and financial supporter groups,' Aylett told author Peter Lalor in his biography of Barassi. 'It was nothing in today's terms, but then it was quite an amount.'

When the Kangaroos broke through for their maiden premiership in 1975 and claimed another two years later, it didn't take long for the other clubs to follow their lead. A spending 'arms race' developed, putting more upward pressure on player payments. With no salary cap in place until 1987, this magnified the disparity between the VFL's rich and poor. The financially troubled South Melbourne club relocated to Sydney in 1982, becoming the Swans. Others were facing the prospect of a merger. By 1984, half the VFL's 12 clubs were technically bankrupt. Temporary salvation came in the form of national expansion. The $4 million licence fees paid on entry by West Coast and Brisbane in 1987 were evenly distributed among the Victorian clubs, helping them keep the debt collectors at bay. Still, it had become clear that new and sustainable sources of revenue were sorely needed.

The Victorian government legislated to allow poker machines in pubs and clubs in 1991. Having lobbied hard for them, the clubs of the rebranded AFL moved quickly. Within two years, the Demons were the only Victorian club without a gaming venue, and the rest were pushing for an increase to the 105-machine cap. Their yield steadily increased through regulatory change, upgrades to their venues, and the acquisition of more attractive and better placed machines. The total pokies take in Victoria had climbed to about $600 per capita by the end of the decade, raising about 10% of Victoria's tax revenue. AFL clubs reaped their own share, using it to support their football programs. The table overleaf shows our best estimates of the gaming-related revenue generated by the clubs that were still involved in the sector in 2016.

As the table shows, the gross takings significantly outweigh the net revenue. This is because the operating costs are substantial. The figures estimated here suggest there are two types of pokies-invested football clubs, separated by the scale of their involvement. Some of the venues that opened in the early 1990s have failed to develop in the way the clubs might have hoped. For instance, St Kilda's social club reportedly made $1.4 million in gross revenue in 1993. Thirteen years later it took in $2.1 million, putting its growth almost in line with inflation. The Saints are one of the smaller players when it comes to gaming, along with the Western Bulldogs, Richmond, Geelong, and Port Adelaide. Most of them operate just one venue and their gross revenue is below $10 million. The Power have pokies at both Alberton Oval and the Prince of Wales Hotel, but their modest returns might partly be explained by the fact South Australia is the only state that prohibits gamblers from using notes in the machines.

	Gross social club revenue ($ million)	Gaming machine revenue from state gambling authority ($ million)	Net revenue from social clubs ($ million)	*Notes
Hawthorn	20.7*	19.8	4.9*	Estimated expenses. Revenue counts 73% stake in WestWaters Hotel and includes $2 million 'accommodation income'
Brisbane	15.2	15.8*	4.2	Regulated income estimated from local average per machine
Melbourne	12.2	10.5	3.9	
Collingwood	22.9*	11.9	3.4*	Can't separate function centre from gaming
Essendon	17.4	12.2	2.5	Excludes fitness centre
Carlton	17.9	17.3	1.6	
Western Bulldogs	5.7*	5.7	1.6*	Includes hospitality
Richmond	7.2	5.6	1.0	Excludes fitness centre
Geelong	9.1	5.1	0.8*	Estimated expenses
Port Adelaide	7.3	4.1*	0.7	Regulated income estimated from local average per machine
St Kilda	2.1	2.2	0.8	

At the other end of the scale are Hawthorn, Brisbane, Collingwood, Essendon, Melbourne, and Carlton. These clubs are heavily invested in gaming, both spending and obtaining well over $10 million per year. Excluding Carlton, their net returns are generally more than $2 million annually. The Melbourne-based clubs in this group tend to run large entertainment and gaming complexes in the city's outer suburbs. Brisbane's single venue in Logan has 200 machines, and its relatively strong net income to expense ratio might be linked to more generous legislation in Queensland. In fact, the Lions are the only club in the AFL that derive more of their net revenue from their side businesses than their football activities. For the others, including the biggest players, such as the Hawks, their gaming income remains secondary to their core revenue.

We won't dwell on the social impact of pokies, except to acknowledge that in 2010 the Productivity Commission estimated that 40% of the money spent on the machines came from problem gamblers. It is perhaps telling, however, that some clubs have since started to divest their gaming interests. Geelong has shut down the pokies it previously operated at Kardinia Park, and in early 2018 Collingwood was reportedly in discussions to sell its machines. 'You have to see that community sentiment regarding pokies has turned sharply, and that makes you question how solid an investment it is,' noted Richmond president Peggy O'Neal. 'Do you want to think that's your future – as volatile as that may be – or do you want to look for something that's more predictable and something that will not have the community backlash?'

The Tigers have signalled their intent to diversify their non-core operations by establishing a subsidiary business called Aligned Leisure, which manages health and fitness centres for local councils on a tendered contract basis. 'When you're in football, you need to find something that doesn't require a lot of capital,' said O'Neal. 'If it's capital intensive, football clubs just don't have that.' It is a sentiment shared by Andrew Fagan. 'The challenge is that most clubs don't have the financial capacity to fund investment outside of their core,' said the Crows' boss. 'That's a challenge we're all looking to overcome.' Adelaide, which does not have any poker machine licences, has focused its attention on innovation and emerging technologies. 'We have acquired a professional eSports [competitive video gaming] team and we have taken equity in a technology start-up that has application across sport, entertainment and health sectors,' said Fagan. 'We are actively looking to extend our wheelhouse to generate growth.'

It won't be easy for all clubs to wean themselves off gaming, but North Melbourne provides an example of the way forward. The Kangaroos sold off their machines in 2008 and rebranded themselves as a community club. 'It's been a pretty long-term stance that we wouldn't be in pokies,' said the club's chief executive, Carl Dilena. 'We took a position not to get back into them at that point and continued on with that.' It was a brave move for a club $8.5 million in debt, but it forced it to become more efficient and resourceful. It signed a deal to take some of its home games each season to Hobart, creating a new membership base in Tasmania. The club also sought to monetise some of its intellectual property. KangaTech, an injury-prevention program developed by North's former high-performance manager Steve Saunders, has been sold to teams in American basketball's NBA, English soccer's Championship, and even other clubs in the AFL. 'When looking at non-core revenue opportunities, we looked internally at the things we were doing well and decided to focus on that as a platform to commercialise,' said the Kangaroos' general manager of commercial and strategy, Nick Haslam. 'After investing in developing the technology, we decided to start selling our expertise to the world.'

Levelling the playing field

Of course, disparities in revenue are not supposed to matter in the modern AFL. Dilena has emphasised that North Melbourne's decision to go without gaming revenue has never disadvantaged it on the field, because the player salary cap has prevented it from being outspent by its richer rivals. Off the field, the league has also pursued a policy of financial equalisation through the distribution and redistribution of AFL revenue. Its distributive function has involved the transfer of centrally collected broadcast revenue to the clubs, while its redistributive function has provided additional funding to those in need. Limited redistribution via the sharing of gate receipts began as early as the 1940s, but for decades it was generally ineffective. Equalisation has only become an effective, game-changing policy in the 21st century. In 2002, the AFL's annual report included an innocuous-looking item noting the Western Bulldogs had been handed an extra million dollars in assistance, and that the Kangaroos would receive the same the following year. A system to help clubs in financial difficulty had quietly been established, which rapidly evolved into a series of unequal payments known as the 'annual special distribution (ASD) fund'.

Seven clubs were drawing ASD funding by 2006, with the Bulldogs (a steady $1.7 million), Kangaroos ($1.4 million) and Melbourne ($1 million) the biggest beneficiaries. The AFL's broadcast deal increased from $150 million per year to $250 million per year in 2012, presenting it with the chance to strengthen its equalisation program without cutting existing funding commitments to wealthy clubs. The new 'club future fund' saw all 18 clubs handed a five-year base payment of $3.25 million, rising according to needs all the way up to $10.2 million for the Bulldogs and Kangaroos. Then, in 2015, the AFL tackled one of the largest remaining bastions of inequality by introducing a soft cap on non-player football expenditure. Under the changed rules, clubs that spent over the cap incurred a luxury tax. 'We're trying to find ways to compensate smaller clubs for structural challenges they face,' explained the league's incoming chief executive, Gillon McLachlan. 'The rate at which non-player footy department spend has grown has been unsustainable, and if we don't do something it'll send the competition broke.' Although the league faced resistance

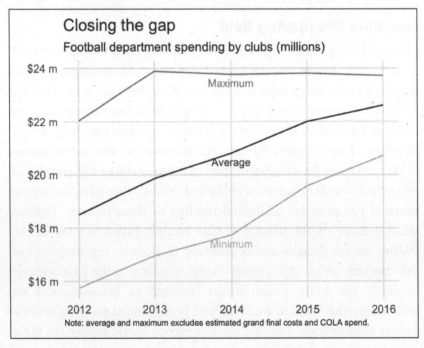

Closing the gap

Football department spending by clubs (millions)

Note: average and maximum excludes estimated grand final costs and COLA spend.

from some of the wealthier clubs, which complained the measure was punishing success, our data shows the introduction of the soft cap achieved its stated aim. The gap in football spending across all teams halved from about $6 million in 2012, to about $3 million in 2016.

The league's equalisation pot grew again in 2017, with the commencement of a six-year, $2.5 billion broadcast deal. McLachlan declared the deal would deliver 'financial security' to the clubs. The few 2017 annual reports that were available at the time of writing indicated significant increases in support for small clubs. Brisbane's AFL funding grew by $4 million year-on-year, while St Kilda's jumped by $3.5 million. In comparison, Hawthorn saw its funding increase by just $1 million.

The Hawks and West Coast were the only two clubs in the league that could have plausibly paid for their football departments without AFL funding in 2016. Even then, Hawthorn would have had to cut its spending to the lower end of the scale, and the Eagles would have been unable to pay royalties to the Western Australian Football Commission. A few more clubs paid their own way if we factor in the minimum level of AFL assistance of about $10.5 million. The average football department cost about $22 million in 2016, so a club would

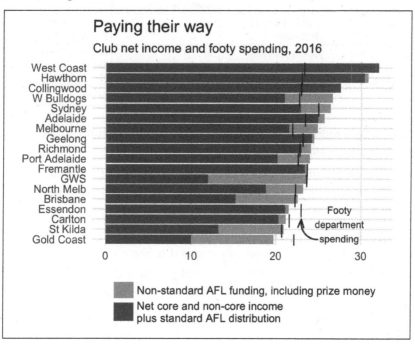

Paying their way

Club net income and footy spending, 2016

have needed about $11.5 million in net core and net non-core income to be considered self-sustainable.

If a club's football department spending, represented by the thin black line, extends more than slightly past the AFL-standard distribution in the graph (previous page), it is evidence that it uses additional AFL support to fund its football spending. Using this data as a rough guide, we have divided the clubs into six different types. Essendon has been classified according to its 'normal' results rather than 2016, which was affected by the suspension of 12 of its players for anti-doping violations.

Category	Clubs	Sustainability test: did the club pay for its football department without extra AFL funding?	Surplus or loss after sustainability test
Super heavyweights	West Coast, Hawthorn, Collingwood, Essendon	Yes, without non–core income	More than $4 million surplus
Heavyweights	Fremantle, Adelaide, Richmond, Geelong	Yes, without non–core income	About $1 million surplus
Middling	Carlton, Sydney, Melbourne, Western Bulldogs	Yes, with caveats (i.e. with non–core income, extra Docklands revenue, or without COLA and Grand Final costs)	Less than $1 million deficit
Smaller	Port Adelaide, North Melbourne	No	Between $1 million and $3 million deficit
Struggling	St Kilda, Brisbane	No	More than $5 million deficit
Expansion	Gold Coast, Greater Western Sydney	No	More than $10 million deficit

Rather than representing actual operating profits, the above categories represent how the league's finances might look if every club got the same flat distribution and no other support. Some of the middling and smaller teams can switch between two of those categories depending on their immediate circumstance. The Western Bulldogs climbed a division in 2016 on the strength of winning the premiership, while Carlton may rise to heavyweight status if it has a sustained period of success. Net core income tends to trend up when clubs win and down when they lose, although it generally remains within a prescribed range determined by structural factors.

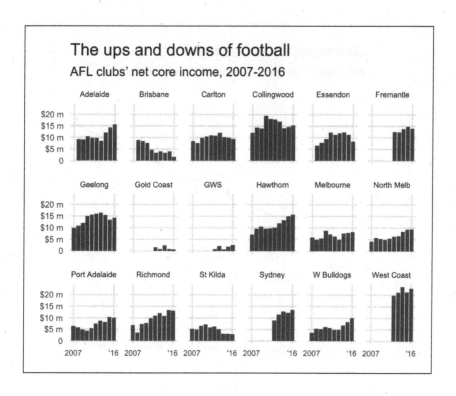

The ups and downs of football
AFL clubs' net core income, 2007-2016

Adelaide Brisbane Carlton Collingwood Essendon Fremantle

Geelong Gold Coast GWS Hawthorn Melbourne North Melb

Port Adelaide Richmond St Kilda Sydney W Bulldogs West Coast

A club's ability to generate core income is largely tied to the size of its supporter base, which can shape everything from its stadium and sponsorship deals to its fixture timeslots and television ratings. North Melbourne, for example, will never make more money than West Coast simply because there are not enough Kangaroos fans. Using the figures from Roy Morgan's 2016 supporter survey, the next graph highlights the correlation between fanbase and revenue. The outliers are Sydney and Brisbane. As discussed in the previous chapter, the Swans and Lions have hundreds of thousands of 'fans' who barely pay attention to them.

But if clubs are hostage to the conditions in which they operate, can they change their structural position by winning? In the short term, premiers will generally experience an above-average spike in core revenue. They sell more tickets and memberships as they build momentum throughout the season, before moving a mountain of merchandise during the finals. They also find it easier to sign new sponsorship deals, and are sometimes handed bonuses from existing partners. 'There's no doubt that winning gives you a blip in positive

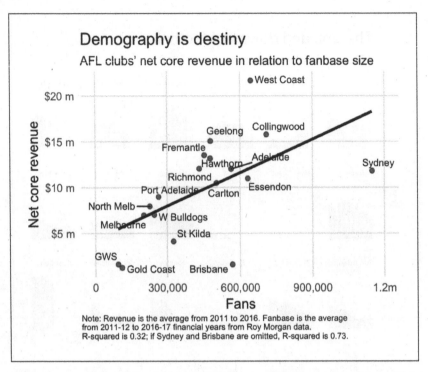

Demography is destiny

AFL clubs' net core revenue in relation to fanbase size

Note: Revenue is the average from 2011 to 2016. Fanbase is the average from 2011-12 to 2016-17 financial years from Roy Morgan data. R-squared is 0.32; if Sydney and Brisbane are omitted, R-squared is 0.73.

revenue,' said Richmond president Peggy O'Neal. 'You receive prize money from the AFL too, so it can be very important.' The bigger challenge, however, is to convert that 'blip' into sustained growth.

Hawthorn is perhaps the only club that has managed to materially improve its outlook through sustained on-field success. For several decades, the Hawks were one of the league's struggling minnows. They joined the VFL alongside Footscray and North Melbourne when the competition expanded to 12 teams in 1925. They finished either last or second-last in 21 of 32 seasons before making their first finals appearance in 1957. Their dismal results were reflected by their lacklustre crowds.

Their fortunes only began to turn when John Kennedy took over as coach and led the club to its first premiership in 1961. After being allocated strong country zones, they won another eight flags between 1971 and 1991. However, it wasn't until they claimed four more premierships between 2008 and 2015 that they consistently exceeded the league average for attendance. 'Hawthorn has managed to increase its supporter base massively, although it has needed to have constant success,' observed AFL Media reporter Peter Ryan in

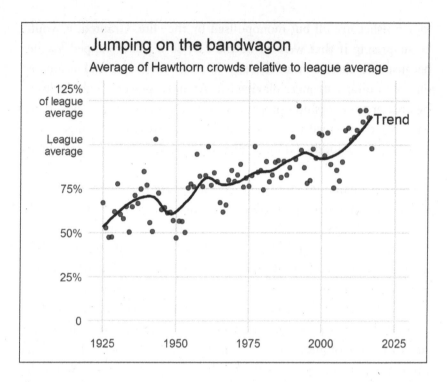

Jumping on the bandwagon

Average of Hawthorn crowds relative to league average

the lead-up to the Hawks' 2014 flag. 'It also made the smart decision to play games in Tasmania, and to use Waverley as a home base to capture the Eastern corridor.' Another club could theoretically follow the Hawks' path to becoming a financial super heavyweight, but it would require decades of on-field success, consistently sound off-field decision-making, and a healthy dose of luck.

Does money buy football happiness?

While sustained on-field success may eventually lead to off-field prosperity, our data shows that the inverse is not necessarily true. That might seem contradictory. Hawthorn's premiership streak, following so soon after Geelong's period of dominance, seemed to contribute to a growing perception that financial clout was vital to winning. Yet, in truth, the modern AFL has been reasonably egalitarian. The financial super heavyweights Collingwood and Essendon have only claimed two flags between them since 2000, while the heavyweights Fremantle and Adelaide have won none. The highest-earning clubs do not dominate as they do in European soccer, where titles and top-four finishes are all but monopolised by the elite. Granted, it would be surprising if that were to be the case in a salary-capped league, because the clubs cannot directly leverage their financial resources into obtaining a stronger playing list. At most, players might be lured by greater sponsorship opportunities at certain clubs, but even these have dried up since the AFL ruled that third-party arrangements, such as Chris Judd's famous 'Visy deal' at Carlton, counted under the cap.

That we came up empty-handed when we tried to correlate the clubs' net incomes with their winning rate would undoubtedly delight the league's administrators. 'The league wants every fan to feel that they genuinely have a realistic chance of success in the medium term,' said the Crows' Andrew Fagan. 'The AFL utopia is that a team only makes finals 10 years out of 18 and wins a flag once every 18 years.' However, as Dr Chris Davies astutely pointed out in a paper entitled 'The AFL's Holy Grail: The Quest for an Even Competition', such an ideal would quickly become as predictable as a league dominated by only a few teams. 'What the AFL is trying to achieve in its competition is reasonable equality, with this being defined as one which produces figures that are in between what an uneven competition would produce, and what a totally even competition would produce,' wrote Dr Davies. 'A reasonably even competition would be one having six to seven different teams winning the premiership in a given decade.' On that measure, the 1990s, the 2000s and the 2010s have all been reasonably equal.

Decade	Unique premiers
1960s	7 of 12
1970s	4 of 12
1980s	4 of 12–14
1990s	7 of 14–16
2000s	7 of 16
2010s	6 of 16–18

Of course, premierships can be a lumpy measure of success. Only one club can win each season, meaning the sample size of premiers is small. A more robust yardstick might be preliminary final appearances, which give us 40 successful teams per decade. Most preliminary finalists are generally considered to be realistic contenders for the flag. If a team makes the final four, it is usually considered to have had a good year. Most of the smaller non-expansion clubs, such as the Western Bulldogs, North Melbourne, Port Adelaide, and St Kilda, have made multiple preliminary finals since 2000. Indeed, every club apart from Gold Coast has reached at least one Grand Final qualifier during that time.

	Last preliminary final	Preliminary finals since 2000
Adelaide	2017	5
Brisbane Lions	2004	4
Carlton	2000	1
Collingwood	2012	7
Essendon	2001	2
Fremantle	2015	3
Geelong	2017	9
Gold Coast	–	0
Greater Western Sydney	2017	2
Hawthorn	2015	7
Melbourne	2000	1
North Melbourne	2015	4
Port Adelaide	2014	5
Richmond	2017	2
St Kilda	2010	5
Sydney	2016	7
West Coast	2015	4
Western Bulldogs	2016	4

The biggest underachievers in the above table span the breadth of the revenue spectrum, from heavyweight Essendon and middling former powerhouse Carlton, to minnow Melbourne. The figures certainly provide no proof of money buying success. Another telling factor is 'ladder churn', which is the degree to which struggling sides ascend the ladder from year to year. The aim of the salary cap and draft is to facilitate such improvement. Since 2000, more than half of all clubs that finished in the bottom four in one year went on to qualify for the finals in at least one of the following three seasons. A third of bottom-four sides became top-four teams within four years.

Movement since 2000 of teams that finished bottom four		
Year	To top 4	To top 8
One year on	7%	19%
Two years on	8%	31%
Cumulative	13%	39%
Three years on	15%	43%
Cumulative	20%	58%
Four years on	20%	46%
Cumulative	33%	67%

The question of a club's profitability appears to be becoming increasingly irrelevant as the AFL's equalisation policies take hold. We have failed to uncover any convincing evidence of financial power leading directly to on-field success since the beginning of the new millennium. Furthermore, the AFL's off-field spending cap has probably neutralised the risk of it happening in the future. The era of clubs facing existential threats like folding or merging seems to have ended, so we might just have to sit back and enjoy the AFL's relatively tranquil socialist enclave.

Credits and Acknowledgements

The writers would like to thank our publisher Helen Littleton for her belief in the project and continued encouragement; our editors Lachlan McLaine and Tony Ryan for their care and thoroughness with the manuscript; our publicist Matthew Howard for his enthusiasm; and, most importantly, our families for their patience and support.

Introduction

Words: James Coventry
Research: James Coventry
Interviews: James Coventry with Mark Evans, Glenn Luff, Karl Jackson, Darren O'Shaughnessy, Liam Pickering, David Rath, and Lawrie Woodman
Acknowledgements: We would like to thank Champion Data for allowing us to observe their operations. Sincere thanks also to Gary and Katherine Adamic, who kindly hosted James Coventry while he conducted his research in Melbourne.

Chapter One – Goal Kicking

Words: Tony Corke, James Coventry, and Daniel Hoevenaars
Research: Tony Corke and Daniel Hoevenaars
Graphs: Tony Corke and Daniel Hoevenaars
Interviews: James Coventry with Dr Kevin Ball, Tory Dickson, Charlie Dixon, David Steventon, and Grant Thomas
Data: afltables.com and Champion Data
More information: insightlane.com and matterofstats.com

Chapter Two – Expected Goals

Words: James Coventry and Robert Younger
Research: Robert Younger
Graphs: Robert Younger
Interviews: James Coventry with Dr Kevin Ball, Aaron Greaves, Trent Hentschel, and David Steventon
Data: afltables.com and Champion Data
Acknowledgements: The cooperation of the Port Adelaide Football Club was greatly appreciated.
More information: figuringfooty.com

Chapter Three – Score Involvements

Words: Robert Younger
Research: Robert Younger
Data: afltables.com and Champion Data
More information: figuringfooty.com

Chapter Four – Win Probabilities

Words: James Coventry and Daniel Hoevenaars
Research: Daniel Hoevenaars
Graphs: Daniel Hoevenaars
Interviews: James Coventry with Craig Jennings
Data: afltables.com and Champion Data
More information: insightlane.com

Chapter Five – Momentum

Words: James Coventry and Robert Younger
Research: Robert Younger
Graphs: Robert Younger
Interviews: James Coventry with Craig Jennings, David Rath and David Steventon
Data: afltables.com and Champion Data

Chapter Six – Statistics

Words: Tony Corke and James Coventry
Research: Tony Corke and James Coventry
Graphs: Tony Corke

Interviews: James Coventry with David Rath and Adam Read
Data: afl.com.au and Champion Data
Acknowledgements: Champion Data provided us with access to their zone-by-zone statistics.
More information: matterofstats.com

Chapter Seven – Home and Away

Words: James Coventry, Matt Cowgill, and Darren O'Shaughnessy
Research: Matt Cowgill and Darren O'Shaughnessy
Graphs: Matt Cowgill
Interviews: James Coventry with Brent Harvey, Glen Jakovich, Hayden Kennedy, Matthew Pavlich, and Peter Schwab; Tony Barker with Damien Drum
Data: afltables.com and Champion Data
Acknowledgements: Ryan Buckland produced the holding-the-ball decision tree.
More information: thearcfooty.com

Chapter Eight – The Draft

Words: Cody Atkinson, James Coventry, and Sean Lawson
Research: Cody Atkinson, James Coventry, and Sean Lawson
Graphs: Cody Atkinson, Matt Cowgill, and Sean Lawson
Interviews: James Coventry with Adrian Caruso, Gerard Neesham, Cameron Schwab, and Emma Quayle
Data: afltables.com, Champion Data, and draftguru.com.au
Acknowledgements: Greater Western Sydney's Adrian Caruso kindly allowed us to observe him while he was working. Ryan Buckland assisted during the editing process.
More information: hpnfooty.com

Chapter Nine – Trading

Words: Cody Atkinson and James Coventry
Research: Cody Atkinson, James Coventry, and Sean Lawson
Graphs: Cody Atkinson
Interviews: James Coventry with Cameron Schwab
Data: afltables.com, Champion Data, and draftguru.com.au
Acknowledgements: Ryan Buckland assisted during the editing process.
More information: hpnfooty.com

Chapter Ten – Shared Experience

Words: James Coventry and Matt Cowgill
Research: Matt Cowgill
Graphs: Matt Cowgill
Interviews: James Coventry with James Kelly and Simon Strachan
Data: afltables.com and Champion Data
Acknowledgements: GAIN LINE chief operating officer Simon Strachan's time and insight was much appreciated.
More information: thearcfooty.com

Chapter Eleven – The Brownlow Medal

Words: James Coventry and Dr Liam Lenten
Research: Cody Atkinson, James Coventry, and Dr Liam Lenten
Graphs: Cody Atkinson and Matt Cowgill
Interviews: James Coventry with Professor Michael Bailey, Murray Bird, Hayden Kennedy, Glenn Luff, Professor David Neumann, Dr Liam Lenten and Professor Lionel Page
Data: afltables.com and Champion Data
Acknowledgements: Professor Michael Bailey generously provided feedback on our research and findings. AFL historian Col Hutchinson supplied a historical record of VFL/AFL tribunal results.

Chapter Twelve – The Hall of Fame

Words: James Coventry and Daniel Hoevenaars
Research: Daniel Hoevenaars
Graphs: Daniel Hoevenaars
Interviews: James Coventry with Brian Atkinson, Max Basheer, and Michelangelo Rucci
Data: afl.com.au and australianfootball.com
Acknowledgements: Our sincere thanks to Greg Wardell-Johnson, Ric Gauci and Steve Davies, who provided a complete list of WAFL premiership players and club best-and-fairest winners, and to Kyle Smith, who supplied a list of SANFL premiership players.
More information: insightlane.com

Chapter Thirteen – Team Ratings

Words: Tony Corke and James Coventry
Research: Tony Corke
Graphs: Ryan Buckland, Tony Corke, and Matt Cowgill
Data: afltables.com, australianfootball.com, and Champion Data
More information: matterofstats.com

Chapter Fourteen – Fandom

Words: James Coventry and Sean Lawson
Research: Sean Lawson
Graphs: Matt Cowgill and Sean Lawson
Data: afltables.com, Australian Bureau of Statistics, Australian Sports Commission, fanfooty.com.au, Google Trends, and Roy Morgan Research
Acknowledgements: Thank you to Roy Morgan Research, which provided us with results from its AFL supporter surveys. The 'Barassi Line' maps were reproduced from work by Colin Ross at colinross.co and Neil Pollock at mahercup.com.au
More information: colinross.co, hpnfooty.com, and mahercup.com.au

Chapter Fifteen – Club Finances

Words: James Coventry and Sean Lawson
Research: Sean Lawson
Graphs: Matt Cowgill and Sean Lawson
Interviews: James Coventry with Peggy O'Neal, Xavier Campbell, Andrew Fagan, and Nick Haslam
Data: Club and AFL annual reports and footyindustry.com
Acknowledgements: Jason Lassey from footyindustry.com provided an extensive repository of financial reports and other administrative documents that were essential to this work.
More information: footyindustry.com, hpnfooty.com

Select Bibliography

Academic papers and articles

M Bailey, *Predicting Sporting Outcomes: A Statistical Approach*, Swinburne University, 2005

R Booth, *Some Economic Effects of Changes to Gate-Sharing Arrangements in the Australian Football League in Football Fever: Moving the Goalposts*, Maribyrnong Press, 2006

A Cardosi, *Neglected Heroes: The Sad Case of the Australian Football Hall of Fame*, australianfootball.com, 2014

S Clarke and R Stefani, *Predictions and Home Advantage in Australian Rules Football*, Journal of Applied Statistics, 1992

C Davies, *The AFL's Holy Grail: The Quest for an Even Competition*, James Cook University Law Review, 2005

J Doughney, *Socioeconomic Banditry: Poker Machines and Income Redistribution in Victoria*, SPRC Report, 2002

T Eardley and B Bradbury (eds), *Competing Visions: Refereed Proceedings of the National Social Policy Conference*, SPRC Report, 2002

G Kendall and L Lenten, *When Sports Rules Go Awry*, European Journal of Operational Research, 2017

L Lenten, *Comparing Attendances and Memberships in the Australian Football League: The Case of Hawthorn*, Economic and Labour Relations Review, 2012

L Lenten, *Racial Discrimination in Umpire Voting: An (Arguably) Unexpected Result*, Applied Economics, 2017

L Lenten, *Sentiment and Bias in Performance Evaluation by Impartial Arbitrators*, La Trobe University, 2018

B Love, L Kopec and O Guest, *Optimism Bias in Fans and Sports Reporters*, PLOS One, 2015

D O'Shaughnessy, *Possession Versus Position: Strategic Evaluation in AFL*, Journal of Sports Science and Medicine, 2006

A Puopolo, *A Home Away From Home: Home Advantage in Shared Stadiums*, Harvard Sports Analysis Collective, 2017

R Stewart, *The Economic Development of the Victorian Football League 1960–1984*, Sporting Traditions, 1985

B Whimpress, *AFL Hall Of Fame – 'See Victoria'*, The Victoria Bulletin of Sport and Culture, 1996

Books

C Anderson and D Sally, *The Numbers Game: Why Everything You Know About Football is Wrong*, 2013

J Button, *Comeback: The Fall and Rise of Geelong*, 2016

J Coventry, *Time and Space: The Tactics That Shaped Australian Rules – and the Players and Coaches Who Mastered Them*, 2015

S Dubner and S Levitt, *SuperFreakonomics: Global Cooling, Patriotic Prostitutes, and Why Suicide Bombers Should Buy Life Insurance*, 2009

M Gladwell, *Outliers: The Story of Success*, 2008

R Hess, B Stewart, M Nicholson and G de Moore, *A National Game: The History of Australian Rules Football*, 2008

T Hopkins, *The Stats Revolution: The Life, Loves and Passion of Football's Futurist*, 2011

S Kuper and S Szymanski, *Soccernomics: Why England Loses, Why Spain, Germany, and Brazil Win, and Why the U.S., Japan, Australia and Even Iraq Are Destined to Become the Kings of the World's Most Popular Sport*, 2009

P Lalor, *Barassi: The Biography*, 2010

M Lewis, *Moneyball: The Art of Winning an Unfair Game*, 2003

M Lewis, *The Undoing Project: A Friendship That Changed Our Minds*, 2016

L Matthews, *Accept the Challenge*, 2013

D Oliver, *Basketball on Paper: Rules and Tools for Performance Analysis*, 2004

M Pavlich, *Purple Heart*, 2015

D Sumpter, *Soccermatics: Mathematical Adventures in the Beautiful Game*, 2016

P Tetlock and D Gardner, *Superforecasting: The Art and Science of Prediction*, 2015

LJ Wertheim and T Moskowitz, *Scorecasting: The Hidden Influences Behind How Sports Are Played and Games Are Won*, 2011

Newspapers, magazines, and periodicals

The Advertiser

The Advocate

AFL Prospectus

AFL Record

The Age

The Argus

The Football Record

The Footballer

Footy Week

Inside Football

Geelong Advertiser

Herald Sun

Sunday Mail

The Sunday Times

The Sydney Morning Herald

The West Australian

Television programs

AFL 360

Footy Classified

The Footy Show

On the Couch

Talking Footy

The Lead Author

JAMES COVENTRY has worked for the ABC since 2002 and is currently the Deputy Sports Editor. He presents the morning sports news across Australia on ABC Radio, and appears on *Grandstand*'s AFL coverage. He is the author of *Time and Space*, a history of Australian football tactics. In 2009 he was the national winner of the AFL's Dream Team competition, and he has written about fantasy football for the *AFL Prospectus*.

Contributors

CODY ATKINSON has been co-authoring the footy website HPN Footy (hpnfooty.com) since 2014. He currently lives and works in Canberra, and is patiently waiting for the Demons to play finals footy again.

RYAN BUCKLAND is a practising economist who writes about sport in his spare time. He wishes it was the other way around. His by-line appears at the sports opinion website The Roar, as well as Onballers (onballers.com) – an alternative sports media site he co-founded in 2017.

TONY CORKE is a freelance data scientist with 20 years of experience helping companies to understand and predict their customers' behaviour. He does sports analytics for his MatterOfStats website (matterofstats.com). He's tried very hard to get the term 'data whisperer' to catch on, but no-one's buying it.

MATT COWGILL is an economist by day and footy stats obsessive by night. His analysis of football data has appeared at *ESPN* and his own site, The Arc (thearcfooty.com).

DANIEL HOEVENAARS currently works as a management consultant, helping firms make better decisions with their data. During the footy season he has provided statistical insight for both Fox Footy's television coverage and the AFL website's Match Centre. He also dabbles in sports analysis at his InsightLane website (insightlane.com).

SEAN LAWSON co-authors the footy website HPN Footy (hpnfooty.com). In his day job, he has worked in non-football statistics compilation and analysis roles since 2010.

DR LIAM LENTEN is a senior lecturer in the Department of Economics and Finance at La Trobe University. His current research agenda is predominantly in sports economics. He has published more than 30 articles in peer-refereed journals, and is also a regular news media contributor on economics and sports-related issues.

DARREN O'SHAUGHNESSY is a researcher and data consultant in several sports. He spent a decade as chief statistician at Champion Data, and has been working with Hawthorn Football Club since 2012.

ROBERT YOUNGER started in football by developing predictive models and writing team analyses for his blog, FiguringFooty (figuringfooty.com). He has since worked as an analyst for Champion Data and Fox Sports, and is currently a performance data scientist at Port Adelaide Football Club.

Also by James Coventry

Time and Space

From Pagan's Paddock to Clarkson's Cluster, from Fitzroy's huddle to Sydney's flood, the tactics of Australian football have become part of the vernacular.

In this groundbreaking book, ABC journalist James Coventry reveals the secrets behind them all. You'll meet the German gymnast who taught Geelong how to break the game from its rugby roots; the two Test cricketers who became footy's first great coaches; and the water polo player who shaped the modern AFL.

Along the way you'll learn how South Australia pioneered the flick pass; how a rule suggested by Tasmania helped Collingwood win four straight flags; and how Fremantle revolutionised the use of the interchange bench.

Time and Space is essential reading for any fan who wants to know why their team does what it does, and why it wins or loses